Michael

C# 7 and .NET Core Cookbook

Quick solutions to common programming problems with the latest features of C# 7.0, .NET Core 1.1, and Visual Studio 2017

Dirk Strauss

BIRMINGHAM - MUMBAI

C# 7 and .NET Core Cookbook

First published: April 2017

Production reference: 1210417

Published by Packt Publishing Ltd.
Livery Place
35 Livery Street
Birmingham
B3 2PB, UK.

ISBN 978-1-78728-627-6

www.packtpub.com

Credits

Author

Dirk Strauss

Reviewer

Fabio Claudio Ferracchiati

Commissioning Editor

Merint Thomas Mathew

Acquisition Editor

Nitin Dasan

Content Development Editor

Vikas Tiwari

Technical Editor

Madhunikita Chindarkar

Copy Editor

Charlotte Carneiro

Project Coordinator

Ulhas Kambali

Proofreader

Safis Editing

Indexer

Tejal Daruwale Soni

Production Coordinator

Shantanu N. Zagade

Foreword

When the author of this book, Dirk Strauss, asked me if I'd write a foreword, it took me about n milliseconds (where n is a small integer) to reply with a "yes". I've known Dirk for a few years, starting when we worked on a project that involved C# Code Contracts. Quite some time ago I worked with the Research in Software Engineering group at Microsoft Research, who originally developed Code Contracts, so when I saw Dirk's explanation of the technology, I knew immediately that Dirk has a rare ability to understand, use, and most importantly with regards to *C# 7 and .NET Core Cookbook*, explain ideas in a clear and precise way.

Most of my colleagues and I believe that a major challenge facing .NET developers, and in fact all software developers, is the astonishing explosion of new technologies and the associated tidal wave of various forms of documentation. It's becoming increasingly difficult to find those few valuable resources that get to the point quickly, and explain technologies and paradigms succinctly so you can get on with your work. This book is one such reference. I hope you'll enjoy and value *C# 7 and .NET Core Cookbook* as much as I do!

Dr. James McCaffrey

Microsoft Research

About the Author

Dirk Strauss is a software developer and Microsoft .NET MVP from South Africa with over 13 years of programming experience. He has extensive experience in SYSPRO Customization (an ERP system), with C# and web development being his main focus.

He works for Evolution Software, but in all fairness, he can't really call it working at all. When you're having fun and loving what you do with incredibly inspirational individuals, you will not work a day in your life.

He authored the *C# Programming Cookbook* in 2016 (also published by Packt) and has written for Syncfusion, contributing to the Succinctly series of eBooks.

He also blogs at `https://dirkstrauss.com/`, whenever he gets a chance.

I would like to thank the team at Evolution Software for being such an incredible source of inspiration to me in my professional and personal life. Working with you folks challenges me to become better at what I do and the way I live my life. Being a part of the Evolution Software team is the most fulfilling experience of my career. It is something that I will always be incredibly grateful for.

Last but by no means least, I would like to thank my wife and kids. Thank you for reminding me what life is actually about. Without your love and support, this book would not have been possible. I love you.

About the Reviewer

Fabio Claudio Ferracchiati is a senior consultant and a senior analyst/developer using Microsoft technologies. He works for Agic Technology (http://www.agictech.com). He is a Microsoft Certified Solution Developer for .NET, Microsoft Certified Application Developer for .NET, and Microsoft Certified Professional. He is also a prolific author and a technical reviewer. Over the last ten years, he's written articles for Italian and international magazines, and coauthored more than 10 books on a variety of computer topics.

www.PacktPub.com

For support files and downloads related to your book, please visit www.PacktPub.com.

Did you know that Packt offers eBook versions of every book published, with PDF and ePub files available? You can upgrade to the eBook version at www.PacktPub.com and as a print book customer, you are entitled to a discount on the eBook copy. Get in touch with us at service@packtpub.com for more details.

At www.PacktPub.com, you can also read a collection of free technical articles, sign up for a range of free newsletters and receive exclusive discounts and offers on Packt books and eBooks.

https://www.packtpub.com/mapt

Get the most in-demand software skills with Mapt. Mapt gives you full access to all Packt books and video courses, as well as industry-leading tools to help you plan your personal development and advance your career.

Why subscribe?

- Fully searchable across every book published by Packt
- Copy and paste, print, and bookmark content
- On demand and accessible via a web browser

Customer Feedback

Thanks for purchasing this Packt book. At Packt, quality is at the heart of our editorial process. To help us improve, please leave us an honest review on this book's Amazon page at `https://www.amazon.com/dp/1787286274`.

If you'd like to join our team of regular reviewers, you can e-mail us at `customerreviews@packtpub.com`. We award our regular reviewers with free eBooks and videos in exchange for their valuable feedback. Help us be relentless in improving our products!

Table of Contents

Preface

Visual Studio 2017 allows developers to harness the latest technology and create world-class applications across a variety of platforms. The new language features in C# 7.0 are powerful tools that will allow you to write better functioning software and deliver complex business requirements quicker.

The book takes a look at all of the awesome new features in C# 7. It also looks at how developers can write diagnostic analyzers to produce better code and adhere to specific code standards. It explores .NET Core 1.1 and looks at creating an ASP.NET Core application using the MVC framework.

If creating mobile apps is something you are interested in, this book will show you how to do so using Cordova. If you want to create native iOS applications, this book shows you how to do just that using Visual Studio for Mac.

If serverless computing is something that want to understand more, then look no further. In the book, we take a look at what the term serverless computing means. We also look at how to create an Azure function and how to use AWS and S3. Lastly, hot off the press from Amazon, we take a look at using C# lambda functions with AWS.

This book will show you the beauty of C#, which when combined with the power of Visual Studio, makes you a very formidable developer, capable of meeting a variety of programming challenges head on.

Whatever your skill level when it comes to programming with C#, this book provides something for everyone and will make you a better developer.

What this book covers

Chapter 1, *New Features in C# 7.0*, shows how C# 7.0 brings a lot of new functionality to the C# language. The biggest of these features by far are Tuples and pattern matching. Getting to grips with what's new in C# 7.0 is essential for developers in order to stay on top of their game.

Chapter 2, *Classes and Generics*, form the building blocks of software development and are essential in building good code. The power of classes, which is to describe the world around us and translate it into a programming language that a compiler can understand, allows developers to create great software.

Chapter 3, *Object-Oriented Programming in C#*, is the foundation of C# and object-oriented programming (OOP). Understanding this concept is essential to .NET developers everywhere.

Chapter 4, *Code Analyzers in Visual Studio*, talks about how code analyzers help developers to write better code. Be sure that the code you or your team ships measures up to your specific set of code quality standards.

Chapter 5, *Regular Expressions*, is about how regex make use of patterns that describe a string through the use of special characters that denote a specific bit of text to match. The use of regex, when applied properly, can be a very powerful approach to certain programming problems.

Chapter 6, *Working with Files, Streams, and Serialization*, teaches the readers that working with files, streams, and serialization is something you as a developer will do many times. Being able to do so correctly will definitely give you an edge as a developer.

Chapter 7, *Making Apps Responsive with Asynchronous Programming*, talks about how asynchronous programming is an exciting feature in C#. It allows you to continue program execution on the main thread while a long-running task finishes its execution. This enables your applications to remain responsive.

Chapter 8, *High Performance Programming Using Parallel and Multithreading in C#*, improves your code's performance. Using multithreading and parallel programming can mean the difference between users experiencing an application as working or broken.

Chapter 9, *Composing Event-Based Programs Using Reactive Extensions*, teaches the reader how Rx is an exciting technology. If you need to create search-as-you-type functionality in an application, have data that changes notify your application instead of having to poll the data all the time (think stock prices), or generally make your app more responsive, the chances are you need to consider using Rx.

Chapter 10, *Exploring .NET Core 1.1*, is about the buzz regarding .NET Core these days. It allows you to create cross-platform applications that run on Windows, Linux, and macOS. Knowing how to use it is essential for all .NET developers.

Chapter 11, *ASP.NET Core on the MVC Framework*, talks about the MVC framework, which is named according to the MVC design pattern it follows. It allows developers to separate the logic by letting each component of the framework focus on one specific thing. It is this separation of concerns that makes MVC so powerful, especially when combined with .NET Core.

Chapter 12, *Choosing and Using a Source Control Strategy*, is about how source control is an essential part of every developer's toolkit. It doesn't matter whether you are a hobbyist or professional programmer; when you get up from your desk to go home, you'd better be sure your code is safe.

Chapter 13, *Creating a Mobile Application in Visual Studio*, allows developers to create mobile applications with ease. It also gives developers more choice about how to go about doing it. From creating a mobile app with Xamarin, to using Cordova, to writing native iOS applications with Visual Studio for Mac, .NET developers can expand their service offering using the IDE they know and love.

Chapter 14, *Writing Secure Code and Debugging in Visual Studio*, talks about how debugging is something developers do more often than not. Being able to do so efficiently is a different story. In a similar way, being able to write secure code is essential to any developer. Creating secure code and being able to efficiently debug that code properly results in a better end product.

Chapter 15, *Creating Microservices on Azure Service Fabric*, is about how, traditionally, developers wrote applications in a monolithic manner, which is one single executable broken up into components via classes and so on. Microservices is a technology that aims to address the issues surrounding traditional monolithic applications. It allows developers to create smaller bits (services) that can function on their own without being dependent on any of the other services.

Chapter 16, *Azure and Serverless Computing*, is about how serverless does not mean the lack of a server, but rather you (or the application) does not know which server is used to provide some functionality to an application. Splitting some of your application logic into a serverless-type architecture allows for extreme scalability when loads increase (or decrease), increased performance, and less code to write and debug.

What you need for this book

You will need the latest version of Visual Studio 2017. For some of the chapters on mobile development, you will need an active Apple iTunes account. Regarding the last chapter, you will need to create a free AWS account. Lastly, some of the recipes might also require access to the Azure portal.

Who this book is for

The book will appeal to C# and .NET developers who have a basic familiarity with C# and the Visual Studio 2015 environment.

Sections

In this book, you will find several headings that appear frequently (Getting ready, How to do it, How it works, There's more, and See also).

To give clear instructions on how to complete a recipe, we use these sections as follows:

Getting ready

This section tells you what to expect in the recipe, and describes how to set up any software or any preliminary settings required for the recipe.

How to do it…

This section contains the steps required to follow the recipe.

How it works…

This section usually consists of a detailed explanation of what happened in the previous section.

There's more…

This section consists of additional information about the recipe in order to make the reader more knowledgeable about the recipe.

See also

This section provides helpful links to other useful information for the recipe.

Conventions

In this book, you will find a number of text styles that distinguish between different kinds of information. Here are some examples of these styles and an explanation of their meaning.

Code words in text, database table names, folder names, filenames, file extensions, pathnames, dummy URLs, user input, and Twitter handles are shown as follows: "You will find the script in the _database scripts folder in the accompanying source code."

A block of code is set as follows:

```
public override void Initialize(AnalysisContext context)
{
    context.RegisterSymbolAction(AnalyzeSymbol,
    SymbolKind.NamedType);
}
```

New terms and **important words** are shown in bold. Words that you see on the screen, for example, in menus or dialog boxes, appear in the text like this: "From the **Tools** menu, select **NuGet Package Manager** and then **Manage NuGet Packages for Solution....**"

Warnings or important notes appear in a box like this.

Tips and tricks appear like this.

Reader feedback

Feedback from our readers is always welcome. Let us know what you think about this book-what you liked or disliked. Reader feedback is important for us as it helps us develop titles that you will really get the most out of.

To send us general feedback, simply e-mail feedback@packtpub.com, and mention the book's title in the subject of your message.

If there is a topic that you have expertise in and you are interested in either writing or contributing to a book, see our author guide at www.packtpub.com/authors.

Customer support

Now that you are the proud owner of a Packt book, we have a number of things to help you to get the most from your purchase.

Downloading the example code

You can download the example code files for this book from your account at `http://www.packtpub.com`. If you purchased this book elsewhere, you can visit `http://www.packtpub.com/support` and register to have the files e-mailed directly to you.

You can download the code files by following these steps:

1. Log in or register to our website using your e-mail address and password.
2. Hover the mouse pointer on the **SUPPORT** tab at the top.
3. Click on **Code Downloads & Errata**.
4. Enter the name of the book in the **Search** box.
5. Select the book for which you're looking to download the code files.
6. Choose from the drop-down menu where you purchased this book from.
7. Click on **Code Download**.

You can also download the code files by clicking on the **Code Files** button on the book's webpage at the Packt Publishing website. This page can be accessed by entering the book's name in the **Search** box. Please note that you need to be logged in to your Packt account.

Once the file is downloaded, please make sure that you unzip or extract the folder using the latest version of:

- WinRAR / 7-Zip for Windows
- Zipeg / iZip / UnRarX for Mac
- 7-Zip / PeaZip for Linux

The code bundle for the book is also hosted on GitHub at `https://github.com/PacktPublishing/CSharp-7-and-DotNET-Core-Cookbook`. We also have other code bundles from our rich catalog of books and videos available at `https://github.com/PacktPublishing/`. Check them out!

Errata

Although we have taken every care to ensure the accuracy of our content, mistakes do happen. If you find a mistake in one of our books-maybe a mistake in the text or the code-we would be grateful if you could report this to us. By doing so, you can save other readers from frustration and help us improve subsequent versions of this book. If you find any errata, please report them by visiting http://www.packtpub.com/submit-errata, selecting your book, clicking on the **Errata Submission Form** link, and entering the details of your errata. Once your errata are verified, your submission will be accepted and the errata will be uploaded to our website or added to any list of existing errata under the Errata section of that title.

To view the previously submitted errata, go to https://www.packtpub.com/books/content/support and enter the name of the book in the search field. The required information will appear under the **Errata** section.

Piracy

Piracy of copyrighted material on the Internet is an ongoing problem across all media. At Packt, we take the protection of our copyright and licenses very seriously. If you come across any illegal copies of our works in any form on the Internet, please provide us with the location address or website name immediately so that we can pursue a remedy.

Please contact us at copyright@packtpub.com with a link to the suspected pirated material.

We appreciate your help in protecting our authors and our ability to bring you valuable content.

Questions

If you have a problem with any aspect of this book, you can contact us at questions@packtpub.com, and we will do our best to address the problem.

1
New Features in C# 7.0

In this first chapter, we will take a look at the C# 7.0 features by covering them in the following recipes:

- Working with Tuples - getting started
- Working with Tuples - going deeper
- Pattern matching
- Out variables
- Deconstruction
- Local functions
- Improvements to literals
- Ref returns and locals
- Generalized async return types
- Expression bodies for accessors, constructors, and finalizers
- throw expressions

Introduction

C# 7.0 brings a lot of new functionality to the C# language. If you were left wanting more after the release of C# 6.0, then C# 7.0 will not disappoint you at all. It focuses on consuming data, simplifying code, and improving performance. Mads Torgersen who is the C# Program Manager noted that C# 7.0's biggest feature by far is **Tuples**. The other is **pattern matching**. These two features (as well as the others) were met with enthusiasm from C# developers worldwide. It is, therefore, no guess that developers will immediately start implementing these new features introduced in C# 7.0. It will, therefore, be very beneficial to get to grips with what C# 7.0 has to offer and implement the new language features in your development projects as soon as possible.

Throughout this book, I will be using the release candidate of Visual Studio 2017. Some features and methods of doing things might change between the time of writing and the final release of Visual Studio 2017.

Working with Tuples - getting started

I have come across many instances where I wanted to return more than one value from a method. As Mads Torgersen pointed out, the existing options available to developers are not optimal. C# 7.0 has, therefore, introduced **Tuple types** and **Tuple literals** to allow developers an easy way of returning multiple values from methods. Developers can also rest easy when creating Tuples. Tuples are structs, which are value types. This means that they are created locally and are passed by copying the contents. Tuples are also mutable and Tuple elements are public mutable fields. I am personally very excited about using Tuples. Let's explore Tuples in closer detail in the following recipe.

Getting ready

Start off by creating a regular console application in Visual Studio 2017. Simply call the project you create **cookbook**. Before I can jump into using Tuples in C# 7.0, I need to add in a NuGet package. Bear in mind that I am using the release candidate of Visual Studio. This process might change between now and the final release of the product.

1. To do this, head on over to **Tools**, **NuGet Package Manager** and then, click on **Manage NuGet Packages for Solution....**

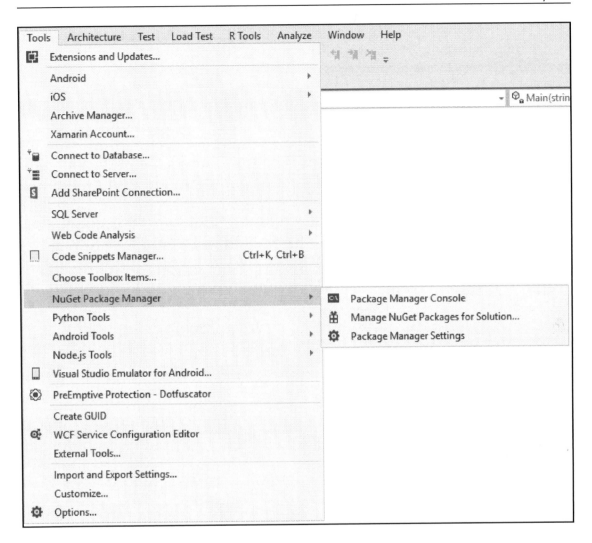

2. Select the **Browse** tab and type in **ValueTuple** in the search box. The
    System.ValueTuple by Microsoft NuGet package should be displayed. Select the
    cookbook project under **Manage Packages for Solution** and click on the **Install**
    button.

Take note that I am using Visual Studio 2017 RC while writing portions of this book. You probably will not need to add `System.ValueTuple` from NuGet some time in the future after the final release. Adding `System.ValueTuple` from NuGet might, however, remain a requirement. Only time will tell.

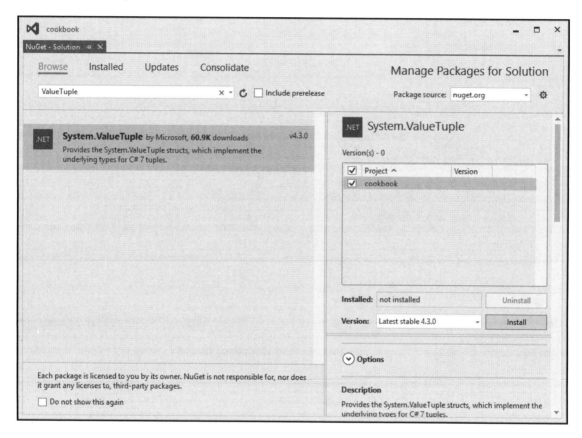

3. Visual Studio will now show you a prompt to review the changes you are about to make to your project. Just click on the **OK** button. Lastly, you will need to provide the **License Agreement** required by Microsoft. Just click on the **I Accept** button. Visual Studio will now start the NuGet package installation. It will show you its progress in the **Output** window.

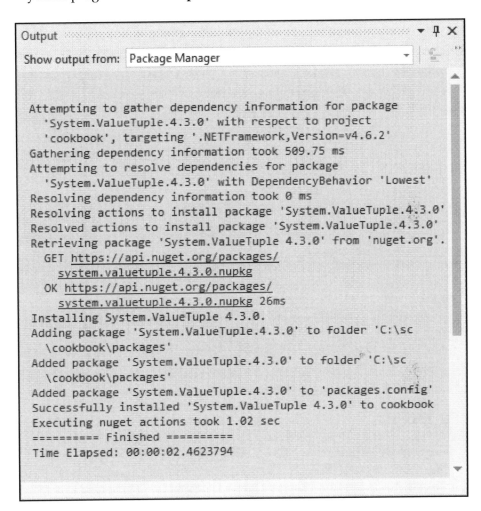

After all this is complete, my Visual Studio solution looks as follows:

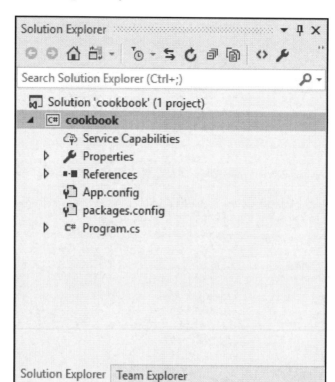

You will now be ready to create your first method that works with Tuples. Let's see how to do that next.

How to do it...

1. Start off by creating a new class in the Program.cs file of your Visual Studio console application. You can call your class anything, but for the purposes of this book I will simply be calling my class Chapter1. Your code should now look as follows:

```
namespace cookbook
{
  class Program
  {
    static void Main(string[] args)
    {
```

```
    }
  }

  public class Chapter1
  {

    }
  }
```

2. This is the format we will be using throughout this chapter. Let's assume that we want to write a method that needs to calculate the average score for a variable number of students. No grade has the same number of students in each class. Therefore, we want our method to return the number of students in the class for the calculated average score. Change the `static void main` method to contain a list of scores. We are also creating a new instance of the `Chapter1` class and calling the method `GetAverageAndCount()`, which will be used to return the two values we need.

 I will be hardcoding this for illustration purposes; in reality, though these scores can be for any number of students. Be sure to add the values exactly as I have in the code listing as I will be illustrating a final gotcha at the end of this recipe.

```
static void Main(string[] args)
{
    int[] scores = { 17, 46, 39, 62, 81, 79, 52, 24 };
    Chapter1 ch1 = new Chapter1();
    var s = ch1.GetAverageAndCount(scores);
}
```

3. It is here that we can use the power of Tuples to declare the `GetAverageAndCount()` method in the `Chapter1` class. It accepts an array of integer scores and looks as follows:

```
public (int, int) GetAverageAndCount(int[] scores)
{

}
```

4. Pay close attention to the return Tuple type `(int, int)`. We are only returning two values from the `GetAverageAndCount()` method, but in reality you can return several values if needed. In order to run your code sample, we will create a dummy implementation of this method. To do this, just include a Tuple literal that returns two zeros.

```
public (int, int) GetAverageAndCount(int[] scores)
{
  var returnTuple = (0, 0);
  return returnTuple;
}
```

5. Go back to the `static void Main` method where the Tuple returning method is called and write code to consume the return values. Every Tuple you create will expose members called `Item1`, `Item2`, `Item3`, and so on. These are used to get the values returned from a Tuple returning method.

```
static void Main(string[] args)
{
  int[] scores = { 17, 46, 39, 62, 81, 79, 52, 24 };
  Chapter1 ch1 = new Chapter1();
  var s = ch1.GetAverageAndCount(scores);
  WriteLine($"Average was {s.Item1} across {s.Item2} students");
  ReadLine();
}
```

6. Be sure to add the following `using` the directive before the namespace.

```
using static System.Console;
```

7. You will notice that we used `s.Item1` and `s.Item2` to reference the return values returned from our `GetAverageAndCount()` method. While this is totally legal, it isn't very descriptive and makes it difficult to infer the usage of the variable returned. It basically means that you would have to remember that `Item1` is the average value and `Item2` is the count value. Perhaps, it is the other way around? Is `Item1` the count and `Item2` the average? It really depends on what you are doing inside the `GetAverageAndCount()` method (which can change over time). Our Tuple returning method can therefore be enhanced as follows:

```
public (int average, int studentCount)
  GetAverageAndCount(int[] scores)
{
  var returnTuple = (0, 0);
  return returnTuple;
```

```
}
```

8. The Tuple return type can now declare variable names for its elements. This makes it easy for the caller of the `GetAverageAndCount()` method to know which value is which. You can still keep on using `s.Item1` and `s.Item2`, but it is now much easier to change the calling code in the `static void Main` method accordingly:

```
static void Main(string[] args)
{
   int[] scores = { 17, 46, 39, 62, 81, 79, 52, 24 };
   Chapter1 ch1 = new Chapter1();
   var s = ch1.GetAverageAndCount(scores);
   WriteLine($"Average was {s.average} across {
      s.studentCount} students");
   ReadLine();
}
```

9. Changing the interpolated string in `WriteLine`, we see that the usage of the values returned by the Tuple is much clearer. You now know that the first value is the average and that the second value is the count of the students used to calculate the average. Tuples, however, allow developers more flexibility. Remember the Tuple literal in the `GetAverageAndCount()` method? We simply added this in the dummy implementation as follows:

```
var returnTuple = (0, 0);
```

10. C# 7.0 also allows developers to add names to Tuple literals. Inside the `GetAverageAndCount()` method, change your Tuple literal as follows:

```
var returnTuple = (ave:0, sCount:0);
```

11. I have just named the first value a name of `ave` (for average) and the second `sCount` (for student count). This is some really exciting stuff! After you have modified your Tuple literal, your dummy implementation of the `GetAverageAndCount()` method should look as follows:

```
public (int average, int studentCount)
   GetAverageAndCount(int[] scores)
{
   var returnTuple = (ave:0, sCount:0);
   return returnTuple;
}
```

Tuples play really nicely together. As long as the Tuple types match up, you do not have to worry that the `ave` and `sCount` names in the Tuple literal don't match the `average` and `studentCount` names of the return type.

How it works...

So far in this recipe, we have seen that Tuples give developers a lot of flexibility when you need to return several values from a method. While the dummy implementation of `GetAverageAndCount()` simply returns the zero-valued Tuple literal, it gives you some idea how Tuples are *wired up*. This recipe is the foundation for the next recipe. I encourage you to go through both recipes thoroughly in order to gain the full benefit from understanding Tuples and how to use them.

Working with Tuples - going deeper

I will now start adding more meat to the dummy implementation of the `GetAverageAndCount()` method we created in the previous recipe. If you are new to Tuples, and have not worked through the previous recipe, I encourage you to do so first before starting to work through this recipe.

Getting ready

You need to have completed the code steps in the recipe *Working with Tuples - getting started*, in order to work through this recipe. Ensure that you have added the required NuGet package as specified in the previous recipe.

How to do it...

1. Let's take a look at the calling code again. We can further simplify the code in the `static void Main` method by getting rid of the `var s`. When we called the `GetAverageAndCount()` method, we returned the Tuple into `var s`.

   ```
   var s = ch1.GetAverageAndCount(scores);
   ```

2. We do not have to do this. C# 7.0 allows us to immediately split the Tuple into its respective parts as follows:

```
var (average, studentCount) = ch1.GetAverageAndCount(scores);
```

3. We can now consume the values returned by the Tuple directly as follows:

```
WriteLine($"Average was {average} across {studentCount} students");
```

4. Before we implement the `GetAverageAndCount()` method, make sure that your `static void Main` method looks as follows:

```
static void Main(string[] args)
{
  int[] scores = { 17, 46, 39, 62, 81, 79, 52, 24 };
  Chapter1 ch1 = new Chapter1();
  var (average, studentCount) = ch1.GetAverageAndCount(scores);
  WriteLine($"Average was {average} across {
    studentCount} students");
  ReadLine();
}
```

5. Secondly, ensure that the `GetAverageAndCount()` method's dummy implementation looks as follows:

```
public (int average, int studentCount)
  GetAverageAndCount(int[] scores)
{
  var returnTuple = (ave:0, sCount:0);
  return returnTuple;
}
```

6. Go ahead and run your console application. You will see that the two values, `average` and `studentCount` are returned from our dummy implementation of `GetAverageAndCount()`.

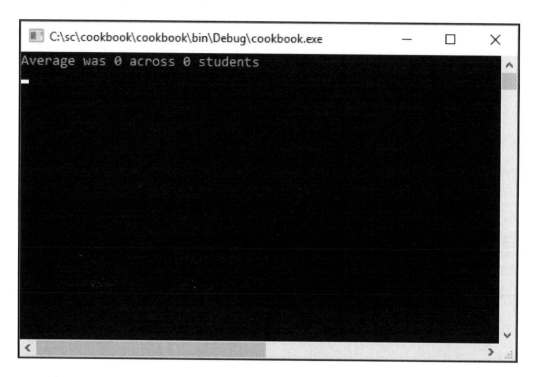

7. The values are obviously still zero because we have not defined any logic inside the method. We will do this next. Before we write the implementation, make sure that you have added the following `using` statement:

```
using System.Linq;
```

8. Because we are using an array of integers for the variable `scores`, we can easily return the results we need. LINQ allows us to get the sum of the student scores contained in the `scores` array, simply by writing `scores.Sum()`. We can also easily get the count of the student scores from the `scores` array by writing `scores.Count()`. The average, therefore, would logically be the sum of the scores divided by the count of the student scores (`scores.Sum()/scores.Count()`). We then put the values into our `returnTuple` literal as follows:

```
public (int average, int studentCount)
```

```
      GetAverageAndCount(int[] scores)
  {
    var returnTuple = (ave:0, sCount:0);
    returnTuple = (returnTuple.ave = scores.Sum()/scores.Count(),
                 returnTuple.sCount = scores.Count());
    return returnTuple;
  }
```

9. Run your console application to see the result displayed as follows:

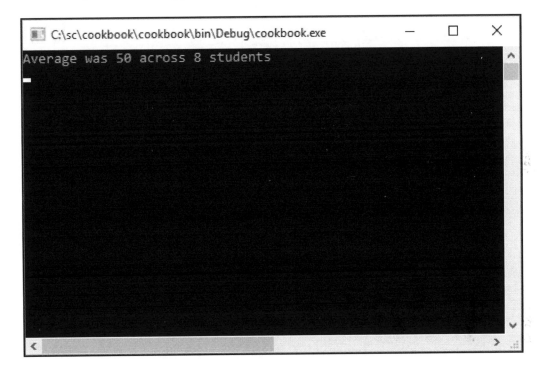

10. We can see that the class average isn't too great, but that is of little importance to our code. Another piece of code that isn't too great is this line:

```
returnTuple = (returnTuple.ave = scores.Sum()/scores.Count(),
             returnTuple.sCount = scores.Count());
```

11. It is clunky and doesn't read very nicely. Let's simplify this a bit. Remember that I mentioned previously that Tuples play nicely together as long as their types match? This means that we can do this:

```
public (int average, int studentCount)
  GetAverageAndCount(int[] scores)
```

```
{
    var returnTuple = (ave:0, sCount:0);
    returnTuple = (scores.Sum()/scores.Count(), scores.Count());
    return returnTuple;
}
```

12. Run your console application again and notice that the result stays the same:

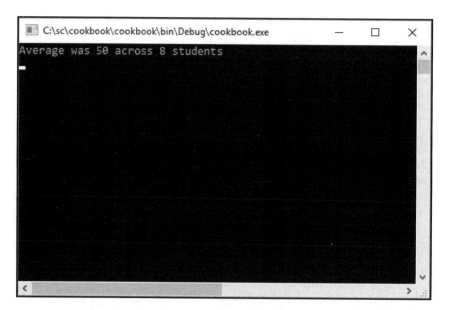

13. So why did we give the Tuple literal names to begin with? Well, it allows you to reference them easily within your GetAverageAndCount() method. It is also really very useful when using a foreach loop in your method. Consider the following scenario. In addition to returning the count and average of the student scores, we need to return an additional Boolean value if the class average is below a certain threshold. For this example, we will be making use of an extension method called CheckIfBelowAverage() and it will take a threshold value as an integer parameter. Start off by creating a new static class called ExtensionMethods.

```
public static class ExtensionMethods
{

}
```

14. Inside the `static` class, create a new method called `CheckIfBelowAverage()` and pass it an integer value called `threshold`. The implementation of this extension method is pretty straightforward, so I will not go into much detail here.

```
public static bool CheckIfBelowAverage(
  this int classAverage, int threshold)
{
  if (classAverage < threshold)
  {
    // Notify head of department
    return true;
  }
  else
    return false;
}
```

15. In the `Chapter1` class, overload the `GetAverageAndCount()` method by changing its signature and passing a value for the threshold that needs to be applied. You will remember that I mentioned that a Tuple return type method can return several values, not just two. In this example, we are returning a third value called `belowAverage` that will indicate if the calculated class average is below the threshold value we pass to it.

```
public (int average, int studentCount, bool belowAverage)
  GetAverageAndCount(int[] scores, int threshold)
{

}
```

16. Modify the Tuple literal, adding it to `subAve` ,and default it to `true`, because a class average of zero will logically be below any threshold value we pass to it.

```
var returnTuple = (ave: 0, sCount: 0, subAve: true);
```

17. We can now call the extension method `CheckIfBelowAverage()` on the `returnTuple.ave` value we defined in our Tuple literal and pass through it the `threshold` variable. Just how useful giving the Tuple literal logical names becomes evident when we use it to call the extension method.

```
returnTuple = (scores.Sum() / scores.Count(), scores.Count(),
              returnTuple.ave.CheckIfBelowAverage(threshold));
```

18. Your completed `GetAverageAndCount()` method will now look as follows:

```
public (int average, int studentCount, bool belowAverage)
  GetAverageAndCount(int[] scores, int threshold)
{
  var returnTuple = (ave: 0, sCount: 0, subAve: true);
  returnTuple = (scores.Sum() / scores.Count(), scores.Count(),
  returnTuple.ave.CheckIfBelowAverage(threshold));
  return returnTuple;
}
```

19. Modify your calling code to make use of the overloaded `GetAverageAndCount()` method as follows:

```
int threshold = 51;
var (average, studentCount, belowAverage) = ch1.GetAverageAndCount(
                                       scores, threshold);
```

20. Lastly, modify the interpolated string to read as follows:

```
WriteLine($"Average was {average} across {studentCount}
        students. {(average < threshold ?
        " Class score below average." :
        " Class score above average.")}");
```

21. The completed code in your `static void Main` method should now look as follows:

```
static void Main(string[] args)
{
  int[] scores = { 17, 46, 39, 62, 81, 79, 52, 24 };
  Chapter1 ch1 = new Chapter1();
  int threshold = 51;
  var (average, studentCount, belowAverage) =
      ch1.GetAverageAndCount(scores, threshold);
  WriteLine($"Average was {average} across {studentCount}
          students. {(average < threshold ?
          " Class score below average." :
          " Class score above average.")}");
  ReadLine();
}
```

22. Run your console application to view the result.

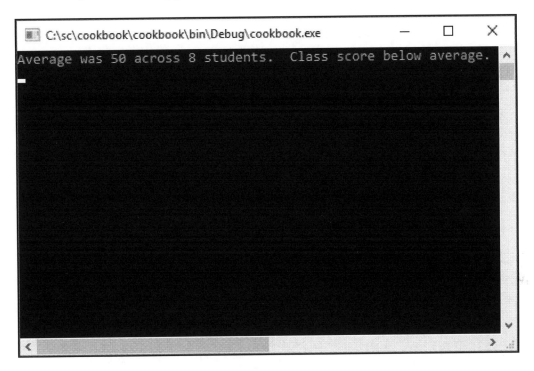

```
C:\sc\cookbook\cookbook\bin\Debug\cookbook.exe          —    □    X
Average was 50 across 8 students.  Class score below average.
```

23. To test that the ternary operator ? is working correctly inside the interpolated string, modify your threshold value to be lower than the average returned.

```
int threshold = 40;
```

24. Running your console application a second time will result in a passing average class score.

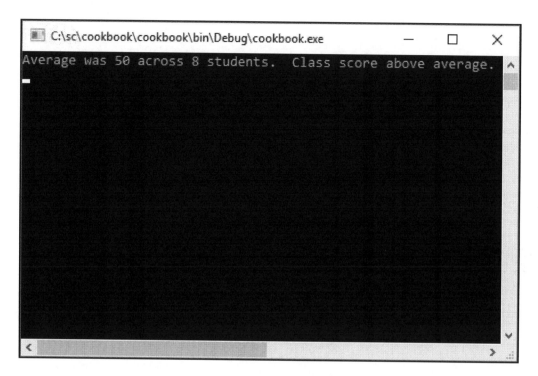

25. Finally, there is one glaring problem that I need to highlight with this recipe. It is one that I am sure you have picked up on already. If not, don't worry. It is a bit of a sneaky one. This is the gotcha I was referring to at the start of this recipe and I intentionally wanted to include it to illustrate the bug in the code. Our array of student scores is defined as follows:

```
int[] scores = { 17, 46, 39, 62, 81, 79, 52, 24 };
```

26. The sum of these equals to 400 and because there are only 8 scores, the value will work out correctly because it divides up to a whole number *(400 / 8 = 50)*. But what would happen if we had another student score in there? Let's take a look. Modify your scores array as follows:

```
int[] scores = { 17, 46, 39, 62, 81, 79, 52, 24, 49 };
```

27. Run your console application again and look at the result.

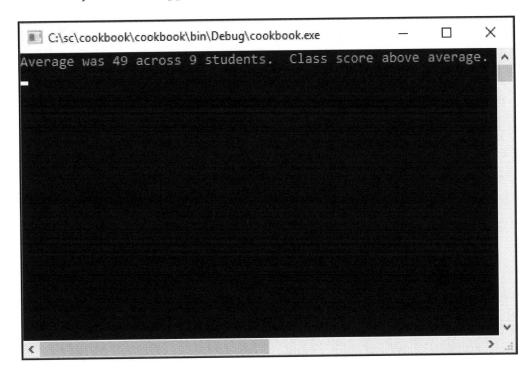

28. The problem here is that the average is incorrect. It should be 49.89. We know that we want a double (unless your application of this is intended to return an integer). We, therefore, need to pay attention to casting the values correctly in the return type and the Tuple literal. We also need to handle this in the extension method `CheckIfBelowAverage()`. Start off by changing the extension method signature as follows to act on a double.

```
public static bool CheckIfBelowAverage(
  this double classAverage, int threshold)
{

}
```

29. Then we need to change the data type of the `average` variable in the Tuple method return type as follows:

```
public (double average, int studentCount, bool belowAverage)
    GetAverageAndCount(int[] scores, int threshold)
{

}
```

30. Then, modify the Tuple literal so `ave` is a double by using `ave: 0D`.

```
var returnTuple = (ave: 0D, sCount: 0, subAve: true);
```

31. Cast the average calculation to a `double`.

```
returnTuple = ((double)scores.Sum() / scores.Count(),
    scores.Count(),
returnTuple.ave.CheckIfBelowAverage(threshold));
```

32. Add the following `using` statement to your application:

```
using static System.Math;
```

33. Lastly, use the `Round` method to format the `average` variable in the interpolated string to two decimals.

```
WriteLine($"Average was {Round(average,2)} across {studentCount}
        students. {(average < threshold ?
                " Class score below average." :
                " Class score above average.")}");
```

34. If everything is done correctly, your `GetAverageAndCount()` method should look as follows:

```
public (double average, int studentCount, bool belowAverage)
    GetAverageAndCount(int[] scores, int threshold)
{
    var returnTuple = (ave: 0D, sCount: 0, subAve: true);
    returnTuple = ((double)scores.Sum() / scores.Count(),
                scores.Count(),
                returnTuple.ave.CheckIfBelowAverage(
                threshold));
    return returnTuple;
}
```

35. Your calling code should also look as follows:

```
static void Main(string[] args)
{
    int[] scores = { 17, 46, 39, 62, 81, 79, 52, 24, 49 };
    Chapter1 ch1 = new Chapter1();
    int threshold = 40;
    var (average, studentCount, belowAverage) =
        ch1.GetAverageAndCount(scores, threshold);
    WriteLine($"Average was {Round(average,2)} across
            {studentCount} students. {(average < threshold ?
            " Class score below average." :
            " Class score above average.")}");
    ReadLine();
}
```

36. Run the console application to see the correctly rounded average for the student scores.

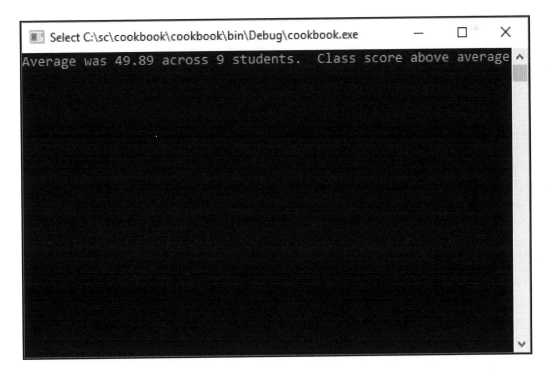

How it works...

Tuples are structs, and therefore value types that are created locally. You, therefore, do not have to worry about using and assigning Tuples on-the-fly or that it creating a lot of allocations. Their contents are merely copied when passed. Tuples are mutable and the elements are publicly scoped mutable fields. Using the code example in this recipe, I can, therefore, do the following:

```
returnTuple = (returnTuple.ave + 15, returnTuple.sCount - 1);
```

C# 7.0 is allowing me to first update the average value (shifting the average up) and then decrementing the count field. Tuples are a very powerful feature of C# 7.0, and it will be of great benefit to many developers when implemented it correctly.

Pattern matching

C# 7.0 introduces an aspect common to functional programming languages with pattern matching. This new kind of construct can test values in different ways. To accomplish this, two language constructs in C# 7.0 have been enhanced to take advantage of patterns. These are as follows:

- The `is` expression
- The `case` clause in `switch` statements

With regard to the is expression, developers can now have a pattern on the right instead of just a type. When it comes to `switch` statements, the `case` clause can now match on patterns. The `switch` statement is no longer limited to primitive types and can switch on anything. Let's start by looking at the `is` expression.

Getting ready

To illustrate the concept of pattern matching, assume the following scenario. We have two object types called `Student` and `Professor`. We want to minimize code, so we want to create a single method to output the data from the object passed to it. This object can be a `Student` or a `Professor` object. The method needs to figure out which object it is working with and act accordingly. But first, we need to do a few things inside our console application to set things up:

1. Ensure that you have added the following `using` statement.

```
using System.Collections.Generic;
```

2. You now need to create two new classes called `Student` and `Professor`. The code for the `Student` class needs to look as follows:

```
public class Student
{
  public string Name { get; set; }
  public string LastName { get; set; }
  public List<int> CourseCodes { get; set; }
}
```

3. Next, the code for the `Professor` class needs to look as follows:

```
public class Professor
{
  public string Name { get; set; }
  public string LastName { get; set; }
  public List<string> TeachesSubjects { get; set; }
}
```

To understand where we are going with pattern matching, we first need to understand where we have come from. I will start the next section off by showing you how developers might have written this code before C# 7.0.

How to do it...

1. In the `Chapter1` class, create a new method called `OutputInformation()` that takes a person object as parameter.

```
public void OutputInformation(object person)
{

}
```

2. Inside this method, we would need to check what type of object is passed to it. Traditionally, we would need to do the following:

```
if (person is Student)
{
  Student student = (Student)person;
  WriteLine($"Student {student.Name} {student.LastName}
```

```
                    is enrolled for courses {String.Join<int>(
                    ", ", student.CourseCodes)}");
    }

    if (person is Professor)
    {
        Professor prof = (Professor)person;
        WriteLine($"Professor {prof.Name} {prof.LastName}
                    teaches {String.Join<string>(",",
prof.TeachesSubjects)}");
    }
```

3. We have two `if` statements. We are expecting either a `Student` object or a `Professor` object. The complete `OutputInformation()` method should look as follows:

```
public void OutputInformation(object person)
{
    if (person is Student)
    {
        Student student = (Student)person;
        WriteLine($"Student {student.Name} {student.LastName}
                    is enrolled for courses {String.Join<int>
                    (", ", student.CourseCodes)}");
    }
    if (person is Professor)
    {
        Professor prof = (Professor)person;
        WriteLine($"Professor {prof.Name} {prof.LastName}
                    teaches {String.Join<string>
                    (",", prof.TeachesSubjects)}");
    }
}
```

4. Calling this method from the `static void Main` is easy enough. The objects are similar, but differ in the list they contain. A `Student` object exposes a list of course codes, while a `Professor` exposes a list of subjects taught to students.

```
static void Main(string[] args)
{
    Chapter1 ch1 = new Chapter1();

    Student student = new Student();
    student.Name = "Dirk";
    student.LastName = "Strauss";
    student.CourseCodes = new List<int> { 203, 202, 101 };
```

```
      ch1.OutputInformation(student);

      Professor prof = new Professor();
      prof.Name = "Reinhardt";
      prof.LastName = "Botha";
      prof.TeachesSubjects = new List<string> {
          "Mobile Development", "Cryptography" };

      ch1.OutputInformation(prof);
  }
```

5. Run the console application and see the OutputInformation() method in action.

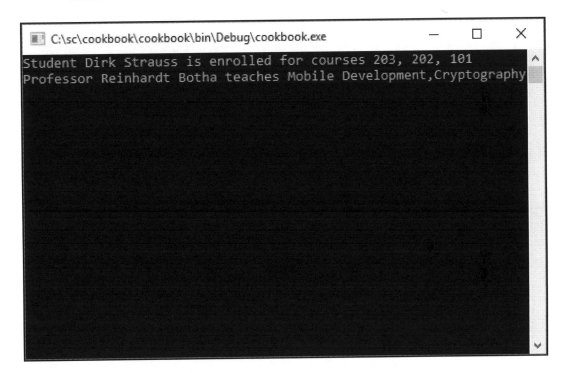

6. While the information we see in the console application is what we expect, we can simplify the code in the `OutputInformation()` method much more with pattern matching. To do this, modify the code as follows:

```csharp
if (person is Student student)
{

}
if (person is Professor prof)
{

}
```

7. The first `if` expression checks to see if the object `person` is of type `Student`. If so, it stores that value in the `student` variable. The same logic is true for the second `if` expression. If true, the value of `person` is stored inside the variable `prof`. For code execution to reach the code between the curly braces of each `if` expression, the condition had to evaluate to true. We can, therefore, dispense with the cast of the `person` object to a `Student` or `Professor` type, and just use the `student` or `prof` variable directly, like so:

```csharp
if (person is Student student)
{
    WriteLine($"Student {student.Name} {student.LastName}
            is enrolled for courses {String.Join<int>
            (", ", student.CourseCodes)}");
}
if (person is Professor prof)
{
    WriteLine($"Professor {prof.Name} {prof.LastName}
            teaches {String.Join<string>
            (",", prof.TeachesSubjects)}");
}
```

8. Running the console application again, you will see that the output is exactly the same as before. We have, however, written better code that uses type pattern matching to determine the correct output to display.

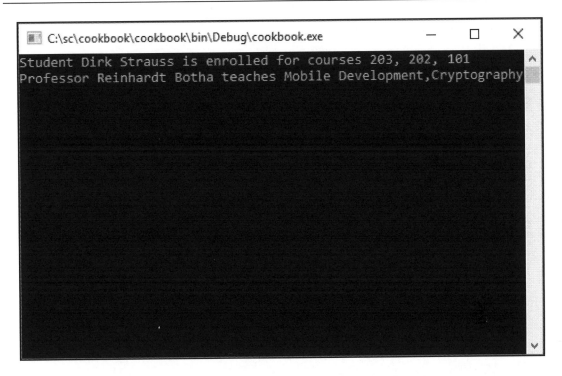

9. Patterns, however, don't stop there. You can also use them in constant patterns, which are the simplest type of pattern to use. Let's take a look at the check for the constant `null`. With pattern matching we can enhance our `OutputInformation()` method as follows:

```
public void OutputInformation(object person)
{
  if (person is null)
  {
    WriteLine($"Object {nameof(person)} is null");
  }
}
```

10. Change the code that is calling the `OutputInformation()` method and set it to `null`.

```
Student student = null;
```

11. Run your console application and see the message displayed.

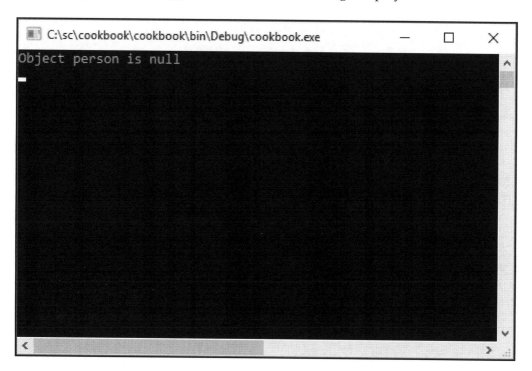

```
C:\sc\cookbook\cookbook\bin\Debug\cookbook.exe

Object person is null
```

It is good practice to use the `nameof` keyword here. If the variable name `person` ever has to change, the corresponding output will be changed also.

12. Lastly, `switch` statements in C# 7.0 have been improved to make use of pattern matching. C# 7.0 allows us to switch on anything, not just primitive types and strings. The `case` clauses now make use of patterns, which is really exciting. Let's have a look at how to implement this in the following code examples. We will keep using the `Student` and `Professor` types to illustrate the concept of pattern matching in `switch` statements. Modify the `OutputInformation()` method and include the boilerplate `switch` statement as follows. The `switch` statement still has defaults, but it can now do so much more.

```
public void OutputInformation(object person)
{
  switch (person)
  {
```

```
      default:
        WriteLine("Unknown object detected");
      break;
    }
  }
```

13. We can expand the `case` statement to check for the `Professor` type. If it matches an object to the `Professor` type, it can act on that object and use it as a `Professor` type in the body of the `case` statement. This means we can call the `Professor`-specific `TeachesSubjects` property. We do it like this:

```
switch (person)
{
  case Professor prof:
    WriteLine($"Professor {prof.Name} {prof.LastName}
              teaches {String.Join<string>
              (",", prof.TeachesSubjects)}");
  break;
  default:
    WriteLine("Unknown object detected");
  break;
}
```

14. We can also do the same for `Student` types. Change the code of the `switch` as follows:

```
switch (person)
{
  case Student student:
    WriteLine($"Student {student.Name} {student.LastName}
              is enrolled for courses {String.Join<int>
              (", ", student.CourseCodes)}");
  break;
  case Professor prof:
    WriteLine($"Professor {prof.Name} {prof.LastName}
              teaches {String.Join<string>
              (",", prof.TeachesSubjects)}");
  break;
  default:
    WriteLine("Unknown object detected");
  break;
}
```

15. One final (and great) feature of `case` statements remains to be illustrated. We can also implement a `when` condition, similar to what we saw in C# 6.0 with exception filters. The `when` condition simply evaluates to a Boolean and further filters the input that it triggers on. To see this in action, change the `switch` accordingly:

```
switch (person)
{
  case Student student when (student.CourseCodes.Contains(203)):
  WriteLine($"Student {student.Name} {student.LastName}
          is enrolled for course 203.");
  break;
  case Student student:
  WriteLine($"Student {student.Name} {student.LastName}
          is enrolled for courses {String.Join<int>
          (", ", student.CourseCodes)}");
  break;
  case Professor prof:
  WriteLine($"Professor {prof.Name} {prof.LastName}
          teaches {String.Join<string>(",",
          prof.TeachesSubjects)}");
  break;
  default:
    WriteLine("Unknown object detected");
  break;
}
```

16. Lastly, to come full circle and check for null values, we can modify our `switch` statement to cater for those too. The completed `switch` statement is, therefore, as follows:

```
switch (person)
{
  case Student student when (student.CourseCodes.Contains(203)):
    WriteLine($"Student {student.Name} {student.LastName}
            is enrolled for course 203.");
  break;
  case Student student:
  WriteLine($"Student {student.Name} {student.LastName}
          is enrolled for courses {String.Join<int>
          (", ", student.CourseCodes)}");
  break;
  case Professor prof:
  WriteLine($"Professor {prof.Name} {prof.LastName}
          teaches {String.Join<string>
          (",", prof.TeachesSubjects)}");
```

```
      break;
    case null:
      WriteLine($"Object {nameof(person)} is null");
      break;
    default:
      WriteLine("Unknown object detected");
      break;
  }
```

17. Running the console application again, you will see that the first case statement containing the when condition is triggered for the Student type.

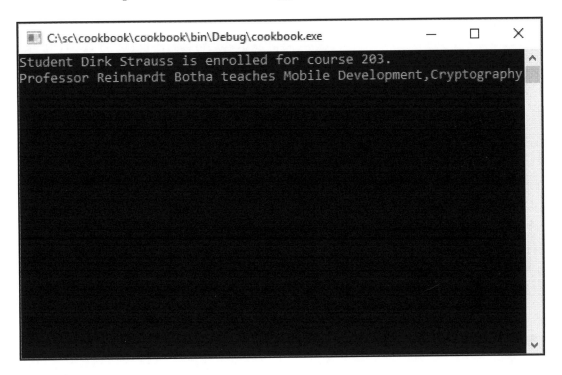

How it works...

With pattern matching, we saw that patterns are used to test whether a value is of a certain type.

You will also hear some developers say that they test whether the value has a certain *shape*.

When we find a match we can get to the information specific to that type (or shape). We saw this in the code where we accessed the `CourseCodes` property, which was specific to the `Student` type and the `TeachesSubjects` property, which was specific to the `Professor` type.

Lastly, you now need to pay careful attention to the order of your `case` statements, which now matters. The `case` statement that uses the `when` clause is more specific than the statement that simply checks for a `Student` type. This means that the `when` case needs to happen before the `Student` case because both of these cases are of type `Student`. If the `Student` case happens before the `when` clause, it will never trigger the `switch` for `Students` that have course code 203.

Another important thing to remember is that the `default` clause will always be evaluated last, irrespective of where it appears in the `switch` statement. It is, therefore, good practice to write it as the last clause in a `switch` statement.

Out variables

C# 7.0 has taken a fresh look at `out` variables. This is a small change, but really one that improves the readability and flow of the code. Previously, we first had to declare a variable to use as an out parameter in a method. In C# 7.0 we no longer need to do that.

Getting ready

We will be using an often used method to test if a value is of a specific type. Yes, you guessed it, we're going to be using `TryParse`. I can already hear some of you groan (or is it just me?). Using `TryParse` is (for me anyway) such a bittersweet thing to do. It's great being able to try and parse something to test if it is valid, but the use of the `out` variable was never as neat and tidy as I would have liked. If you are not familiar with the `TryParse` method, it is a method that tests to see if a value parses to a specific type. If it does, `TryParse` will return a Boolean value of `true`; otherwise, it will return `false`.

How to do it...

1. The following code example will illustrate how we used to have to use `TryParse` to check if a string value is a valid integer. You will notice that we had to declare the integer variable `intVal`, which was used as the `out` variable. The `intVal` variable would just sort of hang there in mid air, usually not initialized and waiting to be used in `TryParse`.

```
string sValue = "500";

int intVal;
if (int.TryParse(sValue, out intVal))
{
  WriteLine($"{intVal} is a valid integer");
  // Do something with intVal
}
```

2. In C# 7.0 this has been simplified, as can be seen in the following code example. We can now declare the `out` variable at the point where it is passed as an out parameter, like so:

```
if (int.TryParse(sValue, out int intVal))
{
  WriteLine($"{intVal} is a valid integer");
  // Do something with intVal
}
```

3. This is a small change, but a very nice one. Run the console application and check the output displayed.

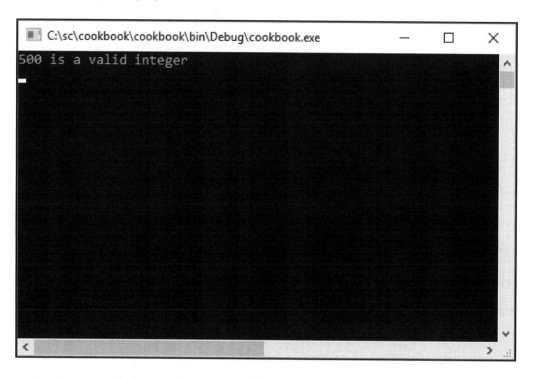

4. As we are declaring the out variable as an argument to the out parameter, the compiler will be able to infer what the type should be. This means that we can also use the var keyword, like this:

```
if (int.TryParse(sValue, out var intVal))
{
  WriteLine($"{intVal} is a valid integer");
  // Do something with intVal
}
```

How it works...

The changes that C# 7.0 has made to out variables are not major. They are, however, a major convenience to those developers who use it often. So far in this chapter, we have seen the use of Tuples, pattern matching, and out variables. We can easily combine some of what we have learned to create something truly unique. Consider the use of extension methods, Tuples, and out variables. We can easily create an extension method called ToInt() that has the following implementation:

```
public static (string originalValue, int integerValue, bool isInteger)
ToInt(this string stringValue)
{
  var t = (original: stringValue, toIntegerValue: 0, isInt: false);
  if (int.TryParse(stringValue, out var iValue))
  {
    t.toIntegerValue = iValue; t.isInt = true;
  }
  return t;
}
```

We create a Tuple literal that will be returned in the event of the TryParse returning false. If the TryParse is true, I set the t.toIntegerValue and t.isInt values. The code that calls the extension method looks as follows:

```
var (original, intVal, isInteger) = sValue.ToInt();
if (isInteger)
{
  WriteLine($"{original} is a valid integer");
  // Do something with intVal
}
```

When you run your console application, you will see that the output is exactly the same as before. This just illustrates the power of the new features in C# 7.0 when combined with each other. Throw some pattern matching into the mix, and we will have a very potent extension method. I'll leave you folks to play around with this some more. There is a lot to discover.

Deconstruction

Tuples can be consumed using a deconstruction declaration. This simply splits a Tuple into its individual parts and assigns these parts to new variables. This is called **deconstruction**, and it is not only reserved for Tuples.

Getting ready

Remember when we used Tuples at the beginning of this chapter? Well we were using code similar to the following to get the values returned by the Tuple literal.

```
var (average, studentCount) = ch1.GetAverageAndCount(scores);
```

This was deconstructing the parts of the Tuple into the new variables `average` and `studentCount`. I do not, however, want to take a look at Tuples again. What I want to do is show how you can implement a deconstruction declaration on any type. To do this, all that we need to do is ensure that the type has a deconstructor method. We will modify our existing `Student` class to add a deconstructor.

How to do it...

1. If you created the `Student` class earlier, you should have something similar to this in your code:

```
public class Student
{
  public string Name { get; set; }
  public string LastName { get; set; }
  public List<int> CourseCodes { get; set; }
}
```

2. To create a deconstructor, add a `Deconstruct` method to your `Student` class. You will notice that this is a `void` method that takes two `out` parameters (in this instance). We then just assign the values of `Name` and `LastName` to the `out` parameters.

If we wanted to deconstruct more values in the `Student` class, we would pass in more `out` parameters, one for each value we wanted to deconstruct.

```
public void Deconstruct(out string name, out string lastName)
{
  name = Name;
  lastName = LastName;
}
```

3. Your modified `Student` class should now look as follows:

```
public class Student
{
  public string Name { get; set; }
  public string LastName { get; set; }
  public List<int> CourseCodes { get; set; }

  public void Deconstruct(out string name, out string lastName)
  {
    name = Name;
    lastName = LastName;
  }
}
```

4. Consuming our `Student` class (just like we did with Tuples) can now be accomplished as follows:

```
Student student = new Student();
student.Name = "Dirk";
student.LastName = "Strauss";

var (FirstName, Surname) = student;
WriteLine($"The student name is {FirstName} {Surname}");
```

5. Running the Console Application will display the deconstructed values returned from the Student class.

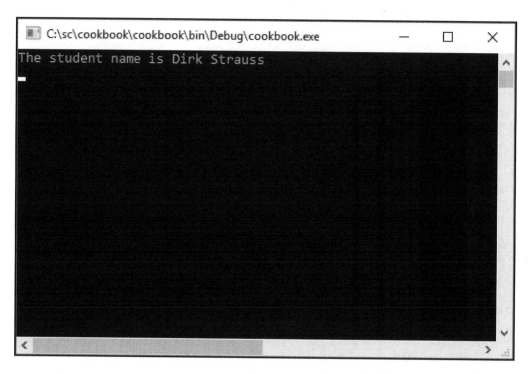

6. Deconstructors can just as easily be used in extension methods. This is quite a nice way to extend the existing type to include a deconstruction declaration. To implement this, we need to remove the deconstructor from our Student class. You can just comment it out for now, but essentially this is what we are after:

```
public class Student
{
  public string Name { get; set; }
  public string LastName { get; set; }
  public List<int> CourseCodes { get; set; }
}
```

7. The `Student` class now does not contain a deconstructor. Head on over to the extension methods class and add the following extension method:

```
public static void Deconstruct(this Student student,
        out string firstItem, out string secondItem)
{
    firstItem = student.Name;
    secondItem = student.LastName;
}
```

8. The extension method acts on a `Student` type only. It follows the same basic implementation of the deconstructor created earlier in the `Student` class itself. Running the console application again, you will see the same result as before. The only difference is that the code is now using the extension method to deconstruct values in the `Student` class.

How it works...

In the code example, we set the student name and last name to specific values. This was just to illustrate the use of deconstruction. A more likely scenario would be to pass a student number to the `Student` class (in the constructor perhaps), as follows:

```
Student student = new Student(studentNumber);
```

The implementation within the `Student` class would then perform a database lookup using the student number passed through in the constructor. This will then return the student details. A more likely implementation of the `Student` class would probably look as follows:

```
public class Student
{
  public Student(string studentNumber)
  {
    (Name, LastName) = GetStudentDetails(studentNumber);
  }
  public string Name { get; private set; }
  public string LastName { get; private set; }
  public List<int> CourseCodes { get; private set; }

  public void Deconstruct(out string name, out string lastName)
  {
    name = Name;
    lastName = LastName;
  }

  private (string name, string surname) GetStudentDetails(string
studentNumber)
  {
    var detail = (n: "Dirk", s: "Strauss");
    // Do something with student number to return the student details
    return detail;
  }
}
```

You will notice that the `GetStudentDetails()` method is just a dummy implementation. This is where the database lookup will start and the values will be returned from here. The code that calls the `Student` class now makes more sense. We call the `Student` class, pass it a student number, and deconstruct it to find the student's first name and surname.

```
Student student = new Student("S20323742");
var (FirstName, Surname) = student;
WriteLine($"The student name is {FirstName} {Surname}");
```

Local functions

The use of local functions might seem a little strange at first. They are in fact quite often used in most functional languages. C# 7.0 now allows us to do the same. So what exactly is a local function? Well, think of it as a helper method for a specific method. This helper method only really makes sense when used from the specific method and will not be useful for other methods in your application. It, therefore, makes sense to use it *inside* your existing method. Some might think that an extension method might be just as well suited, but extension methods should really be used to extend the functionality of many other methods. The usefulness of local functions will become evident in the following code example.

Getting ready

There is nothing you need to specifically get ready or set up beforehand to be able to use local functions. To illustrate the use of local functions, I will create a method that calculates the floor space of a building after the common area space has been subtracted from the total floor space.

How to do it...

1. Create a method called `GetShopfloorSpace()` that takes three parameters: for the common area space, the building width, and the building length.

```
public Building GetShopfloorSpace(int floorCommonArea,
                int buildingWidth, int buildingLength)
{

}
```

2. We are returning a `Building` type, so create a class called `Building` that has a single property called `TotalShopFloorSpace`.

```
public class Building
{
    public int TotalShopFloorSpace { get; set; }
}
```

3. Our local function will simply take the `width` and `length` of the building to calculate the total floor area and then subtract the `common` area from that to get the usable floor space for shops. The local function will look as follows:

```
int CalculateShopFloorSpace(int common, int width, int length)
{
  return (width * length) - common;
}
```

4. This is where it gets interesting. Add the local function inside the `GetShopfloorSpace()` method and add the rest of the code in the following code example:

```
public Building GetShopfloorSpace(int floorCommonArea,
                  int buildingWidth, int buildingLength)
{
  Building building = new Building();

  building.TotalShopFloorSpace = CalculateShopFloorSpace(
        floorCommonArea, buildingWidth, buildingLength);

  int CalculateShopFloorSpace(int common, int width, int length)
  {
    return (width * length) - common;
  }

  return building;
}
```

5. In the calling code, inside the `static void Main` method, call the method as follows:

```
Chapter1 ch1 = new Chapter1();
Building bldng = ch1.GetShopfloorSpace(200, 35, 100);
WriteLine($"The total space for shops is
        {bldng.TotalShopFloorSpace} square meters");
```

6. Run your console application and see the output displayed as follows:

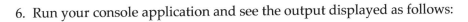

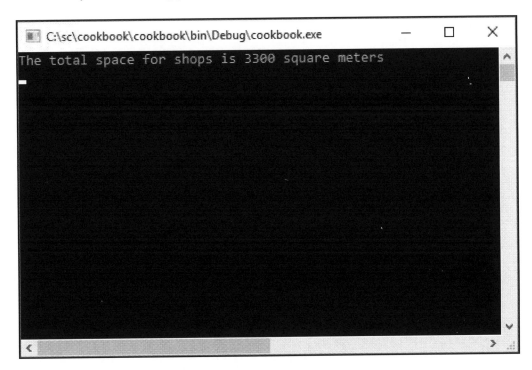

How it works...

The beauty of local functions is that you can call them from anywhere inside your method. To illustrate this, add the following line of code just before the return statement of the GetShopfloorSpace() method. This essentially overrides whatever we passed to the method initially.

```
building.TotalShopFloorSpace = CalculateShopFloorSpace(10, 9, 17);
```

The modified method will now look like this:

```
public Building GetShopfloorSpace(int floorCommonArea, int buildingWidth,
int buildingLength)
{
  Building building = new Building();

  building.TotalShopFloorSpace = CalculateShopFloorSpace(
          floorCommonArea, buildingWidth, buildingLength);
```

```
int CalculateShopFloorSpace(int common, int width, int length)
{
    return (width * length) - common;
}

building.TotalShopFloorSpace = CalculateShopFloorSpace(10, 9, 17);

return building;
}
```

Run your console application again. This time you will see that the values are totally different. The second call to the local function overrode the first call and illustrates that the local function can be called throughout the method containing it.

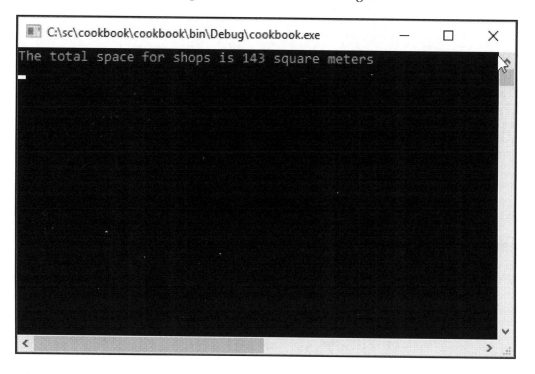

I can think of a few instances where I might have been able to use this in the past. It isn't something I think that I'll use often. It is however a very nice addition to the C# language and great that it is available to developers.

Improvements to literals

This is another minor improvement to the C# language, but one that I'm sure will often be used by developers. One of my first jobs as a young man was working for a logistics company. These folks used to supply parts to Volkswagen, and the most critical parts were flown in by air freight from Germany or elsewhere. I will never forget the 9- and 12-digit shipping numbers the logistics people used to throw around in casual conversation. I wondered how they were able to remember literally hundreds of varying shipping numbers during the course of a year. After listening to them for a while, I noticed that they were saying these numbers with slight pauses after every third number. Even just looking at the 12-digit number 395024102833 is visually taxing. Imagine doing this several times a day, including memorizing the fast movers on the next shipment (I'm not even going to go into the printed shipment manifest, which was a nightmare). It is, therefore, easier to think of the number as 395-024-102-833 and this makes it easier to spot patterns. This is essentially exactly what C# 7.0 now allows developers to do with literals.

Getting ready

Number literals can sometimes be difficult to read. This is why C# 7.0 introduces the underscore (_) to act as a digit separator inside of number literals. C# 7.0 also introduces binary literals, which allow you to specify bit patterns directly without needing to know hexadecimal.

How to do it...

1. Add the following lines of code to your project. It is clear that the newNum literal is easier to read, especially if you read it in groups of three.

```
var oldNum = 342057239127493;
var newNum = 342_057_239_127_493;
WriteLine($"oldNum = {oldNum} and newNum = {newNum}");
```

2. If you run the console application, you will see that the values of the two number literals are exactly the same:

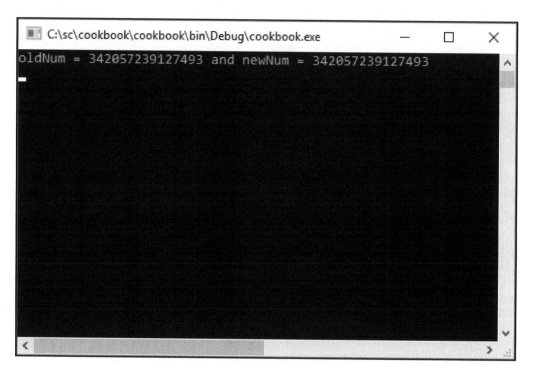

```
C:\sc\cookbook\cookbook\bin\Debug\cookbook.exe                    —    □    ×

oldNum = 342057239127493 and newNum = 342057239127493
```

3. The same logic is true for binary literals. You can now express them as follows:

```
var binLit = 0b1010_1100_0011_0010_0001_0000;
```

How it works...

This is merely syntactical sugar for literals. I'm sure that there is much more to it going on in the background, but the implementation of this in your code is really straightforward.

Ref returns and locals

Passing objects by reference in C# is nothing new. This is done using the `ref` keyword. In C# 7.0, however, you can now return objects by reference and store these objects in a local variable by reference.

Getting ready

It is important to understand the concept of the `ref` keyword. When you pass a `ref` parameter, you are working with the variable itself, not just the value of the variable. This means that, if the value is changed, the original place in memory is updated, not only the value which would be a copy of the parameter. This becomes clearer in the following example.

How to do it...

1. Inside the `Chapter1` class, create a new method called `GetLargest()`. The method is nothing special. It only gets the largest of two values and returns it to the calling code.

```
public int GetLargest(int valueA, int valueB)
{
  if (valueA > valueB)
    return valueA;
  else
    return valueB;
}
```

2. Create a second method with the same name. Only this time, add the `ref` keyword.

```
public ref int GetLargest(ref int valueA, ref int valueB)
{
  if (valueA > valueB)
    return ref valueA;
  else
    return ref valueB;
}
```

3. In the `static void Main` method, create an instance to the `Chapter1` class and call the `GetLargest()` method. Increment the variable `val` and write the variable values to the console window.

```
int a = 10;
int b = 20;
Chapter1 ch1 = new Chapter1();
int val = ch1.GetLargest(a, b);
val += 25;
```

```
WriteLine($"val = {val} a = {a} b = {b} ");
```

4. Then, write the following code just after the previous calling code, but call the ref ch1.GetLargest() method. Increment the refVal variable and write the variable values to the console window.

```
ref int refVal = ref ch1.GetLargest(ref a, ref b);
refVal += 25;

WriteLine($"refVal = {refVal} a = {a} b = {b} ");
```

5. Run your console application and consider the output displayed.

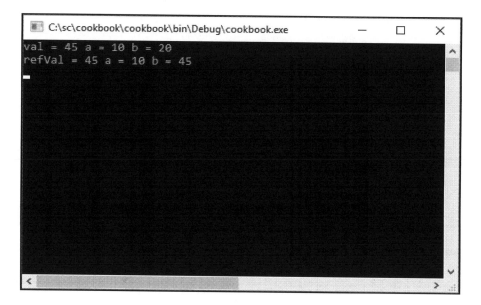

How it works...

In the console window, you will see two very different results. Simply put, in the first line, the variable a is the variable a, the variable b is the variable b, and the variable val is the variable val.

In the second line, the variablea is the variable a, the variable b is the variable b, and the variable refVal is the variable b. This is the whole crux of the ref keyword. In the first GetLargest() method, we returned the largest value into the variable val. This value was 20. The variable val and the variable b had no relation to one another as they were allocated different spaces in memory.

In the second GetLargest() method, we returned the largest variable itself (which was b) into the variable refVal. The variable refVal therefore becomes an alias of the variable b because they both point to the same space allocated in memory. To illustrate this even more clearly, let us have a look at the memory addresses for the variables.

From the **Project** menu, go to the **Properties** of the current project. In the **Build** tab, check the option to **Allow unsafe code** and save the properties.

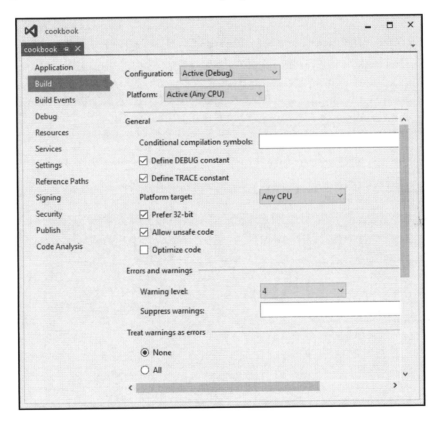

Add the following code to your console application:

```
unsafe
{
  IntPtr a_var_memoryAddress = (IntPtr)(&a);
  IntPtr b_var_memoryAddress = (IntPtr)(&b);
  IntPtr val_var_memoryAddress = (IntPtr)(&val);

  fixed (int* refVal_var = &refVal)
  {
    IntPtr refVal_var_memoryAddress = (IntPtr)(refVal_var);
    WriteLine($"The memory address of a is {a_var_memoryAddress}");
    WriteLine($"The memory address of b is {b_var_memoryAddress}");
    WriteLine($"The memory address of val is {val_var_memoryAddress}");
    WriteLine($"The memory address of refVal is
            {refVal_var_memoryAddress}");
  }
}
```

This code is not really related to the recipe on `ref` returns and locals, so I'm not even going to go into it in any detail. If you want to learn more about pointers in C#, start with the MSDN article on *Pointer types (C# Programming Guide):* `https://msdn.microsoft.com/en-us/library/y31y hkeb.aspx`.

Run your console application and take a look at the memory addresses listed:

```
C:\sc\cookbook\cookbook\bin\Debug\cookbook.exe                    —    □    ✕
The memory address of a is 11531256
The memory address of b is 11531252
The memory address of val is 11531244
The memory address of refVal is 11531252
```

You will notice straightaway that variable `b` and variable `refVal` have the same memory address of `11531252`, while variable `b` and variable `val` have different memory addresses.

So now for the million dollar question: Why is this feature in C# 7.0 even useful? Well, simply put, it can improve performance. Many developers mention that it will be quite useful for game programmers, who can now pass these aliases around to reference large data structures. This means that they don't have to make a copy of a large array (for example) in order to work with it. Using `ref`, they can create an alias that points to the original memory location of the array and read or modify it directly. Thinking of it this way suddenly brings the usefulness of this C# 7.0 feature into perspective.

Will I ever use it? I don't really know. Perhaps not often but, as with local functions, this feature of C# 7.0 is really a great addition to the developer's toolkit. It solves some really tricky problems when you want to get away from copying around large structures in your code.

Generalized async return types

If you use async/await (if not, check it out) the following feature of C# 7.0 will come in really handy. The only supported return types used to be `Task<T>`, `Task`, and `void`. Even then, `void` was also only used with event handlers such as a button click. The challenge, however, was that a `Task<T>` was allocated in situations where the result of the `async` operation was available at the time of awaiting. But, what does this even mean? Well consider an `async` method that returns a `Task<T>` : and that value has a time to live of *n* amount of seconds. If the `async` method is called within the time to live period, why go to the trouble of allocating another `Task<T>` object? This is where the `ValueTask<T>` comes into play; it will allow other types to be defined so that you can return them from an `async` method. This, therefore, reduces the `Task<T>` allocations, which in turn will lead to performance gains.

Getting ready

Start off by creating a new WinForms application and performing the following steps:

1. Add a button, label, timer, and textbox to the Windows form.

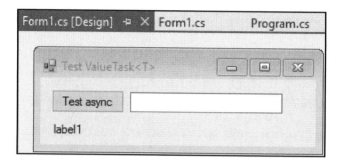

2. We need to add the `System.Threading.Tasks.Extensions` package from NuGet to implement the `ValueTask<T>` struct. This process should be familiar to you if you completed the Tuples recipe. Select the **winform** project and click on the **Install** button.

 Note that I am using Visual Studio 2017 RC while writing this book. You probably will not need to add `System.Threading.Tasks.Extensions` from NuGet in the final release.

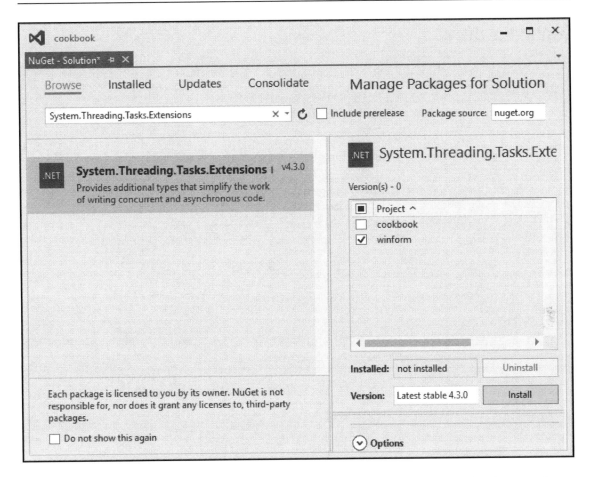

3. A confirmation screen will be displayed to allow you to review the changes that are about to be made. Just click on **OK**. Accept the license agreement. Also make sure that you have added this `using` statement to your project.

```
using System.Threading.Tasks;
```

We are now ready to write our code. The Windows app will call an `async Task<T>` method if the time to live has passed. Once it does that, the method will read a value and cache it. This cached value will be valid for 10 seconds (which is the time to live). If the method is run within the time to live period, then the cached value will be used and returned to the form. If the time to live has passed, the process repeats and the `Task<T>` method is called. The implementation will become clearer when you review the following code samples.

How to do it...

1. Start by adding the following variables to your form.

```
double timerTtl = 10.0D;
private DateTime timeToLive;
private int cacheValue;
```

2. In the form load event, set the label with the timer text.

 Strictly speaking, this is all just fluff. It's not really necessary when it comes to illustrating generalized async return types, but it helps us to visualize and understand the concept.

```
private void Form1_Load(object sender, EventArgs e)
{
    lblTimer.Text = $"Timer TTL {timerTtl} sec (Stopped)";
}
```

3. Set the timer interval on the designer to **1000 ms** and add the following code to the timer1_Tick event.

```
private void timer1_Tick(object sender, EventArgs e)
{
    if (timerTtl == 0)
    {
        timerTtl = 5;
    }
    else
    {
        timerTtl -= 1;
    }
    lblTimer.Text = $"Timer TTL {timerTtl} sec (Running)";
}
```

4. Now create a method that simulates some sort of longer running task. Delay this for a second. Use the Random keyword to generate a random number and assign it to the cacheValue variable. Set the time to live, start the timer, and return the cached value to the calling code.

```
public async Task<int> GetValue()
{
    await Task.Delay(1000);
}
```

```
        Random r = new Random();
        cacheValue = r.Next();
        timeToLive = DateTime.Now.AddSeconds(timerTtl);
        timer1.Start();
        return cacheValue;
    }
```

5. In the calling code, check to see if the time to live is still valid for the current cached value. If the time to live has expired, run the code that allocates and returns a `Task<T>` to get and set the cached value. If the time to live is still valid, just return the cached integer value.

 You will notice that I am passing a Boolean `out` variable to indicate that a cached value has been read or set.

```
        public ValueTask<int> LoadReadCache(out bool blnCached)
        {
          if (timeToLive < DateTime.Now)
          {
            blnCached = false;
            return new ValueTask<int>(GetValue());
          }
          else
          {
            blnCached = true;
            return new ValueTask<int>(cacheValue);
          }
        }
```

6. The code for the button click uses the `out` variable `isCachedValue` and sets the text in the textbox accordingly.

```
        private async void btnTestAsync_Click(object sender, EventArgs e)
        {
          int iVal = await LoadReadCache(out bool isCachedValue);
          if (isCachedValue)
            txtOutput.Text = $"Cached value {iVal} read";
          else
            txtOutput.Text = $"New value {iVal} read";
        }
```

7. When you finish adding all the code, run your application and click on the **Test async** button. This will read a new value from the `GetValue()` method, cache it, and start the time to live count down.

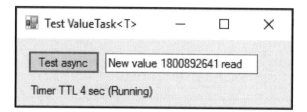

8. If you click on the button again before the time to live has expired, the cached value is returned.

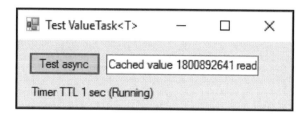

9. When the time to live expires, clicking on the **Test async** button will call the `GetValue()` method again and the process repeats.

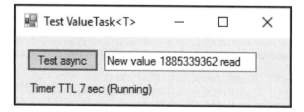

How it works...

`ValueTask<T>` is a very nice addition to C# 7.0. Microsoft, however, does suggest that you benchmark the performance of `Task<T>` versus `ValueTask<T>` when doing additional optimizing of your methods. A simple optimization however would be to simply replace the instances of `Task<T>` with `ValueTask<T>`.

Expression bodies for accessors, constructors, and finalizers

Expression-bodied members have been a big hit with the C# developer community, so much so that Microsoft has expanded the allowed members that can be implemented as expressions. You can now use this feature with:

- Constructors
- Finalizers (used when you need to release unmanaged code)
- get and set accessors on properties and indexers

Getting ready

There is nothing you specifically need to get ready in order to use this recipe. The following code will make use of an old-versus-new approach to demonstrate the differences and implementation of each.

How to do it...

1. Consider the class SomeClass. It contains a constructor, finalizer, and a property.

```
public class SomeClass
{
  private int _initialValue;

  // Property
  public int InitialValue
  {
    get
    {
      return _initialValue;
    }

    set
    {
      _initialValue = value;
    }
  }
```

```
// Constructor
public SomeClass(int initialValue)
{
  InitialValue = initialValue;
}

// Finalizer
~SomeClass()
{
  WriteLine("Release unmanaged code");
}
}
```

2. With expression-bodied members, the class `SomeClass` can be simplified and the number of lines of code reduced.

```
public class SomeClass
{
  private int _initialValue;

  public int InitialValue
  {
    get => _initialValue;
    set => _initialValue = value;
  }

  public SomeClass(int initialValue) =>
          InitialValue = initialValue;

  ~SomeClass() => WriteLine("Release unmanaged code");
}
```

How it works...

If you have used expression-bodied members before in C# 6.0, you will undoubtedly be excited to use the expanded functionality. Personally, I'm really glad that constructors can now be implemented as an expression.

throw expressions

Traditionally, `throw` has been a statement in C#. As we know, because it is a statement and not an expression, we could not use it in certain places. Thanks to expression-bodied members, C# 7.0 introduced `throw` expressions. There isn't any difference in how an exception is thrown, only in where you can throw them from.

Getting ready

Throwing exceptions is nothing new. You have been doing it ever since you have been writing code. I will admit that `throw` expressions are a very welcome addition to C# and it's all thanks to expression-bodied members.

How to do it...

1. To illustrate the use of a `throw` expression, create a method called `GetNameLength()` in the `Chapter1` class. All it does is check to see if the length of a name is not zero. If it is, then the method will throw an exception right there in the expression.

```
public int GetNameLength(string firstName, string lastName)
{
   return (firstName.Length + lastName.Length) > 0 ?
     firstName.Length + lastName.Length : throw new
     Exception("First name and last name is empty");
}
```

2. To see the `throw` expression in action, create an instance of the `Chapter1` class and call the `GetNameLength()` method. Pass it two blank strings as parameters.

```
try
{
   Chapter1 ch1 = new Chapter1();
   int nameLength = ch1.GetNameLength("", "");
}
catch (Exception ex)
{
   WriteLine(ex.Message);
}
```

3. Running your console application will then return the exception message as the output.

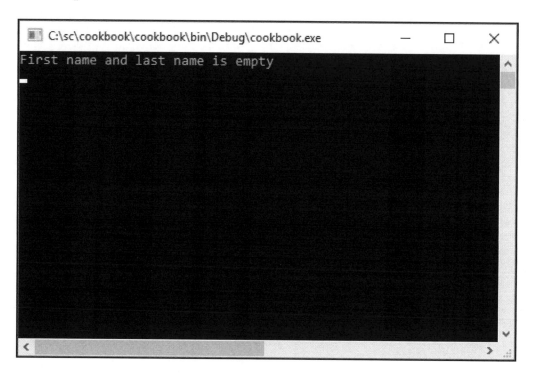

How it works...

Being able to use throw expressions makes your code easier to write and easier to read. The new features in C# 7.0 build on top of the fantastic foundation laid down by C# 6.0.

2

Classes and Generics

Classes form the building blocks of software development and are essential for building good code. In this chapter, we will be looking at classes and generics and why we need to use them. The recipes we will be covering are as follows:

- Creating and implementing an abstract class
- Creating and implementing an interface
- Creating and using a generic class or method
- Creating and using a generic interface

Introduction

As you probably know, classes are simply containers for related methods and properties to describe an object in your software. An object is an instance of a specific class and, sometimes, mimics real-world things. When thinking of a car, you might create a vehicle class that contains certain attributes (properties) that all vehicles contain, such as automatic or manual transmission, wheel count (not all vehicles have only four wheels), or fuel type.

When we create an instance of the vehicle class, we can create a car object, an SUV object, and so on. Here lies the power of classes, which is to describe the world around us and translate it into a programming language that a compiler can understand.

Creating and implementing an abstract class

Many developers have heard about abstract classes, but their implementation is a mystery. How can you as a developer identify an abstract class and decide when to use one? The definition is quite a simple one actually. Once you understand this fundamental definition of an abstract class, when and why to use one becomes obvious.

Imagine for a moment that you are developing an application that manages the animals in a cat sanctuary. The cat sanctuary rehabilitates lions, tigers, jaguars, leopards, cheetahs, pumas, and even domestic cats. The common noun that describes all these animals is the word *cat*. You can, therefore, safely assume that the abstraction of all these animals is a cat, and thus, this word identifies our abstract class. You would then create an abstract class called `Cat`.

However, you need to keep in mind that you will never ever create an instance of the abstract class `Cat`. All the classes that inherit from the abstract class also share some functionality. This means that you will create a `Lion` class and a `Tiger` class that inherit from the abstract class `Cat`. In other words, the inherited classes are a kind of cat. Both classes share functionality in the form of `Sleep()`, `Eat()`, `Hunt()`, and various other methods. In this way, we can ensure that inherited classes all contain this common functionality.

Getting ready

Let's go ahead and create our abstract class for cat. We will then use it to inherit from and create other objects to define different types of cats.

How to do it...

1. Create a new console application in Visual Studio and call it `ClassesAndGenerics`.

2. Add an abstract class called `Cat`. To do this, add the `abstract` keyword to the class. We are now ready to describe the `Cat` abstract class:

```
public abstract class Cat
{

}
```

The `abstract` keyword indicates to us that the object it is applied to has no implementation. When used in a class declaration, it basically tells the compiler that the class is to be used as a base class. This means that no instance of the class can be created. The only way in which implementation of the abstract class happens is when it is implemented by derived classes that inherit from the base class.

3. Your console application code should now look as follows:

```
class Program
{
  static void Main(string[] args)
  {
  }
}

public abstract class Cat
{

}
```

4. Add three methods to the abstract class called `Eat()`, `Hunt()`, and `Sleep()`. You will note that these methods don't contain a body (curly braces). This is because they have been defined as abstract. As with abstract classes, the abstract methods contained within the abstract class contain no implementation. These three methods basically describe functionality that is common to all cats. All cats must eat, hunt, and sleep. Therefore, to ensure that all classes that inherit from the `Cat` abstract class contain this functionality, it is added to the abstract class. These methods are then implemented in the derived classes, which we will see in the upcoming steps:

```
public abstract class Cat
{
  public abstract void Eat();
  public abstract void Hunt();
  public abstract void Sleep();
}
```

5. We want to define two types of cats. The first type of cat we want to define is a lion. For this, we create a `Lion` class:

```
public class Lion
{

}
```

6. At this point in time, the `Lion` class is simply an ordinary class and does not contain any common functionality defined in the `Cat` abstract class. To inherit from the `Cat` abstract class, we need to add : `Cat` after the `Lion` class name. The colon indicates that the `Lion` class inherits from the `Cat` abstract class. The `Lion` class is therefore a derived class of the `Cat` abstract class:

```
public class Lion : Cat
{

}
```

As soon as you specify that the `Lion` class inherits from the `Cat` class, Visual Studio will show you an error. This is expected, because we have told the compiler that the `Lion` class needs to inherit all the features of the `Cat` abstract class, but we have not actually added these features to the `Lion` class. The derived class is said to override the methods in the abstract class, and needs to specifically be written with the `override` keyword.

7. If you hover over the red squiggly line underlining the `Lion` class, Visual Studio will offer an explanation for the error via the lightbulb feature. As you can see, Visual Studio is telling you that while you have defined the class to be inheriting from the abstract class, you have not implemented any of the abstract members of the `Cat` class:

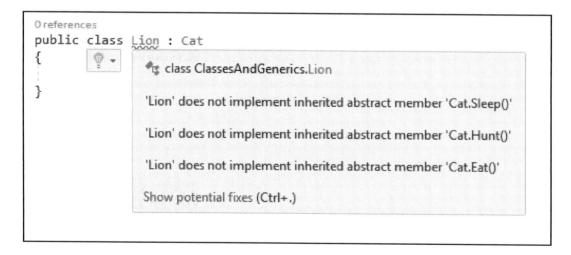

You can, therefore, see that using abstract classes is a fantastic way to enforce specific functionality within your system. If you define abstract members in an abstract class, the derived classes that inherit from that abstract class must implement those members; otherwise, your code will not compile. This can be used to enforce standards and practices adopted by your company or to simply allow other developers to implement certain best practices as they use your base class for their derived classes. With the advent of code analyzers in Visual Studio 2015, the practice of enforcing certain code best practices is easily enforced.

8. To implement these members that Visual Studio is warning us about, place your mouse cursor on the `Lion` class name and hit *Ctrl + .* (period). You can also click on the **Show potential fixes** link in the lightbulb popup. Visual Studio will give you a small heads up, displaying the changes it will make to your code. You can preview these changes by clicking on the **Preview changes** link as well as fix all occurrences in the document, project, or solution by clicking on the appropriate link:

```
0 references
public class Lion : Cat
{

}
```

Implement Abstract Class ▶ ❌ CS0534 'Lion' does not implement inherited abstract member 'Cat.Eat()'

```
...
{
    public override void Eat()
    {
        throw new NotImplementedException();
    }

    public override void Hunt()
    {
        throw new NotImplementedException();
    }

    public override void Sleep()
    {
        throw new NotImplementedException();
    }
}
...
```

Preview changes

Fix all occurrences in: Document | Project | Solution

After Visual Studio has added the changes displayed in the suggestions window, your `Lion` class will be correct and will look like the code listing in the following step.

9. You will notice that Visual Studio automatically adds a `NotImplementedException` exception with the following line of code in each overridden method `throw new NotImplementedException();`:

```
public class Lion : Cat
{
  public override void Eat()
  {
    throw new NotImplementedException();
  }

  public override void Hunt()
  {
    throw new NotImplementedException();
  }

  public override void Sleep()
  {
    throw new NotImplementedException();
  }
}
```

This is the default behavior of Visual Studio when overriding methods in the base class. Basically, if you had to instantiate the `Lion` class without writing any implementation in the overridden methods, a runtime exception would be generated. The idea of inheriting from our abstract class was to extend it and implement common functionality. This is where we need to implement that functionality, and this is the reason there is no implementation in the abstract class. The abstract class just tells us that the following methods need to be implemented. The derived class does the actual implementation.

10. Go ahead and add some implementation to the overridden methods of the `Lion` class. First, add the `using static` statement for the `Console.WriteLine` method to the top of your class file:

```
using static System.Console;
```

11. Then, add the implemented code for the methods as follows:

```
public override void Eat()
{
    WriteLine($"The {LionColor} lion eats.");
}

public override void Hunt()
{
    WriteLine($"The {LionColor} lion hunts.");
}

public override void Sleep()
{
    WriteLine($"The {LionColor} lion sleeps.");
}
```

12. Next, we will create another class called `Tiger` that also derives from the abstract class `Cat`. Follow step 7 to step 10 to create the `Tiger` class and inherit the `Cat` abstract class:

```
public class Tiger : Cat
{
    public override void Eat()
    {
        throw new NotImplementedException();
    }

    public override void Hunt()
    {
        throw new NotImplementedException();
    }

    public override void Sleep()
    {
        throw new NotImplementedException();
    }
}
```

13. Add the same implementation for the `Tiger` class as follows:

```
public override void Eat()
{
    WriteLine($"The {TigerColor} tiger eats.");
}

public override void Hunt()
```

```
{
   WriteLine($"The {TigerColor} tiger hunts.");
}

public override void Sleep()
{
   WriteLine($"The {TigerColor} tiger sleeps.");
}
```

14. For our `Lion` class, add an enumerator for `ColorSpectrum` and a property called `LionColor`. It is here that the implementations of the `Lion` and `Tiger` classes will differ. While they both must implement the common functionality specified in the abstract class, namely, `Eat()`, `Hunt()`, and `Sleep()`, only the lion can have a color of either brown or white in its available range of colors:

```
public enum ColorSpectrum { Brown, White }
public string LionColor { get; set; }
```

15. Next, add the `Lion()` constructor in our `Lion` class. This will allow us to specify a color for the lions in the cat sanctuary. The constructor also takes as a parameter a variable of the `ColorSpectrum` enumerator type:

```
public Lion(ColorSpectrum color)
{
   LionColor = color.ToString();
}
```

16. Slightly similar to this, but quite different in color, the `Tiger` class can only have a `ColorSpectrum` enumeration that defines tigers as being orange, white, gold, blue (yes, you actually get a blue tiger), or black. Add the `ColorSpectrum` enumerator to the `Tiger` class as well as a property called `TigerColor`:

```
public enum ColorSpectrum { Orange, White, Gold, Blue,  Black }
public string TigerColor { get; set; }
```

17. Finally, we will create a `Tiger()` constructor for our `Tiger` class to set the colors of tigers in the cat sanctuary to the valid colors that tigers are found in. By doing this, we are separating certain functionality specific only to tigers and lions in their respective classes, while all the common functionality is contained in the abstract class `Cat`:

```
public Tiger(ColorSpectrum color)
{
   TigerColor = color.ToString();
}
```

18. We now need to instantiate the `Lion` and `Tiger` classes from the console application. You will see that we set the respective cat's color from the constructor:

```
Lion lion = new Lion(Lion.ColorSpectrum.White);
lion.Hunt();
lion.Eat();
lion.Sleep();

Tiger tiger = new Tiger(Tiger.ColorSpectrum.Blue);
tiger.Hunt();
tiger.Eat();
tiger.Sleep();

ReadLine();
```

19. When you run your console application, you see that the methods are called in sequence:

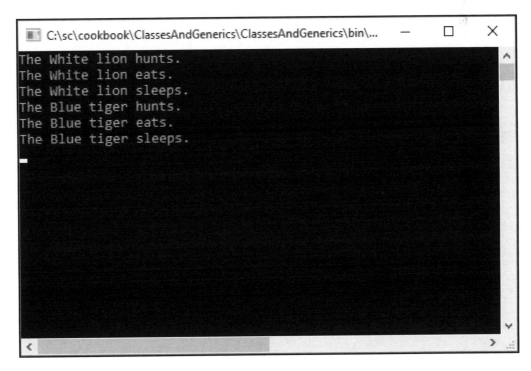

How it works...

While the example illustrated earlier is a rather simplistic one, the theory is sound. The abstract class takes collective functionality across all cats and groups so that it can be shared inside each derived class. No implementation exists in the abstract class; it only defines what needs to happen. Think of abstract classes as a type of blueprint for classes that inherit from the abstract class.

While the content of the implementation is up to you, the abstract class requires that you add the abstract methods it defines. From here on, you can create a solid foundation for similar classes in your applications that are supposed to share functionality. This is the goal of inheritance. Let's recap the features of an abstract class:

- You can't instantiate an abstract class with the `new` keyword.
- You can only add abstract methods and accessors to an abstract class.
- You can never modify an abstract class as `sealed`. The `sealed` modifiers prevents inheritance, while abstract requires inheritance.
- Any class derived from your abstract class must include the implementations of the abstract methods that were inherited from the abstract class.
- Because abstract methods inside the abstract class have no implementation, they don't contain a body either.

Creating and implementing an interface

For many developers, interfaces are equally confusing and their purpose not clearly understood. Interfaces are actually quite easy to get to grips with once you understand the concept that defines an interface.

Interfaces act like verbs. So, for example, if we had to create two classes called `Lion` and `Tiger` that derive from the `Cat` abstract class, the interface would describe some sort of action. Lions and tigers can roar (but not purr). We can then create an interface called `IRoarable`. If we had to derive a class called `Cheetah` from our abstract class `Cat`, we would not be able to use the `IRoarable` interface, because cheetahs purr. We would need to create an `IPurrable` interface.

Getting ready

Creating an interface is very similar to creating an abstract class. The difference is that the interface is describing what the class can do, in the case of the Cheetah class, by implementing IPurrable.

How to do it...

1. If you haven't already done so in the previous recipe, create an abstract class called Cat:

```
public abstract class Cat
{
    public abstract void Eat();
    public abstract void Hunt();
    public abstract void Sleep();
}
```

2. Next, add a class called Cheetah that inherits from the Cat abstract class:

```
public class Cheetah : Cat
{

}
```

3. As soon as you inherit from the Cat abstract class, Visual Studio will show you a warning via the lightbulb feature. As you inherited from the abstract class Cat, you have to implement the abstract members within the abstract class in your derived class Cheetah:

```
0 references
public class Cheetah : Cat
{
    💡 ▾        🔧 class ClassesAndGenerics.Cheetah

                'Cheetah' does not implement inherited abstract member 'Cat.Eat()'
}
                'Cheetah' does not implement inherited abstract member 'Cat.Hunt()'

                'Cheetah' does not implement inherited abstract member 'Cat.Sleep()'

                Show potential fixes (Ctrl+.)
```

4. This is easily fixable by typing *Ctrl +.* (period) and fixing all occurrences in the document. You can also do this for the project or solution. For our purpose, we only select the **Document** link at the bottom of the lightbulb suggestions. Visual Studio will automatically add the abstract methods defined in the abstract class to implement inside your `Cheetah` class:

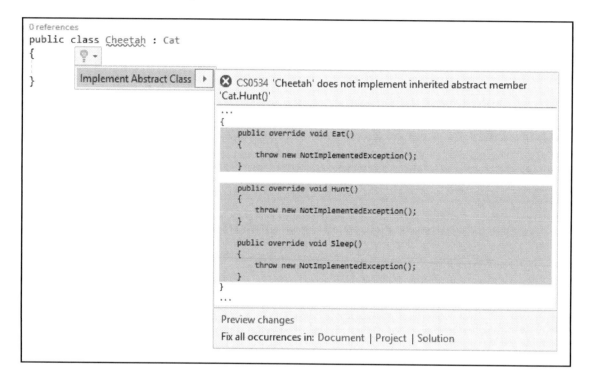

5. You will notice that Visual Studio adds just the methods you need to override but will throw `NotImplementedException` if you try to use the class as is. The reason for using an abstract class is to implement the functionality defined in the abstract class `Cat` in the derived class `Cheetah`. Not doing so contravenes the rules for using abstract classes:

```
public class Cheetah : Cat
{
  public override void Eat()
  {
    throw new NotImplementedException();
  }

  public override void Hunt()
  {
```

```
      throw new NotImplementedException();
    }

    public override void Sleep()
    {
      throw new NotImplementedException();
    }
  }
```

6. To add some implementation, modify your Cheetah class as follows. The implementation in the overridden methods is simple, but this validates the rule of writing some sort of implementation in the overridden methods:

```
public class Cheetah : Cat
{
  public override void Eat()
  {
    WriteLine($"The cheetah eats.");
  }

  public override void Hunt()
  {
    WriteLine($"The cheetah hunts.");
  }

  public override void Sleep()
  {
    WriteLine($"The cheetah sleeps.");
  }
}
```

 You will notice that the WriteLine method is used without the Console class. This is because we are using a new feature introduced in C# 6.0 that allows developers to bring static classes into scope by adding the using static System.Console; statement to the top of your class file.

7. Create an interface called IPurrable that will be implemented in the Cheetah class. A common naming convention for interfaces dictates that the interface name should be prefixed with a capital I:

```
interface IPurrable
{

}
```

8. Next, we will add a method to the interface that any class implementing the interface must implement. You will notice that the interface's `SoftPurr` method contains no implementation at all. It, however, specifies that we will need to pass this method an integer value for the decibel that the `Cheetah` class will purr at:

```
interface IPurrable
{
   void SoftPurr(int decibel);
}
```

9. The next step is to implement the `IPurrable` interface in the `Cheetah` class. To do this, we need to add the `IPurrable` interface name after the `Cat` abstract class name. If the `Cheetah` class did not inherit from the abstract class, then the interface name would simply follow after the colon:

```
public class Cheetah : Cat, IPurrable
{
   public override void Eat()
   {
      WriteLine($"The cheetah eats.");
   }

   public override void Hunt()
   {
      WriteLine($"The cheetah hunts.");
   }

   public override void Sleep()
   {
      WriteLine($"The cheetah sleeps.");
   }
}
```

10. After specifying that the `Cheetah` class implements the `IPurrable` interface, Visual Studio once again displays a warning via the lightbulb feature. It is warning us that the `Cheetah` class does not implement the `SoftPurr` method defined in the interface `IPurrable`:

```
0 references
public class Cheetah : Cat, IPurrable
{
    5 references
    public override void Eat()
    {
        WriteLine($"The cheetah eats.");
    }

    5 references
    public override void Hunt()
    {
        WriteLine($"The cheetah hunts.");
    }
```

11. As we did earlier, we can let Visual Studio suggest possible fixes for the problems encountered by typing *Ctrl + .* (period). Visual Studio suggests that the interface can be implemented implicitly or explicitly:

```
0 references
public class Cheetah : Cat, IPurrable
{
    5 references
    public override voi  Implement interface            ▶   ⊗ CS0535 'Cheetah' does not implement interface member
    {                    Implement interface explicitly       'IPurrable.SoftPurr(int)'
        WriteLine($"The                                     ...
    }                                                       }

    5 references                                            public void SoftPurr(int decibel)
    public override void Hunt()                             {
    {                                                           throw new NotImplementedException();
        WriteLine($"The cheetah hunts.");                   }
    }                                                   }
                                                        ...
    5 references
    public override void Sleep()                        Preview changes
    {                                                   Fix all occurrences in: Document | Project | Solution
        WriteLine($"The cheetah sleeps.");
    }
}
```

12. Knowing when to use an implicit or explicit implementation is also quite easy. We first need to know when using one over the other would be preferred. Let's start off by implementing the `SoftPurr` method implicitly by selecting the first option in the lightbulb suggestion. You will see that this uses the `SoftPurr` method defined in the `IPurrable` interface as if it were part of the `Cheetah` class:

```
public class Cheetah : Cat, IPurrable
{
  public void SoftPurr(int decibel)
  {
    throw new NotImplementedException();
  }

  public override void Eat()
  {
    WriteLine($"The cheetah eats.");
  }

  public override void Hunt()
  {
    WriteLine($"The cheetah hunts.");
  }

  public override void Sleep()
  {
    WriteLine($"The cheetah sleeps.");
  }
}
```

13. If we look at the `SoftPurr` method, it looks like a normal method inside the `Cheetah` class. This would be fine unless our `Cheetah` class already contains a property called `SoftPurr`. Go ahead and add a property called `SoftPurr` to your `Cheetah` class:

```
public class Cheetah : Cat, IPurrable
{
  public int SoftPurr { get; set; }

  public void SoftPurr(int decibel)
  {
    throw new NotImplementedException();
  }

  public override void Eat()
  {
```

```
      WriteLine($"The cheetah eats.");
   }

   public override void Hunt()
   {
      WriteLine($"The cheetah hunts.");
   }

   public override void Sleep()
   {
      WriteLine($"The cheetah sleeps.");
   }
}
```

14. Visual Studio immediately displays a warning by telling us that the `Cheetah` class already contains a definition for `SoftPurr`:

```
0 references
public class Cheetah : Cat, IPurrable
{
    0 references
    public int SoftPurr { get; set; }
    1 reference
    public void SoftPurr(int decibel)
    {
        throw new    ⊘  void Cheetah.SoftPurr(int decibel)

    }                The type 'Cheetah' already contains a definition for 'SoftPurr'

    5 references
    public override void Eat()
    {
        WriteLine($"The cheetah eats.");
    }
```

15. It is here that the use of an explicit implementation becomes evident. This specifies that the `SoftPurr` method is a member of the implementation defined in the `IPurrable` interface:

```
0 references
public class Cheetah : Cat, IPurrable
{
    5 references
    public override voi Implement interface
    {                     Implement interface explicitly  ▶
        WriteLine($"The
    }

    5 references
    public override void Hunt()
    {
        WriteLine($"The cheetah hunts.");
    }

    5 references
    public override void Sleep()
    {
        WriteLine($"The cheetah sleeps.");
    }
}
```

```
⊗ CS0535 'Cheetah' does not implement interface member
  'IPurrable.SoftPurr(int)'
  ...

    void IPurrable.SoftPurr(int decibel)
    {
        throw new NotImplementedException();
    }
  ...

Preview changes
Fix all occurrences in: Document | Project | Solution
```

16. Therefore, selecting the second option to implement the interface explicitly will add the `SoftPurr` method to your `Cheetah` class as follows:

```
public class Cheetah : Cat, IPurrable
{
    public int SoftPurr { get; set; }

    void IPurrable.SoftPurr(int decibel)
    {
        throw new NotImplementedException();
    }

    public override void Eat()
    {
        WriteLine($"The cheetah eats.");
    }

    public override void Hunt()
    {
        WriteLine($"The cheetah hunts.");
    }

    public override void Sleep()
```

```
  {
    WriteLine($"The cheetah sleeps.");
  }
}
```

The compiler now knows that this is an interface that is being implemented and is therefore a valid line of code.

17. For the purposes of this book, let's just use the implicit implementation. Let's write some implementation for the `SoftPurr` method and use the new `nameof` keyword (introduced in C# 6.0) as well as the interpolated string for the output. Also, remove the `SoftPurr` property added earlier:

```
public void SoftPurr(int decibel)
{
    WriteLine($"The {nameof(Cheetah)} purrs at {decibel} decibels.");
}
```

18. Heading over to our console application, we can call our `Cheetah` class as follows:

```
Cheetah cheetah = new Cheetah();
cheetah.Hunt();
cheetah.Eat();
cheetah.Sleep();
cheetah.SoftPurr(60);
ReadLine();
```

19. Running the application will produce the following output:

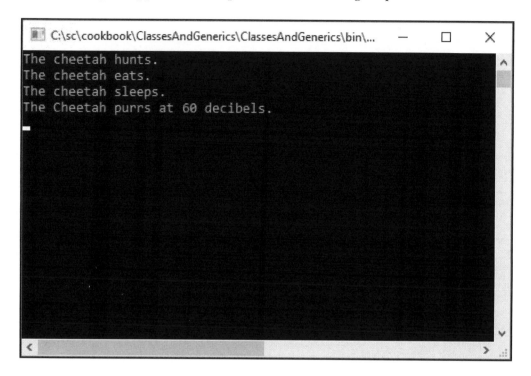

How it works...

So, you might be wondering what the difference between an abstract class and an interface is. It basically comes down to where you want your implementation. If you need to share functionality between derived classes, then an abstract class is the best fit for your needs. In other words, we had specific things that were common to all cats (lions, tigers, and cheetahs) such as hunting, eating, and sleeping. This is then best used within an abstract class.

If your implementation is specific to a class or several classes (but not all classes), then your best course of action would be to use an interface. In this case, the IPurrable interface can be applied to several classes (for example, cheetahs and domestic cats) but can't be applied to all cats (such as lions and tigers), because not all cats can purr.

Knowing this difference and where you need to place your implementation will aid you in deciding whether you need to use an abstract class or an interface.

Creating and using a generic class or method

Generics is a very interesting way of writing code. Instead of specifying the data type of the elements in the code at design time, you can actually delay the specification of those elements until they are used in code. This basically means that your class or method can work with any data type.

Getting ready

We will start off by writing a generic class that can take any data type as a parameter in its constructor and do something with it.

How to do it...

1. Declaring a generic class is actually very easy. All that we need to do is create the class with the generic type parameter <T>:

```
public class PerformAction<T>
{

}
```

 The generic type parameter is basically a placeholder for a specific type that will need to be defined when the class of variable is instantiated. This means that the generic class PerformAction<T> can never just be used without specifying the type argument inside angle brackets when instantiating the class.

2. Next, create a private variable of the generic type parameter T. This will hold the value we pass to the generic class:

```
public class PerformAction<T>
{
  private T _value;
}
```

3. We now need to add a constructor to the generic class. The constructor will take as parameter a value of type T. The private variable _value will be set to the parameterpassed to the constructor:

```
public class PerformAction<T>
{
  private T _value;

  public PerformAction(T value)
  {
    _value = value;
  }
}
```

4. Finally, to complete our generic class, create a void return method called IdentifyDataType(). All that this is going to do is tell us what data type we passed to the generic class. We can find the type of the variable using GetType():

```
public class PerformAction<T>
{
  private T _value;

  public PerformAction(T value)
  {
    _value = value;
  }

  public void IdentifyDataType()
  {
    WriteLine($"The data type of the supplied variable
            is {_value.GetType()}");
  }
}
```

5. To see the true beauty of our generic class in action, instantiate the generic class in the console application and specify different data type arguments inside the angle brackets of each new instantiation:

```
PerformAction<int> iAction = new PerformAction<int>(21);
iAction.IdentifyDataType();

PerformAction<decimal> dAction = new
                          PerformAction<decimal>(21.55m);
dAction.IdentifyDataType();
```

```
PerformAction<string> sAction = new
                    PerformAction<string>("Hello Generics");
sAction.IdentifyDataType();

ReadLine();
```

6. Running your console application will output the given data types that you
   instantiate the generic class with each time:

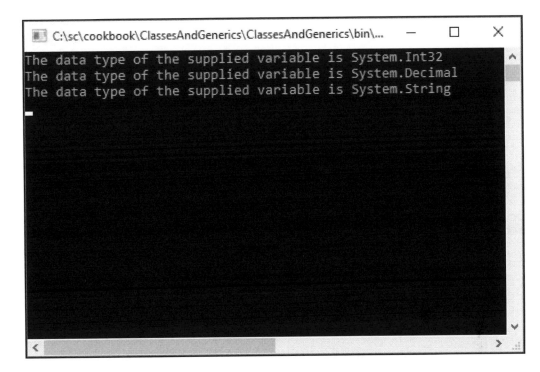

We used the exact same class but let it perform with three very different data
types. This kind of flexibility is a very powerful feature in your code.

Another feature of C# is that you can constrain the generic types implemented:

1. We can do this by telling the compiler that only types that implement the
   IDisposable interface can be used with the generic class. Change your generic
   class by adding where T : IDisposable to it. Your generic class should now
   look like this:

```
public class PerformAction<T> where T : IDisposable
{
    private T _value;
```

```
public PerformAction(T value)
{
  _value = value;
}

public void IdentifyDataType()
{
  WriteLine($"The data type of the supplied variable
          is {_value.GetType()}");
}
}
```

2. Go back to the console application and take a look at the previous instantiations of the generic class:

```
PerformAction<int> iAction = new PerformAction<int>(21);
iAction.IdentifyDataType();

PerformAction<decimal> dAction = new PerformAction<decimal>(21.55m);
dAction.IdentifyDataType();

PerformAction<string> sAction = new PerformAction<string>("Hello Generics");
sAction.IdentifyDataType();
```

Visual Studio will tell you that the types underlined by the red squiggly lines do not implement IDisposable and therefore can't be supplied to the PerformAction generic class.

3. Comment out those lines of code and add the following instantiation to your console application:

```
DataSet dsData = new DataSet();
PerformAction<DataSet> oAction = new
                  PerformAction<DataSet>(dsData);
oAction.IdentifyDataType();
```

 Note that for this to work, you might need to add using System.Data; to your code file. This is needed so that you can declare a DataSet.

4. As you might know, a `DataSet` type implements `IDisposable` and therefore it is a valid type to pass to our generic class. Go ahead and run the console application:

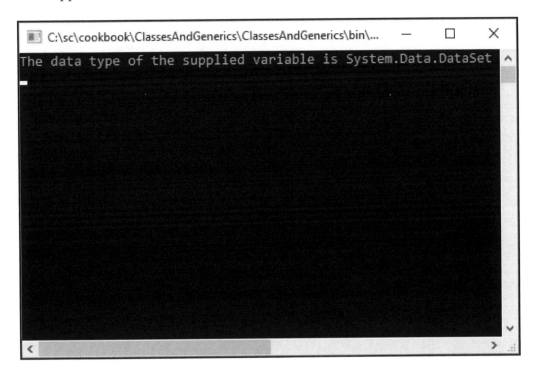

The `DataSet` type is valid, and the generic class performs as expected, identifying the type of the parameter passed to the constructor.

But what about generic methods? Well, just like generic classes, generic methods also do not specify their type at design time. It is only known when the method is called. Let's take a look at the following implementation of the generic methods:

1. Let's go ahead and create a new helper class called `MyHelperClass`:

```
public class MyHelperClass
{
}
```

2. Inside this helper class, we will create a generic method called `InspectType`. What is interesting about this generic method is that it can return multiple types because the return type is also marked with the generic type parameter. Your generic method does not have to return anything. It can also be declared as `void`:

```
public class MyHelperClass
{
  public T InspectType<T>(T value)
  {

  }
}
```

3. To illustrate that this generic method can return multiple types, we will output the type passed to the generic method to the console window and then return that type and display it in the console application. You will notice that you need to cast the return type as `(T)` when returning it:

```
public class MyHelperClass
{
  public T InspectType<T>(T value)
  {
    WriteLine($"The data type of the supplied parameter
             is {value.GetType()}");

    return (T)value;
  }
}
```

4. In the console application, go ahead and create an enumerator called `MyEnum`. The generic method can also accept enumerators:

```
public enum MyEnum { Value1, Value2, Value3 }
```

5. After creating the enumerator, add the following code to the console application. We are instantiating and calling the `oHelper` class and passing different values to it:

```
MyHelperClass oHelper = new MyHelperClass();
var intExample = oHelper.InspectType(25);
WriteLine($"An example of this type is  {intExample}");

var decExample = oHelper.InspectType(11.78m);
WriteLine($"An example of this type is  {decExample}");

var strExample = oHelper.InspectType("Hello Generics");
WriteLine($"An example of this type is  {strExample}");

var enmExample = oHelper.InspectType(MyEnum.Value2);
WriteLine($"An example of this type is  {enmExample}");

ReadLine();
```

6. If you run the console application, you will see that the generic method correctly identifies the type of the parameter passed to it and then returns that type to the calling code in the console application:

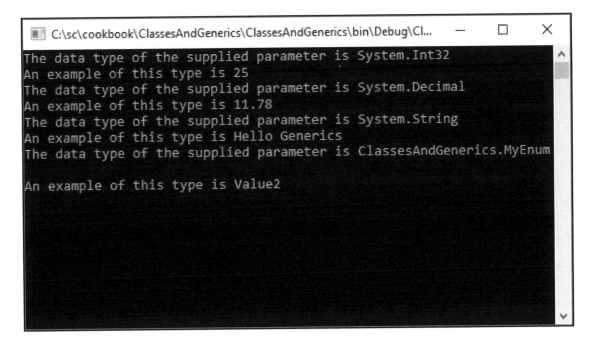

Generic methods can be used in a multitude of situations. This is, however, only an introduction to generic classes and methods. It is recommended that you do further research to learn how to implement generics in your code appropriately.

How it works...

At the heart of generics lies the ability to reuse a single class or method. It allows developers to essentially not repeat similar code throughout your code base. This conforms well to the **Don't Repeat Yourself (DRY)** principle. This design principle states that a specific bit of logic should be represented in code only once.

Using generic classes, for example, also allows developers to create a class that is type safe when compiling. Type safe basically means that the developer can be assured of the type of the object and can use the class in a specific way without experiencing any unexpected behavior. Therefore, the compiler takes over the burden of type safety.

Generics also allow developers to write less code, because code can be reused and less code also performs better.

Creating and using a generic interface

Generic interfaces work in much the same way as the previous examples in generics. Let's assume that we want to find the properties of certain classes in our code, but we can't be sure how many classes we will need to inspect. A generic interface could come in very handy here.

Getting ready

We need to inspect several classes for their properties. To do this, we will create a generic interface that will return a list of all the properties found for a class as a list of strings.

How to do it...

Let's take a look at the following implementation of the generic interface as follows:

1. Go ahead and create a generic interface called `IListClassProperties<T>`. The interface will define a method that needs to be used called `GetPropertyList()` that simply uses a LINQ query to return a `List<string>` object:

```
interface IListClassProperties<T>
{
    List<string> GetPropertyList();
}
```

2. Next, create a generic class called `InspectClass<T>`. Let the generic class implement the `IListClassProperties<T>` interface created in the previous step:

```
public class InspectClass<T> : IListClassProperties<T>
{

}
```

3. As usual, Visual Studio will highlight that the interface member `GetPropertyList()` has not been implemented in the `InspectClass<T>` generic class:

```
O references
public class InspectClass<T> : IListClassProperties<T>
{                          ⚡ ▾    •ᵍ interface ClassesAndGenerics.IListClassProperties<T>

}                                    'InspectClass<T>' does not implement interface member 'IListClassProperties<T>.GetPropertyList()'

                                     Show potential fixes (Ctrl+.)
```

4. To show any potential fixes, type *Ctrl + .* (period) and implement the interface implicitly:

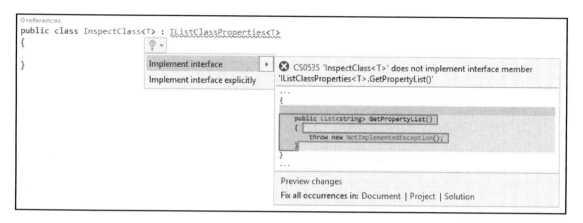

5. This will create the `GetPropertyList()` method in your `InspectClass<T>` class without any implementation. You will add the implementation in a moment. If you try to run your code without adding any implementation to the `GetpropertyList()` method, the compiler will throw `NotImplementedException`:

```
public class InspectClass<T> : IListClassProperties<T>
{
    public List<string> GetPropertyList()
    {
        throw new NotImplementedException();
    }
}
```

6. Next, add a constructor to your `InspectClass<T>` class that takes a generic type parameter and sets it equal to a private variable `_classToInspect` that you also need to create. This is setting up the code that we will use to instantiate out class. We will pass to the object we need a list of properties from the constructor, and the constructor will set the private variable `_classToInspect` so that we can use it in our `GetPropertyList()` method implementation:

```
public class InspectClass<T> : IListClassProperties<T>
{
    T _classToInspect;
    public InspectClass(T classToInspect)
    {
        _classToInspect = classToInspect;
```

```
  }

  public List<string> GetPropertyList()
  {
    throw new NotImplementedException();
  }
}
```

7. To finish off our class, we need to add some implementation to the `GetPropertyList()` method. It is here that the LINQ query will be used to return a `List<string>` object of all the properties contained in the class supplied to the constructor:

```
public List<string> GetPropertyList()
{
  return _classToInspect.GetType()
        .GetProperties().Select(p =>  p.Name).ToList();
}
```

8. Moving to our console application, go ahead and create a simple class called `Invoice`. This is one of several classes that can be used in the system, and the `Invoice` class is one of the smaller classes. It usually just holds invoice data specific to a record in the invoices records of the data store you connect to. We need to find a list of the properties in this class:

```
public class Invoice
{
  public int ID { get; set; }
  public decimal TotalValue { get; set; }
  public int LineNumber { get; set; }
  public string StockItem { get; set; }
  public decimal ItemPrice { get; set; }
  public int Qty { get; set; }
}
```

9. We can now make use of our `InspectClass<T>` generic class that implements the `IListClassProperties<T>` generic interface. To do this, we will create a new instance of the `Invoice` class. We will then instantiate the `InspectClass<T>` class, passing the type in the angle brackets and the `oInvoice` object to the constructor. We are now ready to call the `GetPropertyList()` method. The result is returned to a `List<string>` object called `lstProps`. We can then run `foreach` on the list, writing the value of each `property` variable to the console window:

```
Invoice oInvoice = new Invoice();
```

```
InspectClass<Invoice> oClassInspector = new
                    InspectClass<Invoice>(oInvoice);
List<string> lstProps = oClassInspector.GetPropertyList();

foreach(string property in lstProps)
{
   WriteLine(property);
}
ReadLine();
```

10. Go ahead and run the code to see the output generated by inspecting the properties of the `Invoice` class:

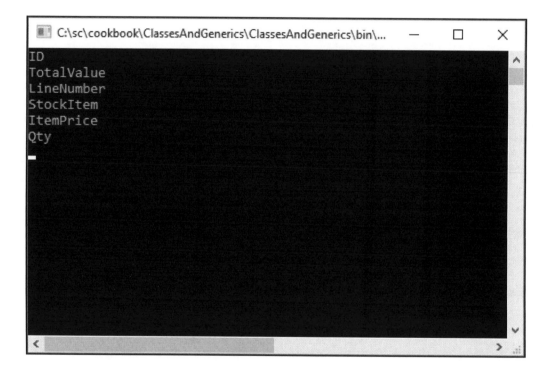

As you can see, the properties are listed as they exist in the `Invoice` class. The `IListClassProperties<T>` generic interface and the `InspectClass<T>` class don't care what type of class they need to inspect. They will take any class and run the code on it and produce a result.

However, the preceding implementation still poses a slight problem. Let's take a look at one of the variations of this problem:

1. Consider the following code in the console application:

```
InspectClass<int> oClassInspector = new InspectClass<int>(10);
List<string> lstProps = oClassInspector.GetPropertyList();
foreach (string property in lstProps)
{
   WriteLine(property);
}
ReadLine();
```

You can see that we have easily passed an integer value and type to the `InspectClass<T>` class, and the code does not show any warnings at all. In fact, if you ran this code, nothing would be returned and nothing outputs to the console window. What we need to do is implement the constraints on our generic class and interface.

2. At the end of the interface implementation after the class, add the `where T :` `class` clause. The code now needs to look like this:

```
public class InspectClass<T> : IListClassProperties<T>
                               where T : class
{
   T _classToInspect;
   public InspectClass(T classToInspect)
   {
      _classToInspect = classToInspect;
   }

   public List<string> GetPropertyList()
   {
      return _classToInspect.GetType().GetProperties()
                      .Select(p => p.Name).ToList();
   }
}
```

3. If we returned to our console application code, you will see that Visual Studio has underlined the `int` type passed to the `InspectClass<T>` class:

```
InspectClass<int> oClassInspector = new InspectClass<int>(10);
List<string> lstProps = oClassInspector.GetPropertyList();
foreach (string property in lstProps)
{
    WriteLine(property);
}
```

The reason for this is because we defined a constraint against our generic class and interface. We told the compiler that we only accept reference types. Therefore, this applies to any class, interface array, type, or delegate. Our `Invoice` class will therefore be a valid type, and the constraint will not apply to it.

We can also be more specific in our type parameter constraints. The reason for this is that we perhaps do not want to constrain the parameters to reference types. If we, for example, wanted to button down the generic class and interface to only accept classes created inside our current system, we can implement a constraint that the argument for T needs to be derived from a specific object. Here, we can use abstract classes again:

1. Create an abstract class called `AcmeObject` and specify that all classes that inherit from `AcmeObject` implement a property called `ID`:

```
public abstract class AcmeObject
{
  public abstract int ID { get; set; }
}
```

2. We can now ensure that objects we create in our code which we need to read the properties from are derived from `AcmeObject`. To apply the constraint, modify the generic class and place the `where T : AcmeObject` constraint after the interface implementation. Your code should now look like this:

```
public class InspectClass<T> : IListClassProperties<T>
                                where T : AcmeObject
{
  T _classToInspect;
  public InspectClass(T classToInspect)
  {
    _classToInspect = classToInspect;
  }
```

```
public List<string> GetPropertyList()
{
    return _classToInspect.GetType().GetProperties()
                    .Select(p => p.Name).ToList();
}
}
```

3. In the console application, modify the `Invoice` class to inherit from the `AcmeObject` abstract class. Implement the `ID` property as defined in the abstract class:

```
public class Invoice : AcmeObject
{
    public override int ID { get; set; }
    public decimal TotalValue { get; set; }
    public int LineNumber { get; set; }
    public string StockItem { get; set; }
    public decimal ItemPrice { get; set; }
    public int Qty { get; set; }
}
```

4. Create two more classes called `SalesOrder` and `CreditNote`. This time, however, only make the `SalesOrder` class inherit from `AcmeObject`. Leave the `CreditNote` object as is. This is so that we can clearly see how the constraint can be applied:

```
public class SalesOrder : AcmeObject
{
    public override int ID { get; set; }
    public decimal TotalValue { get; set; }
    public int LineNumber { get; set; }
    public string StockItem { get; set; }
    public decimal ItemPrice { get; set; }
    public int Qty { get; set; }
}

public class CreditNote
{
    public int ID { get; set; }
    public decimal TotalValue { get; set; }
    public int LineNumber { get; set; }
    public string StockItem { get; set; }
    public decimal ItemPrice { get; set; }
    public int Qty { get; set; }
}
```

5. Create the code needed to get the property list for the `Invoice` and `SalesOrder` classes. The code is straightforward, and we can see that Visual Studio does not complain about either of these two classes:

```
Invoice oInvoice = new Invoice();
InspectClass<Invoice> oInvClassInspector = new
                    InspectClass<Invoice>(oInvoice);
List<string> invProps = oInvClassInspector.GetPropertyList();

foreach (string property in invProps)
{
  WriteLine(property);
}
ReadLine();
SalesOrder oSalesOrder = new SalesOrder();
InspectClass<SalesOrder> oSoClassInspector = new
            InspectClass<SalesOrder>(oSalesOrder);
List<string> soProps = oSoClassInspector.GetPropertyList();

foreach (string property in soProps)
{
  WriteLine(property);
}
ReadLine();
```

6. If, however, we had to try do the same for our `CreditNote` class, we will see that Visual Studio will warn us that we can't pass the `CreditNote` class to the `InspectClass<T>` class because the constraint we implemented only accepts objects that derive from our `AcmeObject` abstract class. By doing this, we have effectively taken control over exactly what we allow to be passed to our generic class and interface by means of constraints:

```
CreditNote oCreditNote = new CreditNote();
InspectClass<CreditNote> oCredClassInspector = new InspectClass<CreditNote>(oCreditNote);
List<string> credProps = oCredClassInspector.GetPropertyList();

foreach (string property in credProps)
{
    WriteLine(property);
}
ReadLine();
```

How it works...

Speaking of generic interfaces, we have seen that we can implement behavior on a generic class by implementing a generic interface. The power of using the generic class and generic interface is well illustrated earlier.

Having said that, we do believe that knowing when to use constraints is also important so that you can close down your generic classes to only accept specific types that you want. This ensures that you don't get any surprises when someone accidentally passes an integer to your generic class.

Finally, the constraints that you can use are as follows:

- `where T: struct`: The type argument must be any value types
- `where T: class`: The type argument must be any reference types
- `where T: new()`: The type argument needs to have a parameterless constructor
- `where T: <base class name>`: The type argument must derive from the given base class
- `where T: <T must derive from object>`: `T` The type arg was must derive must derive from the object after the colon
- `where T: <interface>`: The type argument must implement the interface specified

3

Object-Oriented Programming in C#

This chapter will introduce you to the foundation of C# and **object-oriented programming (OOP)**. In this chapter, you will cover the following recipes:

- Using inheritance in C#
- Using abstraction
- Leveraging encapsulation
- Implementing polymorphism
- Single responsibility principle
- Open/closed principle
- Exception handling

Introduction

During your career as a creator of software, you will hear the term OOP many times. This design philosophy allows for objects to exist independently and can be reused by different sections of code. This is all made possible by what we refer to as the four pillars of OOP: inheritance, encapsulation, abstraction, and polymorphism.

In order to grasp this, you need to start thinking of objects (which are basically instantiated classes) that perform a specific task. Classes need to adhere to the SOLID design principle. This principle is explained here:

- Single responsibility principle (SRP)
- Open/closed principle
- Liskov substitution principle (LSP)
- Interface segregation principle
- Dependency inversion principle

Let's start off with an explanation of the four pillars of OOP, after which we will take a look at the SOLID principle in more detail.

Using inheritance in C#

In today's world, inheritance is usually associated with the end of things. In OOP, however, it is associated with the beginning of something new and better. When we create a new class, we can take an already existing class and inherit it on our new class. This means that our new object will have all the features of the inherited class as well as the additional features added to the new class. This is at the root of inheritance. We call a class that inherits from another a derived class.

Getting ready

To illustrate the concept of inheritance, we will create a few classes that inherit from another to form new, more feature-rich objects.

How to do it...

1. Create a new console application and add a class called `SpaceShip` to your console application.

```
public class SpaceShip
{

}
```

2. Our `SpaceShip` class will contain a few methods that describe the basics of a spaceship. Go ahead and add these methods to your `SpaceShip` class:

```
public class SpaceShip
{
  public void ControlBridge()
  {

  }
  public void MedicalBay(int patientCapacity)
  {

  }
  public void EngineRoom(int warpDrives)
  {

  }
  public void CrewQuarters(int crewCapacity)
  {

  }
  public void TeleportationRoom()
  {

  }
}
```

Because the `SpaceShip` class forms part of all other intergalactic vessels, it becomes the blueprint for every other vessel.

3. Next, we want to create a `Destroyer` class. To accomplish this, we will create a `Destroyer` class and use a colon after the class name to indicate that we want to inherit from another class (the `SpaceShip` class). Therefore, the following needs to be added when creating the `Destroyer` class:

```
public class Destroyer : SpaceShip
{

}
```

We can also say that the `Destroyer` class is derived from the `SpaceShip` class. The `SpaceShip` class is therefore the base class of all other intergalactic vessels.

4. Next, add a few methods to the Destroyer class that are unique to a destroyer. These methods belong only to the Destroyer class and not to the SpaceShip class:

```
public class Destroyer : SpaceShip
{
  public void WarRoom()
  {

  }
  public void Armory(int payloadCapacity)
  {

  }

  public void WarSpecialists(int activeBattalions)
  {

  }
}
```

5. Finally, create a third class called Annihilator. This is the most powerful intergalactic vessel and is used to wage war on planets. Let the Annihilator class inherit from the Destroyer class by creating the class and marking it derived from the Destroyer class as follows:

```
public class Annihilator : Destroyer
{

}
```

6. Finally, add a few methods to the Annihilator class that only belong to this type of SpaceShip class:

```
public class Annihilator : Destroyer
{
  public void TractorBeam()
  {

  }

  public void PlanetDestructionCapability()
  {

  }
}
```

7. What we see now is that when we create a new instance of the `SpaceShip` class in our console application, only the methods defined in that class are available to us. This is because the `SpaceShip` class does not inherit from any other classes:

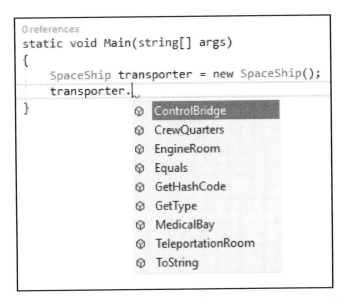

8. Go ahead and create the `SpaceShip` class with its methods in the console application:

```
SpaceShip transporter = new SpaceShip();
transporter.ControlBridge();
transporter.CrewQuarters(1500);
transporter.EngineRoom(2);
transporter.MedicalBay(350);
transporter.TeleportationRoom();
```

You will see that these are the only methods available to us when instantiating a new instance of this class.

9. Next, create a new instance of the Destroyer class. You will notice that the Destroyer class contains more methods than what we defined when we created the class. This is because the Destroyer class is inheriting the SpaceShip class and therefore inherits the methods of the SpaceShip class:

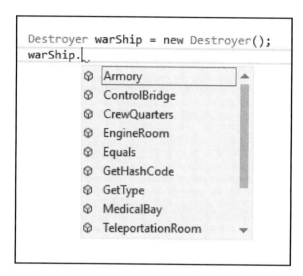

10. Go ahead and create the Destroyer class with all its methods in the console application:

```
Destroyer warShip = new Destroyer();
warShip.Armory(6);
warShip.ControlBridge();
warShip.CrewQuarters(2200);
warShip.EngineRoom(4);
warShip.MedicalBay(800);
warShip.TeleportationRoom();
warShip.WarRoom();
warShip.WarSpecialists(1);
```

11. Finally, create a new instance of the Annihilator class. This class contains all the methods of the Destroyer class as well as the methods from the SpaceShip class. This is because Annihilator inherits from the Destroyer, which, in turn, inherits from SpaceShip:

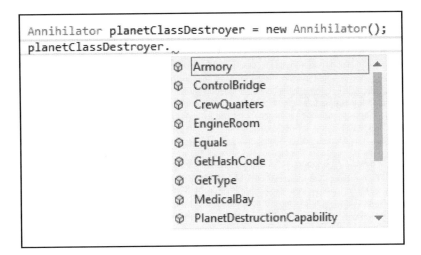

12. Go ahead and create the `Annihilator` class with all its methods in the console application:

```
Annihilator planetClassDestroyer = new Annihilator();
planetClassDestroyer.Armory(12);
planetClassDestroyer.ControlBridge();
planetClassDestroyer.CrewQuarters(4500);
planetClassDestroyer.EngineRoom(7);
planetClassDestroyer.MedicalBay(3500);
planetClassDestroyer.PlanetDestructionCapability();
planetClassDestroyer.TeleportationRoom();
planetClassDestroyer.TractorBeam();
planetClassDestroyer.WarRoom();
planetClassDestroyer.WarSpecialists(3);
```

How it works...

We can see that inheritance allows us to easily extend our classes by reusing functionality that already exists within another class created earlier. You also need to be aware though that any changes to the `SpaceShip` class will be inherited, all the way up to the top-most derived class.

Inheritance is a very powerful feature of C# that allows developers to write less code, and reuse working and tested methods.

Using abstraction

With abstraction, we take from the object we want to create the basic functionality that all objects derived from the abstracted object must have. To explain this in simple terms, we abstract the common functionality and put it in a single class that will be used to provide this shared functionality to all classes that inherit from it.

Getting ready

To explain abstraction, we will use abstract classes. Imagine that you are dealing with trainee space astronauts who need to progress through the ranks as they get trained. The truth is that once you as trainee learn a new skill, that skill is learned and will remain with you even though you learn more advanced ways to do things. You must also implement all the previous skills learned in the new object you create. Abstract classes demonstrate this concept very nicely.

How to do it...

1. Create an abstract class called `SpaceCadet`. This is the first type of astronaut you can get when starting with training. The abstract class and its members are defined using the `abstract` keyword. A thing to note is that abstract classes cannot be instantiated. The members represent the skills that `SpaceCadet` will have, such as negotiation and basic weapons training:

```
public abstract class SpaceCadet
{
    public abstract void ChartingStarMaps();
    public abstract void BasicCommunicationSkill();
    public abstract void BasicWeaponsTraining();
    public abstract void Negotiation();
}
```

2. Next, create another abstract class called `SpacePrivate`. This abstract class inherits from the `SpaceCadet` abstract class. What we are basically saying is that when a space cadet is trained as a space private, they will still have all the skills learned as a space cadet:

```
public abstract class SpacePrivate : SpaceCadet
{
  public abstract void AdvancedCommunicationSkill();
  public abstract void AdvancedWeaponsTraining();
  public abstract void Persuader();
}
```

3. To demonstrate this, create a class called `LabResearcher` and inherit the `SpaceCadet` abstract class. Inheriting from the abstract class is done by defining a colon and abstract class name after the newly created class name. This tells the compiler that the `LabResearcher` class inherits from the `SpaceCadet` class:

```
public class LabResearcher : SpaceCadet
{

}
```

Because we are inheriting an abstract class, the compiler will underline the `LabResearcher` class name to warn us that the derived class does not implement any of the methods in the `SpaceCadet` abstract class.

4. If you hover your mouse over the squiggly line, you will see that the lightbulb tip provides us with the issues discovered:

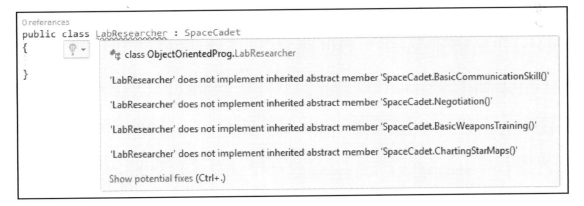

5. Visual Studio does a great job of providing a solution to the issues discovered. By typing *Ctrl + .* (control key and period), you can let Visual Studio show you some potential fixes (in this case, only one fix) for the issues identified:

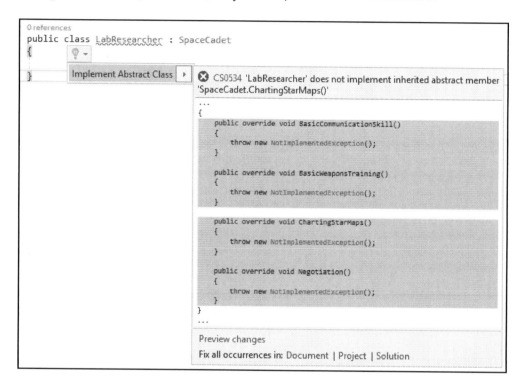

6. After Visual Studio has added the required methods, you will see that these are the same methods defined in the SpaceCadet abstract class. Abstract classes, therefore, require the classes inheriting from the abstract class to implement the methods defined in the abstract class. You will also notice that the methods added to the LabResearcher class contain no implementation and will throw an exception if used as is:

```
public class LabResearcher : SpaceCadet
{
    public override void BasicCommunicationSkill()
    {
        thrownewNotImplementedException();
    }

    publicoverridevoid BasicWeaponsTraining()
    {
```

```
      thrownewNotImplementedException();
   }

   publicoverridevoid ChartingStarMaps()
   {
      thrownewNotImplementedException();
   }

   publicoverridevoid Negotiation()
   {
      thrownewNotImplementedException();
   }
}
```

7. Next, create a class called `PlanetExplorer` and make this class inherit from the `SpacePrivate` abstract class. You will remember that the `SpacePrivate` abstract class inherited from the `SpaceCadet` abstract class:

```
public class PlanetExplorer : SpacePrivate
{

}
```

8. Visual Studio will once again warn you that your new class does not implement the methods of the abstract class that you are inheriting from. Here, however, you will notice that the lightbulb tip informs you that you are not implementing any of the methods in the `SpacePrivate` and `SpaceCadet` abstract classes. This is because the `SpacePrivate` abstract class is inheriting from the `SpaceCadet` abstract class:

9. As before, to fix the issues identified, type *Ctrl +* . (control key and period) and let Visual Studio show you some potential fixes (in this case, only one fix) for the issues identified.

10. After the fixes have been added to your code, you will see that the PlanetExplorer class contains all the methods in the SpacePrivate and SpaceCadet abstract classes:

```
public class PlanetExplorer : SpacePrivate
{
  public override void AdvancedCommunicationSkill()
  {
    throw new NotImplementedException();
  }

  public override void AdvancedWeaponsTraining()
  {
    throw new NotImplementedException();
  }

  public override void BasicCommunicationSkill()
  {
    throw new NotImplementedException();
  }

  public override void BasicWeaponsTraining()
  {
    throw new NotImplementedException();
  }

  public override void ChartingStarMaps()
  {
    throw new NotImplementedException();
  }

  public override void Negotiation()
  {
    throw new NotImplementedException();
  }

  public override void Persuader()
  {
    throw new NotImplementedException();
  }
}
```

How it works...

Abstraction has allowed us to define a common set of functionality that is to be shared among all the classes that derive from the abstract classes. The difference between inheriting from the abstract class and a normal class is that with an abstract class, you have to implement all the methods defined in that abstract class.

This makes the class easy to version and change. If you need to add new functionality, you can do so by adding that functionality to the abstract class without breaking any of the existing code. Visual Studio will require that all inherited classes implement the new method defined in the abstract class.

You can, therefore, be assured that the change applied will be implemented in all your classes that derive from the abstract classes in your code.

Leveraging encapsulation

What is encapsulation? Simply put, it is hiding the inner workings of a class that aren't necessary for the implementation of that class. Think of encapsulation as follows: most people who own a car know that it runs on gas- they don't need to know the inner working of an internal combustion engine to be able to use a car. They only need to know that they need to fill it up with gas when it is close to empty and that they need to check the oil and tyre pressure. Even then, it is usually not done by the car owner. This is true for classes and encapsulation.

The owner of the class is the one who uses it. The inner workings of that class need not be exposed to the developer using the class. The class is, therefore, like a black box. You know that the class will be consistent in its functionality, given the correct set of parameters. How exactly the class gets to the output is of no concern to the developer as long as the input is correct.

Getting ready

To illustrate the concept of encapsulation, we will create a class that is somewhat complex in its inner working. We need to calculate the **thrust-to-weight ratio** (**TWR**) of a space shuttle to determine whether it will be able to take off vertically. It needs to exert more thrust than its weight to counteract gravity and get into a stable orbit. This also depends on which planet the shuttle takes off, because different planets exert different gravitational forces on objects on their surface. In simple terms, the TWR must be greater than one.

How to do it...

1. Create a new class called `LaunchSuttle`. Then, add the following private variables to the class for engine thrust, the mass of the shuttle, the local gravitational acceleration, the constant values for the gravity of the Earth, Moon, and Mars (these are constants because they will never change), the universal gravitational constant, and an enumerator for the planet we are dealing with:

```
public class LaunchShuttle
{
  private double _EngineThrust;
  private double _TotalShuttleMass;
  private double _LocalGravitationalAcceleration;

  private const double EarthGravity = 9.81;
  private const double MoonGravity = 1.63;
  private const double MarsGravity = 3.75;
  private double UniversalGravitationalConstant;

  public enum Planet { Earth, Moon, Mars }
}
```

2. To our class, we will add three overloaded constructors that are essential to perform the calculation of the TWR based on the known facts at the time of instantiation (we assume that we will always know the engine thrust capability and mass of the shuttle). We will pass the gravitational acceleration for the first constructor. This is useful if we know beforehand what that value will be. For example, the gravitational acceleration of the Earth is 9.81 m/s^2.

   The second constructor will use the `Planet` enumerator to calculate the TWR that uses the constant variable values.

   The third constructor will use the radius and mass of the planet to calculate the gravitational acceleration, when those values are known, to return the TWR:

```
public LaunchShuttle(double engineThrust,
  double totalShuttleMass, double gravitationalAcceleration)
{
  _EngineThrust = engineThrust;
  _TotalShuttleMass = totalShuttleMass;
  _LocalGravitationalAcceleration =  gravitationalAcceleration;

}
```

```
public LaunchShuttle(double engineThrust,
   double totalShuttleMass, Planet planet)
{
  _EngineThrust = engineThrust;
  _TotalShuttleMass = totalShuttleMass;
  SetGraviationalAcceleration(planet);


}

public LaunchShuttle(double engineThrust, double
   totalShuttleMass, double planetMass, double planetRadius)
{
  _EngineThrust = engineThrust;
  _TotalShuttleMass = totalShuttleMass;
  SetUniversalGravitationalConstant();
  _LocalGravitationalAcceleration = Math.Round(
    CalculateGravitationalAcceleration (
      planetRadius, planetMass), 2);
}
```

3. In order to use the second overloaded constructor that passes the Planet
   enumerator as a parameter to the class, we need to create another method that
   has been scoped as private to calculate the gravitational acceleration. We also
   need to set the _LocalGravitationalAcceleration variable to the specific
   constant that matches the enumerator value. This method is something that the
   user of the class does not need to see in order to use the class. It is, therefore,
   scoped as private in order to hide that functionality from the user:

```
private void SetGraviationalAcceleration(Planet planet)
{
  switch (planet)
  {
    case Planet.Earth:
      _LocalGravitationalAcceleration = EarthGravity;
    break;
    case Planet.Moon:
      _LocalGravitationalAcceleration = MoonGravity;
    break;
    case Planet.Mars:
      _LocalGravitationalAcceleration = MarsGravity;
    break;
    default:
    break;
  }
}
```

4. Of the following methods, only one is defined as public and will, therefore, be visible to the user of the class. Create the private methods to set the universal gravitational constant and to calculate the TWR and the gravitational acceleration. These are all scoped as private, because the developer does not need to know what these methods do in order to use the class:

```
private void SetUniversalGravitationalConstant()
{
   UniversalGravitationalConstant = 6.6726 * Math.Pow(10, -11);
}

private double CalculateThrustToWeightRatio()
{
   // TWR = Ft/m.g > 1
   return _EngineThrust / (_TotalShuttleMass *
            _LocalGravitationalAcceleration);
}

private double CalculateGravitationalAcceleration(
            double radius, double mass)
{
   return (UniversalGravitationalConstant * mass) /
                           Math.Pow(radius, 2);
}

public double TWR()
{
   return Math.Round(CalculateThrustToWeightRatio(), 2);
}
```

5. Finally, in your console application, create the following variables with their known values:

```
double thrust = 220; // kN
double shuttleMass = 16.12; // t
double gravitationalAccelerationEarth = 9.81;
double earthMass = 5.9742 * Math.Pow(10, 24);
double earthRadius = 6378100;
double thrustToWeightRatio = 0;
```

6. Create a new instance of the `LaunchShuttle` class and pass it the values needed to calculate the TWR:

```
LaunchShuttle NasaShuttle1 = new LaunchShuttle(thrust,
        shuttleMass, gravitationalAccelerationEarth);
thrustToWeightRatio = NasaShuttle1.TWR();
Console.WriteLine(thrustToWeightRatio);
```

7. When you use the dot operator on the `NasaShuttle1` variable, you will notice that the IntelliSense only shows the `TWR` method. The class exposes nothing of the inner workings of how it gets to the calculated TWR value. The only thing that the developer knows is that the `LaunchShuttle` class will consistently return the correct TWR value, given the same input parameters:

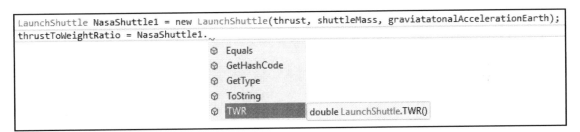

8. To test this, create two more instances of the `LaunchShuttle` class and call a different constructor each time:

```
LaunchShuttle NasaShuttle2 = new LaunchShuttle(thrust,
        shuttleMass, LaunchShuttle.Planet.Earth);
thrustToWeightRatio = NasaShuttle2.TWR();
Console.WriteLine(thrustToWeightRatio);

LaunchShuttle NasaShuttle3 = new LaunchShuttle(
    thrust, shuttleMass, earthMass, earthRadius);
thrustToWeightRatio = NasaShuttle3.TWR();
Console.WriteLine(thrustToWeightRatio);

Console.Read();
```

9. If you run your console application, you will see that the same value is returned for the TWR. The value indicates that a shuttle weighing 16.12 tons with a rocket that puts out 220 kilonewtons of thrust will be able to lift off the surface of the Earth (if only just):

How it works...

The class uses the scoping rules to hide certain functionality inside the class from the developer using the class. As mentioned earlier, the developer does not need to know how the calculations are done to return the value for the TWR. This all aids in making the class more useful and easy to implement. Here is a list of the various scopes available in C# along with their uses:

- `Public`: This is used with variables, properties, types, and methods and is visible anywhere.
- `Private`: This is used with variables, properties, types, and methods and is visible only in the block where they are defined.

- `Protected`: This is used with variables, properties, and methods. Don't think of this in terms of public or private. The protected scope is only visible inside the class in which it is used as well as in any inherited classes.
- `Friend`: This is used with variables, properties, and methods and can only be used by code in the same project or assembly.
- `ProtectedFriend`: This is used with variables, properties, and methods and is a combination (as the name suggests) of the protected and friend scopes.

Implementing polymorphism

Polymorphism is a concept that is quite easy to grasp once you have looked at and understood the other pillars of OOP. Polymorphism literally means that something can have many forms. This means that from a single interface, you can create multiple implementations thereof.

There are two subsections to this, namely, static and dynamic polymorphism. With **static polymorphism**, you are dealing with the overloading of methods and functions. You can use the same method, but perform many different tasks.

With **dynamic polymorphism**, you are dealing with the creation and implementation of abstract classes. These abstract classes act as a blueprint that tells you what a derived class should implement. The following section looks at both.

Getting ready

We will begin by illustrating the use of an abstract class, which is an example of dynamic polymorphism. We will then create overloaded constructors as an example of static polymorphism.

How to do it...

1. Create an abstract class called `Shuttle` and give it a member called `TWR`, which is the calculation of the TWR of the shuttle:

```
public abstract class Shuttle
{
  public abstract double TWR();
}
```

2. Next, create a class called `NasaShuttle` and have it inherit from the abstract class `Shuttle` by putting the abstract class name after a colon at the end of the `NasaShuttle` class declaration:

```
public class NasaShuttle : Shuttle
{

}
```

3. Visual Studio will underline the `NasaShuttle` class because you have told the compiler that the class inherits from an abstract class, but you have not yet implemented the members of that abstract class:

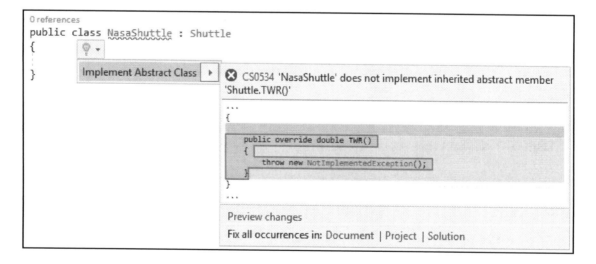

4. To fix the issues identified, type *Ctrl + .* (control key and period) and let Visual Studio show you some potential fixes (in this case, only one fix) for the issues identified:

5. Visual Studio then adds the missing implementation to your NasaShuttle class. By default, it will add it as not implemented, because you are required to provide implementation for the abstract member you overrode in the abstract class:

```
public class NasaShuttle : Shuttle
{
  public override double TWR()
  {
    throw new NotImplementedException();
  }
}
```

6. Create another class called RoscosmosShuttle and inherit from the same Shuttle abstract class:

```
public class RoscosmosShuttle : Shuttle
{

}
```

7. As before, Visual Studio will underline the RoscosmosShuttle class because you have told the compiler that the class inherits from an abstract class, but you have not yet implemented the members of that abstract class.

8. To fix the issues identified, type *Ctrl + .* (control key and period) and let Visual Studio show you some potential fixes (in this case, only one fix) for the issues identified.

9. The overridden method is then added to the RoscosmosShuttle class as not implemented. You have just seen an example of dynamic polymorphism in action:

```
public class RoscosmosShuttle : Shuttle
{
  public override double TWR()
  {
    throw new NotImplementedException();
  }
}
```

10. To see an example of static polymorphism, create the following overloaded constructor for `NasaShuttle`. The constructor name stays the same, but the signature of the constructor changes, which makes it overloaded:

```
public NasaShuttle(double engineThrust,
    double  totalShuttleMass, double gravitationalAcceleration)
{

}

public NasaShuttle(double engineThrust,
    double  totalShuttleMass, double planetMass,
    double planetRadius)
{

}
```

How it works...

Polymorphism is something you will easily be using already by simply applying good object-oriented principles to the design of your classes. With the abstract `Shuttle` class, we saw that the class took on the shape of the `NasaShuttle` class and the `RoscosmosShuttle` class when it was used to derive those new classes from its abstraction. The constructor of the `NasaShuttle` class was then overridden to provide the same method name, but implemented using different signatures.

This is at the heart of polymorphism. Most likely, you have been using it without knowing about it.

Single responsibility principle

When talking about SOLID principles, we will start off with the **single responsibility principle (SRP)**. Here, we are actually saying that a class has a specific task that it needs to fulfill and it should not do anything else.

Getting ready

You will create a new class and write code to log an error to the database when an exception is thrown on adding more troops to the star ship, causing it to be over capacity. For this recipe, ensure that you have added `using System.Data;` and `using System.Data.SqlClient;` namespaces to your application.

How to do it...

1. Create a new class called `StarShip`:

    ```
    public class Starship
    {

    }
    ```

2. To your class, add a new method that will set the maximum troop capacity of the `StarShip` class:

    ```
    public void SetMaximumTroopCapacity(int capacity)
    {

    }
    ```

3. Inside this method, add a `trycatch` clause that will attempt to set the maximum troop capacity, but for some reason, it will fail. Upon failure, it will write the error to the log table inside the database:

    ```
    try
    {
      // Read current capacity and try to add more
    }
    catch (Exception ex)
    {
      string connectionString = "connection string goes  here";
      string sql = $"INSERT INTO tblLog (error, date) VALUES
        ({ex.Message}, GetDate())";
      using (SqlConnection con = new
             SqlConnection(connectionString))
      {
        SqlCommand cmd = new SqlCommand(sql);
        cmd.CommandType = CommandType.Text;
        cmd.Connection = con;
        con.Open();
    ```

```
            cmd.ExecuteNonQuery();
        }
        throw ex;
    }
```

How it works...

If you have code that looks like the preceding one, you are in contravention of the SRP. The StarShip class is no longer responsible for just itself and things that have to do with star ships. It now has to fulfill the role of logging errors to the database too. You see the problem here is that the database-logging code does not belong in the catch clause of the SetMaximumTroopCapacity method. A better approach would be to create a separate DatabaseLogging class with methods to create connections and write exceptions to the appropriate log table. You will also find that you are going to have to write that logging code in multiple places (in every catch clause). If you are finding that you are repeating code (by copying and pasting from other areas), you probably need to put that code into a common class, and you have likely broken the SRP rule.

Open/closed principle

When creating classes, we need to ensure that the class prohibits any breaking modifications by needing to change internal code. We say that such a class is closed. If we need to change it somehow, we can do so by extending the class. This extensibility is where we say that the class is open for extensions.

Getting ready

You will create a class that determines the skills of a trooper by looking at the class of trooper. We will show you the way many developers create such a class and the way it can be created using the open/closed principle.

How to do it...

1. Create a class called `StarTrooper`:

```
public class StarTrooper
{

}
```

2. To this class, add an enumerator called `TrooperClass` to identify the type of trooper we want to return the skills of. Also, create a `List<string>` variable to contain the skills of the specific trooper class. Finally, create a method called `GetSkills` that returns the specific set of skills for the given trooper class.

   The class is quite straightforward, but the implementation of the code is something we see a lot. Sometimes, instead of a `switch` statement, you will see a whole lot of `if...else` statements. While the functionality of the code is clear, it is not easy to add another class of trooper to the `StarTrooper` class without changing code. Assume that you now have to add an additional `Engineer` class to the `StarTrooper` class. You would have to modify the `TrooperClass` enumeration and the code in the `switch` statement.

   This changing of code can cause you to introduce bugs into the code that was previously working fine. We now see that the `StarTrooper` class is not closed and can't be extended easily to accommodate additional `TrooperClass` objects:

```
public enum TrooperClass { Soldier, Medic, Scientist }
List<string> TroopSkill;

public List<string> GetSkills(TrooperClass troopClass)
{
  switch (troopClass)
  {
    case TrooperClass.Soldier:
      return TroopSkill = new List<string>(new string[] {
        "Weaponry", "TacticalCombat",  "HandToHandCombat" });

    case TrooperClass.Medic:
      return TroopSkill = new List<string>(new string[] {
        "CPR", "AdvancedLifeSupport" });

    case TrooperClass.Scientist:
```

```
            return TroopSkill = new List<string>(new string[] {
              "Chemistry",  "MollecularDeconstruction",
              "QuarkTheory" });

        default:
          return TroopSkill = new List<string>(new string[]  {
            "none" });
      }
    }
```

3. The solution to this problem is inheritance. Instead of having to change code, we extend it. Start off by rewriting the preceding `StarTrooper` class and create a `Trooper` class. The `GetSkills` method is declared as `virtual`:

```
public class Trooper
{
  public virtual List<string> GetSkills()
  {
    return new List<string>(new string[] { "none" });
  }
}
```

4. Now, we can easily create derived classes for the `Soldier`, `Medic`, and `Scientist` trooper classes available. Create the following derived classes that inherit from the `Trooper` class. You can see that the `override` keyword is used when creating the `GetSkills` method:

```
public class Soldier : Trooper
{
  public override List<string> GetSkills()
  {
    return new List<string>(new string[] { "Weaponry",
             "TacticalCombat", "HandToHandCombat" });
  }
}

public class Medic : Trooper
{
  public override List<string> GetSkills()
  {
    return new List<string>(new string[] {
        "CPR",  "AdvancedLifeSupport" });
  }
}

public class Scientist : Trooper
{
```

```
public override List<string> GetSkills()
{
  return new List<string>(new string[] { "Chemistry",
    "MollecularDeconstruction", "QuarkTheory" });
}
}
```

5. The code becomes extremely easy to implement when extending the class to add an additional class of `Trooper`. If we now want to add the `Engineer` class, we would simply override the `GetSkills` method after inheriting from the `Trooper` class created earlier:

```
public class Engineer : Trooper
{
  public override List<string> GetSkills()
  {
    return new List<string>(new string[] {
      "Construction", "Demolition" });
  }
}
```

How it works...

The classes derived from the `Trooper` class are extensions of the `Trooper` class. We can say that each class is closed, because modifying it does not necessitate changing the original code. The `Trooper` class is also extensible because we have been able to easily extend the class by creating derived classes from it.

Another byproduct of this design is smaller, more manageable code that is easier to read and understand.

Exception handling

Exception handling is something that you as a developer need to be aware of, and you must also be very good at discerning what information to display to the end user and what information to log. Believe it or not, writing good error messages is harder than it looks. Too much information displayed to the user might instill a sense of distrust in the software. Too little information logged for debugging purposes is also not useful at all to the poor soul that needs to fix the error. This is why you need to have an **exception handling strategy**.

A nice rule of thumb is to display a message to the user stating that something went wrong, but that a notification has been sent to support personnel. Think of Google, Dropbox, Twitter (remember the blue whale?), and other big companies. Humorous error pages with a little robot whose arm fell off, or a popular meme displayed to the user is far better than a threatening error page with a full stack trace and red text. It is something that momentarily takes the user's mind off a frustrating situation. Most importantly of all, it lets you save face.

So let's start off by looking at exception filters. These have been around for some time. Visual Basic.NET (VB.NET) and F# devs have had this functionality for a while. It was introduced in C# 6.0 and does more than meets the eye. At first glance, it looks as if exception filters merely specify a condition when an exception needs to be caught. This is, after all, what the name *exception filter* implies. Upon closer inspection, however, we see that exception filters act as more than just syntactical sugar.

Getting ready

We will create a new class called `Chapter3` and call a method that reads an XML file. The file read logic is determined by a Boolean flag being set to `true`. Imagine that there is some other database flag that when set, also sets our Boolean flag to `true`, and thus, our application knows to read the given XML file.

Begin by ensuring that you have added the following `using` statement:

```
using System.IO;
```

How to do it...

1. Create a class called `Chapter3` (if you have not done so already) that contains two methods. One method reads the XML file, and the second method logs any exception errors:

```
public void ReadXMLFile(string fileName)
{
  try
  {
    bool blnReadFileFlag = true;
    if (blnReadFileFlag)
    {
      File.ReadAllLines(fileName);
    }
  }
```

```
    catch (Exception ex)
    {
      Log(ex);
      throw;
    }
  }

  private void Log(Exception e)
  {
    /* Log the error */
  }
```

2. In the console application, add the following code to call the `ReadXMLFile`
    method, passing it the filename to read:

```
Chapter3 ch3 = new Chapter3();
string File = @"c:tempXmlFile.xml";
ch3.ReadXMLFile(File);
```

3. Running the application will generate an error (assuming that you actually don't
    have a file called `XMLFile.xml` in your `temp` folder. Visual Studio will break on
    the `throw` statement:

4. The `Log(ex)` method has logged the exception, but have a look at the **Watch1** window. We have no idea what the value of `blnReadFileFlag` is. When an exception is caught, the stack is unwound (adding overhead to your code) to whatever the actual catch block is. Therefore, the state of the stack before the exception happened is lost.

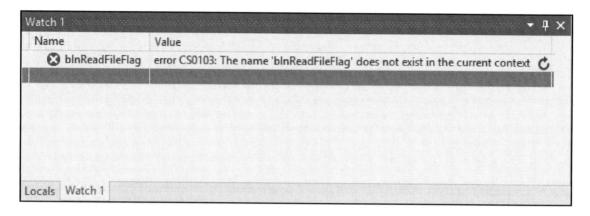

5. Modify your `ReadXMLFile` and `Log` methods as follows to include an exception filter:

```
public void ReadXMLFile(string fileName)
{
  try
  {
    bool blnReadFileFlag = true;
    if (blnReadFileFlag)
    {
      File.ReadAllLines(fileName);
    }
  }
  catch (Exception ex) when (Log(ex))
  {
  }
}
private bool Log(Exception e)
{
  /* Log the error */
  return false;
}
```

6. Running the console application again, Visual Studio will break on the actual line of code that caused the exception:

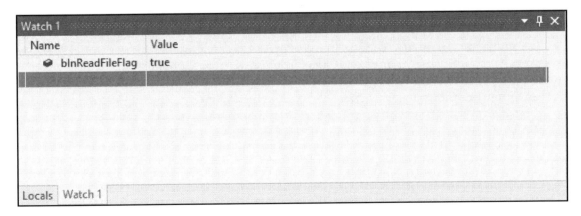

7. More importantly, the value of `blnReadFileFlag` is still in scope. This is because exception filters can see the state of the stack at the point where the exception occurred instead of where the exception was handled. Looking at the locals window in Visual Studio, you will see that the variables are still in scope at the point where the exception occurred:

How it works...

Imagine being able to view the exception information in a log file with all the local variable values available. Another interesting point to note is the return `false` statement in the `Log(ex)` method. Using this method to log the error and return `false` will allow the application to continue and have the exception handled elsewhere. As you know, catching `Exception ex` will catch everything. By returning `false`, the exception filter doesn't run into the `catch` statement, and more specific `catch` exceptions (for example, `catch (FileNotFoundException ex)` after our `catch (Exception ex)` statement) can be used to handle specific errors. Normally, when catching exceptions, `FileNotFoundException` will never be caught in the following code example:

```
catch (Exception ex)
{
}
catch (FileNotFoundException ex)
{
}
```

This is because the order of the exceptions being caught is wrong. Traditionally, developers must catch exceptions in their order of specificity, which means that `FileNotFoundException` is more specific than `Exception` and must, therefore, be placed before `catch (Exception ex)`. With exception filters that call a `false` returning method, we can inspect and log an exception accurately:

```
catch (Exception ex) when (Log(ex))
{
}
catch (FileNotFoundException ex)
{
}
```

The preceding code will catch all exceptions, and in doing so, log the exception accurately but not step into the exception handler because the `Log(ex)` method returns `false`. Another implementation of exception filters is that they can allow developers to retry code in the event of a failure. You might not specifically want to catch the first exception, but implement a type of timeout element to your method. When the error counter has reached the maximum iterations, you can catch and handle the exception. You can see an example of catching an exception based on a `try` clauses' count here:

```
public void TryReadXMLFile(string fileName)
{
  bool blnFileRead = false;
  do
```

```
{
  int iTryCount = 0;
  try
  {
    bool blnReadFileFlag = true;
    if (blnReadFileFlag)
    File.ReadAllLines(fileName);
  }
  catch (Exception ex) when (RetryRead(ex, iTryCount++) == true)
  {
  }
  } while (!blnFileRead);
}

private bool RetryRead(Exception e, int tryCount)
{
  bool blnThrowEx = tryCount <= 10 ? blnThrowEx =
      false : blnThrowEx = true;
  /* Log the error if blnThrowEx = false */
  return blnThrowEx;
}
```

Exception filtering is a very useful and extremely powerful way to handle exceptions in your code. The behind-the-scenes workings of exception filters are not as immediately obvious as one might imagine, but here lies the actual power of exception filters.

4

Code Analyzers in Visual Studio

In this chapter we will take a look at code analyzers and how they can assist developers to write better code. We will cover the following topics:

- Finding and installing analyzers
- Creating a code analyzer
- Creating a custom code analyzer
- Deploying your code analyzer within your organization only

Introduction

With effect from Visual Studio 2015, developers have had the ability to create custom code analyzers that are specific to their project or their development team. Some development teams have a set of standards that they need to adhere to. Perhaps you are an indie developer and you would like to make your code conform to certain best practices. It doesn't really matter what your reason is; code analyzers open doors for developers.

You can be sure that the code you or your team ships measures up to your specific set of code quality standards. There are several code analyzers that can be downloaded from GitHub. We will be looking at one of those called CodeCracker for C#.

Finding and installing analyzers

There are quite a few code analyzers on GitHub. A quick search returns 28 possible C# code analyzers out of 72 repository results. A few of these seem to be student projects. Check those out too; there is some very clever code in some of them. As for this recipe, we will be working with CodeCracker for C# to demonstrate how to install an analyzer from a NuGet package.

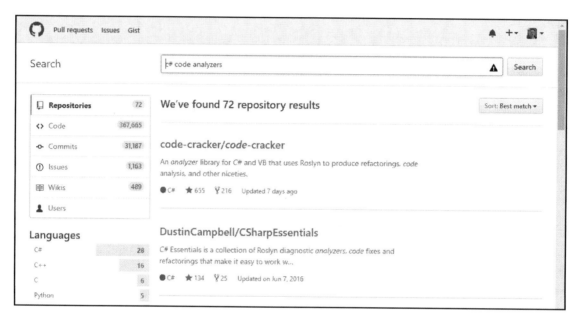

Getting ready

All that you will be doing is downloading a NuGet package for your project. Other than that, there is nothing you specifically need to do in order to get ready.

How to do it...

1. Start off by creating a new console application. You can call it whatever you like. In my example, I simply called it DiagAnalyzerDemo.

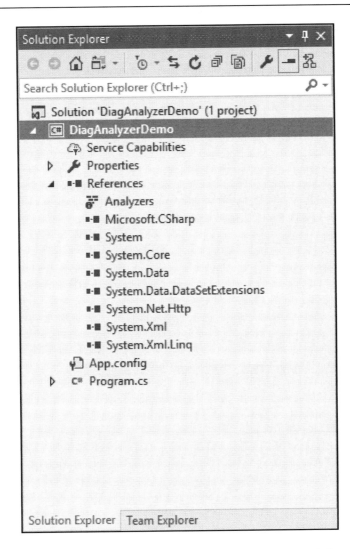

2. From the **Tools** menu, select **NuGet Package Manager** and then **Manage NuGet Packages for Solution...**.

3. In the **Browse** tab, search for `Code-Cracker`. The results should return the **codecracker.CSharp** NuGet package. Check the project you want to apply the NuGet package to and click on the **Install** button.

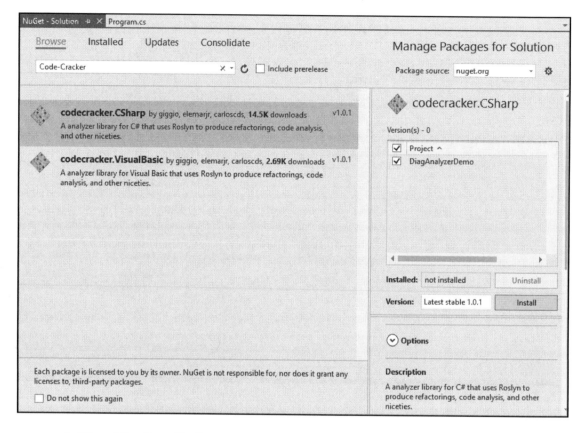

4. Visual Studio will allow you to review the changes that are about to be made. Click on the **OK** button to continue.

5. Click on **I Accept** when the license terms are displayed.

6. When the NuGet package is installed, the results will be displayed in the **Output** window.

7. Looking at your project you will notice that the **CodeCracker.CSharp** analyzer has been added under the **Analyzers** node in your **Solution Explorer**.

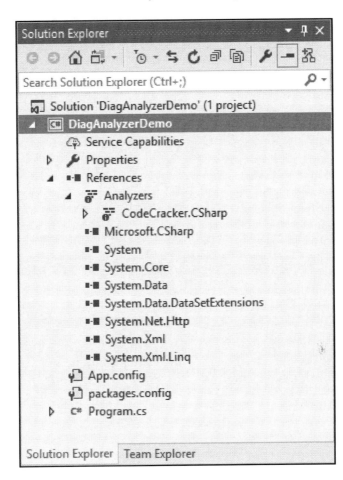

8. If you expand the **CodeCracker.CSharp** analyzer, you will see all the individual analyzers included in the NuGet package.

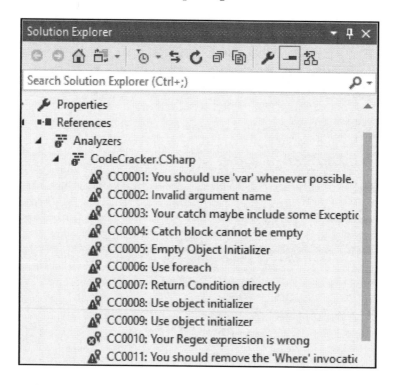

9. There is however a better place to review these analyzers from. From the **Project** menu, go to the [project name] properties menu item. In my case this is **DiagAnalyzerDemo Properties....**

10. Click on the **Open** button to open the rule set.

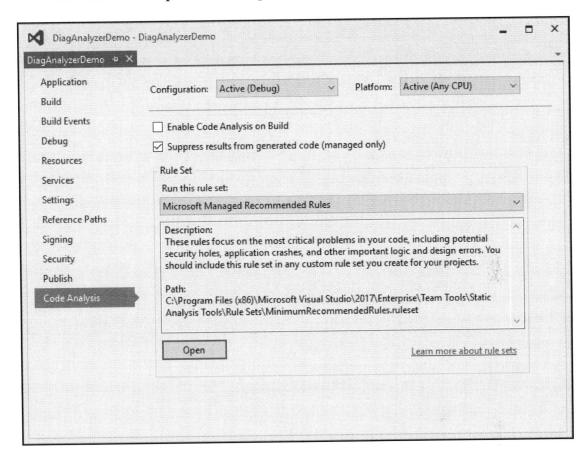

11. Here you will see a collection of all the analyzers available; from this screen, you can modify the action of specific analyzers.

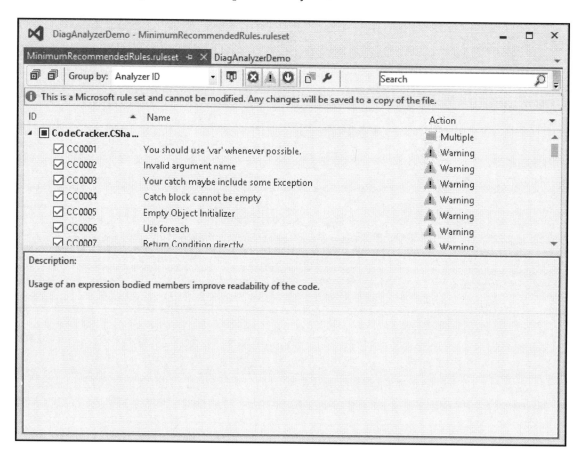

12. In your code, add the following class. You can call it whatever you like, but for simplicity's sake use the following example. You will see that I have a constructor that sets a property called `DimensionWHL`. This property just returns an array with the `width`, `height`, and `length` values. Not very nice code indeed.

```
public class ShippingContainer
{
    public int Width { get; set; }
    public int Height { get; set; }
    public int Length { get; set; }
    public int[] DimensionsWHL { get; set; }
    public ShippingContainer(int width, int height, int length)
    {
```

```
    Width = width;
    Height = height;
    Length = length;

    DimensionsWHL = new int[] { width, height, length };
  }
}
```

13. Return back to the analyzers screen and search for the word `properties`. You will see an analyzer returned called **CA1819,** which specifies that a property should never return an array. The **Action** is changed to **Warning,** but you can change this to **Error** should you wish by clicking on the word **Warning** under the **Action** column and selecting **Error.**

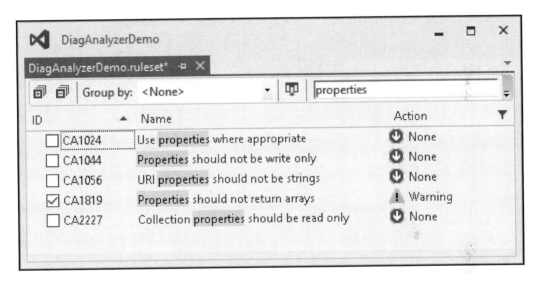

14. Save the changes and go and build your console application. You will see that the warning for the code analyzer **CA1819** is displayed in the **Error List**. If you had changed the action to **Error**, the build would have broken with that error.

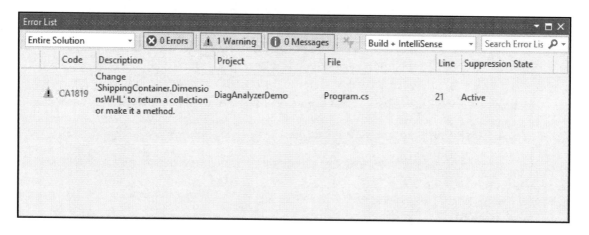

How it works...

Code analyzers can provide you with a lot of functionality and assist developers in writing good code by avoiding common bad coding practices and enforcing specific team guidelines. Each code analyzer can be set to a different severity, with the most severe actually breaking the build. Keeping code analyzers under the references in your projects allows you to check it in to source control; this is evaluated whenever you build your project. You can however also store analyzers on a per-machine basis. These analyzers will be for personal code improvement, prompts, and personal use.

Code analyzers are perfect for modern day developers because they are under the control of the developer and integrate easily into Visual Studio.

Creating a code analyzer

Some of you might already see the benefit of creating your own code analyzer. Being able to control certain design implementations and coding standards specific to your team is invaluable. This is especially true for new developers joining your team. I remember when I started working for a company a couple of years back; the development manager gave me a document of code standards that I needed to adhere to. At the time this was great. It showed me that they cared about code standards. Back then, of course, developers didn't have code analyzers. It was however quite a challenge keeping track of all the standards that I needed to implement. This was especially true for the specific code standards that the company implemented.

Getting ready

Before you can create your own code analyzer, you need to ensure that you have installed the **.NET Compiler Platform SDK**. To do this, perform the following steps:

1. Add a new project to your solution and click on **Extensibility**. Select **Download the .NET Compiler Platform SDK** and click **OK**.

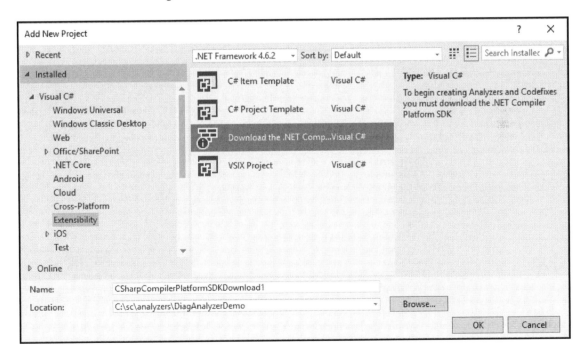

2. This will actually create a project with an index file. The page that opens will provide a download to the **.NET Compiler Platform SDK**. Click on that to start the download.

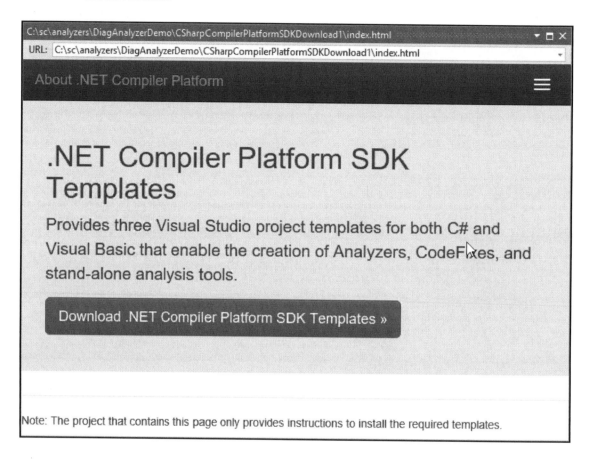

3. Just save the downloaded file to a directory on your hard drive. Then you should close down Visual Studio before clicking on the VSIX file.

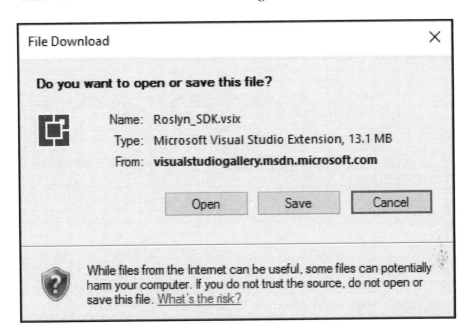

4. The **.NET Compiler Platform SDK** installer will now start and allow you to select the instance of Visual Studio to install to.

When the installation is complete, restart Visual Studio again.

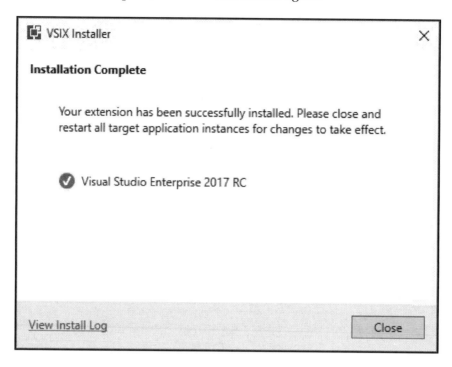

How to do it...

1. Add a new project to your Visual Studio solution and click on **Extensibility** and select the **Analyzer with Code Fix (NuGet + VSIX)** template. Give it a suitable name and click on **OK** to create the Analyzer project.

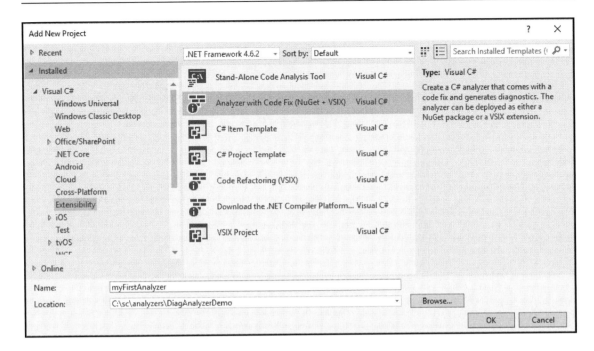

2. You will see that Visual Studio has created three projects for you: `Portable`, `.Test` and `.Vsix`. Ensure that the `.Vsix` project is set as the default startup project.

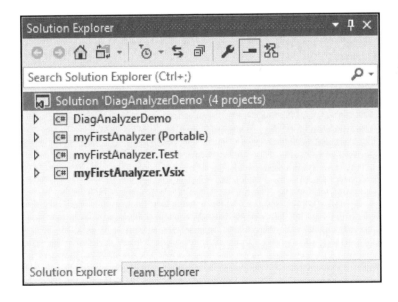

3. In the `Portable` class, take a look at the `DiagnosticAnalyzer.cs` file. You will see a method called `AnalyzeSymbol()`. All that this code analyzer does is simply check for the existence of lowercase letters on the `namedTypeSymbol` variable.

```
private static void AnalyzeSymbol(
  SymbolAnalysisContext context)
{
  // TODO: Replace the following code with your own
     analysis, generating Diagnostic objects for any
     issues you find
  var namedTypeSymbol = (INamedTypeSymbol)context.Symbol;

  // Find just those named type symbols with names
     containing lowercase letters.
  if (namedTypeSymbol.Name.ToCharArray().Any(char.IsLower))
  {
    // For all such symbols, produce a diagnostic.
    var diagnostic = Diagnostic.Create(Rule,
      namedTypeSymbol.Locations[0], namedTypeSymbol.Name);

    context.ReportDiagnostic(diagnostic);
  }
}
```

4. Build your project and click on *F5* to start debugging. This will start a new instance of Visual Studio with its own settings. This means anything you change in this experimental instance of Visual Studio will not affect your current Visual Studio installation. You can open an existing project or create a new one. I simply created a console application. From the start, you will see that the `Program` class name is underlined. Hovering your cursor over this will display the Visual Studio lightbulb and tell you that the type name contains lowercase letters.

5. Clicking on *Ctrl + .* or on the **Show potential fixes** link in the tooltip will display the fixes you can apply to correct the error.

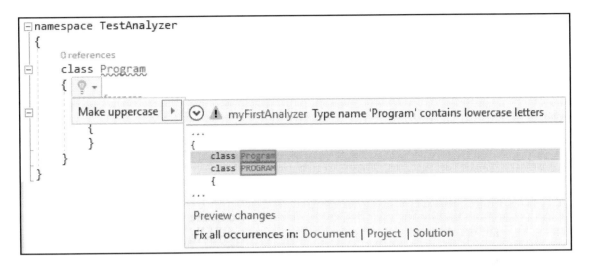

How it works...

Code analyzers will check managed assemblies and report any information relevant. This can be any code that violates the programming and design rules in the .NET *Framework Design Guidelines*. The code analyzer will display the checks it performs as warning messages and if possible suggest a fix like we saw in the aforementioned recipe. To do this, code analyzers use rule sets created by Microsoft or a custom rule set you define to meet a specific need.

Creating a custom code analyzer

The real magic of code analyzers come to the fore when you create one to suit a specific need. What would qualify as a specific need? Well anything that is specific to your own business requirements that is not covered in the out-of-the-box analyzers. Don't get me wrong; the existing analyzers that are available to developers really cover a lot of good programming practices. Just take a look on GitHub by searching for **C# code analyzers**.

Sometimes, however, you might have a case where something is more suited to your workflow or the way your company does business.

An example of this is could be to ensure that comments on all public methods include more information than just the standard `<summary></summary>` and parameter information (if any). You might want to include an additional tag with the internal task ID, for example (think Jira here). Another example is making sure that a created class conforms to a certain XML structure. Are you developing software that writes warehouse stock information to a database? Do you use non-stocked parts? How do you validate non-stocked from stocked parts in code? Code analyzers can provide a solution here.

The preceding examples are perhaps rather unique and not applicable to you or your needs at all, but that is the beauty of code analyzers. You can create them to suit your requirements. Let's take a look at a very simple example. Assume that developers in your organization need to use a specific code library. This code library is a collection of frequently used code and is well maintained. It is included in a Visual Studio template that developers use when creating new projects. We need to ensure that, if a developer creates a specific class (for purchase orders or sales orders), it implements a specific interface. The interfaces exist in the template, but the classes do not. This is because the applications will not always be using sales or purchase orders. The interface is to enable the receipt of sales and purchase orders and is called IReceivable.

Getting ready

Perform the following steps:

1. Create a new Visual Studio project and call it `PurchaseOrderAnalyzer`.

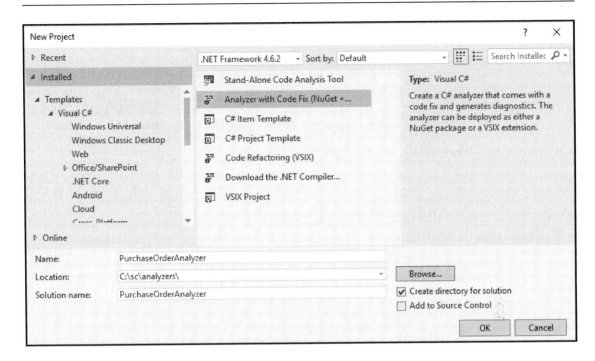

2. Ensure that the following projects are created by default in your solution.

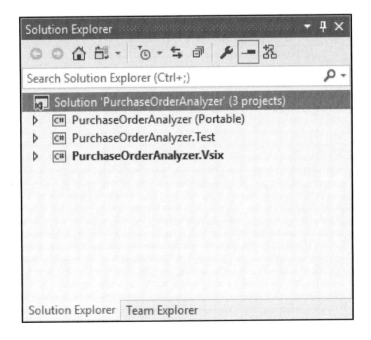

How to do it...

1. Expand the `PurchaseOrderAnalyzer (Portable)` project and open the `DiagnosticAnalyzer.cs` file.

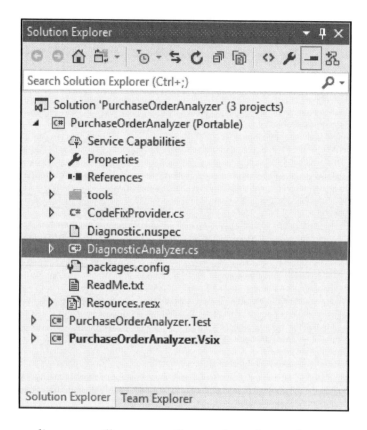

2. As seen earlier, you will see your diagnostic analyzer class. It should read `public class PurchaseOrderAnalyzerAnalyzer : DiagnosticAnalyzer`. Add the following code to the top of this class, replacing the code for the `DiagnosticId`, `Title`, `MessageFormat`, `Description`, `Category`, and `Rule` variables. Note that I have added two enumerators called `ClassTypesToCheck` and `MandatoryInterfaces` to the class. I only want this analyzer to act on a class if it is called `PurchaseOrder` or `SalesOrder`. I also only want the `IReceiptable` interface to be mandatory on the classes defined in the `ClassTypesToCheck` enum.

```
public const string DiagnosticId = "PurchaseOrderAnalyzer";
```

```
public enum ClassTypesToCheck { PurchaseOrder, SalesOrder }
public enum MandatoryInterfaces { IReceiptable }

private static readonly LocalizableString Title =
  "Interface Implementation Available";
private static readonly LocalizableString
  MessageFormat = "IReceiptable Interface not Implemented";
private static readonly LocalizableString Description =
  "You need to implement the IReceiptable interface";
private const string Category = "Naming";

private static DiagnosticDescriptor Rule = new
  DiagnosticDescriptor(DiagnosticId, Title, MessageFormat,
  Category, DiagnosticSeverity.Warning,
  isEnabledByDefault: true, description: Description);
```

3. Make sure that the `Initialize` method contains the following code:

```
public override void Initialize(AnalysisContext context)
{
  context.RegisterSymbolAction(AnalyzeSymbol,
    SymbolKind.NamedType);
}
```

4. Create the `AnalyzeSymbol` method. You can call this method anything you like. Just ensure that, whatever you call this method, it matches the method name in the `RegisterSymbolAction()` method inside `Initialize`.

```
private static void AnalyzeSymbol(SymbolAnalysisContext context)
{

}
```

5. Add to that a Boolean called `blnInterfaceImplemented` that will store a `true` or `false` if the interface is implemented or not. The next check we do is to ignore abstract classes. In reality, you would probably want to check an abstract class too, but I want to exclude it to show the flexibility of code analyzers.

```
bool blnInterfaceImplemented = false;
if (!context.Symbol.IsAbstract)
{

}
```

6. You now need to get the name of the symbol you are checking. To do this, create an object called `namedTypeSymbol` on which you can call the `Name` method to return the symbol name. On a class called `PurchaseOrder`, this should return `PurchaseOrder` as the name. Return the `ClassTypesToCheck` enum as a `List<string>` object called `classesToCheck`. Then, do a check on the class name and see if it is contained in the `classesToCheck` list. It is important to ignore the case by adding `StringComparison.OrdinalIgnoreCase` to the `Equals` check. This will ensure that the analyzer will analyze classes called `purchaseorder`, `PURCHASEORDER`, `PurchaseOrder`, `Purchaseorder`, or `purchaseOrder`. Add the code inside the `if` condition excluding abstract classes.

```
var namedTypeSymbol = (INamedTypeSymbol)context.Symbol;
List<string> classesToCheck = Enum.GetNames(
    typeof(ClassTypesToCheck)).ToList();

if (classesToCheck.Any(s => s.Equals(
    namedTypeSymbol.Name, StringComparison.OrdinalIgnoreCase)))
{

}
```

The capitalization style recommended for class names is PascalCase. PascalCase consists of capitalizing the first letter of an identifier and each subsequent concatenated word. This is applied if the identifier has three or more characters. This means that the concatenated words purchase and order must we written in PascalCase when used in class names. This results in **PurchaseOrder**. Refer to the **Capitalization Styles article** in the MSDN at `https://msdn.microsoft.com/en-us/library/x2dbyw72(v=vs.71).aspx`.

7. Inside the `if` condition, to check if the class name is `PurchaseOrder` or `SalesOrder`, add the following code. Here we are going to check the interfaces defined on the matched `PurchaseOrder` or `SalesOrder` class. We do this by calling the `AllInterfaces()` method and checking to see if it matches the `nameof` the `IReceiptable` enumerator. In reality, we would probably want to check more than one interface, but for our purposes we're only checking for the implementation of the `IReceiptable` interface. If we find the interface as implemented on the class name that was matched in the earlier check, we set `blnInterfaceImplemented = true;` (it is currently initialized to `false`). This means that, if the interface is not matched, then we will produce a diagnostic for the omission of the `IReceiptable` interface. This is done by creating and reporting the diagnostic that contains the `Rule` defined earlier and the location of the class name.

```
string interfaceName = nameof(
  MandatoryInterfaces.IReceiptable);

if (namedTypeSymbol.AllInterfaces.Any(s => s.Name.Equals(
  interfaceName, StringComparison.OrdinalIgnoreCase)))
{
  blnInterfaceImplemented = true;
}

if (!blnInterfaceImplemented)
{
  // Produce a diagnostic.
  var diagnostic = Diagnostic.Create(Rule,
    namedTypeSymbol.Locations[0], namedTypeSymbol.Name);
  context.ReportDiagnostic(diagnostic);
}
```

8. If all the code is added to `AnalyzeSymbol()` the method should look as follows:

```
private static void AnalyzeSymbol(SymbolAnalysisContext context)
{
  bool blnInterfaceImplemented = false;
  if (!context.Symbol.IsAbstract)
  {
    var namedTypeSymbol = (INamedTypeSymbol)context.Symbol;
    List<string> classesToCheck = Enum.GetNames(
      typeof(ClassTypesToCheck)).ToList();

    if (classesToCheck.Any(s => s.Equals(namedTypeSymbol.Name,
      StringComparison.OrdinalIgnoreCase)))
    {
```

```
string interfaceName = nameof(
  MandatoryInterfaces.IReceiptable);

if (namedTypeSymbol.AllInterfaces.Any(s => s.Name.Equals(
  interfaceName, StringComparison.OrdinalIgnoreCase)))
{
  blnInterfaceImplemented = true;
}

if (!blnInterfaceImplemented)
{
  // Produce a diagnostic.
  var diagnostic = Diagnostic.Create(Rule,
    namedTypeSymbol.Locations[0], namedTypeSymbol.Name);
  context.ReportDiagnostic(diagnostic);
}
      }
    }
  }
}
```

9. We now need to create a fix for the code analyzer. If we see that the class does not implement our interface, we want to provide a quick fix for the developer with the lightbulb feature. Open the file called CodeFixProvider.cs. You will see that it contains a class called public class PurchaseOrderAnalyzerCodeFixProvider : CodeFixProvider. The first thing to do is locate the title string constant and change it to a more suitable title. This is the menu flyout displayed when you click on the **lightbulb** in Visual Studio.

```
private const string title = "Implement IReceiptable";
```

10. I have left most of the code-fix code the same except for the code that does the actual fix. Locate the method called RegisterCodeFixesAsync(). I renamed the method to call in the RegisterCodeFix() method to ImplementRequiredInterfaceAsync(). The code should look as follows:

```
public sealed override async Task RegisterCodeFixesAsync(
  CodeFixContext context)
{
  var root = await context.Document.GetSyntaxRootAsync(
    context.CancellationToken).ConfigureAwait(false);

  var diagnostic = context.Diagnostics.First();
  var diagnosticSpan = diagnostic.Location.SourceSpan;

  // Find the type declaration identified by the diagnostic.
```

```
var declaration = root.FindToken(diagnosticSpan.Start)
  .Parent.AncestorsAndSelf().OfType
  <TypeDeclarationSyntax>().First();

// Register a code action that will invoke the fix.
context.RegisterCodeFix(
  CodeAction.Create(
    title: title,
    createChangedSolution: c =>
    ImplementRequiredInterfaceAsync(context.Document,
      declaration, c),
    equivalenceKey: title),
  diagnostic);
}
```

11. You will notice that I have re-purposed the fix used to make the symbol an uppercase to implement the interface. The rest of the code is left as-is. In reality, you would most likely want to check if any other interfaces are implemented on the class and maintain those implementations. For this demonstration, we're just assuming a new class being created called `PurchaseOrder` or `SalesOrder` without existing interfaces.

```
private async Task<Solution> ImplementRequiredInterfaceAsync(
  Document document, TypeDeclarationSyntax typeDecl,
  CancellationToken cancellationToken)
{
  // Get the text of the PurchaseOrder class and return one
    implementing the IPurchaseOrder interface
  var identifierToken = typeDecl.Identifier;

  var newName = $"{identifierToken.Text} : IReceiptable";

  // Get the symbol representing the type to be renamed.
  var semanticModel = await document.GetSemanticModelAsync(
    cancellationToken);
  var typeSymbol = semanticModel.GetDeclaredSymbol(
    typeDecl, cancellationToken);

  // Produce a new solution that has all references to
    that type renamed, including the declaration.
  var originalSolution = document.Project.Solution;
  var optionSet = originalSolution.Workspace.Options;
  var newSolution = await Renamer.RenameSymbolAsync(
    document.Project.Solution, typeSymbol, newName,
    optionSet, cancellationToken).ConfigureAwait(false);

  return newSolution;
```

```
}
```

12. Ensure that the `PurchaseOrderAnalyzer.Vsix` project is set as the start-up project and click on **Debug**. A new instance of Visual Studio will be launched. Create a new console application in this Visual Studio instance and call it `PurchaseOrderConsole`. To this project, add a new interface called `IReceiptable` and add the following code.

```
interface IReceiptable
{
    void MarkAsReceipted(int orderNumber);
}
```

13. Now, add a new class called `PurchaseOrder` to the project with the following code.

```
public class PurchaseOrder
{

}
```

14. After you have done this, your project might look as follows if you added separate files for `IReceiptable` and `PurchaseOrder`.

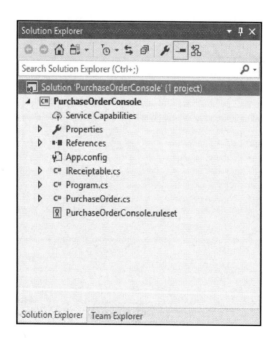

15. Viewing the `PurchaseOrder` class, you will notice a squiggly line under the class name `PurchaseOrder`.

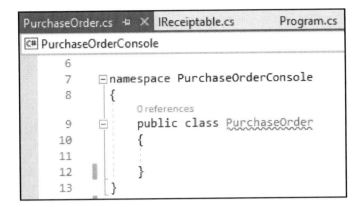

16. Hovering the mouse over the squiggly line, you will see the lightbulb displayed notifying you that the `IReceiptable` interface is not implemented.

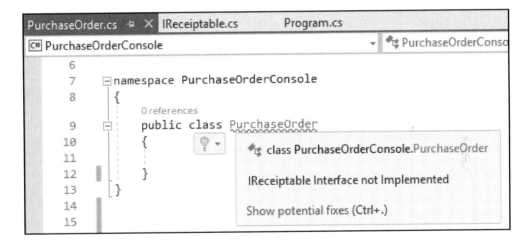

17. When you view potential fixes, you will see that the `title` we changed earlier in the `CodeFixProvider.cs` file to read `private const string title = "Implement IReceiptable";` is displayed as the flyout menu text. The suggested code is then shown as implementing the correct interface `IReceiptable`.

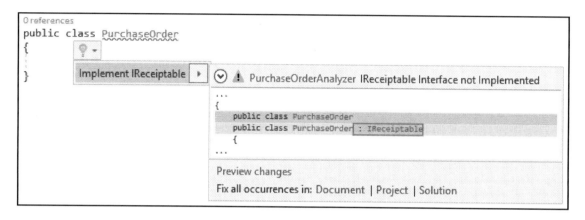

18. Clicking on this modifies our `PurchaseOrder` class to produce the following code:

```
public class PurchaseOrder : IReceiptable
{

}
```

19. Once the code fix has been applied, you will see that the squiggly line under the class name has disappeared. As expected, Visual Studio is now telling us that we need to implement the interface member `IReceiptable.MarkAsReceipted(int)` by underlining the interface name `IReceiptable` with a red squiggly line.

```
PurchaseOrder.cs* ⊕ ✕  IReceiptable.cs      Program.cs
C# PurchaseOrderConsole                              ⧩ Pur

    6
    7        □ namespace PurchaseOrderConsole
    8          {
                   0 references
    9          □     public class PurchaseOrder : IReceiptable
   10                {
   11
   12                }
   13          }
```

20. Hovering over the `IReceiptable` interface name, you will see the lightbulb the code fix. This is the standard Visual Studio analyzer at work here.

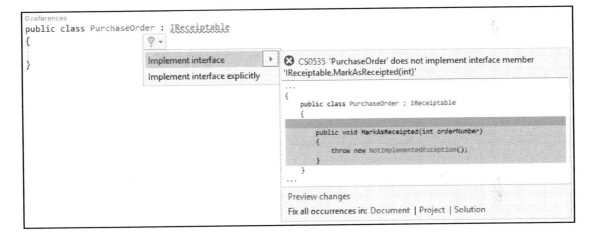

[169]

21. Clicking on the fix to be applied implements the `IReceiptable` member and the `PurchaseOrder` class is correctly defined in the code.

```csharp
namespace PurchaseOrderConsole
{
    0 references
    public class PurchaseOrder : IReceiptable
    {
        1 reference
        public void MarkAsReceipted(int orderNumber)
        {
            throw new NotImplementedException();
        }
    }
}
```

How it works...

The example in this recipe does not even begin to scratch the surface of what is possible with code analyzers. A great way to learn what is possible is to have a look at some of the code analyzers on GitHub. View the code and start writing your own code analyzers. As with most concepts in programming, the only way to learn this is to write the code. There is a wealth of information available on the Internet. A word of advice, though: before you start writing your code analyzers, take a look to see if there isn't an analyzer that already does what you need (or is close to doing what you need).

For example, if you need to ensure method comments include additional information, try to find an analyzer that already does something similar. If you find an analyzer that checks to see if public methods have comments, for example, you could easily retrofit this analyzer to suit your own needs. The best way to learn is to do, but everybody needs a starting point. Standing on the shoulders of others is part of learning new programming concepts.

Deploying your code analyzer within your organization only

Code analyzers are a fantastic method to check and correct code automatically. Sometimes, however, the analyzers you create will not be suitable for public consumption as they might contain proprietary information. With NuGet, you can create private repositories and share these with colleagues. You can use a shared location on a company server, for example, and easily manage NuGet packages from there.

Getting ready

Ensure that you have a shared location accessible to all developers in your organization. This can be anywhere your network administrator has provided for shared file access. You will probably want to restrict the access of these packages to developers only. A nice solution is to create a storage account on Azure to share the NuGet packages to. This is the approach I followed here using a fictitious company I have called Acme Corporation.

I will not go through setting up a storage account on Azure, but I will talk about accessing it from your local machine.

 I encourage you and your organization to consider using Azure. I will not expand much on the benefits of using Azure other than to say that it is an incredible time-saver. If I want to test a specific feature of an application on a particular OS, within minutes I am able to spin up a VM and connect to it via a remote desktop. It is immediately ready to use.

After you have created your storage account on Azure, you will find the access keys on the **Access keys** tab.

1. Make a note of the keys and the **Storage account name**.

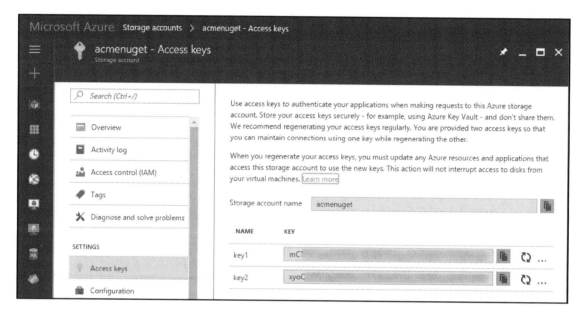

2. I also just created a **File service** called **packages**. To get here, click on **Overview**. Then, under the **Services** heading, click on **Files**. On the **File service** window, select **packages** and view the property information for the file share.

Your storage account might differ from the examples in this book, depending on what you called it.

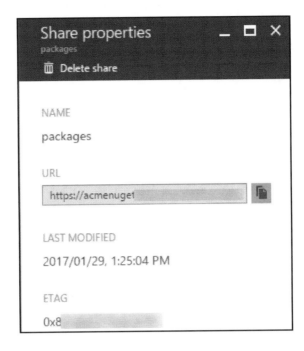

3. Make a note of the URL specified in the properties. Using the URL, map a network drive by changing the `https://` part to `\\` and any subsequent `/` to `\` in the path.

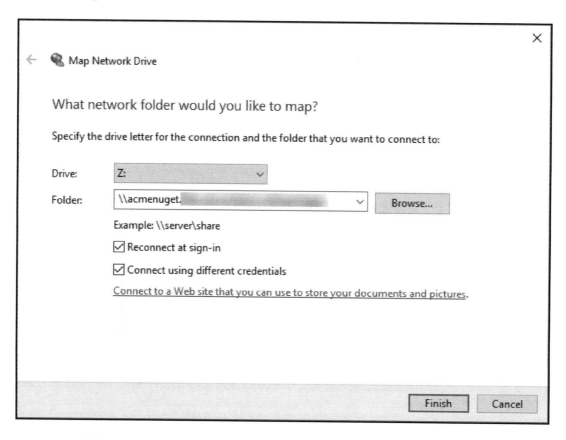

4. Add this path to the **Folder** textbox and ensure that you have checked **Connect using different credentials**.

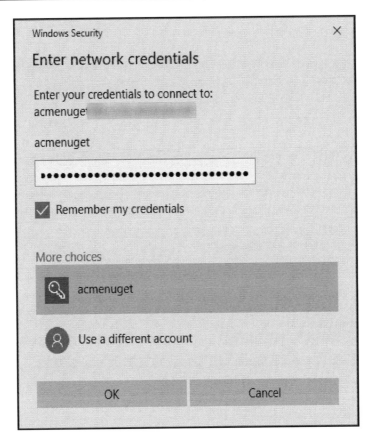

Use the storage account name as the username and one of the keys as the password. You now have a network drive mapped to your Azure Storage account.

How to do it...

1. Have a look at the `PurchaseOrderAnalyzer` project we created. You will see that there is a `tools` folder containing two PowerShell scripts called `install.ps1` and `uninstall.ps1`. It is here that you can specify any installation-specific resources or actions to take when uninstalling the package.

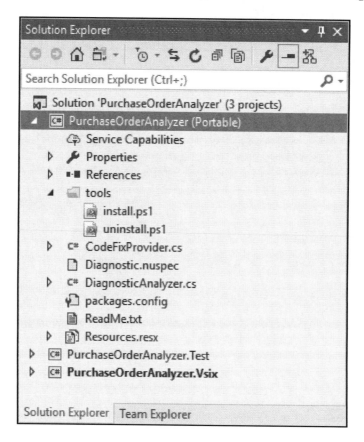

2. Opening the `Diagnostic.nuspec` file, you will note that this contains information regarding the NuGet package you are about to deploy. Make a point of modifying this file accordingly as it contains information important to developers consuming your NuGet package.

```
<?xml version="1.0"?>
<package xmlns="http://schemas.microsoft.com/packaging/
  2011/08/nuspec.xsd">
  <metadata>
```

```
<id>PurchaseOrderAnalyzer</id>
<version>1.1.1.1</version>
<title>Purchase Order Analyzer</title>
<authors>Dirk Strauss</authors>
<owners>Acme Corporation</owners>
<licenseUrl>http://www.acmecorporation.com/poanalyzer/
  license</licenseUrl>
<projectUrl>http://www.acmecorporation.com/poanalyzer
  </projectUrl>
<requireLicenseAcceptance>true</requireLicenseAcceptance>
<description>Validate the creation of Purchase Order Objects
  withing Acme Corporation's development projects
</description>
<releaseNotes>Initial release of the Purchase Order
  Analyzer.</releaseNotes>
<copyright>Copyright</copyright>
<tags>PurchaseOrderAnalyzer, analyzers</tags>
<frameworkAssemblies>
  <frameworkAssembly assemblyName="System"
    targetFramework="" />
</frameworkAssemblies>
</metadata>
<!-- The convention for analyzers is to put language
 agnostic dlls in analyzersportable50 and language
 specific analyzers in either analyzersportable50cs or
 analyzersportable50vb -->
<files>
  <file src="*.dll" target="analyzersdotnetcs"
   exclude="**Microsoft.CodeAnalysis.*;
   **System.Collections.Immutable.*;
   **System.Reflection.Metadata.*;
   **System.Composition.*" />
  <file src="tools*.ps1" target="tools" />
</files>
</package>
```

3. Go ahead and build your code analyzer. You will see that a file called `PurchaseOrderAnalyzer.1.1.1.1.nupkg` has been created in the `bin` folder for your project. Copy that file to the mapped drive you created earlier in the Azure Storage account.

4. Inside Visual Studio, add a new WinForms application. You can call this anything you like. You can now add the Storage account as a NuGet location. Go to **Tools**, **NuGet Package Manager** and click on **Manage NuGet Packages for Solution....** You will notice that, next to the **Package source,** which is currently set to **nuget.org,** there is a small gear icon. Click on this.

I created the Visual Studio WinForms application on a separate machine for this example, but if you do not have access to a separate machine, try using a VM to test this. If you do not have access to Azure, you can use VirtualBox.

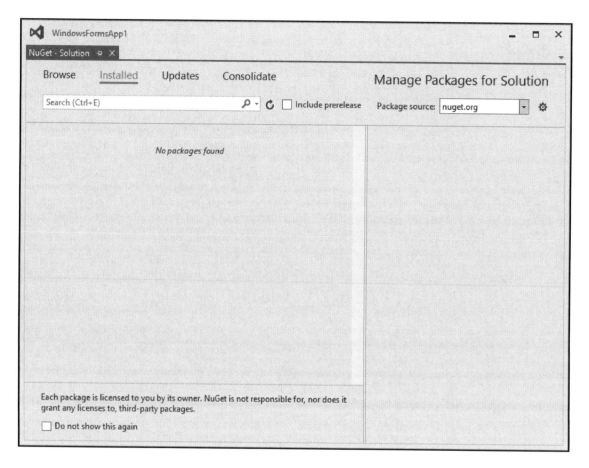

5. The **Options** screen allows you to add an additional source for NuGet packages by clicking on the green plus icon under **Available package sources**.

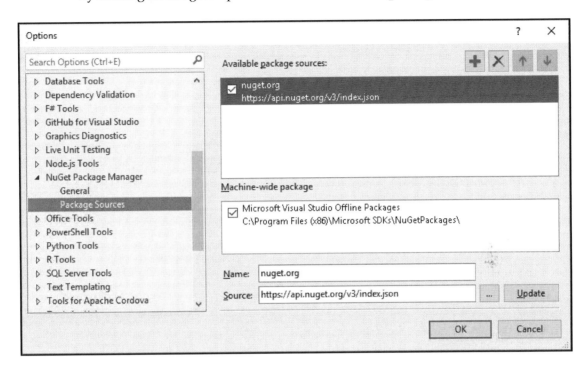

6. At the bottom of the **Options** window, enter a suitable name for the location and enter the path to the Azure Storage account. This is the same path you entered when you mapped the network drive. Before clicking on **OK**, click on the **Update** button. Then click on the **OK** button.

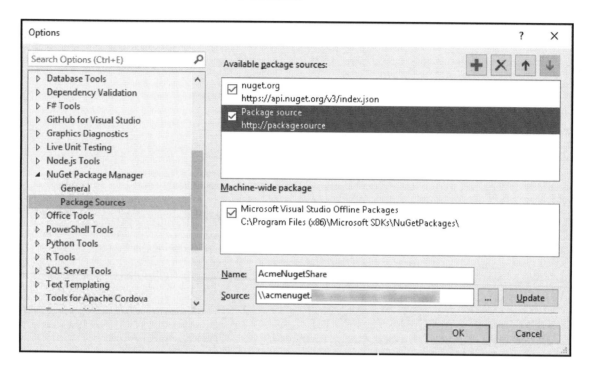

7. You can now change the **Package source** to set it to the Azure Storage account location you mapped to. Doing this and clicking on the **Browse** tab of the NuGet package manager will display all the packages on this file share. The information under the **Options** section to the right is the information you defined in the `Diagnostic.nuspec` file.

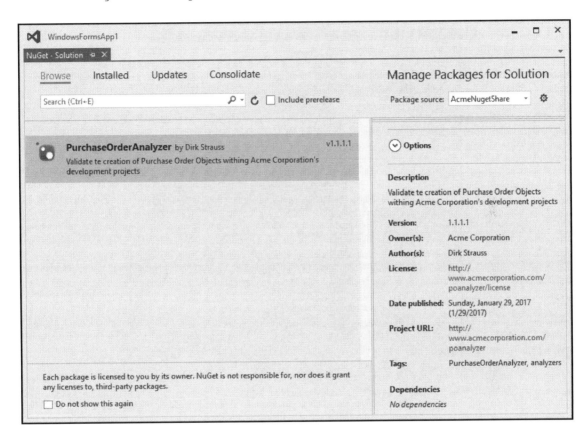

8. You can now go ahead and install the code analyzer NuGet package. When you have completed the installation, the code analyzer will be visible under the `Analyzers` node under `References` in your project.

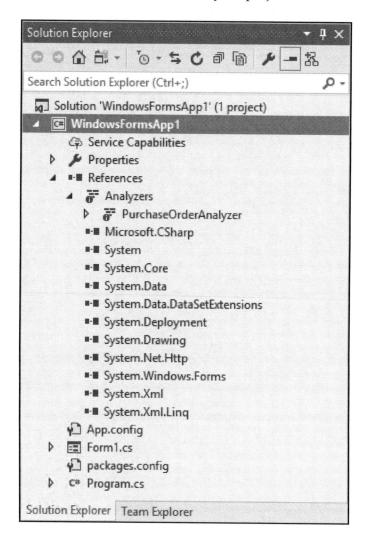

9. The code analyzer also works exactly as expected. Create a class called `PurchaseOrder` and see the analyzer in action.

```
11    namespace WindowsFormsApp1
12    {
          3 references
13        public partial class Form1 : Form
14        {
              1 reference
15            public Form1()
16            {
17                InitializeComponent();
18            }
19
              1 reference
20            private void Form1_Load(object sender, EventArgs e)
21            {
22
23            }
24        }
25
          0 references
26        public class PurchaseOrder
27        {            ᵠ ▾      ᵗₓ class WindowsFormsApp1.PurchaseOrder
28
29        }                    IReceiptable Interface not Implemented
30    }
31                            Show potential fixes (Ctrl+.)
```

How it works...

The NuGet package is the easiest way to deploy code to a large audience or even a few developers. It takes all the heavy lifting out of sharing code and templates. It therefore makes perfect sense to use NuGet to deploy your code analyzers. Setting up a private repository using NuGet for sharing code within your organization is really simple.

5

Regular Expressions

Regular expressions (regex) are something of a mystery to many developers. We admit that they are something that we use often enough to warrant a deeper understanding of how they work. On the flip side, there are so many tried and tested regex patterns on the Internet, that just reusing one that already exists is easier than trying to create one yourself most times. The subject of regex is much larger than what can be explained in a single chapter in this book.

Therefore, in this chapter, we will merely introduce some of the concepts of regex. For a deeper understanding of regex, further study is needed. For the purpose of this book, however, we will take a closer look at how regular expression are created and how they can be applied to some common programming problems. In this chapter, we will cover the following recipes:

- Getting started with regex - Matching a valid date
- Sanitize input
- Dynamic regex matching

Introduction

A regular expression is a pattern that describes a string through the use of special characters that denote a specific bit of text to match. The use of regular expression is not a new concept in programming. For regex to work, it needs to use a regex engine that does all the heavy lifting.

In the .NET Framework, Microsoft has provided for the use of regex. To use regex, you will need to import the `System.Text.RegularExpressions` assembly to your project. This will allow the compiler to use your regex pattern and apply it to the specific text you need to match.

Secondly, regex have a specific set of metacharacters that hold special meaning to the regex engine. These characters are [ ], { }, ( ), *, +, , ?, |, $, ., and ^.

The use of the curly brackets { }, for example, enables developers to specify the number of times a specific set of characters need to occur. Using square brackets, on the other hand, defines exactly what needs to be matched.

If we, for example, specified [abc], the pattern would look for lowercase As, Bs, and Cs. regex, therefore, also allows you to define a range, for example, [a-c], which is interpreted in exactly the same way as the [abc] pattern.

Regular expressions then also allow you to define characters to exclude using the ^ character. Therefore, typing [^a-c] would find lowercase D through Z because the pattern is telling the regex engine to exclude lowercase As, Bs, and Cs.

Regular expressions also define d and D a type of shortcut for [0-9] and [^0-9], respectively. Therefore, d matches all numeric values, and D matches all non-numeric values. Another shortcut is w and W, which match any character from lowercase A to Z, irrespective of the case, all numeric values from 0 to 9, and the underscore character. Therefore, w is [a-zA-Z0-9_], while W is [^a-zA-Z0-9_].

The basics of regex are rather easy to understand, but there is a lot more that you can do with regex.

Getting started with regex - Matching a valid date

If you haven't done so already, create a new console application and add a class to the project called RegExDemo. Your code at this moment should look something like this:

```
class Program
{
    static void Main(string[] args)
    {
    }
}

public class RegExDemo
{

}
```

Getting ready

For the purpose of this book, we are using a console application to illustrate the use of regex. In reality, you would probably not have this logic mixed in between your production code, because this would result in code being rewritten. The best place to add something such as regex is in a helper class within an extension method.

How to do it...

1. In the console application, add the following using statement so that we can use the regex assembly in .NET:

    ```
    using System.Text.RegularExpressions;
    ```

2. We will create a regex to validate a date pattern of yyyy-mm-dd, yyyy/mm/dd, or yyyy.mm.dd. At first, the regex will look daunting, but bear with me. When you have completed the code and run the application, we will dissect the regex. Hopefully, the expression logic will become clear.

3. Inside the RegExDemo class, create a new method called ValidDate() that takes a string as the parameter. This string will be the date pattern we want to validate:

    ```
    public void ValidDate(string stringToMatch)
    {

    }
    ```

4. Add the following regex pattern to your method to a variable in the method:

    ```
    string pattern = $@"^(19|20)dd[-./](0[1-9]|1[0-2])
                        [-./](0[1-9]|[12][0-9]|3[01])$";
    ```

5. Finally, add the regex to match the supplied string parameter:

    ```
    if (Regex.IsMatch(stringToMatch, pattern))
        Console.WriteLine($"The string {stringToMatch}
                        contains a valid date.");
    else
        Console.WriteLine($"The string {stringToMatch} DOES
                        NOT contain a valid date.");
    ```

6. When you have done this, your method should look like this:

```
public void ValidDate(string stringToMatch)
{
    string pattern = $@"^(19|20)dd[-./](0[1-9]|1[0-2])
                     [-./](0[1-9]|[12][0-9]|3[01])$";

    if (Regex.IsMatch(stringToMatch, pattern))
        Console.WriteLine($"The string {stringToMatch} contains
                          a valid date.");
    else
        Console.WriteLine($"The string {stringToMatch} DOES
        NOT contain a valid date.");
}
```

7. Going back to your console application, add the following code and debug your application by clicking on **Start**:

```
RegExDemo oRecipe = new RegExDemo();
oRecipe.ValidDate("1912-12-31");
oRecipe.ValidDate("2018-01-01");
oRecipe.ValidDate("1800-01-21");
oRecipe.ValidDate($"{DateTime.Now.Year}
                  .{DateTime.Now.Month}.{DateTime.Now.Day}");
oRecipe.ValidDate("2016-21-12");
Console.Read();
```

 You will notice that if you add the `using static System.Console;` namespace, you then just need to call `Read()` instead of `Console.Read()`. This new feature where you could import static namespaces was added in C# 6.0.

8. The date strings are passed to the regex, and the pattern is matched against the date string in the parameter. The output is displayed in the console application:

```
The string 1912-12-31 contains a valid date.
The string 2018-01-01 contains a valid date.
The string 1800-01-21 DOES NOT contain a valid date.
The string 2016.4.10 DOES NOT contain a valid date.
The string 2016-21-12 DOES NOT contain a valid date.
```

9. If you look at the output carefully, you will notice that there is a mistake. We are validating the date string in the format yyyy-mm-dd, yyyy/mm/dd, and yyyy.mm.dd. If we use this logic, our regex has incorrectly flagged a valid date as invalid. This is the date 2016.4.10, which is April 10, 2016, and is in fact quite valid.

We will explain shortly why the date 1800-01-21 is invalid.

10. Go back to your ValidDate() method and change the regular expression to read as follows:

```
string pattern = $@"^(19|20)dd[-./](0[1-9]|1[0-2]|[1-9])
[-./](0[1-9]|[12][0-9]|3[01])$";
```

11. Run the console application again and look at the output:

```
The string 1912-12-31 contains a valid date.
The string 2018-01-01 contains a valid date.
The string 1800-01-21 DOES NOT contain a valid date.
The string 2016.4.10 contains a valid date.
The string 2016-21-12 DOES NOT contain a valid date.
```

This time the regex worked for all the given date strings. But what exactly did we do? This is how it works.

How it works...

Let's take a closer look at the two expressions used in the previous code example. Comparing them with each other, you can see the change we made in yellow:

```
string pattern = $@"^(19|20)\d\d[-./](0[1-9]|1[0-2])[-./](0[1-9]|[12][0-9]|3[01])$";
string pattern = $@"^(19|20)\d\d[-./](0[1-9]|1[0-2]|[1-9])[-./](0[1-9]|[12][0-9]|3[01])$";
```

Before we get to what that change means, let's break up the expression and view the individual components. Our regex is basically saying that we must match all string dates that start with 19 or 20 and have the following separators:

- Dash (–)
- Decimal (.)
- Forward slash (/)

To understand the expression better, we need to understand the following format of the expression *<Valid Years><Valid Separators><Valid Months><Valid Separators><Valid Days>*.

We also need to be able to tell the regex engine to consider one *OR* another pattern. The word *OR* is symbolized by the | metacharacter. To make the regex engine consider the word *OR* without splitting up the whole expression, we wrap it in the parenthesis ().

Here are the symbols used in the regex:

The conditional OR	Description
|	This denotes the *OR* metacharacter.
The year portion	**Description**
(19|20)	Only allow 19 or 20
dd	Matches two single digits between 0 and 9. To match only one digit between 0 and 9, you would use d.
The valid separator character set	**Description**
[-./]	Matches any of the following characters in the character set. These are our valid separators. To match a space date separator, you would change this to [- ./], where you add a space anywhere in the character set. We added the space between the dash and the decimal.

Valid digits for months and days	Description
0[1-9]	Matches any part starting with zero followed by any digit between 1 and 9. This will match 01, 02, 03, 04, 05, 06, 07, 08, and 09.
1[0-2]	Matches any part starting with 1 followed by any digit between 0 and 2. This will match 10, 11, or 12.
[1-9]	Matches any digit between 1 and 9.
[12][0-9]	Matches any part starting with 1 or 2 followed by any digit between 0 and 9. This will match all number strings between 10 and 29.
3[01]	Matches any part starting with 3 and followed by 0 or 1. This will match 30 or 31.
Start and end of string	**Description**
^	Tells the regex engine to start at the beginning of the given string to match.
$	Tells the regex engine to stop at the end of the given string to match.

The first regex we created, interprets as follows:

- ^: Start at the beginning of the string to match
- (19|20): Check whether the string starts with 19 or 20
- dd: After the check, follows two single digits between 0 and 9
- [-./]: The year portion ends followed by a date separators
- (0[1-9]|1[0-2]): Find the month logic by looking for digits starting with 0, followed by any digit between 1 and 9, *OR* digits starting with 1, followed by any digit between 0 and 2
- [-./]: The month logic ends followed by a date separator
- (0[1-9]|[12][0-9]|3[01]): Then, find the day logic by looking for digits starting with 0, followed by a digit between 1 and 9, OR digits starting with 1 or 2, followed by any digit between 0 and 9, OR a digit matching 3, followed by any digit between 0 and 1
- $: Do this until the end of the string

Our first regex was incorrect because our month logic was incorrect. Our month logic dictates to find the month logic by looking for digits starting with a 0 followed by any digit between 1 and 9 or digits starting with a 1 followed by any digit between 0 and 2 (0[1-9]|1[0-2]).

This will then find 01, 02, 03, 04, 05, 06, 07, 08, 09, or 10, 11, 12. The date that it didn't match was 2016.4.10 (the date separators don't make a difference here). This is because our month came through as a single digit, and we were looking for months where the single digits started with a zero. To fix this, we had to modify the expression of the month logic to include single digits only between 1 and 9. We did this by adding [1-9] to the expression at the end.

The modified regex then read as follows:

- ^: Start at the beginning of the string to match
- (19|20): Check whether the string starts with 19 or 20
- dd: After the check, follows two single digits between 0 and 9
- [-./]: The year portion ends followed by a date separator
- (0[1-9]|1[0-2]): Find the month logic by looking for digits starting with 0, followed by any digit between 1 and 9, OR digits starting with 1, followed by any digit between 0 and 2 or any single digits between 1 and 9
- [-./]: The month logic ends followed by a date separator
- (0[1-9]|[12][0-9]|3[01]): Then, find the day logic by looking for digits starting with 0, followed by a digit between 1 and 9, OR digits starting with 1 or 2, followed by any digit between 0 and 9, OR a digit matching 3, followed by any digit between 0 and 1
- $: Do this until the end of the string

This is a basic regex, and we say basic because there is a lot more we can do to make the expression better. We can include logic to consider alternative date formats such as mm-dd-yyyy or dd-mm-yyyy. We can add logic to check February and validate that it contains only 28 days, unless it is a leap year, in which case we need to allow the twenty-ninth day of February. Furthermore, we can also extend the regex to check that January, March, May, July, August, October, and December have 31 days while April, June, September, and November contain only 30 days.

Sanitizing input

Sometimes, you will need to sanitize input. This could be to prevent SQL injections or ensure that an entered URL is valid. In this recipe, we will look at replacing the bad words in a string with asterisks. We are sure that there are more elegant and code-efficient methods of writing sanitation logic using regex (especially when we have a large collection of blacklist words), but we want to illustrate a concept here.

Getting ready

Ensure that you have added the correct assembly to your class. At the top of your code file, add the following line of code if you haven't done so already:

```
using System.Text.RegularExpressions;
```

How to do it...

1. Create a new method in your RegExDemo class called SanitizeInput() and let it accept a string parameter:

```
public string SanitizeInput(string input)
{

}
```

2. Add a list of type List<string> to the method that contains the bad words we want to remove from the input:

```
List<string> lstBad = new List<string>(new string[]
{  "BadWord1", "BadWord2", "BadWord3" });
```

 In reality, you might make use of a database call to read the blacklisted words from a table in the database. You would usually not hardcode them in a list like this.

3. Start constructing the regex that we will use to look for the blacklisted words. You concatenate the words with the | (OR) metacharacter so that the regex will match any of the words. When the list is complete, you can append the b expression to either side of the regex. This denotes a word boundary and, therefore, will only match whole words:

```
string pattern = "";
foreach (string badWord in lstBad)
pattern += pattern.Length == 0 ? $"{badWord}"
  :  $"|{badWord}";

pattern = $@"b({pattern})b";
```

4. Finally, we will add the `Regex.Replace()` method that takes the input and looks for the occurrence of the words defined in the pattern, while ignoring case and replacing the bad words with *****:

```
return Regex.Replace(input, pattern, "*****",
                     RegexOptions.IgnoreCase);
```

5. When you have completed this, your `SanitizeInput()` method will look like this:

```
public string SanitizeInput(string input)
{
  List<string> lstBad = new List<string>(new string[]
  { "BadWord1", "BadWord2", "BadWord3" });
  string pattern = "";
  foreach (string badWord in lstBad)
  pattern += pattern.Length == 0 ? $"{badWord}" : $"|{badWord}";

  pattern = $@"b({pattern})b";

  return Regex.Replace(input, pattern, "*****",
                       RegexOptions.IgnoreCase);
}
```

6. In the console application, add the following code to call the `SanitizeInput()` method and run your application (if you have already instantiated an instance of `RegExDemo` in the previous recipe, you don't need to do it again):

```
string textToSanitize = "This is a string that contains a
  badword1, another Badword2 and a third badWord3";
RegExDemo oRecipe = new RegExDemo();
textToSanitize = oRecipe.SanitizeInput(textToSanitize);
WriteLine(textToSanitize);
Read();
```

7. When you run your application, you will see the following in the console window:

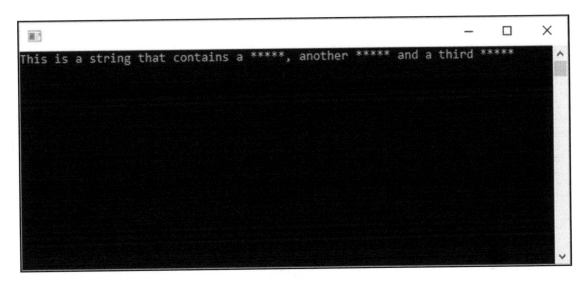

This is a string that contains a *****, another ***** and a third *****

Let's take a closer look at the regular expression generated.

How it works...

Let's step through the code to understand what is happening. We need to get a regex that looks like this: b(wordToMatch1|wordToMatch2|wordToMatch3)b.

What this basically says is "find me any of the words and only whole words which are denoted by b". When we look at the list we created, we will see the words we want to remove from the input string:

```
1 reference
public string SanitizeInput(string input)
{
    List<string> lstBad = new List<string>(new string[] { "BadWord1", "BadWord2", "BadWord3" });
    string pattern ◢ ● lstBad Count = 3 ⊡
    foreach (string b  ● [0]      Q ▾ "BadWord1"
        pattern += pa  ● [1]      Q ▾ "BadWord2" ord}"  : $"|{badWord}";
                       ● [2]      Q ▾ "BadWord3"
    pattern = $@"\b({ ▷ ● Raw View

    return Regex.Replace(input, pattern, "******", RegexOptions.IgnoreCase);
}
```

We then created a simple loop that will create the list of words to match using the OR metacharacter. We ended up with a BadWord1 | BadWord2 | BadWord3 pattern after the foreach loop has completed. However, this is still not a valid regex:

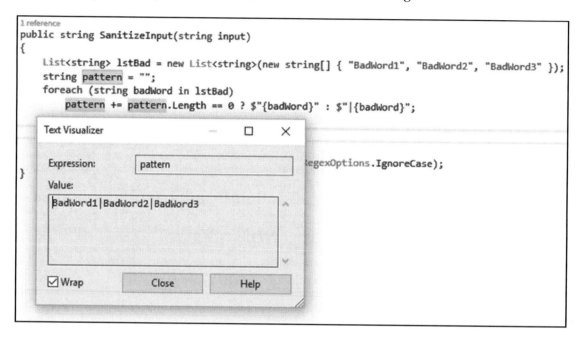

```
1 reference
public string SanitizeInput(string input)
{
    List<string> lstBad = new List<string>(new string[] { "BadWord1", "BadWord2", "BadWord3" });
    string pattern = "";
    foreach (string badWord in lstBad)
        pattern += pattern.Length == 0 ? $"{badWord}" : $"|{badWord}";
```

Text Visualizer — □ ✕

Expression: pattern   egexOptions.IgnoreCase);

Value:

BadWord1|BadWord2|BadWord3

☑ Wrap   Close   Help

```
}
```

To complete the pattern resulting in the valid regex, we need to add the b expression on either side of the pattern to tell the regex engine to only match whole words. As you can see, we are using string interpolation.

It is here, however, that we need to be very careful. Start off by writing the code to complete the pattern without the @ sign as follows:

```
pattern = $"b({pattern})b";
```

If you run your console application, you will see that the bad words are not matched and filtered out. This is because we have not escaped the character before b. The compiler, therefore, interprets this line of code:

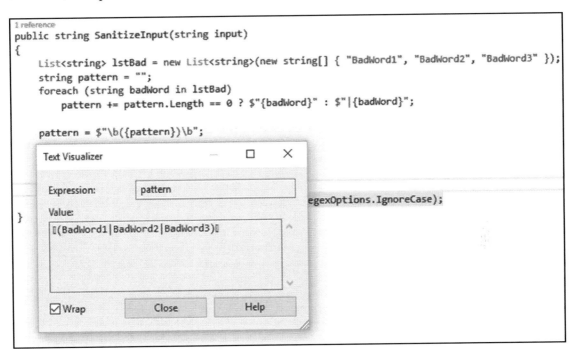

```
1 reference
public string SanitizeInput(string input)
{
    List<string> lstBad = new List<string>(new string[] { "BadWord1", "BadWord2", "BadWord3" });
    string pattern = "";
    foreach (string badWord in lstBad)
        pattern += pattern.Length == 0 ? $"{badWord}" : $"|{badWord}";

    pattern = $"\b({pattern})\b";
```

Text Visualizer

Expression: pattern

Value:
[(BadWord1|BadWord2|BadWord3)]

☑ Wrap   Close   Help

egexOptions.IgnoreCase);

The generated expression `[] (BadWord1| BadWord2| BadWord3) []` is not a valid expression and will, therefore, not sanitize the input string.

To correct this, we need to add the @ symbol before the string to tell the compiler to treat the string as a literal. This means any escape sequences are ignored. The correctly formatted line of code looks like this:

```
pattern = $@"b({pattern})b";
```

Once you do this, the string for the pattern is interpreted literally by the compiler, and the correct regex pattern generated:

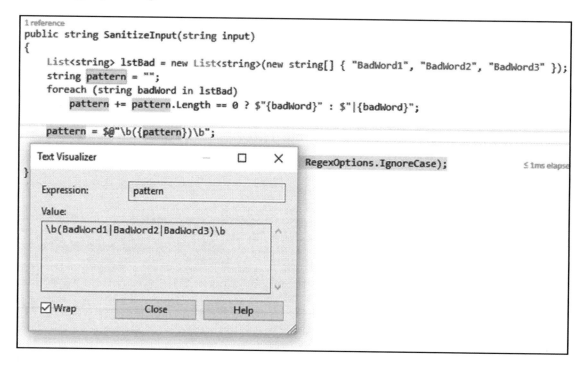

```csharp
1 reference
public string SanitizeInput(string input)
{
    List<string> lstBad = new List<string>(new string[] { "BadWord1", "BadWord2", "BadWord3" });
    string pattern = "";
    foreach (string badWord in lstBad)
        pattern += pattern.Length == 0 ? $"{badWord}" : $"|{badWord}";

    pattern = $@"\b({pattern})\b";
```

Text Visualizer

Expression: pattern

Value:
\b(BadWord1|BadWord2|BadWord3)\b

☑ Wrap   Close   Help

`RegexOptions.IgnoreCase);`

≤ 1ms elapsed

With our correct regex pattern, we called the `Regex.Replace()` method. It takes the input to check, the regex to match, the text to replace the matched words with, and optionally allows for the ignoring of the case:

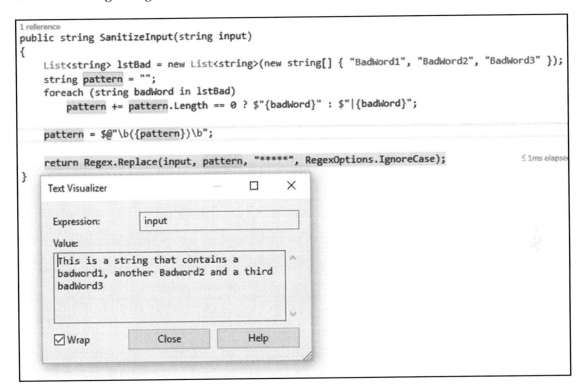

When the string returns to the calling code in the console application, the string will be sanitized properly:

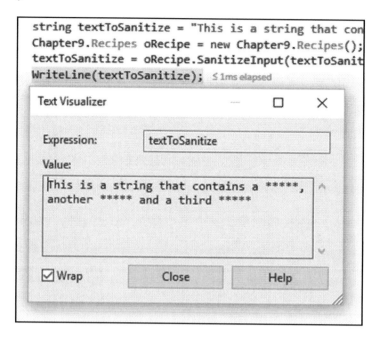

Regex can become quite complex and can be used to perform a multitude of tasks to format and validate input and other text.

Dynamic regex matching

What does dynamic regex matching even mean? Well, it isn't an official term, but it is a term we use to explain a regex that uses variables at runtime to generate a specific expression. Assume for a minute that you are working on a document-management system that needs to implement versioning of documents for a company called ACME Corporation. To do this, the system validates that the document has a valid filename.

A business rule states that the filename of any file uploaded on a specific day must be prefixed with acm (for ACME) and today's date in the yyyy-mm-dd format. They can be only text files, Word documents (only .docx) and Excel documents (only .xlsx). Any documents not conforming to this file format are processed by another method that takes care of archive and invalid documents.

The only task that your method needs to perform is to process fresh documents as version one documents.

 In a production system, further logic will probably be needed to determine whether the same document has been uploaded previously on the same day. This, however, is beyond the scope of this chapter. We are just trying to set the scene.

Getting ready

Ensure that you have added the correct assembly to your class. At the top of your code file, add the following line of code if you haven't already done so:

```
using System.Text.RegularExpressions;
```

How to do it...

1. A really nice way to do this is to use an extension method. This way, you can call the extension method directly on the filename variable and have it validated. In your console application, start off by adding a new class called CustomRegexHelper with public static modifier:

```
public static class CustomRegexHelper
{


}
```

2. Add the usual extension method code to the CustomRegexHelper class and call the ValidAcmeCompanyFilename method:

```
public static bool ValidAcmeCompanyFilename(this string value)
{

}
```

3. Inside your `ValidAcmeCompanyFilename` method, add the following regex. We will explain the makeup of this regex in the *How it works...* section of this recipe:

```
return Regex.IsMatch(value, $@"^^acm[_]{DateTime.Now.Year}[_]
   ({DateTime.Now.Month}|0[{DateTime.Now.Month}])[_]
   ({DateTime.Now.Day}|0[{DateTime.Now.Day}])(.txt|.docx|.xlsx)$");
```

4. When you completed this, your extension method should look like this:

```
public static class CustomRegexHelper
{
    public static bool ValidAcmeCompanyFilename(this String value)
    {
        return Regex.IsMatch(value, $@"^^acm[_]{DateTime.Now.Year}[_]
            ({DateTime.Now.Month}|0[{DateTime.Now.Month}])[_]
({DateTime.Now.Day}|0[{DateTime.Now.Day}])(.txt|.docx|.xlsx)$");
    }
}
```

5. Back in the console application, create a method with `void` return type called `DemoExtensionMethod()`:

```
public static void DemoExtensionMethod()
{

}
```

6. Add some output text to show the current date and the valid filename types:

```
Console.WriteLine($"Today's date is: {DateTime.Now.Year}-
                  {DateTime.Now.Month}-{DateTime.Now.Day}");
Console.WriteLine($"The file must match:  acm_{DateTime.Now.Year}
   _{DateTime.Now.Month}_{DateTime.Now. Day}.txt including
   leading month and day zeros");
Console.WriteLine($"The file must match:  acm_{DateTime.Now.Year}
   _{DateTime.Now.Month}_{DateTime.Now. Day}.docx including
   leading month and day zeros");
Console.WriteLine($"The file must match:  acm_{DateTime.Now.Year}
   _{DateTime.Now.Month}_{DateTime.Now. Day}.xlsx including
   leading month and day zeros");
```

7. Then, add the filename checking code:

```
string filename = "acm_2016_04_10.txt";
if (filename.ValidAcmeCompanyFilename())
  Console.WriteLine($"{filename} is a valid file name");
else
```

```
Console.WriteLine($"{filename} is not a valid file name");

filename = "acm-2016_04_10.txt";
if (filename.ValidAcmeCompanyFilename())
  Console.WriteLine($"{filename} is a valid file name");
else
  Console.WriteLine($"{filename} is not a valid file name");
```

8. You will note that the `if` statement contains the call to the extension method on the variable that contains the filename:

```
filename.ValidAcmeCompanyFilename()
```

9. If you have completed this, your method should look like this:

```
public static void DemoExtensionMethod()
{
  Console.WriteLine($"Today's date is: {DateTime.Now.Year}-
  {DateTime.Now.Month}-{DateTime.Now.Day}");
  Console.WriteLine($"The file must match: acm_{DateTime.Now.Year}
    _{DateTime.Now.Month}_{DateTime.Now.Day}.txt including leading
    month and day zeros");
  Console.WriteLine($"The file must match: acm_{DateTime.Now.Year}
    _{DateTime.Now.Month}_{DateTime.Now.Day}.docx including leading
    month and day zeros");
  Console.WriteLine($"The file must match: acm_{DateTime.Now.Year}
    _{DateTime.Now.Month}_{DateTime.Now.Day}.xlsx including leading
    month and day zeros");

  string filename = "acm_2016_04_10.txt";
  if (filename.ValidAcmeCompanyFilename())
    Console.WriteLine($"{filename} is a valid file name");
  else
    Console.WriteLine($"{filename} is not a valid file name");

  filename = "acm-2016_04_10.txt";
  if (filename.ValidAcmeCompanyFilename())
    Console.WriteLine($"{filename} is a valid file name");
  else
    Console.WriteLine($"{filename} is not a valid file name");
}
```

10. Going back to the console application, add the following code that simply calls the `void` method. This is just to simulate the versioning method talked about earlier:

```
DemoExtensionMethod();
```

11. When you are done, run your console application:

```
Today's date is: 2016-4-10
The file must match: acm_2016_4_10.txt including leading month and day zeros
The file must match: acm_2016_4_10.docx including leading month and day zeros
The file must match: acm_2016_4_10.xlsx including leading month and day zeros
acm_2016_04_10.txt is a valid file name
acm-2016_04_10.txt is not a valid file name
```

How it works...

Let's have a closer look at the regex generated. The line of code we are looking at is the `return` statement in the extension method:

```
return Regex.IsMatch(value,
$@"^acm[_]{DateTime.Now.Year}[_]({DateTime.Now.Month}|0[{DateTime.
Now.Month}])[_]({DateTime.Now.Day}|0[{DateTime.Now.Day}])(.txt|.docx|.xlsx)
$");
```

To appreciate what is happening, we need to break this expression up into the different components:

The conditional OR	Description
|	This denotes the *OR* metacharacter.
The file prefix and separator	**Description**
acm	The file must begin with the text acm.
[_]	The only valid separator between the date components and the prefix in the file name is an underscore.
The date parts	**Description**
{DateTime.Now.Year}	The interpolated year part of the date for the file name.
{DateTime.Now.Month}	The interpolated month part of the date for the file name.
0[{DateTime.Now.Month}]	The interpolated month part of the date with a leading zero for the file name.
{DateTime.Now.Day}	The interpolated day part of the date for the file name.
0[{DateTime.Now.Day}]	The interpolated day part of the date with a leading zero for the file name.
Valid file formats	**Description**
(.txt|.docx|.xlsx)	Match any of these file extensions for text documents, Word documents, or Excel documents.
Start and end of string	**Description**
^	Tells the regex engine to start at the beginning of the given string to match
$	Tells the regex engine to stop at the end of the given string to match

Creating the regex in this manner allows us to always have it stay up to date. As we have to always match the current date to the file being validated, this creates a unique challenge that is easily overcome using string interpolation, DateTime, and regex *OR* statements.

Having a look at some of the more useful bits of regex, you will see that this chapter has not even begun to scratch the surface of what can be accomplished. There is a whole lot more to explore and learn. There are many resources on the Internet as well as some free (some online) and commercial tools that will assist you in creating regex.

6

Working with Files, Streams, and Serialization

Working with files, streams, and serialization is something you as a developer will do many times. Creating import files, exporting data to a file, persisting an application state, using a file definition to build a file, and many other scenarios will present themselves at some point during your career. In this chapter, we will look at the following:

- Creating and extracting ZIP archives
- In-memory stream compression and decompression
- Async and await file processing
- How to make a custom type serializable
- Using ISerializable for custom serialization to a FileStream
- Using XmlSerializer
- JSON serializers

Introduction

Being able to work with files will definitely give you an edge as a developer. There are so many frameworks for working with files available to developers today, that one tends to forget that some of the functionality you want is already rolled up into the .NET Framework itself. Let's look at what exactly we can do with files.

If you ever find that you need to create Excel files in ASP.NET applications, do have a look at the excellent EPPlus .NET library available on CodePlex. At the time of writing, the URL was: `https://epplus.codeplex.com/` and is licensed under the GNU **Library General Public License (LGPL)**. Also consider donating to EPPlus. These folks wrote an incredible library that is very easy to use and well documented.

On March 31, 2017 it was announced that CodePlex would be shut down completely on December 15, 2017. According to the **DISCUSSIONS** tab on the EPPlus CodePlex page (`https://epplus.codeplex.com/discussions/662424`) the source code will be moved to GitHub before CodePlex goes into read-only mode in October 2017.

Creating and extracting ZIP archives

One of the most basic things you can do is work with ZIP files. The .NET Framework does an excellent job at providing this functionality right out of the box. You might need to provide ZIP functionality in an application that needs to upload several files to a network share. Being able to ZIP several files and upload a single ZIP file makes more sense than having to upload several smaller files.

Getting ready

Perform the following steps:

1. Create a console application and call it `FilesExample`:

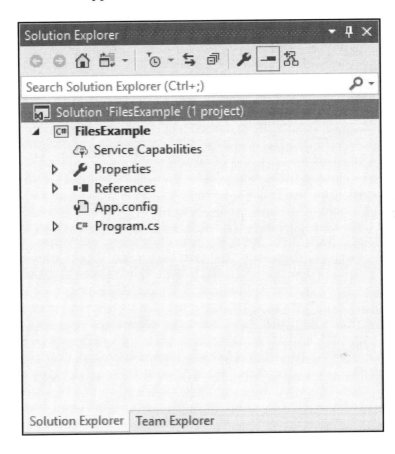

2. Right-click on the **References** node and select **Add Reference...** from the context menu:

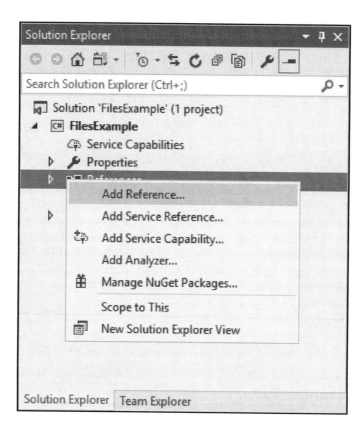

3. In the **Reference Manager**, search for the word `compression`. Add a reference to **System.IO.Compression** and **System.IO.Compression.FileSystem** to your project and click on the **OK** button.

 At the time of writing, there was a **System.IO.Compression** version 4.1.0.0 and **System.IO.Compression** version 4.0.0.0 available from the **Reference Manager**. The example I created just used version 4.1.0.0.

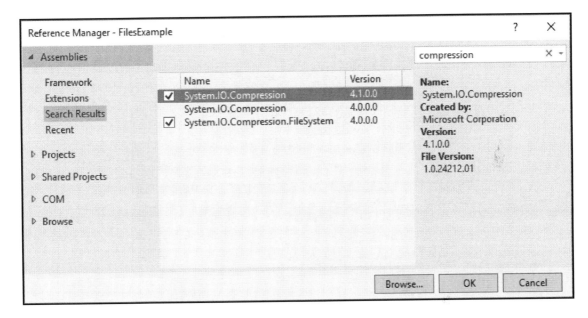

4. When you have added your references, your solution should look as follows:

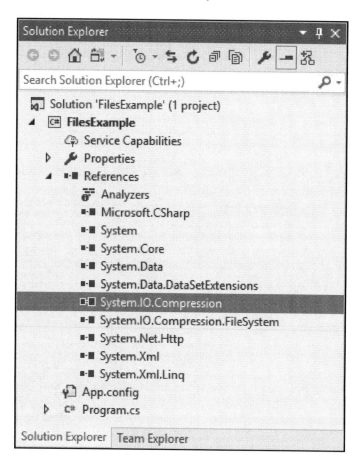

5. Create a folder called `Documents` in your `temp` folder:

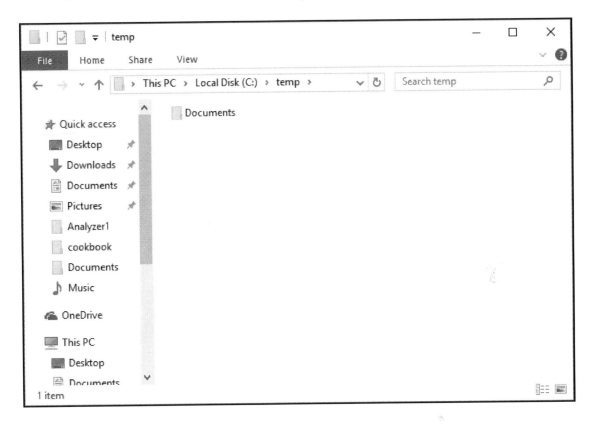

6. Inside this folder, create a few files of varying sizes:

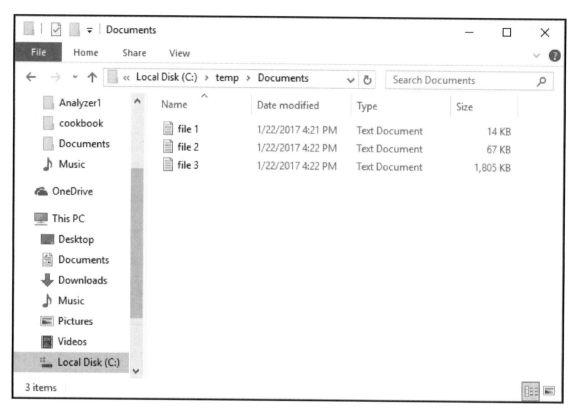

You are now ready to write some code.

How to do it...

1. Add the following using statements to the top of your Program.cs file:

```
using System.IO;
using System.IO.Compression;
```

2. Create a method called `ZipIt()` and add the code to it to ZIP the `Documents` directory. The code is pretty straightforward to understand. I want to, however, highlight the use of the `CreateFromDirectory()` method. Notice that we have set the compression level to `CompressionLevel.Optimal` and set the `includeBaseDirectory` parameter to `false`:

```
private static void ZipIt(string path)
{
  string sourceDirectory = $"{path}Documents";

  if (Directory.Exists(sourceDirectory))
  {
    string archiveName = $"{path}DocumentsArchive.zip";
    ZipFile.CreateFromDirectory(sourceDirectory, archiveName,
                                CompressionLevel.Optimal, false);
  }
}
```

3. Run your console application and look at the `temp` folder again. You will see the following ZIP file created:

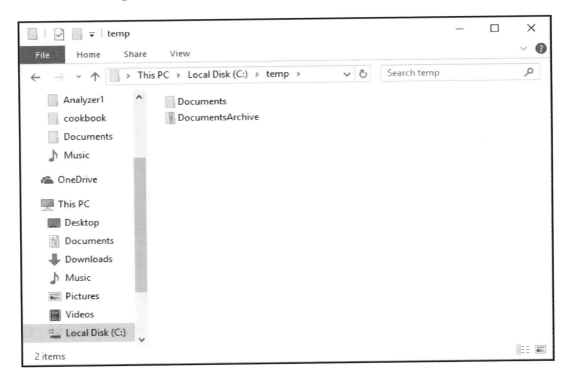

4. Viewing the contents of the ZIP file will display the files contained in the `Documents` folder that we saw earlier:

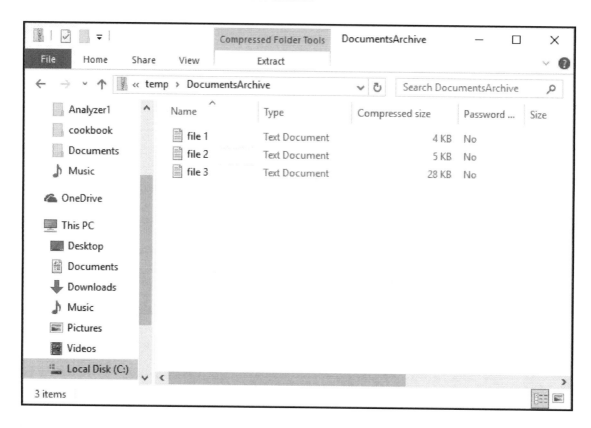

5. Viewing the properties of the ZIP file, you will see that it has been compressed to **36 KB**:

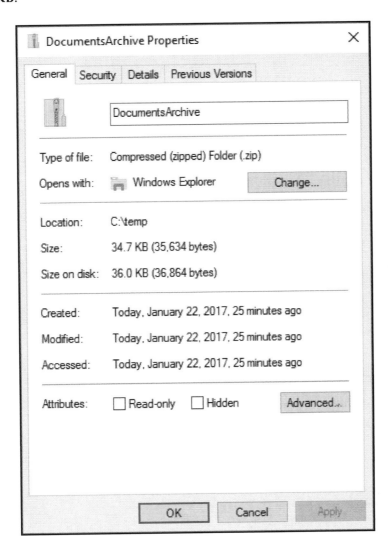

6. Extracting a ZIP file is just as easy to do. Create a method called `UnZipIt()` and pass the path to the `temp` folder to it. Then, specify the directory to unzip the files to and set the variable called `destinationDirectory`. Call the `ExtractToDirectory()` method and pass it the `archiveName` and `destinationDirectory` variables as parameters:

```
private static void UnZipIt(string path)
{
    string destinationDirectory = $"{path}DocumentsUnzipped";

    if (Directory.Exists(path))
    {
        string archiveName = $"{path}DocumentsArchive.zip";
        ZipFile.ExtractToDirectory(archiveName, destinationDirectory);
    }
}
```

7. Run your console application and view the output folder:

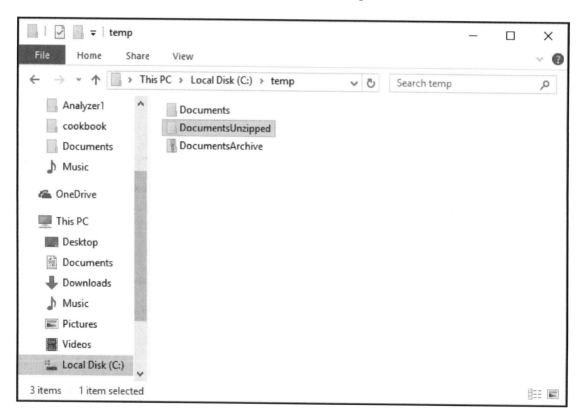

8. Viewing the extracted files in the `DocumentsUnzipped` folder, you will see the original files we started off with:

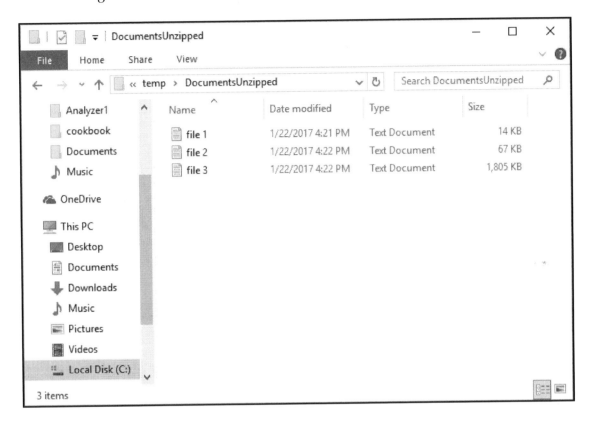

How it works...

Working with ZIP files in .NET is really as easy as it gets. The .NET Framework does a lot of the heavy lifting for mundane tasks such as creating archives. It also allows developers to maintain a certain standard of code without having to "roll their own" archiving methods.

In-memory stream compression and decompression

Sometimes, you need to perform some in-memory compression of a large amount of text. You might want to write this to a file or a database. Perhaps you need to e-mail the text as an attachment that another system will pick up and then decompress. Whatever the reason, in-memory compression and decompression is a very useful feature to have around. The best way to do this is to use extension methods. If you haven't figured this out by now, I quite like using extension methods.

Getting ready

The code is very straightforward. There is not much you will need to get ready beforehand. Just make sure that you include the following `using` statements in your project and that you have a file containing text called `file 3.txt` at the following path `C:\temp\Documents\file 3.txt`. You can continue using the console application created in the preceding recipe.

```
using System.IO.Compression;
using System.Text;
using static System.Console;
```

How to do it...

1. Create a class called `ExtensionMethods` that will contain two extension methods called `CompressStream()` and `DecompressStream()`. Both these extension methods will act on a byte array and return a byte array:

```
public static class ExtensionMethods
{
  public static byte[] CompressStream(this byte[] originalSource)
  {

  }

  public static byte[] DecompressStream(this byte[] originalSource)
  {

  }
}
```

2. Looking at the `CompressStream()` extension method, you need to create a new `MemoryStream` to return to the calling code. Make use of the `using` statement so that objects are properly disposed of when they move out of scope. Next, add a new `GZipStream` object that will compress whatever we give it into the `outStream` object. You will notice that `CompressionMode.Compress` is passed as a parameter to the `GZipStream` object. Lastly, write `originalSource` to the `GZipStream` object, compressing it and returning it to the calling method:

```
public static byte[] CompressStream(this byte[] originalSource)
{
  using (var outStream = new MemoryStream())
  {
    using (var gzip = new GZipStream(outStream,
         CompressionMode.Compress))
    {
      gzip.Write(originalSource, 0, originalSource.Length);
    }

    return outStream.ToArray();
  }
}
```

3. Turn your attention to the `DecompressStream()` extension method next. The process is actually really simple. Create a new `MemoryStream` from `originalSource` and call it `sourceStream`. Create another `MemoryStream` called `outStream` to return to the calling code. Next, create a new `GZipStream` object and pass it `sourceStream` while setting the `CompressionMode.Decompress` value. Copy the decompressed stream to `outStream` and return it to the calling code:

```
public static byte[] DecompressStream(this byte[] originalSource)
{
  using (var sourceStream = new MemoryStream(originalSource))
  {
    using (var outStream = new MemoryStream())
    {
      using (var gzip = new GZipStream(sourceStream,
           CompressionMode.Decompress))
      {
        gzip.CopyTo(outStream);
      }
      return outStream.ToArray();
    }
  }
}
```

4. I created a method called InMemCompressDecompress() to illustrate the use of in-memory compression and decompression. I'm reading the contents of the file at C:tempDocumentsfile 3.txt into a variable called inputString. I then use the default encoding to get the bytes, the original length, compressed length, and decompressed length. If you want to get the original text back, be sure to include the line newString = Encoding.Default.GetString(newFromCompressed); in your code and output that to the console window. A word of warning, though: if you are reading a lot of text, it's probably not going to make much sense to display that in the console window. Write it to a file instead to check if the text is the same as what was compressed:

```
private static void InMemCompressDecompress()
{
    string largeFile = @"C:\temp\Documents\file 3.txt";

    string inputString = File.ReadAllText(largeFile);
    var bytes = Encoding.Default.GetBytes(inputString);

    var originalLength = bytes.Length;
    var compressed = bytes.CompressStream();
    var compressedLength = compressed.Length;

    var newFromCompressed = compressed.DecompressStream();
    var newFromCompressedLength = newFromCompressed.Length;

    WriteLine($"Original string length = {originalLength}");
    WriteLine($"Compressed string length = {compressedLength}");
    WriteLine($"Uncompressed string length =
            {newFromCompressedLength}");

    // To get the original Test back, call this
    //var newString = Encoding.Default.GetString(newFromCompressed);
}
```

5. Ensure that you have a file called `File 3.txt` in the correct directory, as stated previously. Also, ensure that the file contains some text. You can see that the file I am going to compress in-memory is about **1.8 MB** in size:

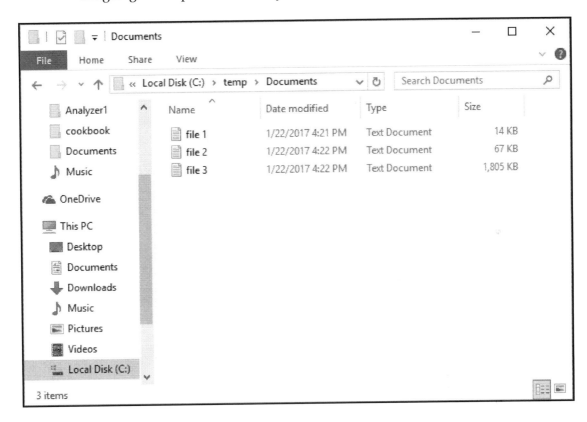

6. Running your console application will display the original length of the file, the compressed length and then the decompressed length. As would be expected, the decompressed length is the same length as the original string length:

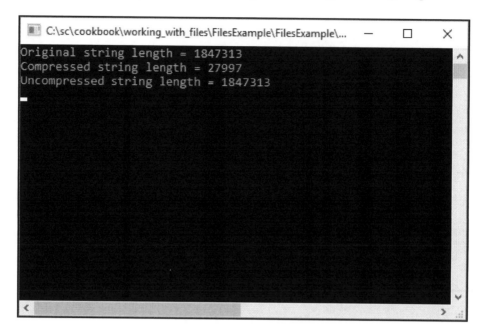

How it works...

In-memory compression and decompression allows developers to use on-the-fly compression and decompression when working with objects containing large data. This can be useful for when you need to read and write log information to a database, for example. This is another example of how the .NET Framework provides developers with the perfect platform to build world-class solutions on.

Async and await file processing

With acync and await, developers can keep their applications fully responsive while performing intensive tasks such as file processing. This makes a perfect candidate for using asynchronous code. If you have several large files that need copying, an async and await method would be a perfect solution for keeping your form responsive.

Getting ready

Ensure that you have added the following `using` statements to the top of your code file:

```
using System.IO;
using System.Threading;
```

For asynchronous code to work, we need to include the threading namespaces.

How to do it...

1. Create two folders called `AsyncDestination` and `AsyncSource`:

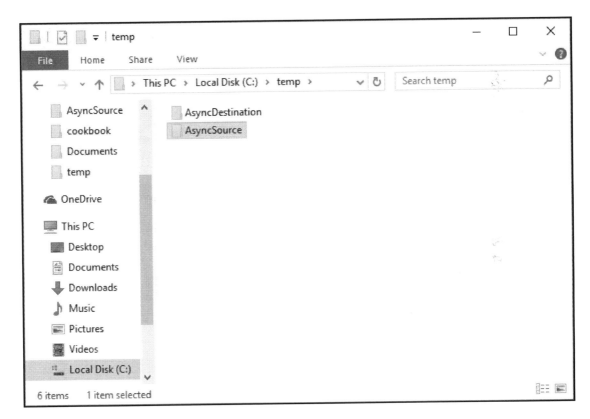

2. To the `AsyncSource` folder, add a couple of large files to process:

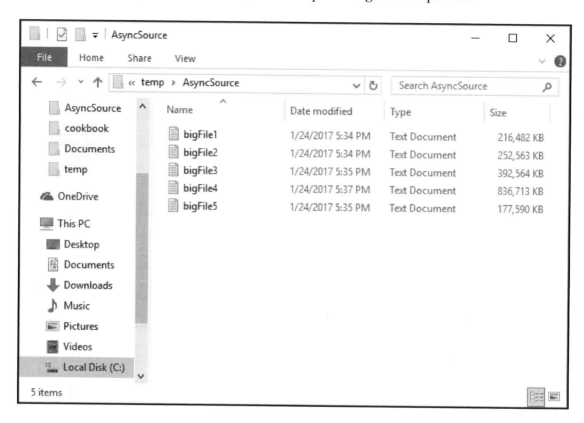

3. Create a new WinForms application and add a forms times control, a button, and a label called `lblTimer` to the form. Call the timer **asyncTimer** and set its **Interval** to `1000` milliseconds (1 second):

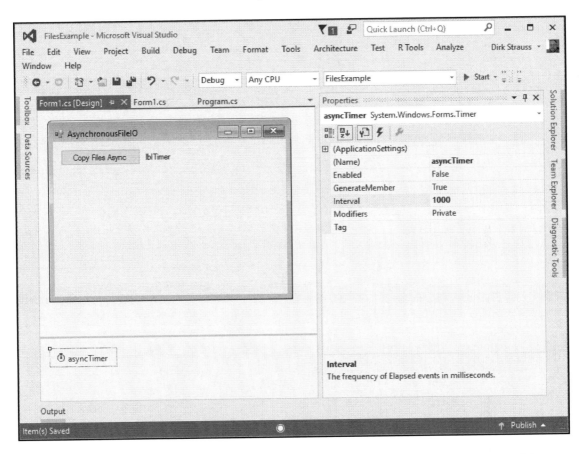

4. In the code above the constructor, add the `CancellationTokenSource` object and the `elapsedTime` variable to the `Form1` class:

```
CancellationTokenSource cts;
int elapsedTime = 0;
```

5. In the constructor, set the timer label text:

```
public Form1()
{
    InitializeComponent();

    lblTimer.Text = "Timer Stopped";
}
```

6. In the button click event handler, add two if conditions. The first will run when the button is clicked first. The second will be run when the button is clicked again to cancel the process. Take note that this is an `async` event handler for `btnCopyFileAsync`:

```
private async void btnCopyFilesAsync_Click(
    object sender, EventArgs e)
{
    if (btnCopyFilesAsync.Text.Equals("Copy Files Async"))
    {

    }

    if (btnCopyFilesAsync.Text.Equals("Cancel Async Copy"))
    {

    }
}
```

7. Add a `Tick` event for the timer and update the timer label text:

```
private void asyncTimer_Tick(object sender, EventArgs e)
{
    lblTimer.Text = $"Duration = {elapsedTime += 1} seconds";
}
```

8. Have a look at the second `if` condition inside the button click. Set the button text back to what it was, and then call the `Cancel()` method of the `CancellationTokenSource` object:

```
if (btnCopyFilesAsync.Text.Equals("Cancel Async Copy"))
{
    btnCopyFilesAsync.Text = "Copy Files Async";
    cts.Cancel();
```

9. In the first `if` statement, set the source and destination directory. Also update the button text so that when it is clicked again, it will run the cancel logic. Instantiate `CancellationTokenSource`, set the `elapsedTime` variable to 0 and then start the timer. We can now start enumerating the files in the source folder and store the result in the `fileEntries` variable:

```
if (btnCopyFilesAsync.Text.Equals("Copy Files Async"))
{
    string sourceDirectory = @"C:\temp\AsyncSource\";
    string destinationDirectory = @"C:\temp\AsyncDestination\";
    btnCopyFilesAsync.Text = "Cancel Async Copy";
    cts = new CancellationTokenSource();
    elapsedTime = 0;
    asyncTimer.Start();

    IEnumerable<string> fileEntries = Directory
        .EnumerateFiles(sourceDirectory);
}
```

10. Start by iterating over the files in the source folder and copying the file from the source folder to the destination folder asynchronously. This can be seen in the line of code `await sfs.CopyToAsync(dfs, 81920, cts.Token);`. The value `81920` is just the buffer size and the cancellation token `cts.Token` is passed to the async method:

```
foreach (string sourceFile in fileEntries)
{
    using (FileStream sfs = File.Open(sourceFile, FileMode.Open))
    {
        string destinationFilePath = $"{destinationDirectory}{
            Path.GetFileName(sourceFile)}";
        using (FileStream dfs = File.Create(destinationFilePath))
        {
            try
            {
                await sfs.CopyToAsync(dfs, 81920, cts.Token);
            }
            catch (OperationCanceledException ex)
            {
                asyncTimer.Stop();
                lblTimer.Text = $"Cancelled after {elapsedTime} seconds";
            }
        }
    }
}
```

11. Lastly, if the token isn't canceled, stop the timer and update the timer label:

```
if (!cts.IsCancellationRequested)
{
  asyncTimer.Stop();
  lblTimer.Text = $"Completed in {elapsedTime} seconds";
}
```

12. Putting the code all together, you will see how this all fits together:

```
private async void btnCopyFilesAsync_Click(object sender,
  EventArgs e)
{
  if (btnCopyFilesAsync.Text.Equals("Copy Files Async"))
  {
    string sourceDirectory = @"C:\temp\AsyncSource\";
    string destinationDirectory = @"C:\temp\AsyncDestination\";
    btnCopyFilesAsync.Text = "Cancel Async Copy";
    cts = new CancellationTokenSource();
    elapsedTime = 0;
    asyncTimer.Start();

    IEnumerable<string> fileEntries = Directory
      .EnumerateFiles(sourceDirectory);

    //foreach (string sourceFile in Directory
    //            .EnumerateFiles(sourceDirectory))
    foreach (string sourceFile in fileEntries)
    {
      using (FileStream sfs = File.Open(sourceFile, FileMode.Open))
      {
        string destinationFilePath = $"{destinationDirectory}
        {Path.GetFileName(sourceFile)}";
        using (FileStream dfs = File.Create(destinationFilePath))
        {
          try
          {
            await sfs.CopyToAsync(dfs, 81920, cts.Token);
          }
          catch (OperationCanceledException ex)
          {
            asyncTimer.Stop();
            lblTimer.Text = $"Cancelled after {elapsedTime}
              seconds";
          }
        }
      }
    }
  }
}
```

```
    if (!cts.IsCancellationRequested)
    {
      asyncTimer.Stop();
      lblTimer.Text = $"Completed in {elapsedTime} seconds";
    }
  }
  if (btnCopyFilesAsync.Text.Equals("Cancel Async Copy"))
  {
    btnCopyFilesAsync.Text = "Copy Files Async";
    cts.Cancel();
  }
}
```

How it works...

When the Windows form opens up for the first time, you will see that the timer label defaults to **Timer Stopped**. Click on the **Copy Files Async** button to start the copy process:

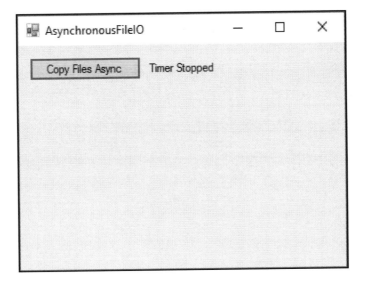

When the application has finished processing, you will see that the large files have been copied to the destination folder:

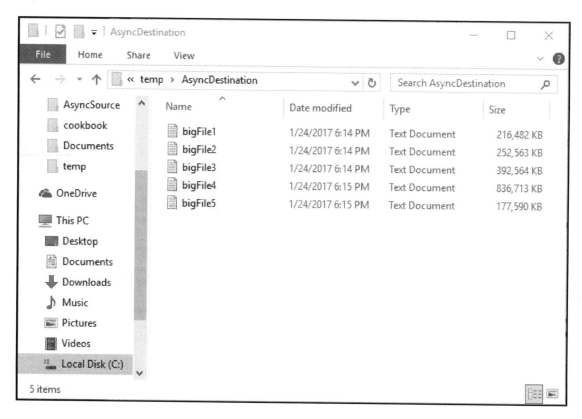

While the copy process is running, your Windows form remains active and responsive. The timer label also continues to count. Usually, with processes such as these, the form would be unresponsive:

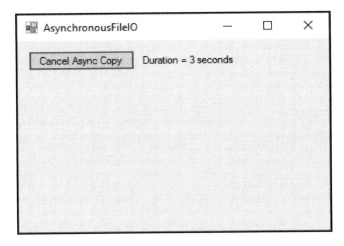

When the files have finished copying, the timer label will display the duration of the async copy process. A fun experiment is to play around with this code to see how much you can optimize it to improve the copy speed:

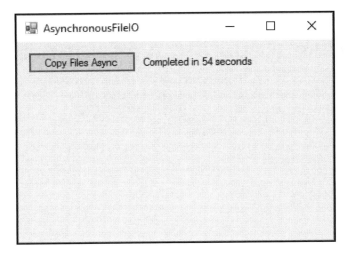

The Windows form not only remains responsive, but also allows you to cancel the process whenever you like. When you click on the **Copy Files Async** button, the text changes to **Cancel Async Copy**:

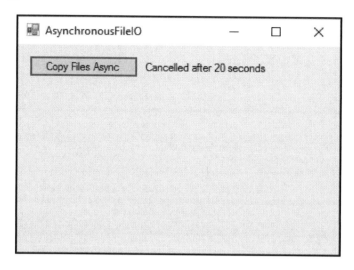

Clicking on the **Cancel** button or sets the `CancellationTokenSource` object to canceled, which in turns stops the async file copy process.

How to make a custom type serializable?

Serialization is the process by which an object's state is transformed into a set of bytes (depending on the serialization type used, it could be XML, binary, JSON), which can then be saved in a stream (think `MemoryStream` or `FileStream`) or transmitted via WCF or Web API. Making a custom type serializable means that you can apply serialization to custom types by adding the `System.SerializableAttribute`. Examples of custom types are as follows:

- Classes and generic classes
- Structs
- Enums

A real-world example of serialization could be to create a recovery mechanism for a specific object. Think of a workflow scenario. At some point in time, the state of the workflow needs to be persisted. You can serialize the state of that object and store this in a database. When the workflow needs to continue at a future point in time, you can read the object from the database and deserialize it to the exact state as it was before it was persisted to the database.

Trying to serialize a non-serializable type will result in your code throwing a `SerializationException`.

Getting ready

If you are running this example from your console application, ensure that the console application imports the `System` namespace by adding `using System` to the top of your `Program.cs` file. Also ensure that `using System.Runtime.Serialization.Formatters.Binary` is added.

How to do it...

1. Start by adding an abstract class called `Cat`. This class simply defines fields for `Weight` and `Age`. Note that in order to make your class serializable, you need to add the `[Serializable]` attribute to it.

```
[Serializable]
public abstract class Cat
{
    // fields
    public int Weight;
    public int Age;
}
```

2. Next, create a class called `Tiger` that is derived from the `Cat` class. Note that the `Tiger` class must also have the `[Serializable]` attribute added. This is because the serialization isn't inherited from the base class. Each derived class must implement serialization on its own:

```
[Serializable]
public class Tiger : Cat
{
    public string Trainer;
```

```
    public bool IsTamed;
  }
```

3. Next, we need to create a method to serialize the `Tiger` class. Create a new object of type `Tiger` and set some values to it. We then use a `BinaryFormatter` to serialize the `Tiger` class into a `stream` and return it to the calling code:

```
private static Stream SerializeTiger()
{
  Tiger tiger = new Tiger();
  tiger.Age = 12;
  tiger.IsTamed = false;
  tiger.Trainer = "Joe Soap";
  tiger.Weight = 120;

  MemoryStream stream = new MemoryStream();
  BinaryFormatter fmt = new BinaryFormatter();
  fmt.Serialize(stream, tiger);
  stream.Position = 0;
  return stream;
}
```

4. Deserialization is even easier. We create a `DeserializeTiger` method and pass the `stream` to it. We then use the `BinaryFormatter` again to deserialize the `stream` into an object of type `Tiger`:

```
private static void DeserializeTiger(Stream stream)
{
  stream.Position = 0;
  BinaryFormatter fmt = new BinaryFormatter();
  Tiger tiger = (Tiger)fmt.Deserialize(stream);
}
```

5. To see the results of our serialization and deserialization, read the result from the `SerializeTiger()` method into a new `Stream` and display it in the console window. Then, call the `DeserializeTiger()` method:

```
Stream str = SerializeTiger();
WriteLine(new StreamReader(str).ReadToEnd());
DeserializeTiger(str);
```

How it works...

When the serialized data is written to the console window, you will see some identifying information. Most of it will, however, look jumbled up. This is because it's binary serialized data that is being displayed.

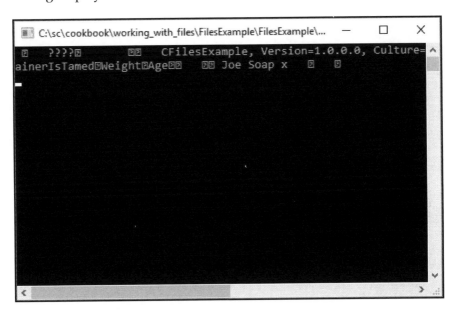

When this serialized data is deserialized, it is cast back to an object of the type `Tiger`. You can clearly see how the original values of the fields are visible in the deserialized object.

Using ISerializable for custom serialization to a FileStream

If you want more control over what is serialized, you should implement `ISerializable` on your object. This gives a developer complete control over what is serialized. Note that you still need to add the `[ISerializable]` attribute to your object. Lastly, the developer also needs to implement a deserialization constructor. Using `ISerializable`, however, does have a caveat. According to the MSDN, the forward compatibility of your object with newer versions of the .NET Framework and any improvements made to the serialization framework might not be applicable on your object. You also need to implement `ISerializable` on all the derived types of your object.

Getting ready

We will create a new class that wants to control its own serialization using `ISerializable`. Ensure that your application has the `using System.Runtime.Serialization;` added to the `using` statements.

How to do it...

1. Create a class called `Vehicle`. You will notice that this class implements `ISerializable` while still having the `[Serializable]` attribute. You must do this so that the Common Language Runtime can identify this class as serializable:

   ```
   [Serializable]
   public class Vehicle : ISerializable
   {

   }
   ```

2. To this class, add the following fields and the constructor:

   ```
   // Primitive fields
   public int VehicleType;
   public int EngineCapacity;
   public int TopSpeed;

   public Vehicle()
   {
   ```

}

3. When you implement ISerilizable on your Vehicle class, Visual Studio will alert you that the ISerializable interface has not been implemented inside your class. Add the implementation by clicking on the lightbulb next to the underlined interface name and accepting the correction. Visual Studio will now add the GetObjectData() method inside your class. Note that the method is added with an exception that will throw a NotImplementedException if you don't add some code to the method. Add very basic code here that simply adds the values of the fields to the SerializationInfo object:

```
public void GetObjectData(SerializationInfo info,
  StreamingContext context)
{
  info.AddValue("VehicleType", VehicleType);
  info.AddValue("EngineCapacity", EngineCapacity);
  info.AddValue("TopSpeed", TopSpeed);
}
```

4. As mentioned previously, we need to add the deserialization constructor that will deserialize the fields. This, you add manually:

```
// Deserialization constructor
protected Vehicle(SerializationInfo info, StreamingContext context)
{
  VehicleType = info.GetInt32("VehicleType");
  EngineCapacity = info.GetInt32("EngineCapacity");
  TopSpeed = info.GetInt32("TopSpeed");
}
```

5. After adding all the code, your class should look as follows:

```
[Serializable]
public class Vehicle : ISerializable
{
  // Primitive fields
  public int VehicleType;
  public int EngineCapacity;
  public int TopSpeed;

  public Vehicle()
  {

  }
  public void GetObjectData(SerializationInfo info,
    StreamingContext context)
```

```
    {
      info.AddValue("VehicleType", VehicleType);
      info.AddValue("EngineCapacity", EngineCapacity);
      info.AddValue("TopSpeed", TopSpeed);
    }

    // Deserialization constructor
    protected Vehicle(SerializationInfo info,
      StreamingContext context)
    {
      VehicleType = info.GetInt32("VehicleType");
      EngineCapacity = info.GetInt32("EngineCapacity");
      TopSpeed = info.GetInt32("TopSpeed");
    }
  }
```

6. We are simply going to write the serialized class to a file. For the purposes of this recipe, simply hardcode an output path for the file. Next, create a new instance of the `Vehicle` class and set some values to the fields:

```
string serializationPath = @"C:\temp\vehicleInfo.dat";
Vehicle vehicle = new Vehicle();
vehicle.VehicleType = (int)VehicleTypes.Car;
vehicle.EngineCapacity = 1600;
vehicle.TopSpeed = 230;

if (File.Exists(serializationPath))
  File.Delete(serializationPath);
```

7. Also be sure to add the `VehicleTypes` enumerator to the top of your class:

```
public enum VehicleTypes
{
  Car = 1,
  SUV = 2,
  Utility = 3
}
```

8. We then add the code that will serialize the class to the file you specified in the hardcoded path. To do this, we add a `FileStream` and a `BinaryFormatter` object to serialize the `vehicle` to the file:

```
using (FileStream stream = new FileStream(serializationPath,
  FileMode.Create))
{
  BinaryFormatter fmter = new BinaryFormatter();
  fmter.Serialize(stream, vehicle);
```

```
    }
```

9. Lastly, we add the code to read the file containing the serialized data and create the `Vehicle` object containing the state of the `Vehicle` at the time it was serialized. While the deserialize code runs immediately after the serialize code, note that this is just for demonstration purposes. The `Vehicle` deserialization could occur at any future point in time by reading from the file:

```
using (FileStream stream = new FileStream(serializationPath,
  FileMode.Open))
{
  BinaryFormatter fmter = new BinaryFormatter();
  Vehicle deserializedVehicle = (Vehicle)fmter.Deserialize(stream);
}
```

How it works...

After you run your code, you will find that the `vehicleInfo.dat` file has been created at the path you specified:

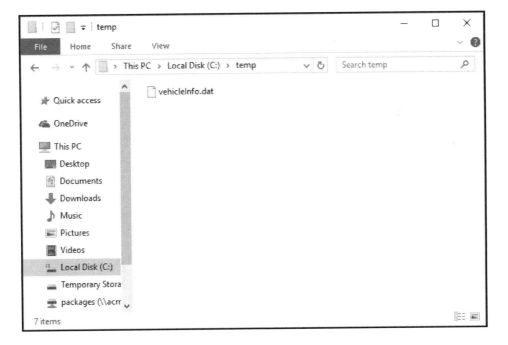

Opening the file in a text editor will show the serialized information. As you may notice, some of the class information is still visible:

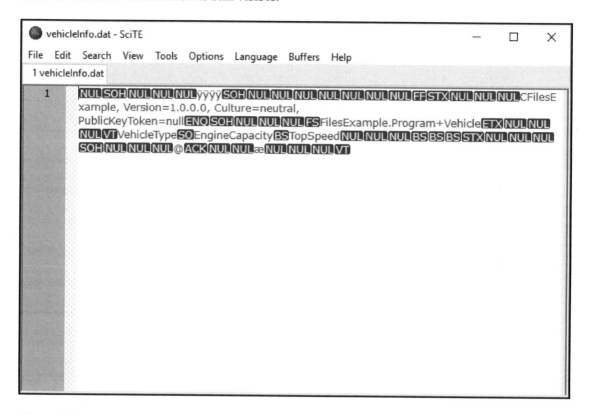

If we add a breakpoint in the deserialization code and inspect the created `deserializedVehicle` object, you will see that the `Vehicle` state has been *rehydrated* to the state it was before serialization:

```
using (FileStream stream = new FileStream(serializationPath, FileMode.Open))
{
    BinaryFormatter fmter = new BinaryFormatter();
    Vehicle deserializedVehicle = (Vehicle)fmter.Deserialize(stream);
}   ≤ 1ms elapsed        deserializedVehicle  {FilesExample.Program.Vehicle}
                            EngineCapacity  1600
                            TopSpeed        230
                            VehicleType     1
```

Using XmlSerializer

From the name you probably guessed that the XmlSerializer serializes data into XML. It gives you more control over the XML structure of the serialized data. Typical real-world examples for using this serializer would be to maintain compatibility with XML web services. It is also an easy medium to use when transmitting data using some type of message queuing (such as MSMQ or RabbitMQ).

The default behavior of XmlSerializer is to serialize public fields and properties. Using attributes from the System.Xml.Serialization namespace, you can control the structure of your XML.

Getting ready

Since we are going to use List<> in this example, ensure that you have added the using System.Collections.Generic; namespace. We also want to have more control over the structure of the XML, so also include the using System.Xml.Serialization; namespace so that we can use the appropriate attributes. Lastly, for the LINQ query, you will need to add the using System.Linq; namespace.

How to do it...

1. Start off by creating a Student class.

```
public class Student
{
    public string StudentName;
    public double SubjectMark;
}
```

2. Next, create a class for a subject called FundamentalProgramming. Several attributes have been applied to the fields of this class:
   - XmlRoot
   - XmlElement
   - XmlIgnore
   - XmlAttribute
   - XmlArray

We can see that the XmlRoot attribute specifies that ElementName be called FundamentalsOfProgramming. This attribute thus defines the root of your generated XML. The XmlElement specifies an element called LecturerFullName instead of Lecturer. XmlIgnore attribute will cause XmlSerializer to ignore this field during serialization, while XmlAttribute will create an attribute on the root element of the generated XML. Lastly, we are serializing the List<Student> collection with the XmlArray attribute:

```
[XmlRoot(ElementName = "FundamentalsOfProgramming",
  Namespace = "http://serialization")]
public class FundamentalProgramming
{
  [XmlElement(ElementName = "LecturerFullName",
    DataType = "string")]
  public string Lecturer;

  [XmlIgnore]
  public double ClassAverage;

  [XmlAttribute]
  public string RoomNumber;

  [XmlArray(ElementName = "StudentsInClass",
    Namespace = "http://serialization")]
  public List<Student> Students;
}
```

3. In the calling code, set up the Student objects and add them to the List<Student> object students:

```
string serializationPath = @"C:tempclassInfo.xml";
Student studentA = new Student()
{
  StudentName = "John Smith"
  , SubjectMark = 86.4
};
Student studentB = new Student()
{
  StudentName = "Jane Smith"
  , SubjectMark = 67.3
};
List<Student> students = new List<Student>();
students.Add(studentA);
students.Add(studentB);
```

4. Now we create our FundementalProgramming class and populate the fields. The reason why ClassAverage is ignored is because we will always calculate this field value:

```
FundamentalProgramming subject = new FundamentalProgramming();
subject.Lecturer = "Prof. Johan van Niekerk";
subject.RoomNumber = "Lecture Auditorium A121";
subject.Students = students;
subject.ClassAverage = (students.Sum(mark => mark.SubjectMark) /
   students.Count());
```

5. Add the following code to serialize the subject object, taking note to pass the type of object to XmlSerializer as typeof(FundamentalProgramming):

```
using (FileStream stream = new FileStream(serializationPath,
   FileMode.Create))
{
  XmlSerializer xmlSer = new XmlSerializer(typeof(
     FundamentalProgramming));
  xmlSer.Serialize(stream, subject);
}
```

6. Lastly, add the code to deserialize the XML back into the FundamentalProgramming object:

```
using (FileStream stream = new FileStream(serializationPath,
   FileMode.Open))
{
  XmlSerializer xmlSer = new XmlSerializer(typeof(
     FundamentalProgramming));
  FundamentalProgramming fndProg = (FundamentalProgramming)
     xmlSer.Deserialize(stream);
}
```

How it works...

When you run the console application, you will find that it creates an XML document at the path you specified in the code. Viewing this XML document, you can see that the XML elements are defined exactly as we specified on the class by using the attributes. Note that the `FundamentalsOfProgramming` root element has the `RoomNumber` field as an attribute. The field `ClassAverage` has been ignored and is not present in the XML. Lastly, you can see how nicely the `List<Student>` object has been serialized to the XML file.

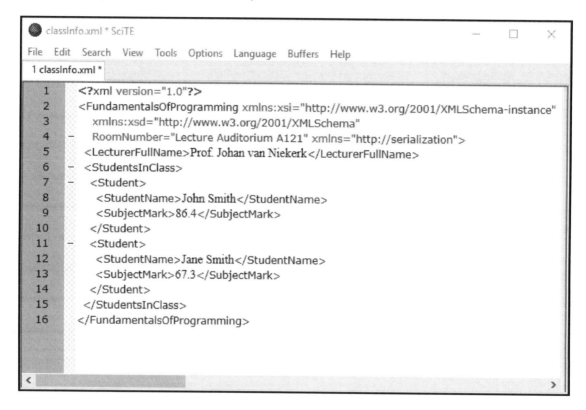

On deserialization of the XML, you will notice that the serialized values are displayed. `ClassAverage`; however, does not have a value as it was never serialized to begin with.

```
using (FileStream stream = new FileStream(serializationPath, FileMode.Open))
{
    XmlSerializer xmlSer = new XmlSerializer(typeof(FundamentalProgramming));
    FundamentalProgramming fndProg = (FundamentalProgramming)xmlSer.Deserialize(stream);
}
#endregion
```

▲ ● fndProg [FilesExample.FundamentalProgramming] ➕	
● ClassAverage	0
● Lecturer	🔍 ▾ "Prof. Johan van Niekerk"
● RoomNumber	🔍 ▾ "Lecture Auditorium A121"
▷ ● Students	Count = 2

JSON serializers

Unlike `BinaryFormatter`, JSON serialization serializes data in a human-readable format. Using `XmlSerializer` also produces XML that is human-readable, but JSON serialization produces a smaller data size than `XmlSerializer`. JSON is primarily used to exchange data and can be used with many different programming languages (as can XML).

Getting ready

From the **Tools** menu, go to **NuGet Package Manager** and click on the **Manage NuGet Packages for Solution...** menu. In the **Browse** tab, search for **Newtonsoft.Json** and install the NuGet package. **Newtonsoft.Json** is a high-performance JSON framework for .NET. Once it is installed, you will see that the reference **Newtonsoft.Json** has been added to your project, **References**.

In the `using` statements for your class, add the following namespaces `using Newtonsoft.Json;` and `using Newtonsoft.Json.Linq;` to your code.

How to do it...

1. Start off by creating the `FundamentalProgramming` and `Student` classes we used before for `XmlSerializer`. This time, remove all the attributes to produce the following code:

```
public class FundamentalProgramming
{
  public string Lecturer;
  public double ClassAverage;
  public string RoomNumber;
  public List<Student> Students;
}

public class Student
{
  public string StudentName;
  public double SubjectMark;
}
```

2. In the calling code, set up the `Student` object, as previously and add them to `List<Student>`:

```
string serializationPath = @"C:\temp\classInfo.txt";
Student studentA = new Student()
{
  StudentName = "John Smith"
  , SubjectMark = 86.4
};
Student studentB = new Student()
{
  StudentName = "Jane Smith"
  , SubjectMark = 67.3
};
List<Student> students = new List<Student>();
students.Add(studentA);
students.Add(studentB);
```

3. Create the `subject` object of type `FundamentalProgramming` and assign the values to the fields:

```
FundamentalProgramming subject = new FundamentalProgramming();
subject.Lecturer = "Prof. Johan van Niekerk";
subject.RoomNumber = "Lecture Auditorium A121";
subject.Students = students;
subject.ClassAverage = (students.Sum(mark => mark.SubjectMark) /
    students.Count());
WriteLine($"Calculated class average = {subject.ClassAverage}");
```

4. Add a `JsonSerializer` object to your code and set the formatting to indented. Using a `JsonWriter`, serialize the `subject` to the `serializationPath` to the file `classInfo.txt`:

```
JsonSerializer json = new JsonSerializer();
json.Formatting = Formatting.Indented;
using (StreamWriter sw = new StreamWriter(serializationPath))
{
  using (JsonWriter wr = new JsonTextWriter(sw))
  {
    json.Serialize(wr, subject);
  }
}
WriteLine("Serialized to file using JSON Serializer");
```

5. The next section of code will read the text from the file `classInfo.txt` created previously and create a `JObject` called `jobj` that uses the `Newtonsoft.Json.Linq` namespace to query JSON objects. Use `JObject` to parse the string returned from the file. This is where the power of using the `Newtonsoft.Json.Linq` namespace becomes evident. I can query the `jobj` object using LINQ to return the student marks and calculate an average:

```
using (StreamReader sr = new StreamReader(serializationPath))
{
  string jsonString = sr.ReadToEnd();
  WriteLine("JSON String Read from file");
  JObject jobj = JObject.Parse(jsonString);
  IList<double> subjectMarks = jobj["Students"].Select(
    m => (double)m["SubjectMark"]).ToList();
  var ave = subjectMarks.Sum() / subjectMarks.Count();
  WriteLine($"Calculated class average using JObject = {ave}");
}
```

6. If you need to deserialize the JSON object, the deserializer logic is quite easy to implement. We use a `JsonReader` to get the text from the file and deserialize it:

```
using (StreamReader sr = new StreamReader(serializationPath))
{
  using (JsonReader jr = new JsonTextReader(sr))
  {
    FundamentalProgramming funProg = json.Deserialize
      <FundamentalProgramming>(jr);
  }
}
```

How it works...

After you run your console application, you can view the file created by the JSON serializer.

The results of the class average calculation on the class and from the LINQ query on the JSON object are exactly the same.

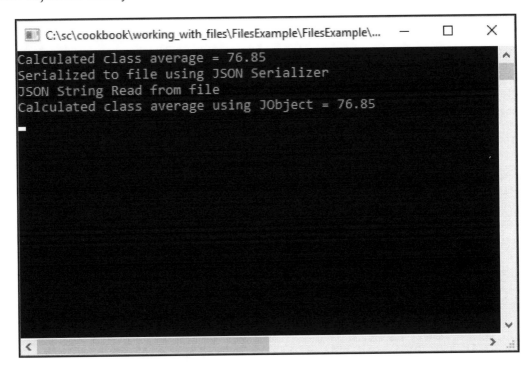

Lastly, the deserialized object from the JSON text in the file can be seen when adding a break point to the code and inspecting the funProg object. As you can see, the object state is the same as before it was serialized to the file.

```
using (StreamReader sr = new StreamReader(serializationPath))
{
    using (JsonReader jr = new JsonTextReader(sr))
    {
        FundamentalProgramming funProg = json.Deserialize< FundamentalProgramming>(jr);
    }
}
    //json.Deserialize()
```

⊿ ● funProg	{FilesExample.FundamentalProgramming}	⊞
● ClassAverage	76.85	
● Lecturer	Q ▾ "Prof. Johan van Niekerk"	
● RoomNumber	Q ▾ "Lecture Auditorium A121"	
▷ ● Students	Count = 2	

Do you remember at the beginning of this recipe I mentioned that JSON produces much less data than XML? I created the `Student` class containing 10,000 students in `List<Student>` and serialized using XML and JSON. The comparison between the two file sizes is quite stunning. JSON clearly produces a much smaller file.

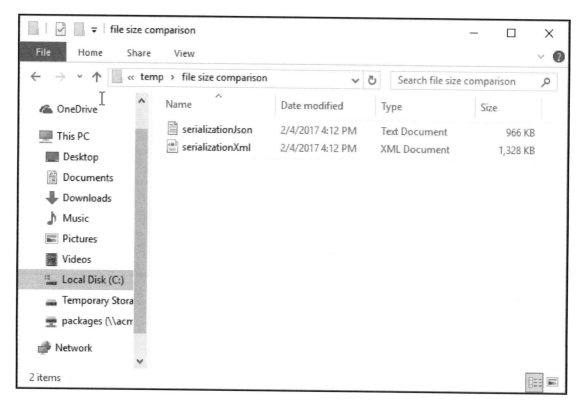

7

Making Apps Responsive with Asynchronous Programming

This chapter will introduce you to asynchronous programming. It will cover the following recipes:

- Return types of asynchronous functions
- Handling tasks in asynchronous programming
- Exception handling in asynchronous programming

Introduction

Asynchronous programming is an exciting feature in C#. It allows you to continue program execution on the main thread while a long-running task finishes its execution. When this long-running task is complete, a thread from the thread pool will return to the method containing so that the long-running task can continue execution. The best way to learn and understand asynchronous programming is to experience it. The following recipes will illustrate some of the basics to you.

Return types of asynchronous functions

In asynchronous programming, the `async` methods can have three possible return types. These are as follows:

- `void`
- `Task`
- `Task<TResult>`

We will take a look at each return type in the following recipe.

Getting ready

What could be the use of a `void` return type in asynchronous methods? Generally, `void` is used with event handlers. Just bear in mind that `void` returns nothing, so you can't wait for it. Therefore, if you call a `void` return type asynchronous method, your calling code should be able to continue executing code without having to wait for the asynchronous method to complete.

With asynchronous methods that have a return type of `Task`, you can utilize the `await` operator to pause the execution of the current thread until the called asynchronous method has completed. Keep in mind that an asynchronous method that returns a type of `Task` basically does not return an operand. Therefore, if it was written as a synchronous method, it would be a `void` return type method. This statement might be confusing, but it will become clear in the following recipes.

Finally, asynchronous methods that have a `return` statement have a return type of `TResult`. In other words, if the asynchronous method returns a boolean, you would create an asynchronous method with a return type of `Task<bool>`.

Let's start with the `void` return type asynchronous method.

How to do it...

1. Create a new Windows forms project in Visual Studio called `winformAsync`. We will be creating a new Windows forms application so that we can create a button-click event.

2. On the **winformAsync** Forms Designer, open**Toolbox** and select the **Button** control, which is found under the **All Windows Forms** node:

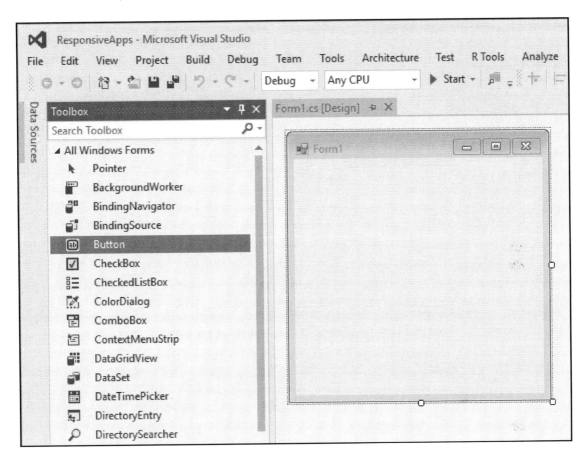

3. Drag the **Button** control onto the **Form1** designer.

4. With the **Button** control selected, double-click on the control to create the click event in the code behind. Visual Studio will insert the event code for you:

```
namespace winformAsync
{
    public partial class Form1 : Form
    {
        public Form1()
        {
            InitializeComponent();
        }
```

```
                    private void button1_Click(object sender, EventArgs e)
                    {

                    }
            }
    }
```

5. Change the `button1_Click` event and add the `async` keyword to the click event. This is an example of a `void` returning an asynchronous method:

```
private async void button1_Click(object sender, EventArgs e)
{
}
```

6. Next, create a new class called `AsyncDemo`:

```
public class AsyncDemo
{
}
```

7. The next method to add to the `AsyncDemo` class is the asynchronous method that returns `TResult` (in this case, a boolean). This method simply checks whether the current year is a leap year. It then returns a boolean to the calling code:

```
async Task<bool> TaskOfTResultReturning_AsyncMethod()
{
    return await Task.FromResult<bool>
    (DateTime.IsLeapYear(DateTime.Now.Year));
}
```

8. The next method to add is the `void` returning method that returns a `Task` type so that it allows you to `await` the method. The method itself does not return any result, making it a `void` returning method. However, in order to use the `await` keyword, you to return the `Task` type from this asynchronous method:

```
async Task TaskReturning_AsyncMethod()
{
    await Task.Delay(5000);
    Console.WriteLine("5 second delay");
}
```

9. Finally, add a method that will call the previous asynchronous methods and display the result of the leap year check. You will notice that we are using the `await` keyword with both method calls:

```
public async Task LongTask()
{
    bool isLeapYear = await TaskOfTResultReturning_AsyncMethod();
    Console.WriteLine($"{DateTime.Now.Year} {(isLeapYear ? " is " :
                    " is not  ")} a leap year");
    await TaskReturning_AsyncMethod();
}
```

10. In the button click, add the following code that calls the long-running task asynchronously:

```
private async void button1_Click(object sender, EventArgs e)
{
    Console.WriteLine("Button Clicked");
    AsyncDemo oAsync = new AsyncDemo();
    await oAsync.LongTask();
    Console.WriteLine("Button Click Ended");
}
```

11. Running your application will display the Windows forms application:

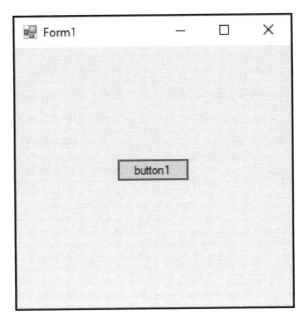

12. Before clicking on the **button1** button, ensure that the **Output** window is visible. To do this, click on **View** and then **Output**. You can also just hold down *Ctrl + W + O*.

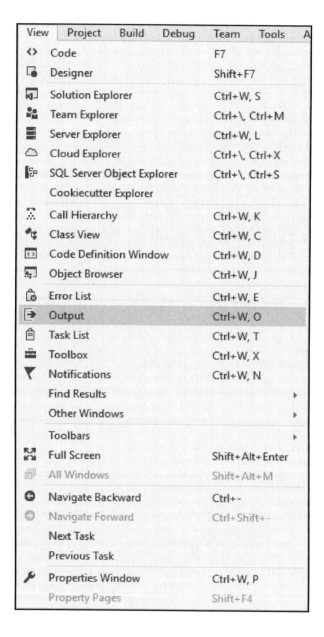

13. Displaying the **Output** window will allow us to see the `Console.Writeline()` outputs that we added to the code in the `AsyncDemo` class and in the Windows application.

14. Clicking on the **button1** button will display the outputs to our **Output** window. Throughout this code execution, the form remains responsive:

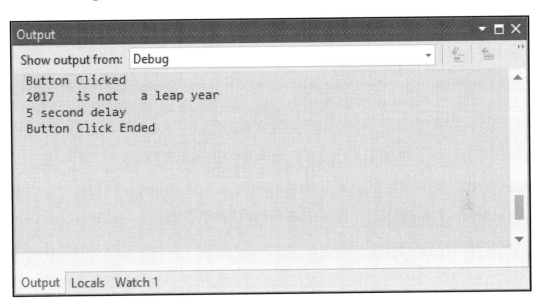

15. Finally, you can also use the `await` operator in separate calls. Modify the code in the `LongTask()` method as follows:

```
public async Task LongTask()
{
    Task<bool> blnIsLeapYear = TaskOfTResultReturning_AsyncMethod();

    for (int i = 0; i <= 10000; i++)
    {
        // Do other work that does not rely on
        // blnIsLeapYear before awaiting
    }

    bool isLeapYear = await TaskOfTResultReturning_AsyncMethod();
    Console.WriteLine($"{DateTime.Now.Year} {(isLeapYear ?
                       " is " : " is not ")} a leap year");

    Task taskReturnMethhod = TaskReturning_AsyncMethod();

    for (int i = 0; i <= 10000; i++)
```

```
    {
        // Do other work that does not rely on
        // taskReturnMethhod before awaiting
    }

    await taskReturnMethhod;
}
```

How it works...

In the preceding code, we saw the `void` returning type asynchronous method that was used in the `button1_Click` event. We also created a `Task` returning method that returns nothing (that would be a `void` if used in synchronous programming), but returning a `Task` type allows us to `await` the method. Finally, we created a `Task<TResult>` returning method that performs a task and returns the result to the calling code.

Handling tasks in asynchronous programming

Task-based Asynchronous Pattern (TAP) is now the recommended method to create asynchronous code. It executes asynchronously on a thread from the thread pool and does not execute synchronously on the main thread of your application. It allows us to check the task's state by calling the `Status` property.

Getting ready

We will create a task to read a very large text file. This will be accomplished using an asynchronous `Task`. Be sure that you have added the `using System.IO;` namespace to your Windows forms application.

How to do it...

1. Create a large text file (we called ours `taskFile.txt`) and place it in a folder called `C:\temp\taskFile\`:

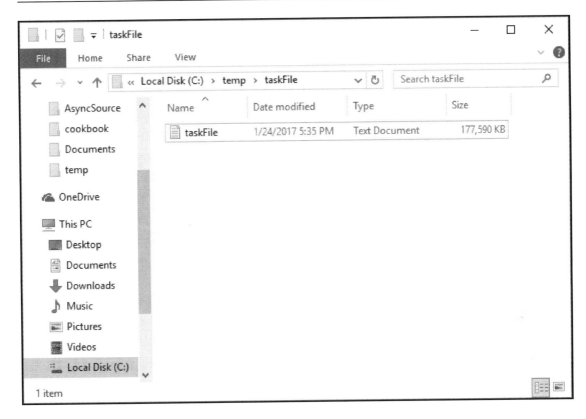

2. In the `AsyncDemo` class, create a method called `ReadBigFile()` that returns a `Task<TResult>` type, which will be used to return an integer of bytes read from our big text file:

```
public Task<int> ReadBigFile()
{
}
```

3. Add the following code to open and read the file bytes. You will see that we are using the `ReadAsync()` method that asynchronously reads a sequence of bytes from the stream and advances the position of that stream by the number of bytes read from that stream. You will also notice that we are using a buffer to read those bytes:

```
public Task<int> ReadBigFile()
{
    var bigFile = File.OpenRead(@"C:\temp\taskFile\taskFile.txt");
    var bigFileBuffer = new byte[bigFile.Length];
    var readBytes = bigFile.ReadAsync(bigFileBuffer, 0,
```

```
    (int)bigFile.Length);

    return readBytes;
}
```

 The exceptions you can expect to handle from the ReadAsync() method
are ArgumentNullException, ArgumentOutOfRangeException,
ArgumentException, NotSupportedException,
ObjectDisposedException, and InvalidOperatorException.

4. Finally, add the final section of code just after the var readBytes =
   bigFile.ReadAsync(bigFileBuffer, 0, (int)bigFile.Length); line
   that uses a lambda expression to specify the work that the task needs to perform.
   In this case, it is to read the bytes in the file:

```
public Task<int> ReadBigFile()
{
    var bigFile = File.OpenRead(@"C:temptaskFile.txt");
    var bigFileBuffer = new byte[bigFile.Length];
    var readBytes = bigFile.ReadAsync(bigFileBuffer, 0,
    (int)bigFile.Length);
    readBytes.ContinueWith(task =>
    {
        if (task.Status == TaskStatus.Running)
            Console.WriteLine("Running");
        else if (task.Status == TaskStatus.RanToCompletion)
            Console.WriteLine("RanToCompletion");
        else if (task.Status == TaskStatus.Faulted)
            Console.WriteLine("Faulted");

        bigFile.Dispose();
    });
    return readBytes;
}
```

5. If you've not done so in the previous recipe, add a button to your Windows forms
   application's Forms Designer. In the **winformAsync** Forms Designer, open
   Toolbox and select the **Button** control, which is found under the **All Windows
   Forms** node:

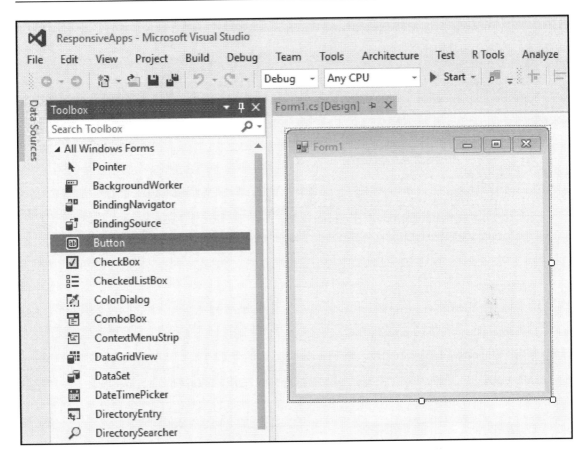

6. Drag the **Button** control onto the **Form1** designer:

7. With the **Button** control selected, double-click on the control to create the click
   event in the code behind. Visual Studio will insert the event code for you:

```
namespace winformAsync
{
    public partial class Form1 : Form
    {
        public Form1()
        {
            InitializeComponent();
        }

        private void button1_Click(object sender, EventArgs e)
        {
```

```
        }
      }
    }
```

8. Change the `button1_Click` event and add the `async` keyword to the click event. This is an example of a `void` returning asynchronous method:

```
private async void button1_Click(object sender, EventArgs e)
{

}
```

9. Now, make sure that you add code to call the `AsyncDemo` class's `ReadBigFile()` method asynchronously. Remember to read the result from the method (which are the bytes read) into an integer variable:

```
private async void button1_Click(object sender, EventArgs e)
{
    Console.WriteLine("Start file read");
    AsyncDemo oAsync = new AsyncDemo();
    int readResult = await oAsync.ReadBigFile();
    Console.WriteLine("Bytes read = " + readResult);
}
```

10. Running your application will display the Windows forms application:

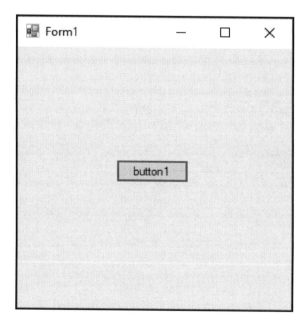

11. Before clicking on the **button1** button, ensure that the **Output** window is visible:

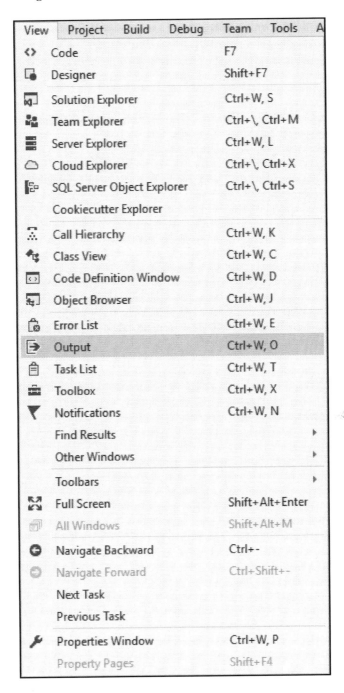

12. From the **View** menu, click on the **Output** menu item or type *Ctrl + W + O* to display the **Output** window. This will allow us to see the `Console.Writeline()` outputs that we added to the code in the `AsyncDemo` class and in the Windows application.

13. Clicking on the **button1** button will display the outputs to our **Output** window. Throughout this code execution, the form remains responsive:

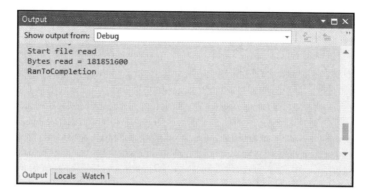

 Take note, though, that the information displayed in your **Output** window will differ from the screenshot. This is because the file you used is different from mine.

How it works...

The task is executed on a separate thread from the thread pool. This allows the application to remain responsive while the large file is being processed. Tasks can be used in multiple ways to improve your code. This recipe is but one example.

Exception handling in asynchronous programming

Exception handling in asynchronous programming has always been a challenge. This was especially true in the catch blocks. The following feature (introduced in C# 6.0) allows you to write asynchronous code inside the `catch` and `finally` blocks of your exception handlers.

Getting ready

The application will simulate the action of reading a log file. Assume that a third-party system always makes a backup of the log file before processing it in another application. While this processing is happening, the log file is deleted and recreated. Our application, however, needs to read this log file on a periodic basis. We therefore need to be prepared for the case where the file does not exist in the location we expect it in. Therefore, we will purposely omit the main log file so that we can force an error.

How to do it...

1. Create a text file and two folders to contain the log files. We will, however, only create a single log file in the BackupLog folder. Name your text file taskFile.txt and copy it to the BackupLog folder. The MainLog folder will remain empty:

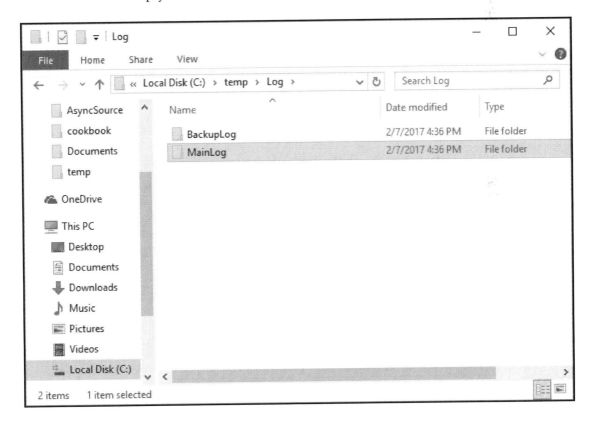

2. In our `AsyncDemo` class, write a method to read the log file in the folder specified by the `enum` value:

```
private async Task<int> ReadLog(LogType logType)
{
    string logFilePath = String.Empty;
    if (logType == LogType.Main)
        logFilePath = @"C:\temp\Log\MainLog\taskFile.txt";
    else if (logType == LogType.Backup)
        logFilePath = @"C:\temp\Log\BackupLog\taskFile.txt";

    string enumName = Enum.GetName(typeof(LogType), (int)logType);

    var bigFile = File.OpenRead(logFilePath);
    var bigFileBuffer = new byte[bigFile.Length];
    var readBytes = bigFile.ReadAsync(bigFileBuffer, 0,
    (int)bigFile.Length);
    await readBytes.ContinueWith(task =>
    {
        if (task.Status == TaskStatus.RanToCompletion)
            Console.WriteLine($"{enumName} Log RanToCompletion");
        else if (task.Status == TaskStatus.Faulted)
            Console.WriteLine($"{enumName} Log Faulted");

        bigFile.Dispose();
    });
    return await readBytes;
}
```

3. Create the `enum` value as shown here:

```
public enum LogType { Main = 0, Backup = 1 }
```

4. We will then create a main `ReadLogFile()` method that tries to read the main log file. As we have not created the log file in the `MainLog` folder, the code will throw a `FileNotFoundException`. It will then run the asynchronous method and `await` it in the `catch` block of the `ReadLogFile()` method (something that was impossible in the previous versions of C#), returning the bytes read to the calling code:

```
public async Task<int> ReadLogFile()
{
    int returnBytes = -1;
    try
    {
        returnBytes = await ReadLog(LogType.Main);
```

```
    }
    catch (Exception ex)
    {
        try
        {
            returnBytes = await ReadLog(LogType.Backup);
        }
        catch (Exception)
        {
            throw;
        }
    }
    return returnBytes;
}
```

5. If you've not done so in the previous recipe, add a button to your Windows forms application's Forms Designer. On the **winformAsync** Forms Designer, open **Toolbox** and select the **Button** control, which is found under the **All Windows Forms** node:

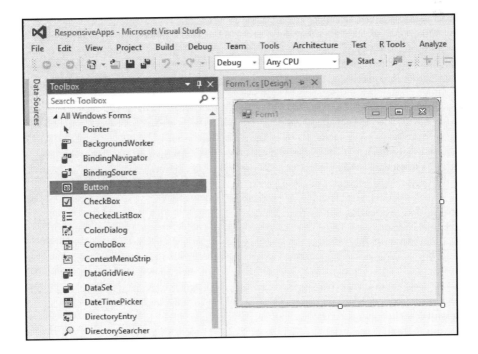

6. Drag the **Button** control onto the **Form1** designer:

7. With the **Button** control selected, double-click on the control to create the click event in the code behind. Visual Studio will insert the event code for you:

```
namespace winformAsync
{
    public partial class Form1 : Form
    {
        public Form1()
        {
            InitializeComponent();
        }

        private void button1_Click(object sender, EventArgs e)
        {

        }
    }
}
```

8. Change the button1_Click event and add the async keyword to the click event. This is an example of a void returning an asynchronous method:

```
private async void button1_Click(object sender, EventArgs e)
{

}
```

9. Next, we will write the code to create a new instance of the AsyncDemo class and attempt to read the main log file. In a real-world example, it is at this point that the code does not know that the main log file does not exist:

```
private async void button1_Click(object sender, EventArgs  e)
{
    Console.WriteLine("Read backup file");
    AsyncDemo oAsync = new AsyncDemo();
    int readResult = await oAsync.ReadLogFile();
    Console.WriteLine("Bytes read = " + readResult);
}
```

10. Running your application will display the Windows forms application:

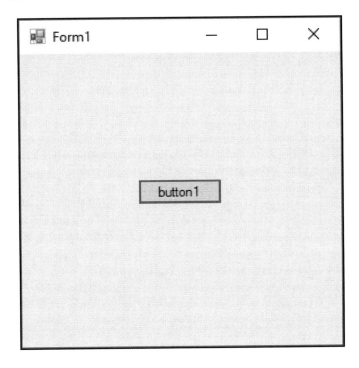

11. Before clicking on the **button1** button, ensure that the **Output** window is visible:

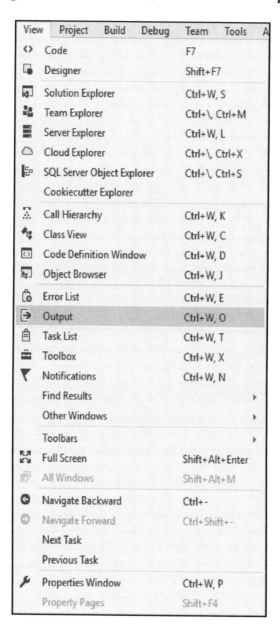

12. From the **View** menu, click on the **Output** menu item or type *Ctrl + W + O* to display the **Output** window. This will allow us to see the `Console.Writeline()` outputs that we added to the code in the `AsyncDemo` class and in the Windows application.

13. To simulate a file not found exception, we deleted the file from the `MainLog` folder. You will see that the exception is thrown, and the `catch` block runs the code to read the backup log file instead:

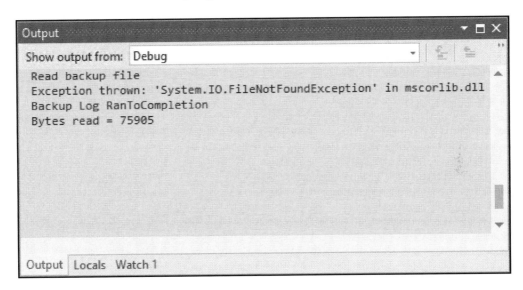

How it works...

The fact that we can await in `catch` and `finally` blocks allows developers much more flexibility because asynchronous results can consistently be awaited throughout the application. As you can see from the code we wrote, as soon as the exception was thrown, we asynchronously read the file read method for the backup file.

8

High Performance
Programming Using Parallel
and Multithreading in C#

This chapter takes a look at improving your code's performance using multithreading and parallel programming. In this chapter, we will cover the following recipes:

- Creating and aborting a low-priority background thread
- Increasing the maximum thread pool size
- Creating multiple threads
- Locking one thread until the contended resources are available
- Invoking parallel calls to methods using Parallel.Invoke
- Using a parallel foreach loop
- Cancelling a parallel foreach loop
- Catching errors in parallel foreach loops
- Debugging multiple threads

Introduction

If you can find a single core CPU in a computer today, it will probably mean that you are standing in a museum. Every new computer today utilizes the advantages of multiple cores. Programmers can take advantage of this extra processing power in their own applications. As applications have grown in size and complexity, in many cases they actually need to utilize multithreading.

While not every situation is always suited to the implementation of multithreaded code logic, it is good to know how to use multithreading to improve the performance of your applications. This chapter will take you through the fundamentals of this exciting technology in C# programming.

Creating and aborting a low-priority background thread

The reason we want to take a look at a background thread specifically is because, by default, all threads created by the main app thread or `Thread` class constructor are foreground threads. So, what exactly separates a foreground thread from a background thread? Well, background threads are identical to foreground threads with the exception that if all foreground threads are terminated, the background threads are stopped too. This is useful if you have a process in your application that must not stop the application from terminating. In other words, while your application is running, the background threads must continue to run.

Getting ready

We will create a simple application that defines the thread created as a background thread. It will then suspend, resume, and abort the thread.

How to do it...

1. Create a new console application in Visual Studio.

2. Next, add a class called `Demo` to your console application.

3. Inside the `Demo` class, add a method called `DoBackgroundTask()` with the `public void` modifiers, and add the following console output to it:

```
public void DoBackgroundTask()
{
    WriteLine($"Thread {Thread.CurrentThread.ManagedThreadId} has
    a threadstate of {Thread.CurrentThread.ThreadState} with
    {Thread.CurrentThread.Priority} priority");
    WriteLine($"Start thread sleep at {DateTime.Now.Second}
            seconds");
    Thread.Sleep(3000);
    WriteLine($"End thread sleep at {DateTime.Now.Second} seconds");
}
```

 Make sure that you have added the `using` statements for `System.Threading` and `static System.Console` to your `using` statements.

4. In the `void Main` method of your console application, create a new instance of your `Demo` class and add it to a new thread called `backgroundThread`. Define this newly created thread to be a background thread and then start it. Finally, set the thread to sleep for 5 seconds. We need to do this because we created a background thread that is set to sleep for 3 seconds. Background threads do not prohibit foreground threads from terminating. Therefore, if the main application thread (which is by default a foreground thread) terminates before the background thread completes, the application will terminate and also terminate the background thread:

```
static void Main(string[] args)
{
    Demo oRecipe = new Demo();
    var backgroundThread = new Thread(oRecipe.DoBackgroundTask);
    backgroundThread.IsBackground = true;
    backgroundThread.Start();
    Thread.Sleep(5000);
}
```

5. Run your console application by pressing *F5*. You will see that we have created a background thread with a normal priority:

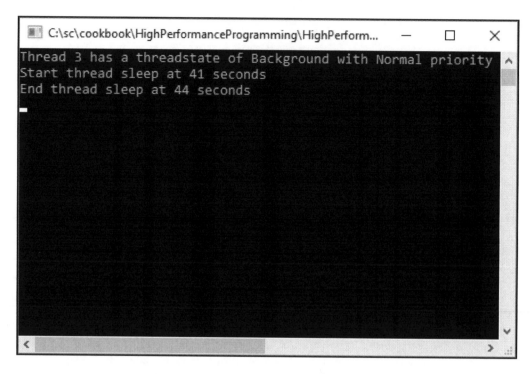

6. Let's modify our thread and set its priority down to low. Add this line of code to your console application:

```
backgroundThread.Priority = ThreadPriority.Lowest;
```

This line will downgrade the thread priority:

```
Demo oRecipe = new Demo();
var backgroundThread = new Thread(oRecipe.DoBackgroundTask);
backgroundThread.IsBackground = true;
backgroundThread.Priority = ThreadPriority.Lowest;
backgroundThread.Start();
Thread.Sleep(5000);
```

7. Run your console application again. This time, you will see that the thread priority has been set to the lowest priority:

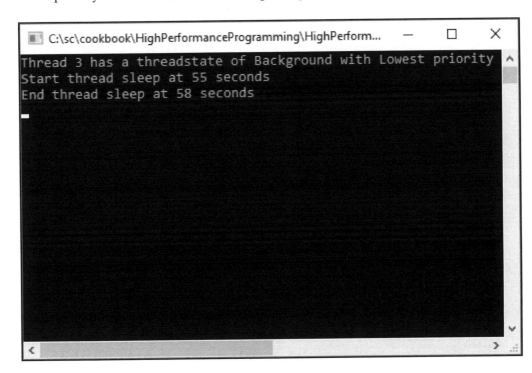

8. Go back to your `DoBackgroundTask()` method and add `Thread.CurrentThread.Abort();` right before `Thread.Sleep(3000);` is called. This line will prematurely kill the background thread. Your code should look like this:

```
public void DoBackgroundTask()
{
  WriteLine($"Thread {Thread.CurrentThread.ManagedThreadId} has a
  threadstate of {Thread.CurrentThread.ThreadState} with
  {Thread.CurrentThread.Priority} priority");
  WriteLine($"Start thread sleep at {DateTime.Now.Second}
            seconds");
  Thread.CurrentThread.Abort();
  Thread.Sleep(3000);
  WriteLine($"End thread sleep at {DateTime.Now.Second} seconds");
}
```

9. When you run your console application, you will see that the thread is aborted before the `Thread.Sleep` method is called. Aborting a thread in this way, however is, generally, not recommended:

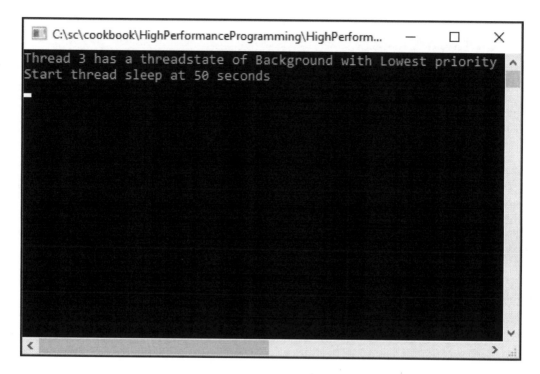

How it works...

Being able to create a background thread is a great way to work on a different thread from the main thread while not interfering with the process of the main application thread. Another added benefit is that the background thread is terminated as soon as the main application thread is completed. This process ensures that your application will terminate gracefully.

Increasing the maximum thread pool size

The thread pool in .NET resides in the `System.Threading.ThreadPool` class. Generally, there is a lot of discussion around creating your own threads, as opposed to using the thread pool. Popular thinking dictates that the thread pool should be used for brief jobs. This is because the thread pool is limited in size. There are many other processes in the system that will use the thread pool. You, therefore, do not want your application to hog all the threads in the thread pool.

The rule is that you can't set the number of maximum worker or completion threads to be fewer than the number of processors on your computer. You are also not allowed to set the maximum worker or completion threads to less than the minimum thread pool size.

Getting ready

We will read the number of processors on the current computer. Then, we will get the minimum and maximum allowable thread pool size, generate a random number between the minimum and maximum thread pool size, and set the maximum number of threads on the thread pool.

How to do it...

1. Create a new method called `IncreaseThreadPoolSize()` in the `Demo` class.

2. Start by adding the code to read the number of processors on the current machine using `Environment.ProcessorCount`:

```
public class Demo
{
  public void IncreaseThreadPoolSize()
  {
     int numberOfProcessors = Environment.ProcessorCount;
     WriteLine($"Processor Count = {numberOfProcessors}");
  }
}
```

3. Next, we retrieve the maximum and minimum threads available in the thread pool:

```
int maxworkerThreads;
int maxconcurrentActiveRequests;
int minworkerThreads;
int minconcurrentActiveRequests;
ThreadPool.GetMinThreads(out minworkerThreads,
   out  minconcurrentActiveRequests);
WriteLine($"ThreadPool minimum Worker = {minworkerThreads}
   and minimum Requests = {minconcurrentActiveRequests}");
ThreadPool.GetMaxThreads(out maxworkerThreads,
   out  maxconcurrentActiveRequests);
WriteLine($"ThreadPool maximum Worker = {maxworkerThreads}
   and maximum Requests = {maxconcurrentActiveRequests}");
```

4. Then, we generate a random number between the maximum and minimum number of threads in the thread pool:

```
Random rndWorkers = new Random();
int newMaxWorker = rndWorkers.Next(minworkerThreads,
  maxworkerThreads);
WriteLine($"New Max Worker Thread generated = {newMaxWorker}");

Random rndConRequests = new Random();
int newMaxRequests = rndConRequests.Next(
minconcurrentActiveRequests, maxconcurrentActiveRequests);
WriteLine($"New Max Active Requests generated = {newMaxRequests}");
```

5. We now need to attempt to set the maximum number of threads in the thread pool by calling the SetMaxThreads method, and setting it to our new random maximum value for the worker threads and the completion port threads. Any requests above this maximum number will be queued until the thread pool threads become active again. If the SetMaxThreads method is successful, the method will return true; otherwise, it will return false. It is a good idea to ensure that the SetMaxThreads method is successful:

```
bool changeSucceeded = ThreadPool.SetMaxThreads(
  newMaxWorker, newMaxRequests);
if (changeSucceeded)
{
   WriteLine("SetMaxThreads completed");
   int maxworkerThreadCount;
   int maxconcurrentActiveRequestCount;
   ThreadPool.GetMaxThreads(out maxworkerThreadCount,
```

```
      out maxconcurrentActiveRequestCount);
      WriteLine($"ThreadPool Max Worker = {maxworkerThreadCount}
      and Max Requests = {maxconcurrentActiveRequestCount}");
  }
  else
      WriteLine("SetMaxThreads failed");
```

 Worker threads is the maximum number of worker threads in the thread pool while the completion port threads is the maximum number of asynchronous I/O threads in the thread pool.

6. When you've added all the code in the steps listed, your `IncreaseThreadPoolSize()` method should look like this:

```
public class Demo
{
  public void IncreaseThreadPoolSize()
  {
    int numberOfProcessors = Environment.ProcessorCount;
    WriteLine($"Processor Count = {numberOfProcessors}");

    int maxworkerThreads;
    int maxconcurrentActiveRequests;
    int minworkerThreads;
    int minconcurrentActiveRequests;
    ThreadPool.GetMinThreads(out minworkerThreads,
      out minconcurrentActiveRequests);
    WriteLine($"ThreadPool minimum Worker = {minworkerThreads}
      and minimum Requests = {minconcurrentActiveRequests}");
    ThreadPool.GetMaxThreads(out maxworkerThreads,
      out maxconcurrentActiveRequests);
    WriteLine($"ThreadPool maximum Worker = {maxworkerThreads}
      and maximum Requests = {maxconcurrentActiveRequests}");

    Random rndWorkers = new Random();
    int newMaxWorker = rndWorkers.Next(minworkerThreads,
      maxworkerThreads);
    WriteLine($"New Max Worker Thread generated = {newMaxWorker}");

    Random rndConRequests = new Random();
    int newMaxRequests = rndConRequests.Next(
      minconcurrentActiveRequests,
      maxconcurrentActiveRequests);
    WriteLine($"New Max Active Requests generated =
                {newMaxRequests}");
```

```
bool changeSucceeded = ThreadPool.SetMaxThreads(
  newMaxWorker, newMaxRequests);
if (changeSucceeded)
{
  WriteLine("SetMaxThreads completed");
  int maxworkerThreadCount;
  int maxconcurrentActiveRequestCount;
  ThreadPool.GetMaxThreads(out maxworkerThreadCount,
    out maxconcurrentActiveRequestCount);
  WriteLine($"ThreadPool Max Worker = {maxworkerThreadCount}
  and Max Requests = {maxconcurrentActiveRequestCount}");
}
else
  WriteLine("SetMaxThreads failed");

  }
}
```

7. Head on over to your console application, create a new instance of your Demo class, and call the `IncreaseThreadPoolSize()` method:

```
Demo oRecipe = new Demo();
oRecipe.IncreaseThreadPoolSize();
Console.ReadLine();
```

8. Finally, run your console application and take note of the output:

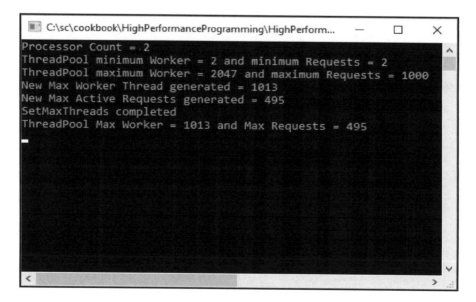

How it works...

From the console application, we can see that the processor count is 2. The minimum number of thread pool threads, therefore, also equals 2. We then read the maximum thread pool size and generate a random number between the minimum and maximum numbers. Lastly, we set the maximum thread pool size, to our randomly generated minimum and maximum.

While this is only a proof of concept and not something one would do in a production application (setting the thread pool to a random number), it clearly illustrates the ability to set the thread pool to a value specified by the developer.

The code in this recipe was compiled for 32-bit. Try changing your application to a 64-bit application and run the code again. See the difference a 64-bit makes.

Creating multiple threads

Sometimes, we need to create multiple threads. Before we can continue, however, we need to wait for these threads to complete doing whatever they need to do. For this, the use of tasks is best suited.

Getting ready

Make sure that you add the `using System.Threading.Tasks;` statement to the top of your `Recipes` class.

How to do it...

1. Create a new method called `MultipleThreadWait()` in your `Demo` class. Then, create a second method called `RunThread()` with the `private` modifier that takes an integer of seconds to make the thread sleep. This will simulate the process of doing some work for a variable amount of time:

    ```
    public class Demo
    {
        public void MultipleThreadWait()
    ```

```
    {

    }

    private void RunThread(int sleepSeconds)
    {

    }
}
```

 In reality, you would probably not call the same method. You could, for all intents and purposes, call three separate methods. Here, however, for simplicity's sake, we will call the same method with different sleep durations.

2. Add the following code to your `MultipleThreadWait()` method. You will notice that we are creating three tasks that then create three threads. We then fire off these three threads and make them sleep for 3, 5, and 2 seconds. Finally, we call the `Task.WaitAll` method to wait before continuing the execution of the application:

```
Task thread1 = Task.Factory.StartNew(() => RunThread(3));
Task thread2 = Task.Factory.StartNew(() => RunThread(5));
Task thread3 = Task.Factory.StartNew(() => RunThread(2));

Task.WaitAll(thread1, thread2, thread3);
WriteLine("All tasks completed");
```

3. Then, in the `RunThread()` method, we read the current thread ID and then make the thread sleep for the amount of milliseconds supplied. This is just the integer value for the seconds multiplied by 1000:

```
int thread
ID = Thread.CurrentThread.ManagedThreadId;

WriteLine($"Sleep thread {threadID} for {sleepSeconds}
    seconds at {DateTime.Now.Second} seconds");
Thread.Sleep(sleepSeconds * 1000);
WriteLine($"Wake thread {threadID} at {DateTime.Now.Second}
        seconds");
```

4. When you have completed the code, your Demo class should look like this:

```
public class Demo
{
    public void MultipleThreadWait()
```

```
{
    Task thread1 = Task.Factory.StartNew(() => RunThread(3));
    Task thread2 = Task.Factory.StartNew(() => RunThread(5));
    Task thread3 = Task.Factory.StartNew(() => RunThread(2));

    Task.WaitAll(thread1, thread2, thread3);
    WriteLine("All tasks completed");
}

private void RunThread(int sleepSeconds)
{
    int threadID = Thread.CurrentThread.ManagedThreadId;
    WriteLine($"Sleep thread {threadID} for {sleepSeconds}
        seconds at {DateTime.Now.Second}        seconds");
    Thread.Sleep(sleepSeconds * 1000);
    WriteLine($"Wake thread {threadID} at {DateTime.Now.Second}
            seconds");
}
}
```

5. Finally, add a new instance of the Demo class to your console application and call the MultipleThreadWait() method:

```
Demo oRecipe = new Demo();
oRecipe.MultipleThreadWait();
Console.ReadLine();
```

6. Run your console application and view the output produced:

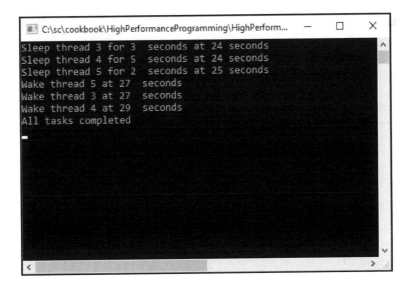

How it works...

You will notice that three threads (`thread 3`, `thread 4`, and `thread 5`) are created. These are then paused by making them sleep for various amounts of time. After each thread wakes, the code waits for all three threads to complete before continuing the execution of the application code.

Locking one thread until the contended resources are available

There are instances where we want to give sole access to a process to a specific thread. We can do this using the `lock` keyword. This will, therefore, execute this process in a thread-safe manner. Hence, when a thread runs the process it will gain exclusive access to the process for the duration of the lock scope. If another thread tries to gain access to the process inside the locked code, it will be blocked and have to wait its turn until the lock is released.

Getting ready

For this example, we will use tasks. Make sure that you've added the `using System.Threading.Tasks;` statement to the top of your `Demo` class.

How to do it...

1. In the `Demo` class, add an object called `threadLock` with the `private` modifier. Then, add two methods called `LockThreadExample()` and `ContendedResource()` that take an integer of seconds to sleep as a parameter:

```
public class Demo
{
  private object threadLock = new object();
  public void LockThreadExample()
  {

  }

  private void ContendedResource(int sleepSeconds)
  {
```

```
   }
}
```

It is considered to be a best practice to define the object to lock on as private.

2. Add three tasks to the `LockThreadExample()` method. They will create threads that try to access the same section of code simultaneously. This code will wait until all the threads have completed before terminating the application:

```
Task thread1 = Task.Factory.StartNew(() => ContendedResource(3));
Task thread2 = Task.Factory.StartNew(() => ContendedResource(5));
Task thread3 = Task.Factory.StartNew(() => ContendedResource(2));

Task.WaitAll(thread1, thread2, thread3);
WriteLine("All tasks completed");
```

3. In the `ContendedResource()` method, create a lock using the `private` `threadLock` object and then make the thread sleep for the amount of seconds passed to the method as a parameter:

```
int threadID = Thread.CurrentThread.ManagedThreadId;
lock (threadLock)
{
  WriteLine($"Locked for thread {threadID}");
  Thread.Sleep(sleepSeconds * 1000);
}
WriteLine($"Lock released for thread {threadID}");
```

4. Back in the console application, add the following code to instantiate a new `Demo` class and call the `LockThreadExample()` method:

```
Demo oRecipe = new Demo();
oRecipe.LockThreadExample();
Console.ReadLine();
```

5. Run the console application and look at the information output to the console window:

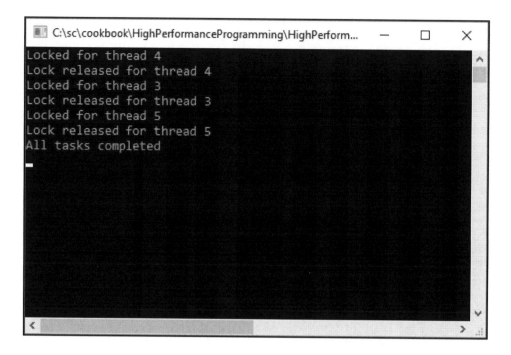

How it works...

We can see that `thread 4` gained exclusive access to the contended resource. At the same time, `thread 3` and `thread 5` tried to access the contended resource locked by `thread 4`. This then caused the other two threads to wait until `thread 4` had completed and released the lock. The result of this is that the code is executed in an orderly manner, as can be seen in the console window output. Each thread waits its turn until it can access the resource and lock its thread.

Invoking parallel calls to methods using Parallel.Invoke

`Parallel.Invoke` allows us to execute tasks in (you guessed it) parallel. Sometimes, you need to perform operations simultaneously and, in so doing, speed up the processing. You can, therefore, expect that the total time taken to process the tasks is equal to the longest running process. Using `Parallel.Invoke` is quite easy.

Getting ready

Make sure that you've added the `using System.Threading.Tasks;` statement to the top of your `Demo` class.

How to do it...

1. Start off by creating two methods in the `Demo` class called `ParallelInvoke()` and `PerformSomeTask()` that take an integer of seconds to sleep as the parameter:

```
public class Demo
{
  public void ParallelInvoke()
  {

  }

  private void PerformSomeTask(int sleepSeconds)
  {

  }
}
```

2. Add the following code to the `ParallelInvoke()` method. This code will call `Paralell.Invoke` to run the `PerformSomeTask()` method:

```
WriteLine($"Parallel.Invoke started at
  {DateTime.Now.Second} seconds");
Parallel.Invoke(
  () => PerformSomeTask(3),
  () => PerformSomeTask(5),
  () => PerformSomeTask(2)
);

WriteLine($"Parallel.Invoke completed at
  {DateTime.Now.Second} seconds");
```

3. In the `PerformSomeTask()` method, make the thread sleep for the amount of seconds passed to the method as the parameter (converting the seconds to milliseconds by multiplying it by 1000):

```
int threadID = Thread.CurrentThread.ManagedThreadId;
WriteLine($"Sleep thread {threadID} for
  {sleepSeconds}  seconds");
Thread.Sleep(sleepSeconds * 1000);
WriteLine($"Thread {threadID} resumed");
```

4. When you've added all the code, your Demo class should look like this:

```
public class Demo
{
  public void ParallelInvoke()
  {
    WriteLine($"Parallel.Invoke started at
              {DateTime.Now.Second} seconds");
    Parallel.Invoke(
      () => PerformSomeTask(3),
      () => PerformSomeTask(5),
      () => PerformSomeTask(2)
    );

    WriteLine($"Parallel.Invoke completed at {DateTime.Now.Second}
              seconds");
  }

  private void PerformSomeTask(int sleepSeconds)
  {
    int threadID = Thread.CurrentThread.ManagedThreadId;
    WriteLine($"Sleep thread {threadID} for {sleepSeconds}
              seconds");
```

```
            Thread.Sleep(sleepSeconds * 1000);
            WriteLine($"Thread {threadID} resumed");
        }
    }
```

5. In the console application, instantiate a new instance of the Demo class and call the ParallelInvoke() method:

    ```
    Demo oRecipe = new Demo();
    oRecipe.ParallelInvoke();
    Console.ReadLine();
    ```

6. Run the console application and look at the output produced in the console window:

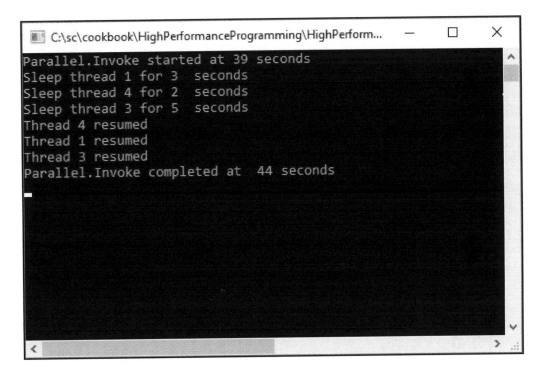

```
C:\sc\cookbook\HighPerformanceProgramming\HighPerform...        —    □    ×
Parallel.Invoke started at 39 seconds
Sleep thread 1 for 3  seconds
Sleep thread 4 for 2  seconds
Sleep thread 3 for 5  seconds
Thread 4 resumed
Thread 1 resumed
Thread 3 resumed
Parallel.Invoke completed at  44 seconds
```

How it works...

Because we are running all these threads in parallel, we can assume that the longest process will denote the total duration of all the tasks. This means that the total duration of the process will be 5 seconds because the longest task will take 5 seconds to complete (we set `thread 3` to sleep for a maximum of 5 seconds).

As we can see, the time difference between the start and the end of `Parallel.Invoke` is exactly 5 seconds.

Using a parallel foreach loop

A while ago, during a work retreat (yes, the company I work for is really that cool), Graham Rook, who is one of my colleagues, showed me a parallel `foreach` loop. It certainly speeds up processing a great deal. But here's the rub. It makes no sense to use a parallel `foreach` loop if you're dealing with small amounts of data or little tasks. The parallel `foreach` loop excels when there is bulk processing to do or huge amounts of data to process.

Getting ready

We will start off by looking at where the parallel `foreach` loop does not perform better than the standard `foreach` loop. For this, we will create a small list of 500 items and just iterate over the list, writing the items to the console window.

For the second example, which illustrates the power of the parallel `foreach` loop, we will use the same list and create a file for each item in the list. The power and benefit of the parallel `foreach` loop will be evident in the second example. You will need to add the `using System.Diagnostics;` and `using System.IO;` namespaces to run this recipe.

How to do it...

1. Start off by creating two methods in the `Demo` class. Call one method `ReadCollectionForEach()` and pass it a parameter of `List<string>`. Create a second method called `ReadCollectionParallelForEach()` that also accepts a parameter of `List<string>`:

   ```
   public class Demo
   {
   ```

```
public double ReadCollectionForEach(List<string> intCollection)
{

}

public double ReadCollectionParallelForEach(List<string>
   intCollection)
{

}
}
```

2. In the `ReadCollectionForEach()` method, add a standard `foreach` loop that will iterate over the collection of strings passed to it and write the value it finds to the console window. Then, clear the console window. Use a timer to keep track of the total seconds elapsed during the `foreach` loop:

```
var timer = Stopwatch.StartNew();
foreach (string integer in intCollection)
{
  WriteLine(integer);
  Clear();
}
return timer.Elapsed.TotalSeconds;
```

3. In the second method, called `ReadCollectionParallelForEach()`, do the same. However, instead of using a standard `foreach` loop, add a `Parallel.ForEach` loop. You will notice that the `Parallel.ForEach` loop looks slightly different. The signature of `Parallel.ForEach` requires that you pass it an enumerable data source (`List<string> intCollection`) and define an action, which is the delegate that is invoked for every iteration (`integer`):

```
var timer = Stopwatch.StartNew();
Parallel.ForEach(intCollection, integer =>
{
  WriteLine(integer);
  Clear();
});
return timer.Elapsed.TotalSeconds;
```

4. When you have added all the required code, your Demo class should look like this:

```
public class Demo
{
  public double ReadCollectionForEach(List<string> intCollection)
```

```
    {
      var timer = Stopwatch.StartNew();
      foreach (string integer in intCollection)
      {
        WriteLine(integer);
        Clear();
      }
      return timer.Elapsed.TotalSeconds;
    }

    public double ReadCollectionParallelForEach(List<string>
      intCollection)
    {
      var timer = Stopwatch.StartNew();
      Parallel.ForEach(intCollection, integer =>
      {
        WriteLine(integer);
        Clear();
      });
      return timer.Elapsed.TotalSeconds;
    }
  }
```

5. In the console application, create the `List<string>` collection and pass it to the two methods created in the `Demo` class. You will notice that we are only creating a collection of 500 items. After the code is completed, return the time elapsed in seconds and output it to the console window:

```
List<string> integerList = new List<string>();
for (int i = 0; i <= 500; i++)
{
  integerList.Add(i.ToString());
}
Demo oRecipe = new Demo();
double timeElapsed1 = oRecipe.ReadCollectionForEach(integerList);
double timeElapsed2 = oRecipe.ReadCollectionParallelForEach(
  integerList);
WriteLine($"foreach executed in {timeElapsed1}");
WriteLine($"Parallel.ForEach executed in {timeElapsed2}");
```

6. Run your application. From the output displayed, you will see the difference in performance. The `Parallel.ForEach` loop actually took longer to complete than the `foreach` loop:

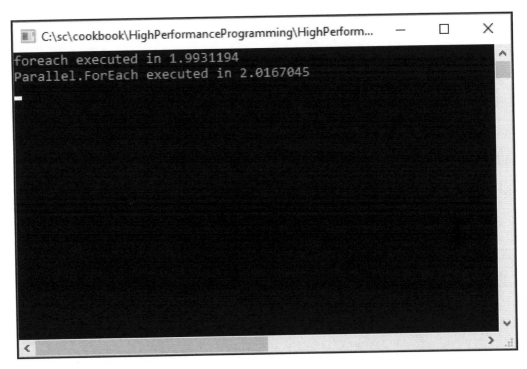

7. Let's use a different example now. We will create a process-intensive task and measure the performance gain that the `Parallel.ForEach` loop will give us. Create two methods called `CreateWriteFilesForEach()` and `CreateWriteFilesParallelForEach()` that both take the `List<string>` collection as the parameter:

```
public class Demo
{
  public void CreateWriteFilesForEach(List<string> intCollection)
  {

  }

  public void CreateWriteFilesParallelForEach(List<string>
    intCollection)
  {
```

```
        }
    }
```

8. Add the following code to the `CreateWriteFilesForEach()` method. This code starts the timer and executes the standard `foreach` loop on the `List<string>` object. It then writes the elapsed time out to the console window:

```
WriteLine($"Start foreach File method");
var timer = Stopwatch.StartNew();
foreach (string integer in intCollection)
{

}
WriteLine($"foreach File method executed in
    {timer.Elapsed.TotalSeconds} seconds");
```

9. Inside the `foreach` loop, add the code to check whether a file exists with the specific name created by appending the `integer` value to the filename portion of the `filePath` variable. Create the file (ensuring that you use the `Dispose` method so as not to lock the file when trying to write to it) and write some text to the newly created file:

```
string filePath =  $"C:\temp\output\ForEach_Log{integer}.txt";
if (!File.Exists(filePath))
{
    File.Create(filePath).Dispose();
    using (StreamWriter sw = new StreamWriter(filePath, false))
    {
        sw.WriteLine($"{integer}. Log file start:
            {DateTime.Now.ToUniversalTime().ToString()}");
    }
}
```

10. Next, add this code to the `CreateWriteFilesParallelForEach()` method, which basically performs the same function as the `CreateWriteFilesForEach()` method, but uses a `Parallel.ForEach` loop to create and write files:

```
WriteLine($"Start Parallel.ForEach File method");
var timer = Stopwatch.StartNew();
Parallel.ForEach(intCollection, integer =>
{

});
WriteLine($"Parallel.ForEach File method executed in
{timer.Elapsed.TotalSeconds} seconds");
```

11. Add the slightly modified file-creation code inside the `Parallel.ForEach` loop:

```
string filePath = $"C:\temp\output\ParallelForEach_Log{
  integer}.txt";
if (!File.Exists(filePath))
{
  File.Create(filePath).Dispose();
  using (StreamWriter sw = new StreamWriter(filePath, false))
  {
    sw.WriteLine($"{integer}. Log file start:
      {DateTime.Now.ToUniversalTime().ToString()}");
  }
}
```

12. When you are done, your code needs to look like this:

```
public class Demo
{
  public void CreateWriteFilesForEach(List<string> intCollection)
  {
    WriteLine($"Start foreach File method");
    var timer = Stopwatch.StartNew();
    foreach (string integer in intCollection)
    {
      string filePath = $"C:\temp\output\ForEach_Log{integer}.txt";
      if (!File.Exists(filePath))
      {
        File.Create(filePath).Dispose();
        using (StreamWriter sw = new StreamWriter(filePath, false))
        {
            sw.WriteLine($"{integer}. Log file start:
            {DateTime.Now.ToUniversalTime().ToString()}");
        }
      }
    }
    WriteLine($"foreach File method executed in {
            timer.Elapsed.TotalSeconds} seconds");
  }

  public void CreateWriteFilesParallelForEach(List<string>
    intCollection)
  {
    WriteLine($"Start Parallel.ForEach File method");
    var timer = Stopwatch.StartNew();
    Parallel.ForEach(intCollection, integer =>
    {
      string filePath = $"C:\temp\output\ParallelForEach_Log
        {integer}.txt";
```

```
        if (!File.Exists(filePath))
        {
          File.Create(filePath).Dispose();
          using (StreamWriter sw = new StreamWriter(filePath, false))
          {
            sw.WriteLine($"{integer}. Log file start:
              {DateTime.Now.ToUniversalTime().ToString()}");
          }
        }
      });
      WriteLine($"Parallel.ForEach File method executed in
      {timer.Elapsed.TotalSeconds} seconds");
    }
  }
```

13. Head over to the console application, modify the `List<string>` object slightly, and increase the count from 500 to 1000. Then, call the file methods created in the Demo class:

```
List<string> integerList = new List<string>();
for (int i = 0; i <= 1000; i++)
{
  integerList.Add(i.ToString());
}

Demo oRecipe = new Demo();
oRecipe.CreateWriteFilesForEach(integerList);
oRecipe.CreateWriteFilesParallelForEach(integerList);
ReadLine();
```

14. Finally, when you are ready, make sure that you have the C:\tempoutput directory and that there aren't any other files in that directory. Run your application and review the output in the console window. This time round, we can see that the Parallel.ForEach loop has made a huge difference. The performance gain is massive and heralds a 47.42 percent performance increase over the standard foreach loop:

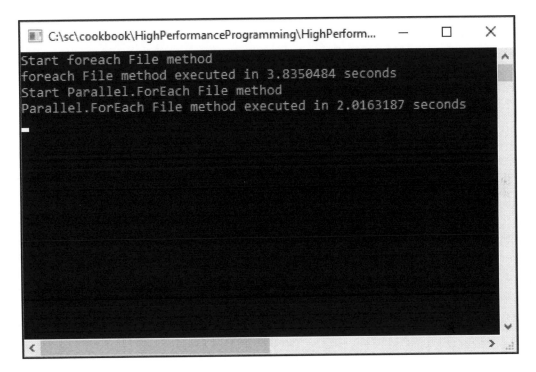

```
Start foreach File method
foreach File method executed in 3.8350484 seconds
Start Parallel.ForEach File method
Parallel.ForEach File method executed in 2.0163187 seconds
```

How it works...

From the examples used in this recipe, it is clear that use of the parallel foreach loop should be considered carefully. If you are dealing with relatively low volumes of data or non-process intensive transactions, the parallel foreach loop will not benefit your application's performance much. In some instances, the standard foreach loop could be much faster than the parallel foreach loop. If, however, you find your application running into performance issues when processing large amounts of data or running processor-intensive tasks, give the parallel foreach loop a try. It just might surprise you.

Cancelling a parallel foreach loop

When dealing with parallel `foreach` loops, the obvious question is how one would terminate the loop prematurely based on a certain condition, such as a timeout. As it turns out, the parallel `foreach` loop is quite easy to terminate prematurely.

Getting ready

We will create a method that takes a collection of items and loops through this collection in a parallel `foreach` loop. It will also be aware of a timeout value that, if exceeded, will terminate the loop and exit the method.

How to do it...

1. Start off by creating a new method called `CancelParallelForEach()` in the `Demo` class, which takes two parameters. One is a collection of `List<string>`, while the other is an integer specifying a timeout value. When the timeout value is exceeded, the `Parallel.ForEach` loop must terminate:

```
public class Demo
{
  public void CancelParallelForEach(List<string> intCollection,
    int timeOut)
  {

  }
}
```

2. Inside the `CancelParallelForEach()` method, add a timer to keep track of the elapsed time. This will signal the loop that the timeout threshold has been exceeded and that the loop needs to exit. Create a `Parallel.ForEach` method defining a state. In each iteration, check the elapsed time against the timeout, and if the time is exceeded, break out of the loop:

```
var timer = Stopwatch.StartNew();
Parallel.ForEach(intCollection, (integer, state) =>
{
  Thread.Sleep(1000);
  if (timer.Elapsed.Seconds > timeOut)
  {
    WriteLine($"Terminate thread {Thread.CurrentThread
      .ManagedThreadId}. Elapsed time {
      timer.Elapsed.Seconds} seconds");
    state.Break();
  }
  WriteLine($"Processing item {integer} on thread
    {Thread.CurrentThread.ManagedThreadId}");
});
```

3. In the console application, create the `List<string>` object and add 1000 items to it. Call the `CancelParallelForEach()` method with a timeout of only 5 seconds:

```
List<string> integerList = new List<string>();
for (int i = 0; i <= 1000; i++)
{
  integerList.Add(i.ToString());
}

Demo oRecipe = new Demo();
oRecipe.CancelParallelForEach(integerList, 5);
WriteLine($"Parallel.ForEach loop terminated");
ReadLine();
```

4. Run your console application and review the output results:

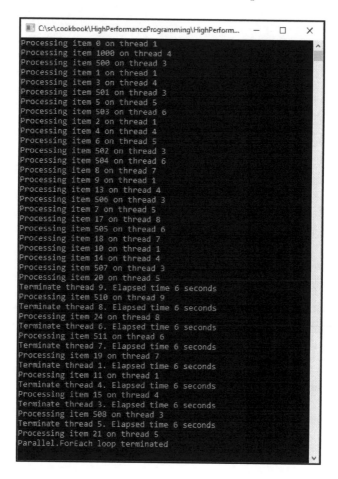

```
C:\sc\cookbook\HighPerformanceProgramming\HighPerform...    —    □    ×
Processing item 0 on thread 1
Processing item 1000 on thread 4
Processing item 500 on thread 3
Processing item 1 on thread 1
Processing item 3 on thread 4
Processing item 501 on thread 3
Processing item 5 on thread 5
Processing item 503 on thread 6
Processing item 2 on thread 1
Processing item 4 on thread 4
Processing item 6 on thread 5
Processing item 502 on thread 3
Processing item 504 on thread 6
Processing item 8 on thread 7
Processing item 9 on thread 1
Processing item 13 on thread 4
Processing item 506 on thread 3
Processing item 7 on thread 5
Processing item 17 on thread 8
Processing item 505 on thread 6
Processing item 18 on thread 7
Processing item 10 on thread 1
Processing item 14 on thread 4
Processing item 507 on thread 3
Processing item 20 on thread 5
Terminate thread 9. Elapsed time 6 seconds
Processing item 510 on thread 9
Terminate thread 8. Elapsed time 6 seconds
Processing item 24 on thread 8
Terminate thread 6. Elapsed time 6 seconds
Processing item 511 on thread 6
Terminate thread 7. Elapsed time 6 seconds
Processing item 19 on thread 7
Terminate thread 1. Elapsed time 6 seconds
Processing item 11 on thread 1
Terminate thread 4. Elapsed time 6 seconds
Processing item 15 on thread 4
Terminate thread 3. Elapsed time 6 seconds
Processing item 508 on thread 3
Terminate thread 5. Elapsed time 6 seconds
Processing item 21 on thread 5
Parallel.ForEach loop terminated
```

How it works...

You can see from the console window output that, as soon as the elapsed time exceeded the timeout value, the parallel loop was notified to cease the execution of iterations beyond the current iteration at the system's earliest convenience. Having this kind of control over the Parallel.ForEach loop allows developers to avoid runaway loops, and gives the user control to cancel a loop operation by clicking on a button or automatically having the application terminate when the timeout value has been reached.

Catching errors in parallel foreach loops

With parallel `foreach` loops, developers can wrap the loop in a `try...catch` statement. Care needs to be taken, however, because the `Parallel.ForEach` will throw an `AggregatedException`, which has the exceptions it encounters over several threads rolled into one.

Getting ready

We will create a `List<string>` object that contains a collection of machine IP addresses. The `Parallel.ForEach` loop will check the IP addresses to see whether the machines on the other end of the given IPs are alive. It does this by pinging the IP address. The method that performs the `Parallel.ForEach` loop will also be given the minimum required alive machines as an integer value. If the minimum number of machines alive is not met, an exception is thrown.

How to do it...

1. In the `Demo` class, add a method called `CheckClientMachinesOnline()`, which takes as parameters a `List<string>` collection of IP addresses and an integer that specifies the minimum number of machines required to be online. Add a second method called `MachineReturnedPing()`, which will receive an IP address to ping. For our purpose, we will just return `false` to mimic a dead machine (the ping to the IP address timed out):

```
public class Recipes
{
  public void CheckClientMachinesOnline(List<string> ipAddresses,
    int minimumLive)
  {

  }

  private bool MachineReturnedPing(string ip)
  {
    return false;
  }
}
```

2. Inside the `CheckClientMachinesOnline()` method, add the `Parallel.ForEach` loop and create the `ParallelOptions` variable that will specify the degree of parallelism. Wrap all this code inside a `try...catch` statement and catch an `AggregateException`:

```
try
{
    int machineCount = ipAddresses.Count();
    var options = new ParallelOptions();
    options.MaxDegreeOfParallelism = machineCount;
    int deadMachines = 0;

    Parallel.ForEach(ipAddresses, options, ip =>
    {

    });
}
catch (AggregateException aex)
{
    WriteLine("An AggregateException has occurred");
    throw;
}
```

3. Inside the `Parallel.ForEach` loop, write the code to check whether the machine is online by calling the `MachineReturnedPing()` method. In our example, this method will always return `false`. You will notice that we are keeping track of the offline machine count via the `Interlocked.Increment` method. This is just a way of incrementing a variable across the threads of the `Parallel.ForEach` loop:

```
if (MachineReturnedPing(ip))
{

}
else
{
    if (machineCount - Interlocked.Increment(ref deadMachines)
        < minimumLive)
    {
        WriteLine($"Machines to check = {machineCount}");
        WriteLine($"Dead machines = {deadMachines}");
        WriteLine($"Minimum machines required = {minimumLive}");
        WriteLine($"Live Machines = {machineCount - deadMachines}");
        throw new Exception($"Minimum machines requirement of
            {minimumLive} not met");
    }
```

}

4. If you have added all the code correctly, your Demo class will look like this:

```
public class Demo
{
  public void CheckClientMachinesOnline(List<string> ipAddresses,
    int minimumLive)
  {
    try
    {
      int machineCount = ipAddresses.Count();
      var options = new ParallelOptions();
      options.MaxDegreeOfParallelism = machineCount;
      int deadMachines = 0;

      Parallel.ForEach(ipAddresses, options, ip =>
      {
        if (MachineReturnedPing(ip))
        {

        }
        else
        {
          if (machineCount - Interlocked.Increment(
              ref deadMachines) < minimumLive)
          {
            WriteLine($"Machines to check = {machineCount}");
            WriteLine($"Dead machines = {deadMachines}");
            WriteLine($"Minimum machines required =
                    {minimumLive}");
            WriteLine($"Live Machines = {machineCount -
                    deadMachines}");
            throw new Exception($"Minimum machines requirement
                          of {minimumLive} not met");
          }
        }
      });
    }
    catch (AggregateException aex)
    {
      WriteLine("An AggregateException has occurred");
      throw;
    }
  }

  private bool MachineReturnedPing(string ip)
  {
```

```
        return false;
    }
}
```

5. In the console application, create the `List<string>` object to store a collection of dummy IP addresses. Instantiate your `Demo` class and call the `CheckClientMachinesOnline()` method, passing the collection of IP addresses and the minimum number of machines required to be online to it:

```
List<string> ipList = new List<string>();
for (int i = 0; i <= 10; i++)
{
    ipList.Add($"10.0.0.{i.ToString()}");
}

try
{
    Demo oRecipe = new Demo();
    oRecipe.CheckClientMachinesOnline(ipList, 2);
}
catch (Exception ex)
{
    WriteLine(ex.InnerException.Message);
}
ReadLine();
```

6. Run your application and review the output in the console window:

Just a point to note. If you have **Just My Code** enabled, in some cases Visual Studio will break on the line that throws the exception. It might also say that the exception is not handled by the user code. You can just press *F5* to continue. To prevent this from happening, uncheck **Enable Just My Code** under **Tools**, **Options**, **Debugging**, and **General**.

How it works...

From the console window output, you can see that the minimum number of machines required to be online was not achieved. The application then threw an exception and caught it from the `Parallel.ForEach` loop. Being able to handle exceptions in parallel loops such as this one is essential for maintaining the stability of your application by being able to handle exceptions as they occur.

I encourage you to play around a little with the `Parallel.ForEach` loop and drill into some of the inner methods of the `AggregareException` class to really understand it better.

Debugging multiple threads

Debugging multiple threads in Visual Studio is tricky, especially since these threads are all running at the same time. Luckily, we have a few tools available to us as developers to use to get a better understanding of what is happening in our multithreaded applications.

Getting ready

While debugging multithreaded applications, you can access various windows by navigating to **Debug** | **Windows** in Visual Studio.

How to do it...

1. Start debugging your multithreaded application after adding a break point somewhere in the code. You can access various debugging windows by going to **Debug | Windows** in Visual Studio:

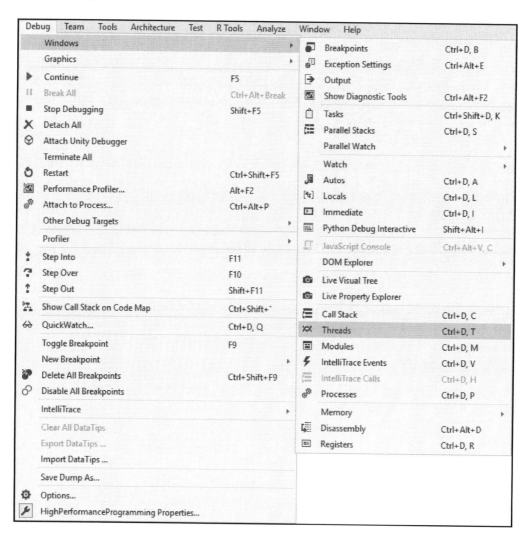

2. The first window available to you is the **Threads** window. Access it by going to **Debug | Windows** in Visual Studio or type *Ctrl + D, T*. In here, you can right-click on a thread to watch and flag it. If you have given your threads names, you will see those names appear in the **Name** column. To give your thread a name, modify the `LockThreadExample()` method created in an earlier recipe.

```
public void LockThreadExample()
{
  Task thread1 = Task.Factory.StartNew(() => ContendedResource(3));
  Task thread2 = Task.Factory.StartNew(() => ContendedResource(5));
  Task thread3 = Task.Factory.StartNew(() => ContendedResource(2));

  int threadID = Thread.CurrentThread.ManagedThreadId;
  Thread.CurrentThread.Name = $"New Thread{threadID}";

  Task.WaitAll(thread1, thread2, thread3);
  WriteLine("All tasks completed");
}
```

You will also be able to see the currently active thread in the debugger. It will be marked with a yellow arrow. Then, there is the managed ID, which is the same ID you will have used to create the unique thread name earlier on.

The **Location** column displays the current method that the thread is in. The **Threads** window allows you to view the stack of the thread by double-clicking on the **Location** field. You can also freeze and thaw threads. Freezing stops a thread from executing, while thawing allows the frozen thread to continue as normal.

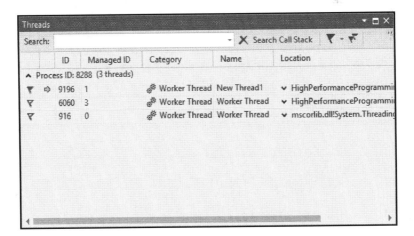

3. The **Tasks** window can be accessed by going to **Debug** I **Windows** or by holding down *Ctrl* + *Shift* + *D, K*. To see this in action, place a break point in your `LockThreadExample()` method on the line that reads `Task.WaitAll(thread1, thread2, thread3);`. Debug your application again and look at the **Status** column for each thread created. The status of the task shows the status at that moment, and we can see that the three threads are **Active**, **Blocked**, and **Scheduled**:

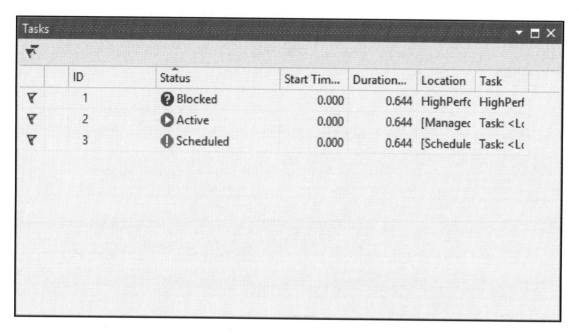

4. The **Parallel Stacks** window can be accessed by going to **Debug** I **Windows** in Visual Studio or by holding down *Ctrl* + *D* + *S* key. Here, you can see a graphical view of the tasks and threads. You can switch between the **Threads** and **Tasks** view by making a selection in the drop-down list in the upper-left corner of the **Parallel Stacks** window:

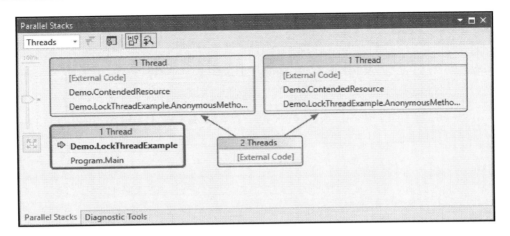

5. Changing the selection to **Tasks** will show you the current tasks in the debug session:

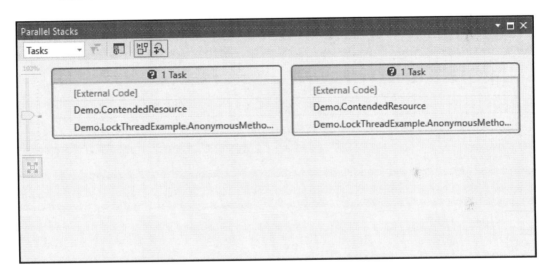

6. The next window, undoubtedly my favorite, is the **Parallel Watch** window. It is in fact identical to the standard **Watch** window in Visual Studio, but this watches values across all threads in your application. You can type any valid C# expression into **Parallel Watch** and see the values as they are at that moment in the debug session. Try it out by adding several break points and adding expressions into the **Parallel Watch**.

How it works...

Being able to use the debugging tools for multithreaded applications effectively in Visual Studio makes it much easier to understand the structure of your application and helps you identify possible bugs, bottlenecks, and areas of concern.

I encourage you to learn more about these various debugging windows available to you.

9

Composing Event-Based Programs Using Reactive Extensions

This chapter deals with **Reactive Extensions (Rx)**. To understand Rx, we will cover the following recipes:

- Installing Rx
- Events versus observables
- Using LINQ to perform queries
- Using schedulers in Rx
- Debugging lambda expressions

Introduction

Often, during your day-to-day dealings with developing applications in C#, you will have to use asynchronous programming. You might also have to deal with many data sources. Think of a web service that returns the current exchange rates, a Twitter search returning a stream of related data, or even different events generated by multiple computers. Rx provides an elegant solution in the form of the `IObserver<T>` interface.

You use the `IObserver<T>` interface to subscribe to the events. Then, the `IObservable<T>` interface, which maintains a list of `IObserver<T>` interfaces, will notify them of the change of state. In essence, Rx will stick together multiple data sources (social media, RSS feeds, UI events, and so on) that generate data. Rx, therefore, brings these data sources together in one interface. In fact, Rx can be thought of as consisting of three sections:

- **Observables**: The interface that brings together and represents all these datastreams
- **Language-Integrated Query (LINQ)**: The ability to use LINQ to query these multiple datastreams
- **Schedulers**: Parameterizing concurrency using schedulers

The question on many minds might be why developers should use (or find a use for) Rx. Here are a few examples where Rx is really useful.

- Creating a search that has an autocomplete function. You don't want the code to perform a search for each value you type into the search area. Rx allows you to throttle the search.
- Making the UI of your application more responsive.
- Being notified when data changes instead of having to poll the data for changes. Think of real-time stock prices.

To keep up to date with Rx, you can take a look at the `https://github.com/Reactive-Extensions/Rx.NET` GitHub page.

Installing Rx

Before we can begin exploring Rx, we need to install it. The easiest way to do this is using NuGet.

Getting ready

For this chapter on Rx, we will not create a separate class. All the code will be written in a console application.

How to do it...

1. Create a console application, and then right-click on your solution and select **Manage NuGet Packages for Solution...** from the context menu.

2. In the window that is displayed afterwards, type in `System.Reactive` in the search textbox and search for the NuGet installer:

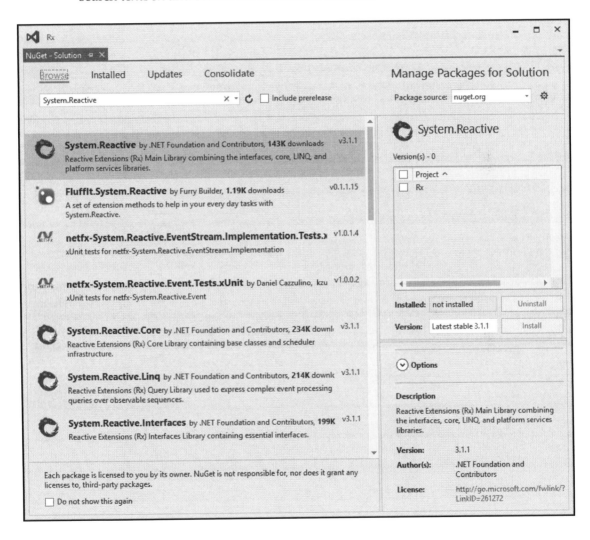

3. At the time of writing this book, the last stable release was version 3.1.1. If you have more than a single project, select the projects that you want to install Rx on. Seeing that we only have a single Console application, just select Rx to be installed for the whole project.

4. The next screen that is displayed is a confirmation dialog box, asking you to confirm the changes to the project. It will show a preview of the changes it will be making to each project. If you are happy with the changes, click on the **OK** button.

5. A license agreement might be presented to you in the last dialog screen, which you will need to accept. To continue, click on the **I Accept** button.

6. After the installation is complete, you will see the references added to the Rx under the **References** node in your project. These are as follows:

   - `System.Reactive.Core`
   - `System.Reactive.Interfaces`
   - `System.Reactive.Linq`
   - `System.Reactive.PlatformServices`

How it works...

NuGet is by far the easiest way to add additional components to your projects. As you can see from the added references, `System.Reactive` is the main assembly. To gain a better understanding of `System.Reactive`, view the assemblies in **Object Browser**. To do this, double-click on any of the assemblies in the **References** option of your project. This will display the **Object Browser**:

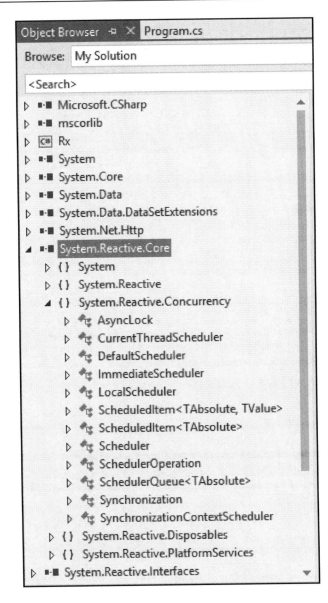

`System.Reactive.Linq` contains all the querying functionality in Rx. You will also notice that `System.Reactive.Concurrency` contains all the schedulers.

Events versus observables

Being developers, we should all be quite familiar with events. Most developers have been creating events since we started writing code. In fact, if you have even dropped a button control on a form and double-clicked the button to create the method that handles the click of the button, you have created an event. In .NET, we can declare events using the `event` keyword, publish to the event by invoking it, and subscribe to that event by adding a handler to the event. We, therefore, have the following operations:

- Declare
- Publish
- Subscribe

With Rx, we have a similar structure where we declare a datastream, publish data to that stream, and subscribe to it.

Getting ready

First, we will see how an event works in C#. We will then see the working of an event using Rx and, in doing so, highlight the differences.

How to do it...

1. In your console application, add a new class called `DotNet`. To this class, add a property called `AvailableDatatype`:

```
public class DotNet
{
    public string  AvailableDatatype { get; set; }
}
```

2. In the main program class, add a new static action event called `types`. Basically, this is just a delegate and will receive some value; in our case, the available .NET data types:

```
class Program
{
    // Static action event
    static event Action<string> types;
```

```
static void Main(string[] args)
{

}
}
```

3. Inside `void Main`, create a `List<DotNet>` class called `lstTypes`. Inside this list, add several values of type `DotNet` class. Here, we will just add hardcoded data of some of the data types in .NET:

```
List<DotNet> lstTypes = new List<DotNet>();
DotNet blnTypes = new DotNet();
blnTypes.AvailableDatatype = "bool";
lstTypes.Add(blnTypes);

DotNet strTypes = new DotNet();
strTypes.AvailableDatatype = "string";
lstTypes.Add(strTypes);

DotNet intTypes = new DotNet();
intTypes.AvailableDatatype = "int";
lstTypes.Add(intTypes);

DotNet decTypes = new DotNet();
decTypes.AvailableDatatype = "decimal";
lstTypes.Add(decTypes);
```

4. Our next task is to subscribe to this event with an event handler that is simply outputting the value of *x* to the console window. We then raise the event each time we loop through our `lstTypes` list by adding the line `types(lstTypes[i].AvailableDatatype);`:

```
types += x =>
{
  Console.WriteLine(x);
};

for (int i = 0; i <= lstTypes.Count - 1; i++)
{
  types(lstTypes[i].AvailableDatatype);
}

Console.ReadLine();
```

In reality, before raising an event we should always check that the event isn't null. Only after this check should we raise the event. For brevity, we have not added this check before raising the event.

5. When you have added all the code from step 1 to step 4, your console application should look like this:

```
class Program
{
  // Static action event
  static event Action<string> types;

  static void Main(string[] args)
  {
    List<DotNet> lstTypes = new List<DotNet>();
    DotNet blnTypes = new DotNet();
    blnTypes.AvailableDatatype = "bool";
    lstTypes.Add(blnTypes);

    DotNet strTypes = new DotNet();
    strTypes.AvailableDatatype = "string";
    lstTypes.Add(strTypes);

    DotNet intTypes = new DotNet();
    intTypes.AvailableDatatype = "int";
    lstTypes.Add(intTypes);

   DotNet decTypes = new DotNet();
    decTypes.AvailableDatatype = "decimal";
    lstTypes.Add(decTypes);

    types += x =>
    {
      Console.WriteLine(x);
    };

    for (int i = 0; i <= lstTypes.Count - 1; i++)
    {
      types(lstTypes[i].AvailableDatatype);
    }

    Console.ReadLine();
  }
}
```

6. Running your application will set our list with values and then raise the event created to output the values of the list to the console window:

7. Let's see the working of events using Rx. Add a static `Subject` of `string`. You might also need to add the `System.Reactive.Subjects` namespace to your project as `Subjects` live in this separate namespace:

```
class Program
{

    static Subject<string> obsTypes = new Subject<string>();

  static void Main(string[] args)
    {

    }
  }
}
```

8. After the code that created the list of `DotNet`, we used `+=` to wire up an event handler. This time round, we will use `Subscribe`. This is the `IObservable` portion of the code. After you've added this, raise the event using the `OnNext` keyword. This is the `IObserver` portion of the code. Therefore, as we loop through our list, we will call `OnNext` to pump out the values to the subscribed `IObservable` interface:

```
// IObservable
obsTypes.Subscribe(x =>
{
  Console.WriteLine(x);
});

// IObserver
for (int i = 0; i <= lstTypes.Count - 1; i++)
{
  obsTypes.OnNext(lstTypes[i].AvailableDatatype);
}

Console.ReadLine();
```

9. When you've completed adding all the code, your application should look like this:

```
class Program
{
  static Subject<string> obsTypes = new Subject<string>();

  static void Main(string[] args)
  {
    List<DotNet> lstTypes = new List<DotNet>();
    DotNet blnTypes = new DotNet();
    blnTypes.AvailableDatatype = "bool";
    lstTypes.Add(blnTypes);

    DotNet strTypes = new DotNet();
    strTypes.AvailableDatatype = "string";
    lstTypes.Add(strTypes);

    DotNet intTypes = new DotNet();
    intTypes.AvailableDatatype = "int";
    lstTypes.Add(intTypes);

    DotNet decTypes = new DotNet();
    decTypes.AvailableDatatype = "decimal";
    lstTypes.Add(decTypes);
```

```
// IObservable
obsTypes.Subscribe(x =>
{
    Console.WriteLine(x);
});

// IObserver
for (int i = 0; i <= lstTypes.Count - 1; i++)
{
    obsTypes.OnNext(lstTypes[i].AvailableDatatype);
}

Console.ReadLine();
    }
}
```

10. When you run your application, you will see the same items are output to the console window, as it did earlier.

How it works...

In Rx, we can declare an event stream with the `Subject` keyword. So, we have a source of events that we can publish to using `OnNext`. To see those values in the console window, we subscribed to the event stream using `Subscribe`.

Rx allows you to have objects that are just publishers or just subscribers. This is because the `IObservable` and `IObserver` interfaces are in fact separate. Also, note that in Rx, the observables can be passed as parameters, returned as results, and stored in variables, which makes them first class.

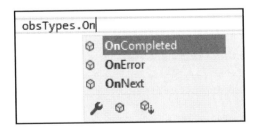

Rx also allows you to specify that the event stream is completed or that an error occurred. This really sets Rx apart from events in .NET. Also, it is important to note that including the `System.Reactive.Linq` namespace in your project allows developers to write queries over the `Subject` type because a `Subject` is an `IObservable` interface:

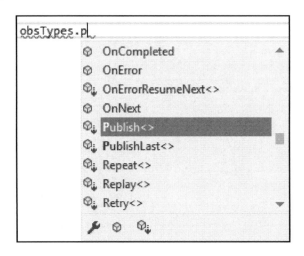

This is another feature that sets Rx apart from the events in .NET.

Using LINQ to perform queries

Rx allows developers to use the `IObservable` interface, which represents synchronous datastreams, to write queries using LINQ. To recap, Rx can be thought of as consisting of three sections:

- **Observables**: The interface that brings together and represents all these datastreams
- **Language-Integrated Query (LINQ)**: The ability to use LINQ to query these multiple datastreams
- **Schedulers**: Parameterizing concurrency using schedulers

In this recipe, we will be looking at the LINQ functionality of Rx in more detail.

Getting ready

As observables are just datastreams, we can use LINQ to query them. In the following recipe, we will output text to the screen based on a LINQ query.

How to do it...

1. Start by adding a new Windows forms project to your solution.

2. Call the project `winformRx` and click on the **OK** button:

3. In **Toolbox**, search for the **TextBox** control and add it to your form.

4. Finally, add a label control to your form:

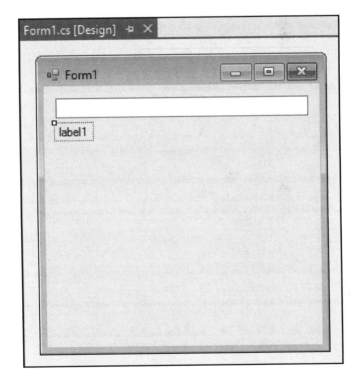

5. Right-click on your `winformRx` project and select **Manage NuGet Packages...** from the context menu.

6. In the search textbox, enter `System.Reactive` to search for the NuGet package and click on the **Install** button.

7. Visual Studio will ask you to review the changes it's about to make to your project. Click on the **OK** button.

8. Before the installation starts, you might need to accept the license agreement by clicking on the **I Accept** button.

9. After the installation completes, you should see the newly added references to your `winformRx` project if you expand the **References** for the project:

10. Finally, right-click on the project and set `winformRx` as your startup project by clicking on the **Set as StartUp Project** from the context menu.

11. Create the form load event handler for the form by double-clicking anywhere on the Windows form. To this form, add the `Observable` keyword. You will notice that the keyword is immediately underlined. This is because you are missing the reference to the LINQ assembly of `System.Reactive`.

12. To add this, press *Ctrl + .* (period) to bring up the possible suggestions to fix the issue. Select to add the `using System.Reactive.Linq` namespace to your project.

13. Continue adding the following code to your form load event. Basically, you are using LINQ and telling the compiler that you want to select the text from the event pattern that matches the text changed event of the textbox on the form called `textBox1`. After you have done that, add a subscription to the variable and tell it to output whatever it finds in the text to the label on the form called `label1`:

```
private void Form1_Load(object sender, EventArgs e)
{
    var searchTerm = Observable.FromEventPattern<EventArgs>(
        textBox1, "TextChanged").Select(x => ((TextBox)x.Sender).Text);

    searchTerm.Subscribe(trm => label1.Text = trm);
}
```

When we added the textbox and label to our form, we left the control names as default. If, however, you changed the default names, you would need to specify those names instead of `textBox1` and `label1` for the controls on the form.

14. Click on the run button to run your application. The Windows form will be displayed with the textbox and label on it.

15. Notice that as you type, the text is output to the label on the form:

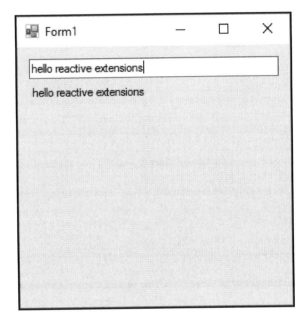

16. Let's jazz things up a bit by adding in a `Where` condition to the LINQ statement. We will specify that the `text` string must only select the text when it ends with a period. This means that the text will only be displayed in the label after each full sentence. As you can see, we aren't doing anything special here. We are merely using standard LINQ to query our datastream and return the results to our `searchTerm` variable:

```
private void Form1_Load(object sender, EventArgs e)
{
    var searchTerm = Observable.FromEventPattern<EventArgs>(
      textBox1, "TextChanged").Select(x => ((TextBox)x.Sender)
      .Text).Where(text => text.EndsWith("."));

    searchTerm.Subscribe(trm => label1.Text = trm);
}
```

17. Run your application and start typing in a line of text. You will see that nothing is output to the label control as you type, as was evident in the previous example before we added in our `Where` condition:

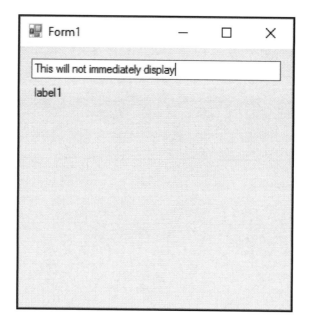

18. Add a period and start adding a second line of text:

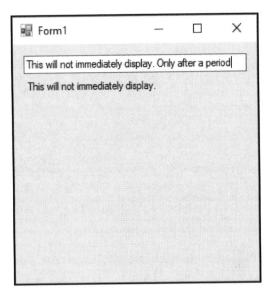

19. You will see that only after each period, the text entered is added to the label. Our `Where` condition is, therefore, working perfectly:

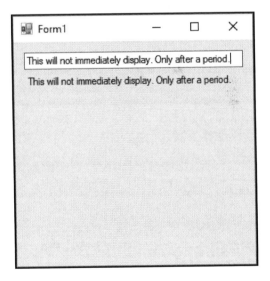

How it works...

The LINQ aspect of Rx allows developers to construct observables. Here are some examples:

- `Observable.Empty<>`: This returns an empty observable sequence
- `Observable.Return<>`: This returns an observable sequence containing a single element
- `Observable.Throw<>`: This returns an observable sequence terminating with an exception
- `Observable.Never<>`: This returns a non-terminating observable sequence that is infinite in duration

The use of LINQ in Rx allows the developer to manipulate and filter the datastream to return exactly what they need.

Using schedulers in Rx

Sometimes, we need to have an `IObservable` subscription run at a specific time. Imagine having to synchronize events across servers in different geographical areas and time zones. You might also need to read data from a queue while preserving the order in which the events occur. Another example would be to perform some kind of I/O task that could take some time to complete. Schedulers come in very handy in these situations.

Getting ready

Additionally, you can consider reading up more on using schedulers on MSDN. Take a look at `https://msdn.microsoft.com/en-us/library/hh242963(v=vs.103).aspx`.

How to do it...

1. If you haven't already done so, create a new Windows form application and call it `winformRx`. Open the form designer and in **Toolbox**, search for the **TextBox** control and add it to your form.

2. Next, add a label control to your form.

3. Double-click on your Windows form designer to create the onload event handler. Inside this handler, add some code to read the text entered into the textbox and only display that text 5 seconds after the user has stopped typing. This is achieved using the `Throttle` keyword. Add a subscription to the `searchTerm` variable, writing the result of the text input to the label control's text property:

```
private void Form1_Load(object sender, EventArgs e)
{
    var searchTerm = Observable.FromEventPattern<EventArgs>(
        textBox1, "TextChanged").Select(x => ((TextBox)x.Sender)
        .Text).Throttle(TimeSpan.FromMilliseconds(5000));

    searchTerm.Subscribe(trm => label1.Text = trm);
}
```

 Note that you might need to add `System.Reactive.Linq` in your `using` statements.

4. Run your application and start typing some text into the textbox. Immediately, we will receive an exception. It is a cross-thread violation. This occurs when there is an attempt to update the UI from a background thread. The `Observable` interface is running a timer from `System.Threading`, which isn't on the same thread as the UI. Luckily, there is an easy way to overcome this. Well, it turns out that the UI-threading capabilities lie in a different assembly, which we find easiest to get via the **Package Manager Console**:

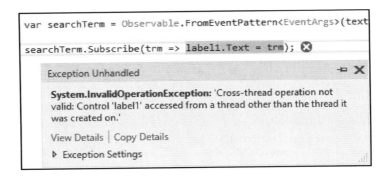

5. Navigate to **View | Other Windows | Package Manager Console** to access the **Package Manager Console**.

6. Enter the following command:

```
PM> Install-Package System.Reactive.Windows.Forms
```

This will add the **System.Reactive.Windows.Forms.3.1.1** to your `winformRx` project. You should, therefore, see the following in the output: **Successfully installed 'System.Reactive.Windows.Forms 3.1.1' to winformRx**

 Note that you need to ensure that the **Default project** selection is set to `winformRx` in the **Package Manager Console**. If you don't see this option, resize the **Package Manager Console** screen width ways until the option is displayed. This way you can be certain that the package is added to the correct project.

7. After the installation completes, modify your code in the onload event handler and change `searchTerm.Subscribe(trm => label1.Text = trm);`, which does the subscription, to look like this:

```
searchTerm.ObserveOn(new ControlScheduler(this)).Subscribe(trm =>
label1.Text = trm);
```

You will notice that we are using the `ObserveOn` method here. What this basically tells the compiler is that the `this` keyword in `new ControlScheduler(this)` is actually a reference to our Windows form. Therefore, `ControlScheduler` will use the Windows forms timers to create the interval to update our UI. The message happens on the correct thread, and we no longer have our cross-thread violation.

8. If you have not added the `System.Reactive.Concurrency` namespace to your project, Visual Studio will underline the `ControlScheduler` line of code with a squiggly line. Pressing *Ctrl + . (period)* will allow you to add the missing namespace.

9. This means that `System.Reactive.Concurrency` contains a scheduler that can talk to Windows forms controls so that it can do the scheduling. Run your application again and start typing some text into your textbox:

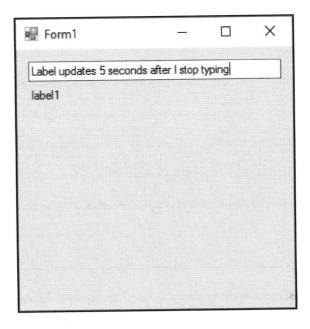

10. Around 5 seconds after we stop typing, the throttle condition is fulfilled and the text is output to our label:

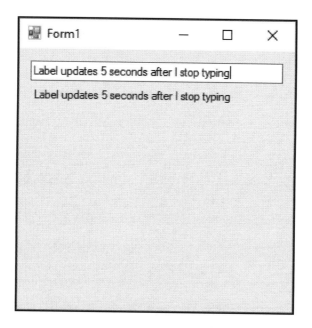

How it works...

What we need to keep in mind here from the code we created is that there is ObserveOn and Subscribe. You should not confuse the two. In most cases, when dealing with schedulers, you will use ObserveOn. The ObserveOn method allows you to parameterize where the OnNext, OnCompleted, and OnError messages run. With Subscribe, we parameterize where the actual subscribe and unsubscribe code runs.

We also need to remember that Rx uses the threading timers (System.Threading.Timer) as a default, which is why we encountered the cross-thread violation earlier. As you saw though, we used schedulers to parameterize which timer to use. The way schedulers do this is by exposing three components. These are as follows:

- The scheduler's ability to perform some action
- The order in which the action or work to be performed is executed
- A clock that allows the scheduler to have a notion of time

The use of a clock is important because it allows the developer to use timers on remote machines; for example (where there might be a time difference between you and them), to tell them to perform an action at a particular time.

Debugging lambda expressions

The ability to debug lambda expressions has been around since Visual Studio 2015. This is a fantastic addition to the features of our favorite IDE. It allows us to check the results of a lambda expression on the fly and modify the expression to test different scenarios.

Getting ready

We will create a very basic lambda expression and change it in the **Watch** window to produce a different value.

How to do it...

1. Create a console application and add a class called `LambdaExample` to the console application. Add a property to this class called `FavThings`:

```
public class LambdaExample
{
    public string FavThings { get; set; }
}
```

2. In the console application, create a `List<LambdaExample>` object and add a few of your favorite things to this list:

```
List<LambdaExample> MyFavoriteThings = new List<LambdaExample>();
LambdaExample thing1 = new LambdaExample();
thing1.FavThings = "Ice-cream";
MyFavoriteThings.Add(thing1);

LambdaExample thing2 = new LambdaExample();
thing2.FavThings = "Summer Rain";
MyFavoriteThings.Add(thing2);

LambdaExample thing3 = new LambdaExample();
thing3.FavThings = "Sunday morning snooze";
MyFavoriteThings.Add(thing3);
```

3. Then, create an expression to return only the things starting with the string "Sum". Here, we would obviously expect to see Summer Rain as a result:

```
var filteredStuff = MyFavoriteThings.Where(feature =>
feature.FavThings.StartsWith("Sum"));
```

4. Place a breakpoint on the expression and run your application. When the code stops at the breakpoint, you can copy the lambda expression:

```
static void Main(string[] args)
{
    List<LambdaExample> MyFavoriteThings = new List<LambdaExample>();
    LambdaExample thing1 = new LambdaExample();
    thing1.FavoriteFeature = "Ice-cream";
    MyFavoriteThings.Add(thing1);

    LambdaExample thing2 = new LambdaExample();
    thing2.FavoriteFeature = "Summer Rain";
    MyFavoriteThings.Add(thing2);

    LambdaExample thing3 = new LambdaExample();
    thing3.FavoriteFeature = "Sunday morning snooze";
    MyFavoriteThings.Add(thing3);

    var filteredStuff = MyFavoriteThings.Where(feature =>
    feature.FavoriteFeature.StartsWith("Sum"));
}
```

5. Paste the lambda expression MyFavoriteThings.Where(feature => feature.FavThings.StartsWith("Sum")) into your **Watch** windows and change the string in the StartsWith method from Sum to Ice. You will see that the result has changed and now displays an Ice-cream string:

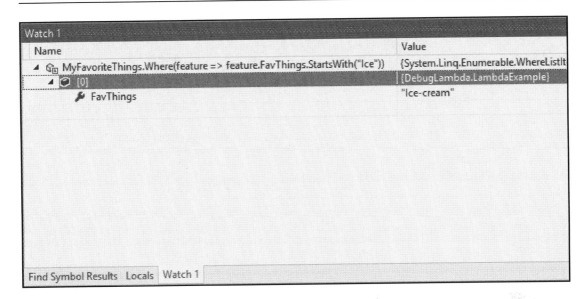

Name	Value
▲ MyFavoriteThings.Where(feature => feature.FavThings.StartsWith("Ice"))	{System.Linq.Enumerable.WhereListIt
▲ [0]	{DebugLambda.LambdaExample}
FavThings	"Ice-cream"

Find Symbol Results Locals Watch 1

Note that if you are using Visual Studio 2017 RC, debugging lambda expressions will probably not work. You will receive anything from **Internal error in the expression evaluator** to a message stating **Expression cannot contain lambda expression**.

How it works...

In this way, we're able to change and debug a lambda expression easily. This is something that was not possible in the previous versions before Visual Studio 2015. It is obviously of great importance to know this tip when working with these expressions.

Another point to note is that you can do the same thing from the **Immediate** window in Visual Studio 2017, as well as pinned variables from the lambda expression.

10
Exploring .NET Core 1.1

This chapter will explore .NET Core 1.1. We will see what .NET Core is and what you can do with it. We will be looking at:

- Creating a simple .NET Core application and running it on a Mac
- Creating your first ASP.NET Core application
- Publishing your ASP.NET Core application

Introduction

There is a lot of buzz these days regarding .NET Core. There are really a lot of articles explaining what .NET Core is and what it does. Simply put, .NET Core allows you to create cross-platform applications that run on Windows, Linux, and macOS. It does this by leveraging a .NET Standard Library that targets all these platforms with the exact same code. You can, therefore, use the language and tools you are comfortable with to create applications. It supports C#, VB, and F#, and even allows the use of constructs such as generics, async support, and LINQ. For more information and documentation on .NET Core, go to `https://www.microsoft.com/net/core`.

Creating a simple .NET Core application and running it on a Mac

We will take a look at how to create an application on Windows using Visual Studio 2017 and then running that application on a Mac. This kind of application development was previously impossible as you could not run code compiled for Windows on a Mac. .NET Core changes all this.

Getting ready

You will need access to a Mac in order to run the application you created. I'm using a Mac mini (late 2012) with a 2.5 GHz Intel Core i5 CPU running macOS Sierra with 4GB of memory.

In order to use your .NET Core apps on a Mac, there are a few things you need to do:

1. We need to install Homebrew, which is used to get the latest version of OpenSSL. Open the Terminal on your Mac by typing `Terminal` into your Spotlight search:

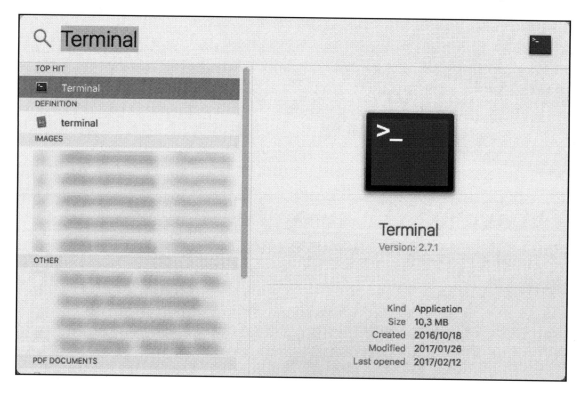

 The following steps can also be completed by going to `https://www.microso ft.com/net/core#macos` and performing these on your Mac.

2. Paste the following at the Terminal prompt and press *Enter*:

```
/usr/bin/ruby -e "$(curl -fSSL
https://raw.githubusercontent.com/Homebrew/install/master/install)"
```

3. If the Terminal asks you for your password, enter your password and press *Enter*. You will not see anything as you type. This is normal. Just type your password and press *Enter* to continue.

 The requirements for installing Homebrew are an Intel CPU, OS X 10.10 or higher, **Command Line Tools (CLT)** for Xcode, and a Bourne-compatible shell for installation, such as bash or zsh. Terminal is thus well suited.

Depending on the speed of your Internet connection and whether you have CLT for Xcode installed, the process of installing Homebrew can take some time to complete. When completed, the Terminal should look as follows:

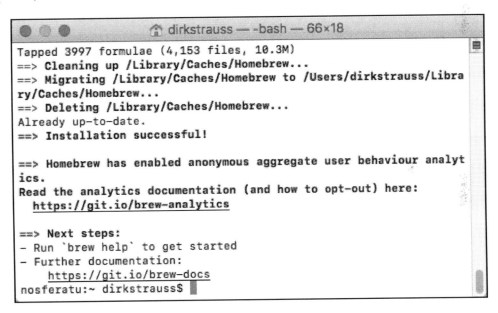

Typing in `brew help` will show you some useful commands you can use:

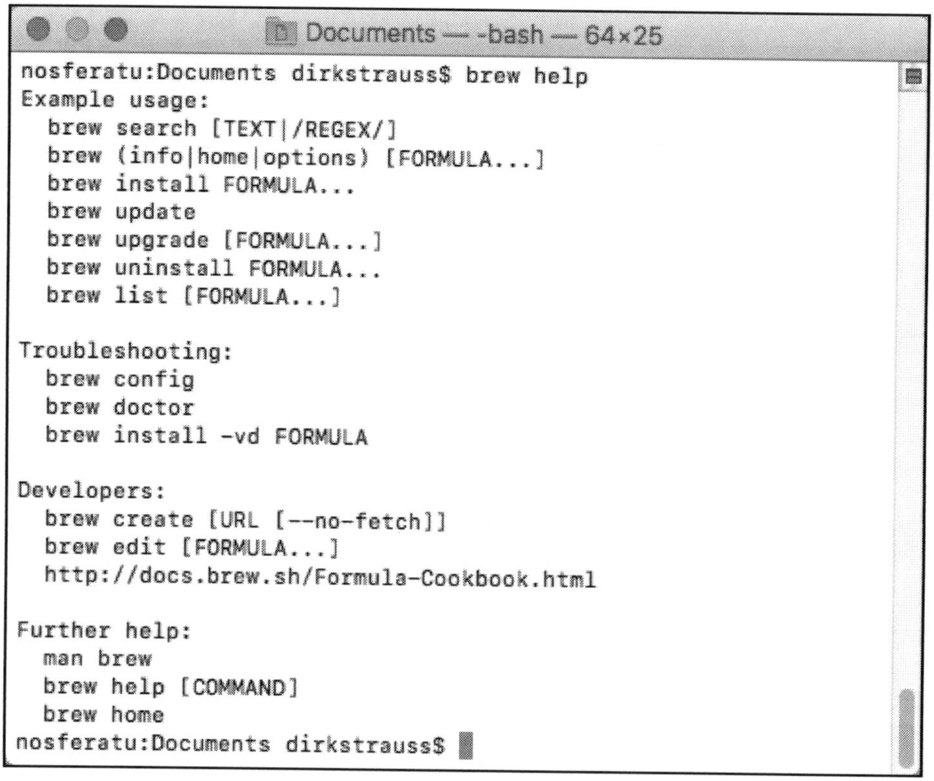
Documents — -bash — 64×25
nosferatu:Documents dirkstrauss$ brew help
Example usage:
brew search [TEXT|/REGEX/]
brew (info|home|options) [FORMULA...]
brew install FORMULA...
brew update
brew upgrade [FORMULA...]
brew uninstall FORMULA...
brew list [FORMULA...]
Troubleshooting:
brew config
brew doctor
brew install -vd FORMULA
Developers:
brew create [URL [--no-fetch]]
brew edit [FORMULA...]
http://docs.brew.sh/Formula-Cookbook.html
Further help:
man brew
brew help [COMMAND]
brew home
nosferatu:Documents dirkstrauss$

Run the following commands one after the other in the Terminal:

- `brew update`
- `brew install openssl`
- `mkdir -p /usr/local/lib`
- `ln -s /usr/local/opt/openssl/lib/libcrypto.1.0.0.dylib /usr/local/lib/`
- `ln -s /usr/local/opt/openssl/lib/libssl.1.0.0.dylib /usr/local/lib/`

We then need to install the .NET Code SDK. From the URL `https://www.microsoft.com/n et/core#macos` click on the **Download .NET Core SDK** button. After the download has completed, click on the `.pkg` file downloaded. Click on the **Continue** button to install the .NET Core 1.1.0 SDK:

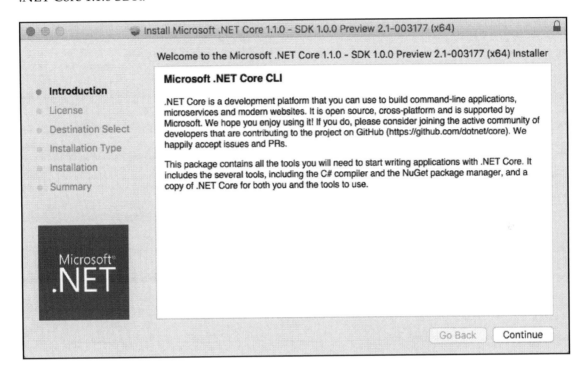

How to do it...

1. We will create a .NET Core console application in Visual Studio 2017. Under Visual C# templates, select **.NET Core** and a **Console App (.NET Core)** project:

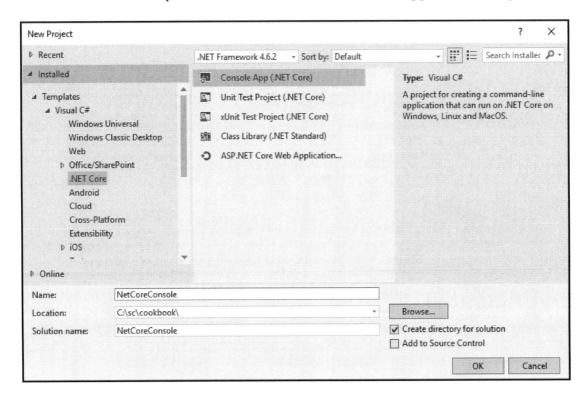

2. When you created your console application, the code will look as follows:

```
using System;

class Program
{
  static void Main(string[] args)
  {
    Console.WriteLine("Hello World!");
  }
}
```

3. Modify your code to look as follows:

```
static void Main(string[] args)
{
  Console.WriteLine("I can run on Windows, Linux and macOS");
  GetSystemInfo();
  Console.ReadLine();
}

private static void GetSystemInfo()
{
    var osInfo =
System.Runtime.InteropServices.RuntimeInformation.OSDescription;
    Console.WriteLine($"Current OS is: {osInfo}");
}
```

4. The method `GetSystemInfo()` just returns the current operating system the console application currently runs on. The `csproj` file for my application looks as follows:

```xml
<Project ToolsVersion="15.0"
  xmlns="http://schemas.microsoft.com/developer/msbuild/2003">
  <Import Project="$(MSBuildExtensionsPath)$(MSBuildToolsVersion)
    Microsoft.Common.props" />
    <PropertyGroup>
      <OutputType>Exe</OutputType>
      <TargetFramework>netcoreapp1.1</TargetFramework>
    </PropertyGroup>
    <ItemGroup>
      <Compile Include="***.cs" />
      <EmbeddedResource Include="***.resx" />
    </ItemGroup>
    <ItemGroup>
      <PackageReference Include="Microsoft.NETCore.App">
        <Version>1.1.0</Version>
      </PackageReference>
      <PackageReference Include="Microsoft.NET.Sdk">
        <Version>1.0.0-alpha-20161104-2</Version>
        <PrivateAssets>All</PrivateAssets>
      </PackageReference>
    </ItemGroup>
  <Import Project="$(MSBuildToolsPath)Microsoft.CSharp.targets" />
</Project>
```

The `<version>` is defined as `1.1.0`.

If you are still running Visual Studio 2017 RC, it would be a good idea to check your installed NuGet packages to see whether there is an update available for your .NET Core version from .NET Core 1.0 to .NET Core 1.1.

How it works...

Press *F5* to run your console application. You will see that the OS is displayed in the output:

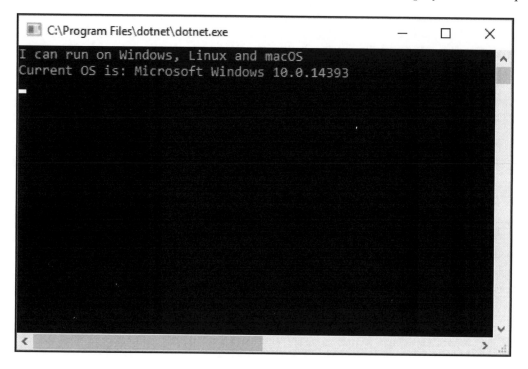

Go to the `bin` folder of your console application and copy the files to a folder on the desktop of your Mac. Call that folder `consoleApp`. In Terminal, navigate to the folder with the copied files. You can do this by typing the command `cd ./Desktop` and then type `ls` to list the contents of your desktop. Check if the folder you created is listed, and if so, in Terminal type `cd ./consoleApp`. List the contents of the `consoleApp` folder again by typing `ls`. In my case, the DLL was called `NetCoreConsole.dll`. To run the code you wrote earlier, type `dotnet NetCoreConsole.dll` and press *Enter*:

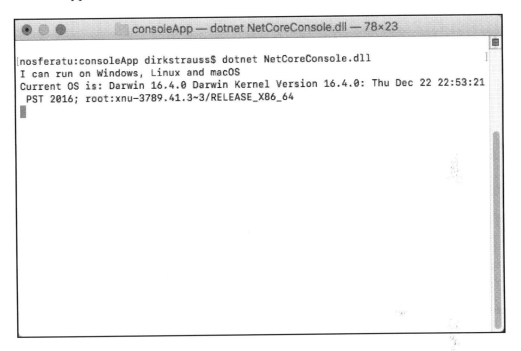

You can see that the code is run and the text output in Terminal.

If, by any chance, you find that trying to run the `dotnet` command (after installing the .NET Core SDK) results in an error saying `command not found`, try the following. In Terminal type the following and press Enter: `ln -s /usr/local/share/dotnet/dotnet /usr/local/bin/`, which adds a symbolic link. Running the `dotnet` command should work after this.

Creating your first ASP.NET Core application

Let's take a look at building your first ASP.NET Core app. In this recipe, we will just create a very basic ASP.NET Core application and briefly discuss the `Startup` class. Further reading on the subject will be required and is not included in this brief introduction to ASP.NET Core.

Getting ready

Start off by creating a new project in Visual Studio 2017. Under **Visual C#**, select the **.NET Core** node and click on the **ASP.NET Core Web Application....** Click on **OK**:

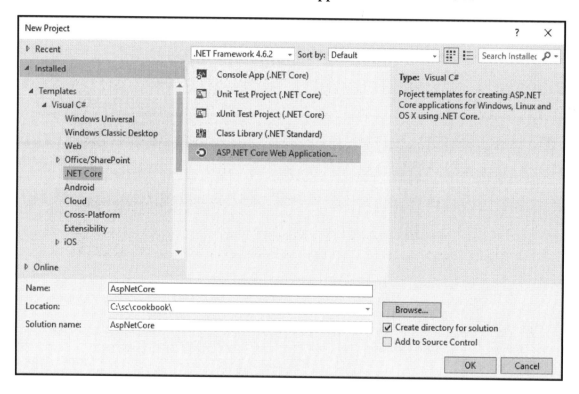

You will then be presented with the project template selection. You can choose to create an empty application, a **Web API** (allows you to create an HTTP-based API), or a full **Web Application**. Select the **Empty** template, make sure that **Host in the cloud** is unchecked, and and click on **OK**:

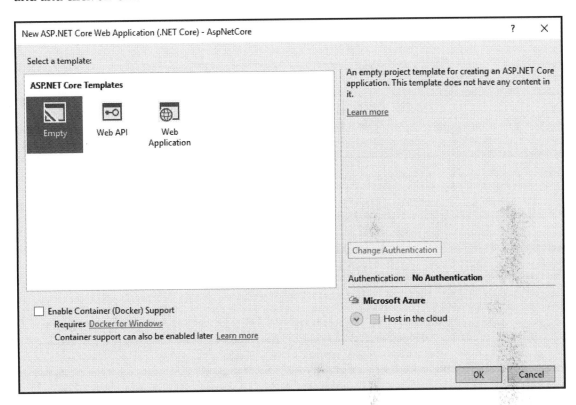

 Note how the templates window allows you to enable Docker support. Docker allows you to develop applications inside containers that contain a complete file system and everything else required to run your application. This means that your software will always function exactly the same, regardless of the environment it is in. For more on Docker, visit
www.docker.com.

When your ASP.NET Core application is created, your **Solution Explorer** will look as follows:

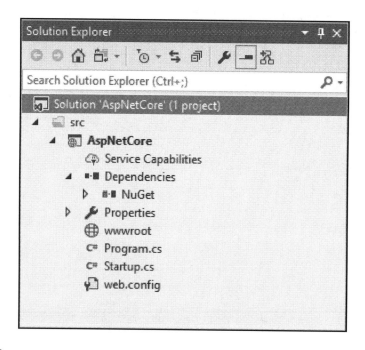

 If you are running Visual Studio 2017 RC, what you need to do is click on **Tools, NuGet Package Manager, Manage NuGet Packages for Solution...** and see if there are any updates to .NET Core. If you are on .NET Core 1.01, there should be an update to .NET Core 1.1 available via NuGet. Let NuGet update your project dependencies for you. After doing this, you must browse to https://www.microsoft.com/net/download/core#/curr ent and make sure that you have selected the **Current** option under **All downloads**. Download the current .NET Core SDK installer for Windows and install it.

At this point, you can press *Ctrl + F5* to **Start without Debugging** and launch your ASP.NET Core application. This will start IIS Express, which is the default host for ASP.NET Core applications. The only thing it does now is to display the text **Hello World!**. You have successfully created and run an ASP.NET Core application. Don't close your browser yet. Keep it open:

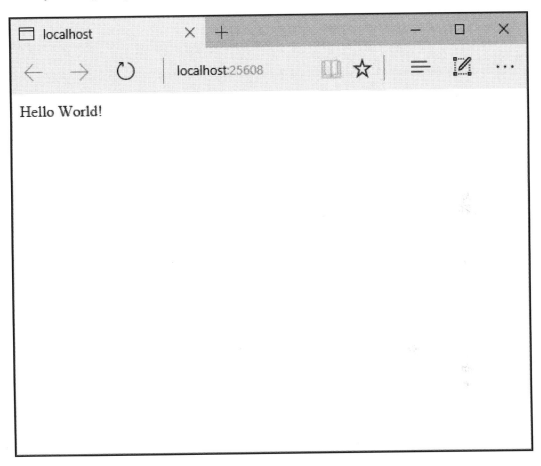

 Note that the port number **25608** in the URL of the browser is a randomly selected port. The port number you will see will most likely be different than in the book.

How to do it...

1. Right-click on the solution in your**Solution Explorer** and click on **Open Folder in File Explorer**. You will notice that you have a folder called `src`. Click into this folder and click on the `AspNetCore` sub-folder inside it:

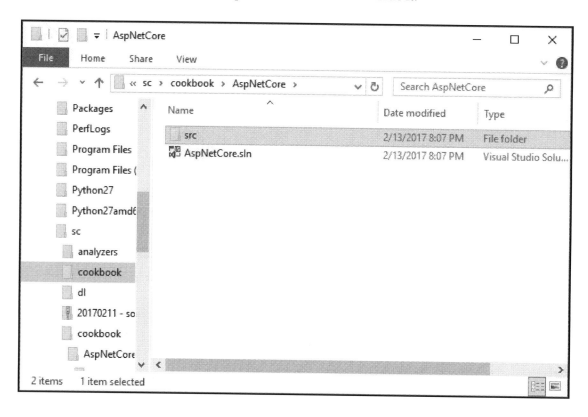

2. Comparing the contents of the `AspNetCore` folder and the **Solution Explorer** in Visual Studio will show you that they are virtually the same. This is because in ASP.NET Core, the Windows file system determines the solution in Visual Studio:

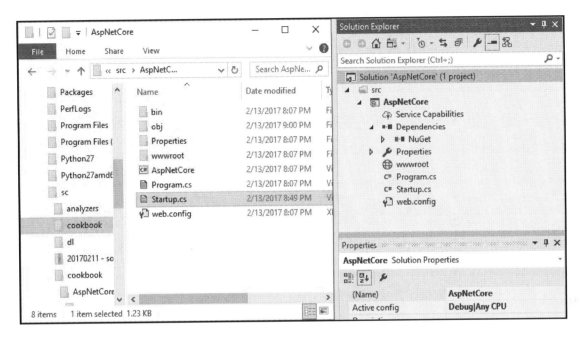

3. In the Windows file explorer, right-click on the `Startup.cs` file and edit it in Notepad. You will see the following code in Notepad:

```
using System;
using System.Collections.Generic;
using System.Linq;
using System.Threading.Tasks;
using Microsoft.AspNetCore.Builder;
using Microsoft.AspNetCore.Hosting;
using Microsoft.AspNetCore.Http;
using Microsoft.Extensions.DependencyInjection;
using Microsoft.Extensions.Logging;
```

```
namespace AspNetCore
{
  public class Startup
  {
    // This method gets called by the runtime. Use this method
       to add services to the container.
    // For more information on how to configure your application,
       visit https://go.microsoft.com/fwlink/?LinkID=398940
    public void ConfigureServices(IServiceCollection services)
    {
    }

    // This method gets called by the runtime. Use this method
       to configure the HTTP request pipeline.
    public void Configure(IApplicationBuilder app,
      IHostingEnvironment env, ILoggerFactory loggerFactory)
    {
      loggerFactory.AddConsole();

      if (env.IsDevelopment())
      {
        app.UseDeveloperExceptionPage();
      }

      app.Run(async (context) =>
      {
        await context.Response.WriteAsync("Hello World!");
      });
    }
  }
}
```

4. Still in Notepad, edit the line that reads `await`
   `context.Response.WriteAsync("Hello World!");` and change it to
   read `await context.Response.WriteAsync($"The date is`
   `{DateTime.Now.ToString("dd MMM yyyy")}");`. Save the file in Notepad
   and go to the browser and refresh it. You will see that the changes are displayed
   in the browser without me having to edit it in Visual Studio at all. This is because
   (as mentioned earlier) Visual Studio uses the file system to determine the project
   structure and ASP.NET Core detected the changes to the `Startup.cs` file and
   automatically recompiled it on the fly:

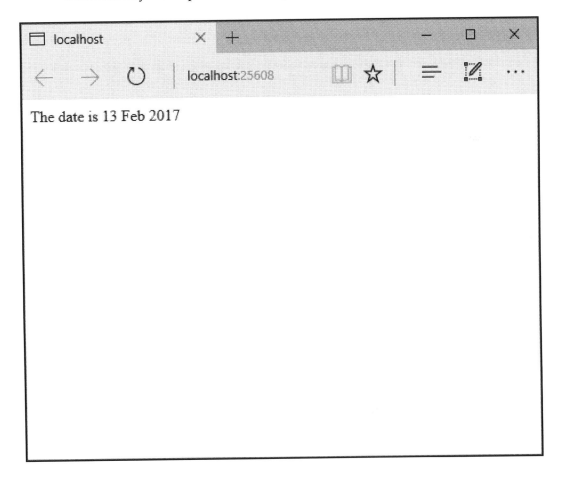

5. Looking at the **Solution Explorer** a little more in detail, I want to highlight some of the files in the project. The `wwwroot` folder will represent the root of the website when hosted. It is here that you will place static files such as images, JavaScript, and CSS style sheet files. Another file of interest is the `Startup.cs` file, which essentially replaces the `Global.asax` file. It is here in the `Startup.cs` file that you can write code to execute when your ASP.NET Core application starts up:

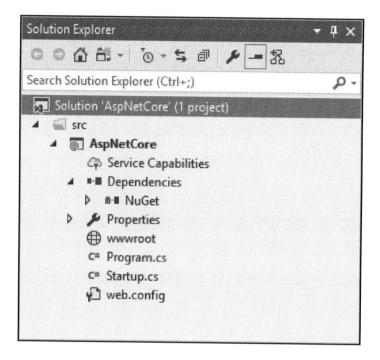

How it works

The `Startup.cs` file contains the `Startup` class. ASP.NET Core requires a `Startup` class and will look for this class by default. By convention the `Startup` class is called `Startup`, but you can call it something else if you want. If you need to rename it, then you also need to ensure that the `Program.cs` file is modified so that the `WebHostBuilder()` specifies the correct class name for `.UseStartup`:

```
public static void Main(string[] args)
{
    var host = new WebHostBuilder()
        .UseKestrel()
        .UseContentRoot(Directory.GetCurrentDirectory())
        .UseIISIntegration()
        .UseStartup<Startup>()
        .Build();

    host.Run();
}
```

Going back to our `Startup` class in the `Startup.cs` file, when you look inside this class you will see two methods. The methods are `Configure()` and `ConfigureServices()`. As you can see from the comment on the `Configure()` method, it is used *to configure the HTTP request pipeline*. Basically, incoming requests are handled by the application here and all it currently does in our application is to display the current date for every incoming request. The `ConfigureServices()` method is called before `Configure()` and is optional. Its explicit purpose is to add any services required by the application. ASP.NET Core supports dependency Injection natively. This means that if I can leverage services by injecting them into methods in the `Startup` class. For more information on DI, be sure to read `https://docs.microsoft.com/en-us/aspnet/core/fundamentals/dependency-injection`.

Publishing your ASP.NET Core application

Publishing an ASP.NET Core application is quite straightforward. We will take a look at publishing the application via Command Prompt (run as administrator) and then publishing the ASP.NET Core application to IIS on a Windows server.

Getting ready

You will need to have IIS set up in order to do this. Start **Programs and Features** and click on **Turn Windows features on or off** in the left-hand side of the **Programs and Features** form. Ensure that **Internet Information Services** is selected. When you select IIS, click **OK** to turn the feature on:

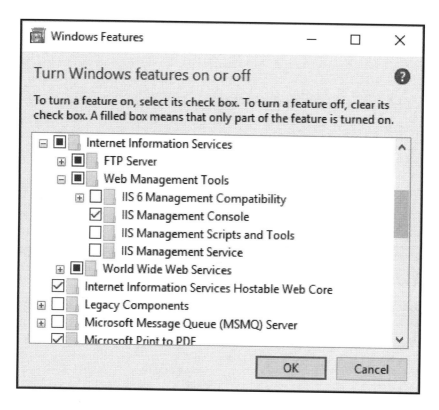

You also need to ensure that you have installed the .NET Core Windows Server Hosting bundle, which will create a reverse-proxy between IIS and the Kestrel server.

 At the time of this writing, the .NET Core Windows Server Hosting bundle is available at the following link:
`https://docs.microsoft.com/en-us/aspnet/core/publishing/iis#install-the-net-core-windows-server-hosting-bundle`

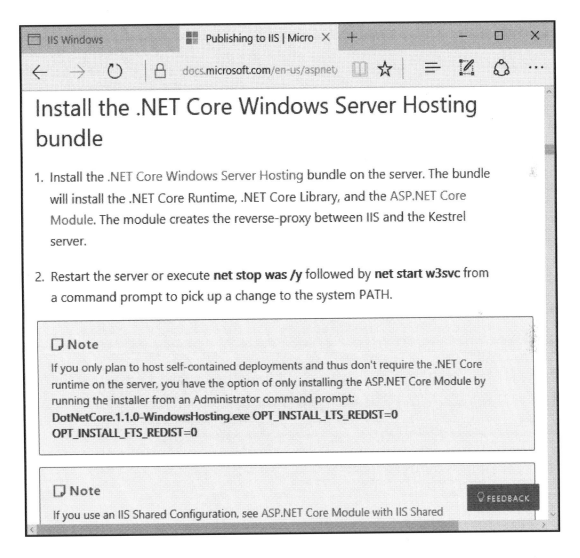

After installing the .NET Core Windows Server Hosting bundle, you need to restart IIS:

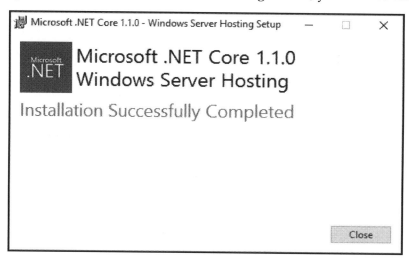

Open Command Prompt as administrator, type `iisreset` and press *Enter*. This will stop and then start IIS:

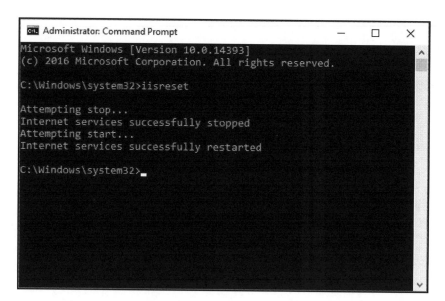

How to do it...

1. Open up Command Prompt by running it as administrator. In Command Prompt, go to the src\AspNetCore directory of your project. Ensure that you have a folder called publish in your temp folder on the C:\ drive of your computer, then type in the following command, and press *Enter*. This will build and publish your project:

```
dotnet publish --output "c:temppublish" --configuration release
```

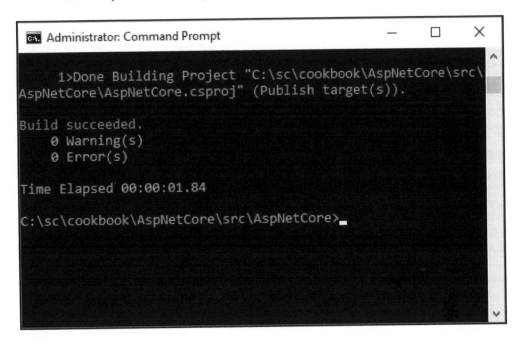

 Depending on what you called your ASP.NET Core application, the folder name under your src folder will be different to what mine is.

2. After the app has been published you will see the published files along with all their dependencies in the output folder:

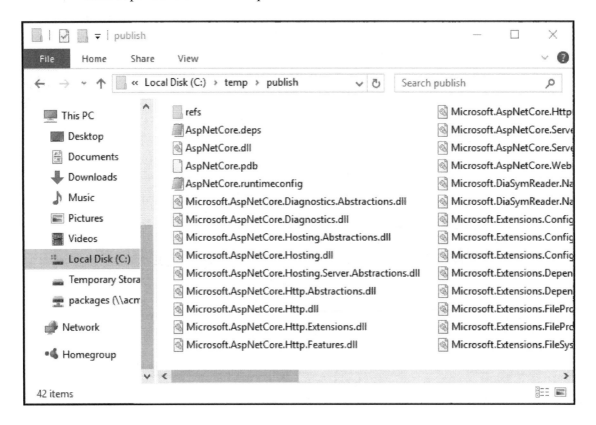

3. Going back to Command Prompt, run the application by typing in `dotnet AspNetCore.dll`. Take note that if your ASP.NET Core application is called something else, the DLL you will run will be different from the example in the book.

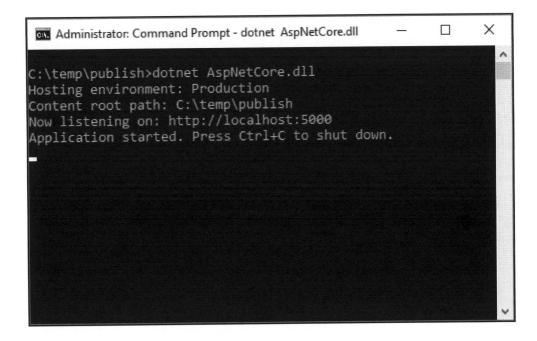

You can now go to your browser and type in `http://localhost:5000`. This will display your ASP.NET Core application for you:

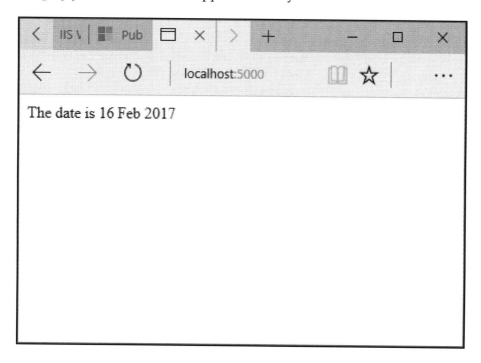

4. You can do exactly the same on macOS by copying the published files to a folder and typing `dotnet AspNetCore.dll` in Terminal:

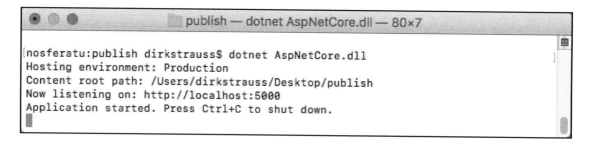

Then in Safari on your Mac, type in `http://localhost:5000` and press *Enter*. This will load the site in Safari:

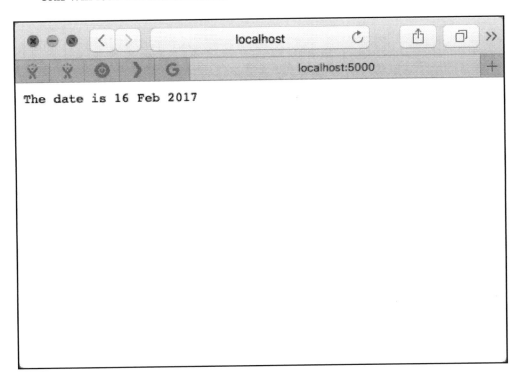

 While I have just shown Safari running on macOS as an alternative, the ASP.NET Core application will run happily on Linux too.

5. Publishing the application to IIS is also easily done. In Visual Studio, right-click on the project in the **Solution Explorer** and click on **Publish...** from the context menu:

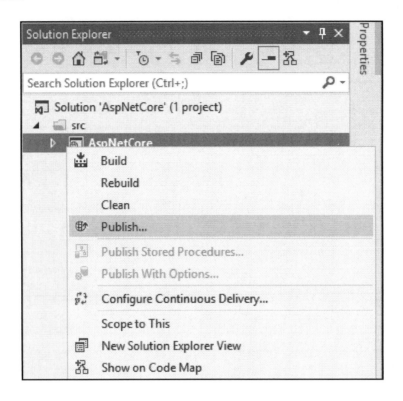

6. You then need to select a publish target. There are a few options available to you, but for this example, you need to select the **File System** option and click on **OK**:

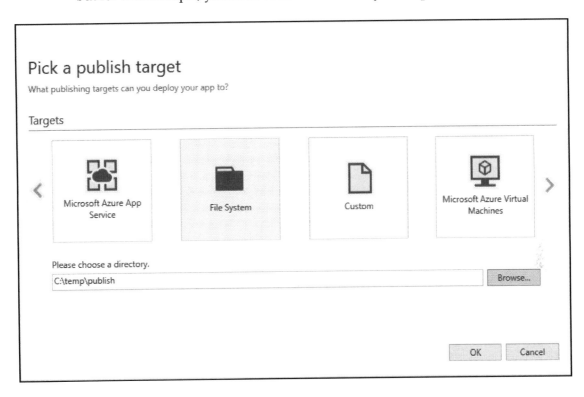

[**369**]

7. Back in the publish screen you can modify additional settings by clicking on **Settings...** next to the **Target Location** path. Here you need to select the publishing to be done in **Release** mode. Finally, click on the **Publish** button.

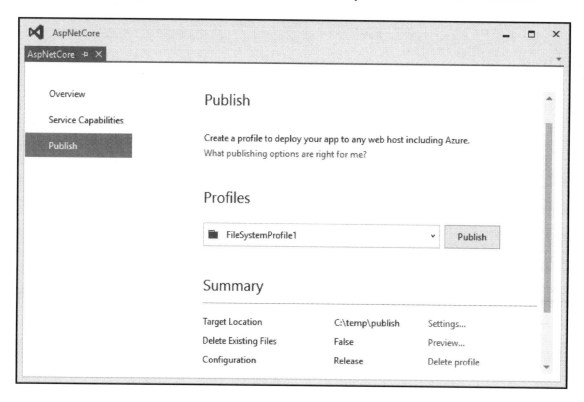

8. When the app has been published, Visual Studio will display the results in the
   Output window along with the publish location you selected:

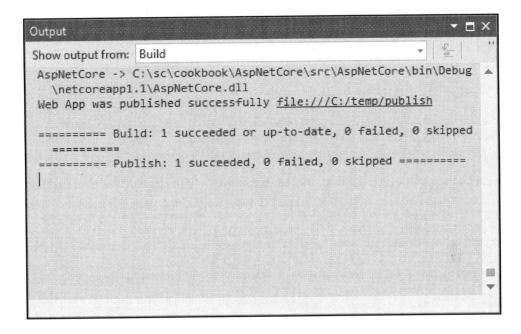

9. In your browser, if you enter `http://localhost` you will see the default page for IIS. This means that IIS is set up:

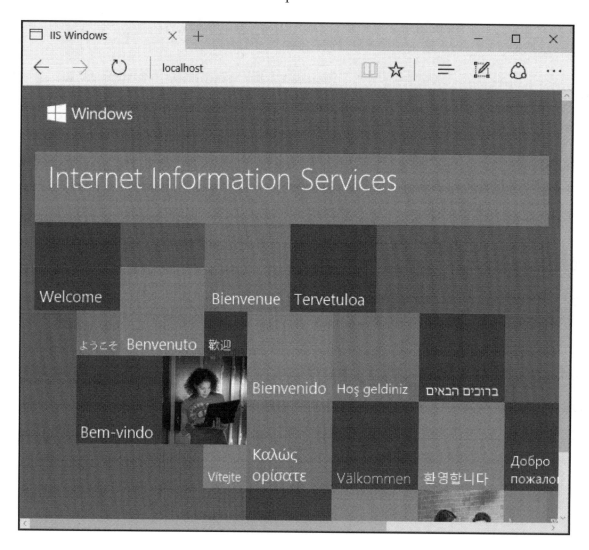

10. In Windows Explorer, browse to `C:\inetpub\wwwroot` and create a new folder called `netcore`. Copy the published files from your ASP.NET Core application into this new folder you created. In IIS, add a new website by right-clicking on the `Sites` folder and selecting **Add Website**. Give the site a name and select the path you copied the published files to in the **Physical path** setting. Lastly, change the **Port** to `86` as port `80` is used by the default website and click on **OK**:

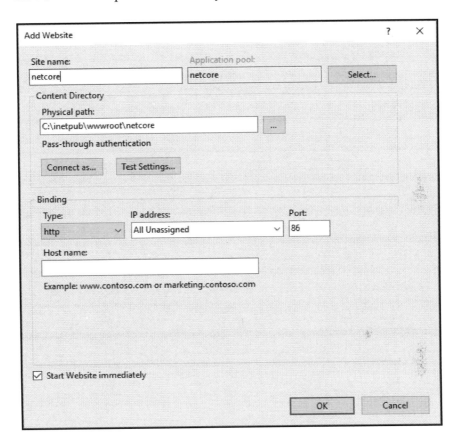

11. You will see your website added to the **Sites** folder in IIS. Under the **Browse Website** heading in the right-hand panel of IIS Manager, click on **Browse *.86 (http)**:

15. This will launch your ASP.NET Core application inside your default browser:

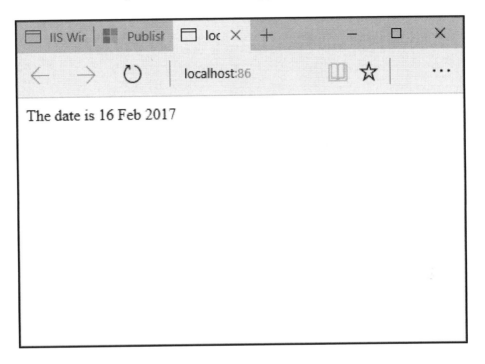

How it works...

Creating an ASP.NET Core application on Windows allows us to run the application on Windows, as well as macOS and Linux. Running it standalone is done easily via the `dotnet` command in Windows Command Prompt or in Terminal on macOS. This is what makes .NET Core so powerful for the future of application development. You can use the IDE you are used to in order to develop applications that are platform independent. There is a lot more to know surrounding .NET Core and you would really need to dig in to understand the concept and learn what it is capable of.

11

ASP.NET Core on the MVC Framework

This chapter will explore creating an ASP.NET Core application with the MVC framework. The previous chapter introduced you to ASP.NET Core, and we started with the basics needed for this chapter. If you are not familiar with ASP.NET Core, take a look at what `Chapter 10`, *Exploring .NET Core 1.1* has to offer. We will be looking at:

- Including middleware and why it is useful
- Creating Controllers and using routing
- Rendering Views

Introduction

The MVC framework is named according to the MVC design pattern it follows. MVC stands for **Model-View-Controller**. An HTTP request is sent to a Controller, which is then mapped to a method inside the *Controller* class. Inside that method, the Controller decides what to do with the HTTP request. It then constructs a *model* that is agnostic to the Controller and request. The model brings all the logic together that contains the information the Controller needs. The *view* is then used to display the information contained inside the model to build an HTML page that gets sent back to the requesting client in the HTTP response.

What the MVC framework allows us to do is separate the logic by letting each component of the framework focus on one specific thing:

- The Controller receives the HTTP request and builds a model
- The model contains the data we requested and sends it to the view
- The view then creates the HTML page from the data contained in the model

Including middleware and why it is useful

This recipe will show you how to set up middleware in your ASP.NET Core application. Middleware in ASP.NET defines how our application responds to any HTTP requests it receives. It is also useful for controlling how our application responds to user authentication or errors. It can also perform logging operations regarding incoming request.

Getting ready

We need to modify the code contained inside the Configure() method of our Startup class. It is here that we set up middleware in an ASP.NET Core application. In Chapter 10, *Exploring .NET Core 1.1*, we saw that our Configure() method already contained two pieces of middleware. The first is a piece of middleware that will display a developer exception page when an unhandled exception is caught. The code looks as follows:

```
if (env.IsDevelopment())
{
    app.UseDeveloperExceptionPage();
}
```

This will display any error messages which is useful for debugging the application. Typically, this page would contain information such as a stack trace. It is only installed when the application is in development mode. When you first create an ASP.NET Core application, it is in development mode.

The second middleware is the `app.Run()` and will always be present in your application. In `Chapter 10`, *Exploring .NET Core 1.1*, it would always respond with the current date. Think of middleware as gate keepers. All HTTP requests coming in to your application must pass through your middleware.

It is also important to know that the order you add your middleware is important. In the `app.Run()` middleware, we did a `context.Response.WriteAsync()`. Any middleware added after this will not be reached because the processing pipeline terminates in `app.Run()`. This will become clearer as we move on.

How to do it...

1. Your current ASP.NET Core application should contain a `Configure()` method that looks as follows:

```
public void Configure(IApplicationBuilder app,
  IHostingEnvironment env,
  ILoggerFactory loggerFactory)
{
  loggerFactory.AddConsole();

  if (env.IsDevelopment())
  {
    app.UseDeveloperExceptionPage();
  }

  app.Run(async (context) =>
  {
    await context.Response.WriteAsync($"The date is
      {DateTime.Now.ToString("dd MMM yyyy")}");
  });
}
```

2. From the **Debug** menu, click on **Start Without Debugging** or press *Ctrl + F5*. You will see the date displayed as follows:

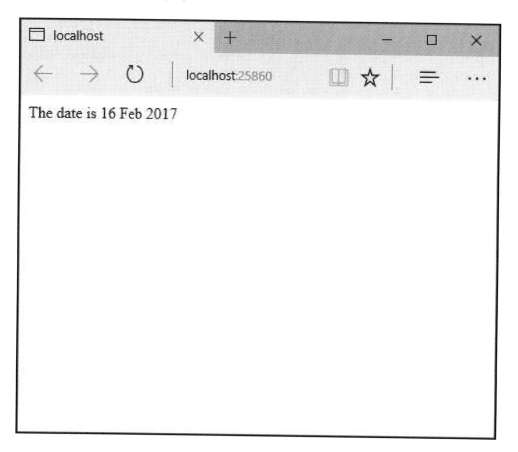

3. Go back to your code and tell your application to display the welcome page middleware. You can do this by adding `app.UseWelcomePage();` just before the `app.Run()`. Your code needs to look as follows:

```
if (env.IsDevelopment())
{
   app.UseDeveloperExceptionPage();
}

app.UseWelcomePage();

app.Run(async (context) =>
{
   await context.Response.WriteAsync($"The date is
```

```
        {DateTime.Now.ToString("dd MMM yyyy")}");
    });
```

4. Save your `Startup.cs` file and refresh your browser.

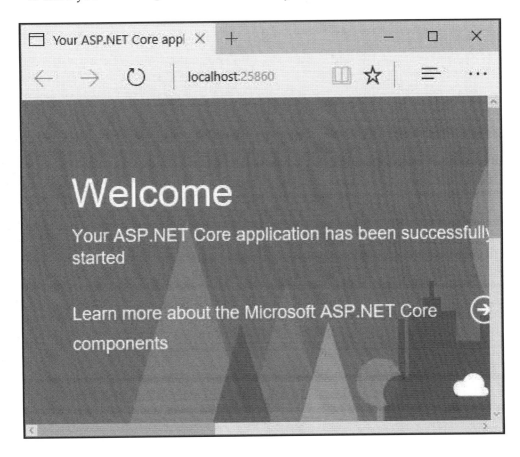

5. You now no longer see the date displayed on the screen. This is because the welcome page is the terminating middleware and any HTTP requests do not pass through that. Go ahead and modify the welcome page middleware to look as follows:

```
app.UseWelcomePage("/hello");
```

6. If you save your file and refresh your browser now, you will see the date displayed in the browser again. So what happened? Well you just told the welcome page middleware to only respond to requests for a /hello page.

7. Change the URL in the browser as follows http://localhost:25860/hello and press *Enter*. The welcome page is displayed again.

8. Let's take a look at the UseDeveloperExceptionPage() middleware. Modify app.Run() to look as follows:

```
app.Run(async (context) =>
{
    throw new Exception("Error in app.Run()");
    await context.Response.WriteAsync($"The date is
      {DateTime.Now.ToString("dd MMM yyyy")}");
});
```

9. Save your changes and refresh your browser. You will see that the browser now displays a page that a developer will find extremely useful. It displays the stack information, the incoming query, any cookies as well as the header info. It even tells us on what line the exception happened (line 36 in the `Startup.cs` file). The `UseDeveloperExceptionPage()` middleware allows the request to pass through it to the lower middleware. If an exception happens, this would then allow the `UseDeveloperExceptionPage()` middleware to do its job. As mentioned earlier, the placement of middleware is important. If we had this `UseDeveloperExceptionPage()` middleware at the end of the page, it wouldn't catch any unhandled exceptions. It is, therefore, a good idea to have this at the top of your `Configure()` method:

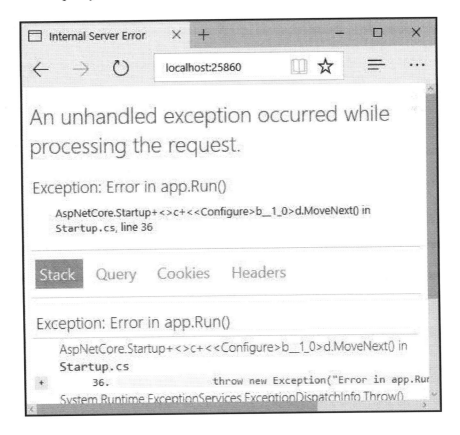

10. Let's take this concept further. When we are in a production environment, we would typically not want the user to see the exception page. Assume that they need to be directed to a friendly error page. Start off by adding a static HTML page to the **wwwroot** of your application. Right-click on the **wwwroot** and select **Add**, **New Item** from the context menu:

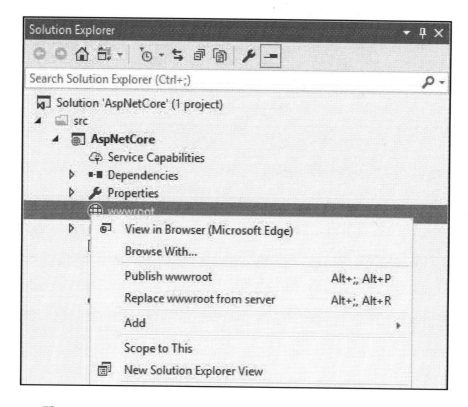

 The **wwwroot** is where you would serve static pages such as JavaScript files, CSS files, images, or static HTML pages.

11. Select an HTML page, call it `friendlyError.html` and click on **Add**.

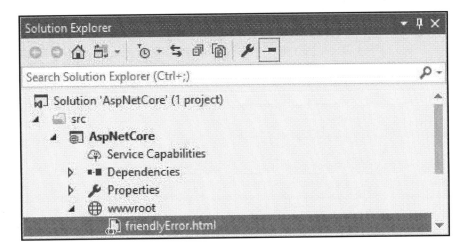

12. Modify the HTML of `friendlyError.html` as follows:

```
<!DOCTYPE html>
<html>
  <head>
    <meta charset="utf-8" />
    <title>Friendly Error</title>
  </head>
  <body>
    Something went wrong. Support has been notified.
  </body>
</html>
```

13. What we need to do next is add a NuGet package to our application so that we can serve static files. In the **NuGet Package Manager**, search for **Microsoft.AspNetCore.StaticFiles** and add that to the application.

14. Now, we need to modify the code slightly to simulate that it is running in a production environment. We do this by setting the`EnvironmaneName` property of the `IHostingEnvironment` interface as follows: `env.EnvironmentName = EnvironmentName.Production;`.

15. We then need to add an `else` statement to the `if (env.IsDevelopment())` condition and write the code to call our custom, static error page. It is here that we will add the `friendlyError.html` file to our `DefaultFileNames()` collection and tell our application that we want to use this error file on any exceptions in the production environment. Lastly, we need to tell our application to use static files by calling the `UseStaticFiles()` method. When complete, your code should look as follows:

```
env.EnvironmentName = EnvironmentName.Production;
if (env.IsDevelopment())
{
  app.UseDeveloperExceptionPage();
}
else
{
  DefaultFilesOptions options = new DefaultFilesOptions();
  options.DefaultFileNames.Add("friendlyError.html");
  app.UseDefaultFiles(options);

  app.UseExceptionHandler("/friendlyError");
}

app.UseStaticFiles();
```

How it works...

Press *Ctrl* + *F5* again to restart IIS Express and launch our application. You will see that our custom error page has been displayed inside the browser:

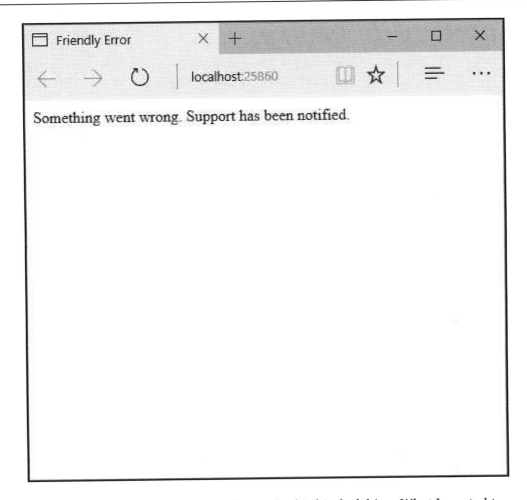

In reality, we will probably use a controller to do this kind of thing. What I wanted to illustrate here was the use of adding a custom default page and to display that page when an exception happens in the production environment.

As you can see, middleware in ASP.NET Core is really useful. There is a lot of documentation regarding his topic, and I encourage you to do some further reading on the topic. Start with the Microsoft documentation at `https://docs.microsoft.com/en-us/asp net/core/fundamentals/middleware`.

Creating Controllers and using routing

Inside the MVC framework, the Controllers, Models, and Views need to work together to form the HTTP request and response cycle. The fundamental starting point, however, is calling the correct Controller based on the HTTP request it receives. Without that, our application built on the MVC framework can't work. In the MVC framework, the process of calling the correct Controller for the HTTP request is known as routing.

Getting ready

We can route HTTP requests to the correct Controllers by looking at what routing information is contained in the middleware of our application. The middleware then uses this routing information to see if the HTTP request needs to get sent to a Controller or not. Middleware will have a look at the incoming URL and match that up with the configuration information we provide it with. We can define this routing information in the `Startup` class using one of two routing approaches, namely:

- Convention-based routing
- Attribute-based routing

This recipe will explore these routing approaches. Before we can do that, we need to add the ASP.NET MVC NuGet package to our application. You should be rather familiar with adding NuGet packages to your application by now. Inside the **NuGet Package Manager**, browse for and install the **Microsoft.AspNetCore.Mvc** NuGet package. This will expose new middleware for our application, one of which is `app.UseMvc();`. This is used to map an HTTP request to a method in one of our Controllers. Modify the code in your `Configure()` method as follows:

```
loggerFactory.AddConsole();

if (env.IsDevelopment())
{
    app.UseDeveloperExceptionPage();
}
else
{
    DefaultFilesOptions options = new DefaultFilesOptions();
    options.DefaultFileNames.Add("friendlyError.html");
    app.UseDefaultFiles(options);

    app.UseExceptionHandler("/friendlyError");
}
```

```
app.UseStaticFiles();
app.UseMvc();
```

Next, we need to register our MVC services that the MVC framework requires in order to function. Inside `ConfigureServices()` add the following:

```
public void ConfigureServices(IServiceCollection services)
{
    services.AddMvc();
}
```

After this is complete, we have the basics set up for MVC to function.

How to do it...

1. Add another folder to your application called `Controllers`:

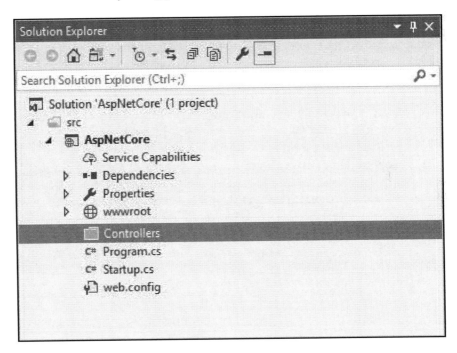

2. Inside the `Controllers` folder, add a new class called `StudentController`. Inside the `StudentController`, add a method called `Find()`. When you are done, your class will look as follows:

```
public class StudentController
{
  public string Find()
  {
    return "Found students";
  }
}
```

3. Back in the `Startup` class, add a `private void` method called `FindController()` that takes a parameter of type `IRouteBuilder`. Make sure that you also add the `using Microsoft.AspNetCore.Routing;` namespace to your class. Your method should look as follows:

```
private void FindController(IRouteBuilder route)
{

}
```

4. In the `Configure()` method, change the `app.UseMvc();` to `app.UseMvc(FindController);`.

5. We now need to tell our application how to look at a URL to determine which Controller to call. We will use convention-based routing here which uses a template that we define, to determine which Controller to call. Consider the following template `{controller}/{action}`. Our application will then use this template to split apart a URL and identify which part of a URL is the Controller part and which part of the URL is the Action. Using our `StudentController` class, the method `Find()` is the Action the template refers to. Therefore, when the application receives an incoming HTTP request with a URL `/Student/Find`, it will know to look for the `StudentController` class and go to the `Find()` method inside that Controller.

 We do not need to have the URL explicitly named `/StudentController/Find` because the MVC framework will, by convention, automatically take the word `Student` in the `{controller}` portion of the template and apply `Controller` to it to identify the name of the Controller to find.

6. Add the route mapping to the `FindController()` method. This tells the application that the template name is default and the template needs to look for a `{controller}/{action}` template in the URL. Your code should now look as follows:

```
private void FindController(IRouteBuilder route)
{
    route.MapRoute("Default", "{controller}/{action}");
}
```

7. Putting it all together, your `Startup` class will look as follows:

```
public void ConfigureServices(IServiceCollection services)
{
    services.AddMvc();
}

public void Configure(IApplicationBuilder app,
    IHostingEnvironment env, ILoggerFactory loggerFactory)
{
    loggerFactory.AddConsole();

    if (env.IsDevelopment())
    {
        app.UseDeveloperExceptionPage();
    }
    else
    {
        DefaultFilesOptions options = new DefaultFilesOptions();
        options.DefaultFileNames.Add("friendlyError.html");
        app.UseDefaultFiles(options);

        app.UseExceptionHandler("/friendlyError");
    }

    app.UseStaticFiles();
    app.UseMvc(FindController);
}

private void FindController(IRouteBuilder route)
{
    route.MapRoute("Default", "{controller}/{action}");
}
```

8. Save your code and enter the following to the end of your URL in your browser: /student/find. My URL looks as follows, but yours will differ because the port number will most likely be different to mine: http://localhost:25860/student/find. Entering that in your browser will route the incoming HTTP request to the correct Controller.

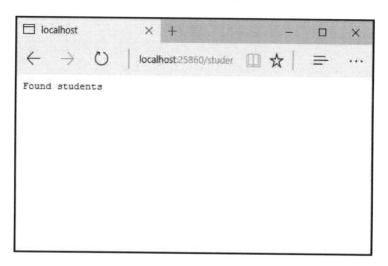

9. What should we do, however, if the URL is not in the correct format or the Controller can't be found. Well, this is where we can add defaults to our template. Remove the /student/find portion of the URL and hit enter. You should now see an error 404 in the browser. This is because the application could not find the Controller based on our URL. Add another class to our Controllers folder. Call this class ErrorController. Then, create a method inside this controller called Support(). Your code should look as follows:

```
public class ErrorController
{
  public string Support()
  {
    return "Content not found. Contact Support";
  }
}
```

10. Back in the `Startup` class, modify the template in the `FindController()` method. It should look as follows:

```
route.MapRoute("Default", "{controller=Error}/{action=Support}");
```

11. What this does is tell our application that if it does not find a Controller, it should default to the `ErrorController` class and execute the `Support()` method inside that class. Save your code and refresh your browser to see the application default to the `ErrorController`.

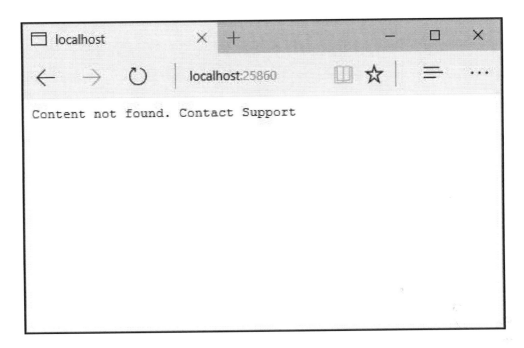

12. As you can see, the routing in ASP.NET MVC is very flexible. The previous steps listed discussed what we call convention-based routing. There is another routing method called attribute-based routing that uses attributes on our Controllers. Go to the `ErrorController` class and add the following `using Microsoft.AspNetCore.Mvc;` namespace to the class. Then, add an attribute `[Route("Error")]` to the class name and an attribute `[Route("Support")]` to your method. Your code should look as follows:

```
[Route("Error")]
public class ErrorController
{
    [Route("Support")]
```

```
public string Support()
{
  return "Content not found. Contact Support";
}
}
```

13. In the `Startup` class inside the `FindController()` method, comment out the line `route.MapRoute("Default",` `"{controller=Error}/{action=Support}");`. In the browser, add the text `/Error/Support` to the end of your URL and enter. You will see that the application correctly matches the `ErrorController`, based on the attributes defined inside the `ErrorController` class.

How it works...

Routing inside the MVC framework is a very flexible method of accessing specific Controllers, based on HTTP requests. If you need more control over the Controller that is accessed, attribute-based routing would probably be a better fit than convention-based routing. That said, there are additional things you can do when using attribute-based routing. Take a look at what is available to you as a developer when using attribute-based routing.

Rendering Views

So far we have been using plain C# classes as Controllers, but it is far more common have your Controllers inherit from the `Controller` base class which the MVC framework provides. This allows developers to return complex objects from their Controllers, students in our case. These complex return types are returned in a result that implements the `IActionResult` interface. We can, therefore, return JSON, XML, and even HTML to return to the client. The usage of this and creating Views is what we will be looking at next in this recipe.

Getting ready

Open up the `StudentController` class and modify it to contain attribute-based routing. Be sure to add the `using Microsoft.AspNetCore.Mvc;` namespace to the `StudentController` class. Also, inherit from the `Controller` base class.

```
[Route("Student")]
public class StudentController : Controller
{
    [Route("Find")]
    public string Find()
    {
        return "Found students";
    }
}
```

Then, add another folder to your project called `Models`. Inside the `Models` folder, add a class called `Student` because our application will be returning student information. This will be a simple class with properties for the student number, first name, and last name. Your `Student` class should look as follows:

```
public class Student
{
    public int StudentNumber { get; set; }
    public string FirstName { get; set; }
    public string LastName { get; set; }
}
```

Back in the `StudentController`, we want to instantiate our `Student` model and give it some data. We then change the return type of the `Find()` method from `string` to `IActionResult`. Also, add the `using AspNetCore.Models;` namespace to your `StudentController` class.

 Note, if your project is called something other than `AspNetCore`, your namespace will change accordingly:
`using [projectname].Models;`

Your code should now look as follows:

```
[Route("Find")]
public IActionResult Find()
{
    var studentModel = new Student
    {
        StudentNumber = 123
```

```
        , FirstName = "Dirk"
        , LastName = 'Strauss"
    };
    return View(studentModel);
}
```

Ultimately, we want to return a view result from our `StudentController`. We now have everything set up to do that next.

How to do it...

1. Add a new folder to your project called `Views`. Inside that folder, add another folder called `Student`. Inside the `Student` folder, add an new item by right-clicking on the `Student` folder and selecting **New Item...** from the context menu. From the **Add New Item** dialog screen, search for the **MVC View Page** template and call it `Find.cshtml`.

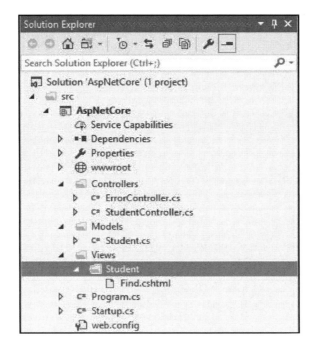

2. You should begin to notice that the `Views` folder, sub folders, and views follow a very specific naming convention. This is because the MVC framework follows a very specific convention, and when you look at the `StudentController`, this convention will become clear. The `Views` folder are `Views`, `Student`, `Find`, and the `StudentController` contains the word `Student` in the class name and has a method called `Find()`.

You can also create a `Shared` folder in the `Views` folder. This is where you place views that are shared across all Controllers and the Controllers will look in the `Shared` folder by default.

3. Heading back to the `Find.cshtml` Razor view, delete the code that is currently in there and replace it with the following:

```
<html xmlns="http://www.w3.org/1999/xhtml">
  <head>
    <title></title>
  </head>
  <body>
  </body>
</html>
```

You can also use the HTML code snippet. Type `html` and press *Tab* twice to insert the boilerplate HTML code into the **Find** view.

4. The deal with Razor views is that you are able to write C# expressions directly inside the `Find.cshtml` file. Before we do this, however, we need to set the type of the model we will be bringing in to our view. We do this using the following directive: `@model AspNetCore.Models.Student`. We can now reference our `Student` model directly inside our Razor view with full IntelliSense support. This is done using `@Model` with an upper case `M`. Take a look at the changes to the Razor view:

```
@model AspNetCore.Models.Student
<html xmlns="http://www.w3.org/1999/xhtml">
  <head>
    <title>Student</title>
  </head>
  <body>
    <div>
      <h1>Student Information</h1>
```

```
        <strong>Student number:</strong>@Model.StudentNumber<br />
        <strong>First name: </strong>@Model.FirstName<br />
        <strong>First name: </strong>@Model.LastName<br />
      </div>
    </body>
  </html>
```

How it works...

Save your code and refresh your browser. Your URL should be `http://localhost:[your port number]/student/find` for this to work correctly.

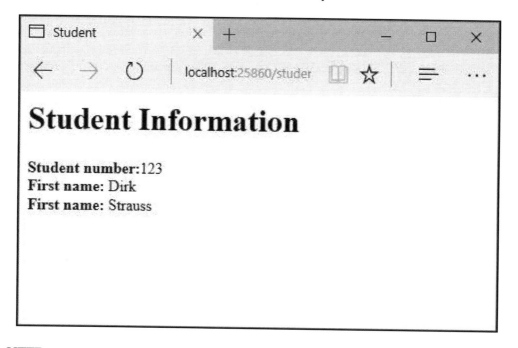

The HTTP request is routed to the `StudentController` that in turn populates and returns the `Student` model containing the data we need and sends it to the **Find** Razor view. This is the essence of what the MVC framework is all about. There is a lot more to cover when it comes to the MVC framework and ASP.NET Core, but this chapter just deals with the basic introduction to these topics.

We as developers are continually challenged to stay up to date with the latest and greatest technologies. There is a drive in us to learn more and become better at what we do. The very fact that you are reading this book is a testament to that. Regarding this chapter, however, .NET Core and the MVC framework are areas that definitely need more learning. It is not possible to cover all there is to know in a single chapter. There are various online resources available to developers. I find that one of the best (and free) resources for learning new tech is the Microsoft Virtual Academy at h ttps://mva.microsoft.com. Free Microsoft training is delivered by experts.

Hopefully, this is enough to pique your interest and will encourage you to research the topics further.

12

Choosing and Using a Source Control Strategy

Source control is an essential part of every developer's toolkit. It doesn't matter whether you are a hobbyist or professional programmer, when you get up from your desk to go home, you better be sure your code is safe. In this chapter, we will be looking at choosing and using a source control strategy. Some of the topics we will be taking a look at are:

- Setting up Visual Studio account management and determining which source control solution is best for you
- Setting up Visual Studio GitHub integration, checking in code for the first time, and checking in changes
- Working as a team using GitHub, handling and resolving conflicts in code

Introduction

During my career, I used Visual SourceSafe, SVN, VSTS, Bitbucket, and GitHub. It really does not matter how you approach it, the important thing is that you keep your source code safe and versioned. When I first started working with source control, the company I worked at used Visual SourceSafe. If you are unfamiliar with the software, just Google it. You will see results come back containing words such as hate, unpleasant, bad, and Microsoft's source destruction system. You get the point.

We had an employee leave files exclusively checked out to him, after he resigned and emigrated to another country. I'm beginning to wonder if the company policy to enforce the use of SourceSafe wasn't the reason he emigrated. But jokes apart, it gave us endless problems. Slap SourceSafe on a large project, and you could end up with a disaster. These days, however, developers have excellent choices available to them.

The two that stand out are obviously Microsoft Team Services and GitHub. Both have a free tier, but the decision of using one over the other depends entirely on your unique situation.

Setting up Visual Studio account management and determining which source control solution is best for you

Visual Studio allows developers to create an account and sign in. This is particularly beneficial if you hot desk often or work in multiple locations on different machines (think work and home PCs), because Visual Studio will then automatically sync your settings between the machines you're signed in to.

Getting ready

This recipe will assume that you have just completed installing Visual Studio 2017 on your machine. It doesn't matter whether you have installed the trial or licensed version of Visual Studio 2017.

How to do it...

1. After installation completes, open up Visual Studio.

2. At the top right of Visual Studio, you will see that there is a **Sign in** link:

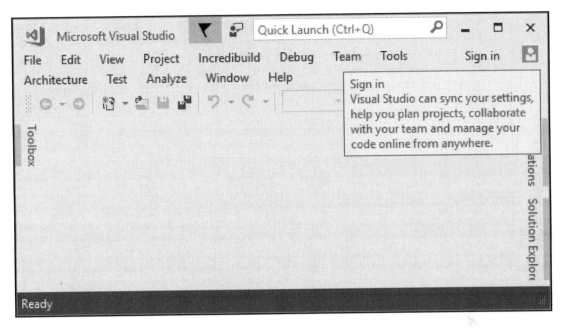

3. Clicking on the **Sign in** link, you will be allowed to enter your e-mail address here. I find it useful to just use my Outlook e-mail address. In my opinion, it is one of the best web e-mails available.

 Note that I'm not endorsing Outlook for any other reason other than I really think it is a great product. I also have a Gmail account as well as an iCloud e-mail account.

4. After adding your e-mail account, Visual Studio will redirect you to a sign in page.

5. Because I already have an Outlook account, Visual Studio simply allows me to sign in with it. If, however, you need to create an account, you can do so from the sign up link on the **Sign in to Visual Studio** form:

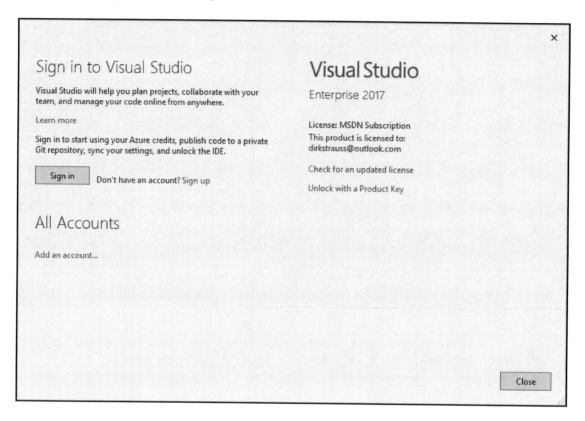

6. Visual Studio will now redirect you to a sign up page where you can go and create an account:

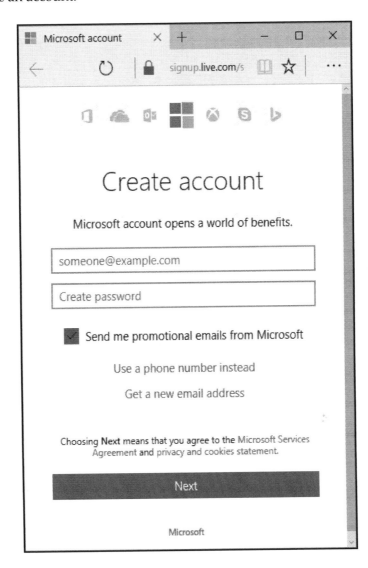

7. After your account is created, you will be prompted to return to Visual Studio to sign in. After you have signed in, Visual Studio will display your details in the right-hand corner of the IDE:

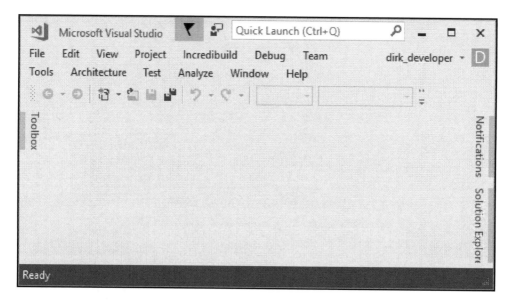

8. Clicking on the down arrow next to your account name, you can view your **Account settings....**

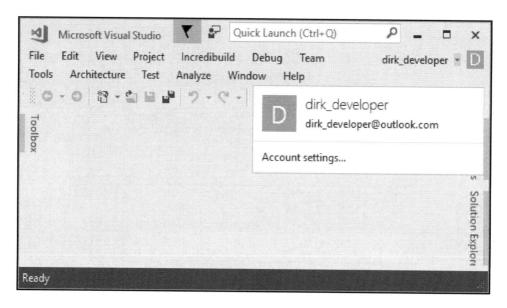

9. This will show you a summary of your account, from where you can further personalize your account:

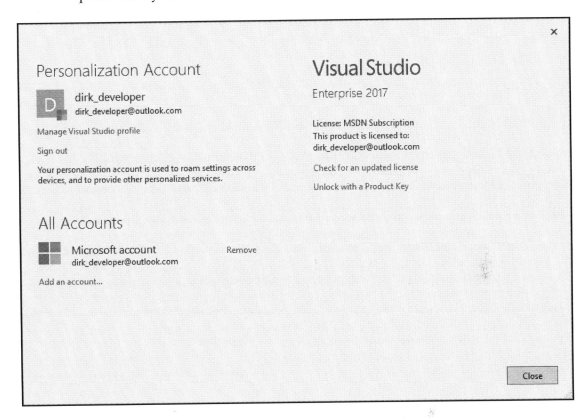

How it works...

The choice of source control is a topic every developer has a strong opinion about. Unfortunately, if you work for a boss, that decision might not even be up to you. Many companies have already set up their source control system just the way they like it, and you will need to fall in with company procedure. That is just the way it is. It is, however, good to know about the options available to you as an indie developer.

All good developers should be writing code in their own time too. You are not only a developer while you sit at work. We eat, breathe, sleep, and live code. It is part of who and what we are. I will say that in order for you to become better at your job as a developer, you must play with code in your own time. Start a pet project, get some friends together, and decide to write some software together. Not only will this make you all better at what you do, but you will learn a lot from each other.

If you are a remote developer who does not commute to and work in an office every day, you can still connect with the developer community. There are so many resources available to developers, and the developer community is more than happy to rally around newbies and help them grow. Starting a solo or pet project is useless if you don't commit (pun intended) to keeping your code safe. To do this, you don't have to pay a single dollar either. **Visual Studio Online** (now called **Team Services**) and GitHub provide developers with a fantastic platform to keep your code safe.

Let's start by looking at Team Services. The site can be found by pointing your browser to `h ttps://www.visualstudio.com/team-services/`.

Here you will see that Microsoft has given developers a fantastic opportunity to use Team Services. It is absolutely free for up to five users. This means that you and your mates can collaboratively work on the next big thing while ensuring that your code remains secure. Signing up is as simple as clicking on the **Get started for free** link:

For information on pricing, visit the following link:
`https://www.visualstudio.com/team-services/pricing/`

The second excellent option is GitHub. It differs slightly in its free offering by requiring developers to use a public repository on the free account. If you don't mind your code being essentially open source, then GitHub is a great choice. With GitHub though, you can have unlimited collaborators and public repositories:

For information on pricing, visit the following link:
`https://github.com/pricing`

The choice of source control essentially comes down to the openness of your code. If you can afford to let other developers see and download your code, then GitHub is a great choice. If you need your code to remain private and only shared between specific people, then a paid GitHub account will suit you better. If you don't want to fork out money yet, then Team Services will be your best bet.

Setting up Visual Studio GitHub integration, checking in code for the first time, and checking in changes

GitHub has been a tour de force for so many years. There are developers that swear by it. In fact, it is the default option when using Apple's Xcode IDE. For whatever reason you decide to use GitHub, rest assured that you and your code are in good hands.

Getting ready

The following recipe will assume that you have already signed up for GitHub and that you have enabled **Two-factor authentication**. If you have not signed up for a GitHub account, you can do so by going to `https://github.com/` and creating a new account. To enable **Two-factor authentication** on your GitHub account (something I personally strongly advise), do the following:

1. Click on the down arrow next to your profile image, and select **Settings**:

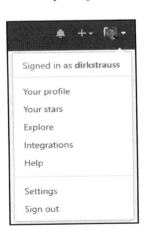

2. From the **Personal settings** menu that appears on the left of the next web page, select **Security**:

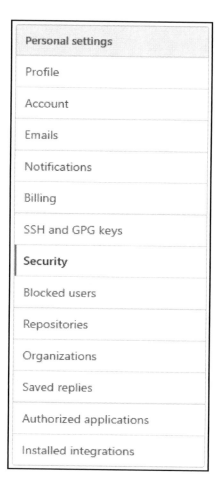

3. The first section on the security page will be your **Two-factor authentication** status. To get started with setting it up, click on the **Set up two-factor authentication** button.

4. You will then be presented with a brief overview of what **Two-factor authentication** is and you will be given the choice of **Set up using an app** (which I recommend) or **Set up using SMS**. Using an app is by far the easiest, and if you have a smartphone or tablet, you can download an authenticator application from the applicable app store. From there on, follow the prompts that GitHub give you to complete the **Two-factor authentication** setup.

5. After you have completed the setup, your Two-factor authentication will be switched on.

How to do it...

1. Adding the GitHub extension to Visual Studio is easily done by downloading the visx from the following link and installing it:
   `https://visualstudio.github.com/downloads/GitHub.VisualStudio.vsix.`

2. Assuming that you have an existing application you want to add to GitHub, the process of adding it to a new repository is quite simple. I have simply created a console application with nothing but the template code, but you can add any project type and size to GitHub.

3. On the **View** menu in Visual Studio 2017, select the **Team Explorer** option.

4. You will be presented with two options under the **Hosted Service Providers** section. For now, we will select **GitHub** and, seeing as we already have an account, we will click on **Connect...**

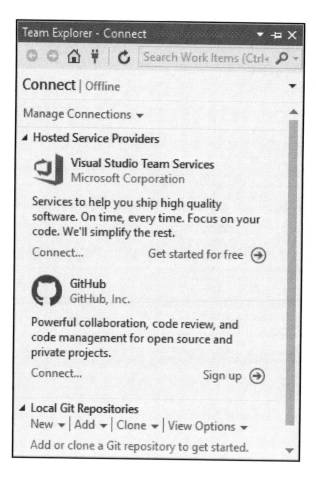

5. You will now be presented with the GitHub login page. You are also offered the chance to sign up from here if you do not have an existing GitHub account:

6. Because I have **Two-factor authentication** set up on my GitHub account, I am prompted to use my authenticator application to enter the generated authentication code and authenticate myself:

7. After you have been authenticated, you will return to the **Manage Connections** screen. If your project isn't displayed under the **Local Git Repositories**, you can add it:

8. Next, you will want to click on the Home icon, which is a picture of a little house at the top of the **Team Explorer** window. From the **Home** screen, click on the **Sync** button:

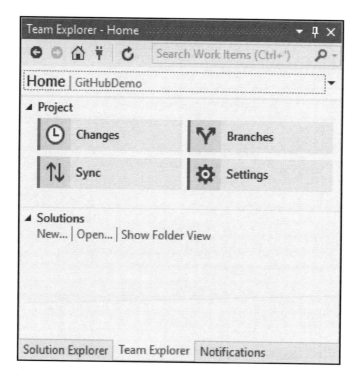

9. This will display the **Publish** window to you. Under GitHub, click on the **Publish to GitHub** button. This is going to publish your project to a new repository on GitHub.

Remember, if you are using the free GitHub, all your repositories are public. If you are writing code that can't be made public (is not open source), then sign up for one of the paid GitHub accounts that include private repositories.

10. GitHub will then prompt you to add in the details for this publish. Because you connected to GitHub earlier, your username will already be selected in the drop-down menu. When you are ready, click on **Publish**:

11. When the project has been published to GitHub, you will automatically be returned to the **Home** screen:

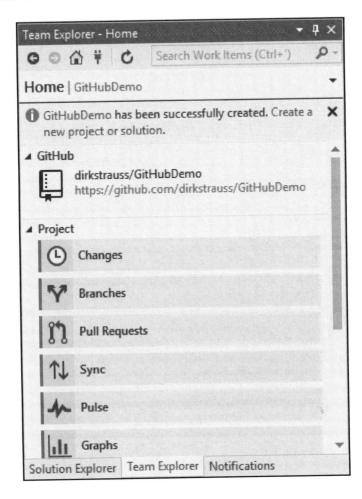

12. Looking at your GitHub account online, you will see that the project has been added:

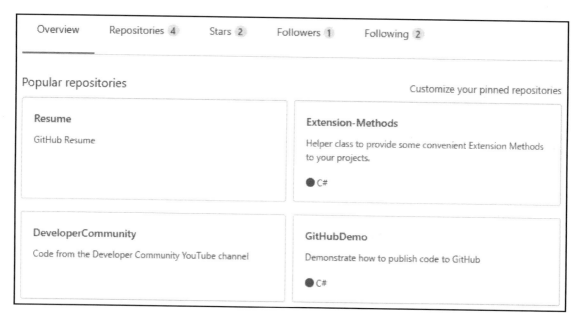

13. Next, let's go and make some changes to the `GitHubDemo` application. Just go ahead and add a new class to your project. I called mine `NewClass.cs`, but you can call yours whatever you like.

14. You will notice that as soon as a change is made to your project, that the solution will mark the changed items with a red tick. Your class is marked with a green plus sign:

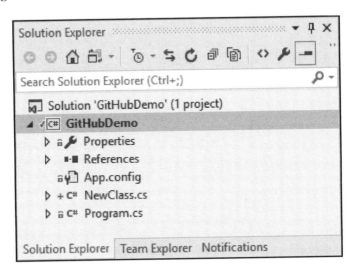

15. To add the changes to your GitHub repository, you can follow two routes. The first option is to go to the **Team Explorer - Home** window and click on the **Changes** button.

16. The second (and in my opinion more convenient) option, is to right-click the solution in **Solution Explorer** and click on the **Commit...** menu item from the context menu.

17. GitHub might ask you for your user information the first time you perform a commit.

18. Before you are allowed to commit your changes, you must fill in the required commit message. In a real team project, be as descriptive as possible in your commit message. Consider using task item code (or backlog codes) to uniquely identify the code being added. This will save your (or another developer's) bacon sometime in the future, I guarantee it:

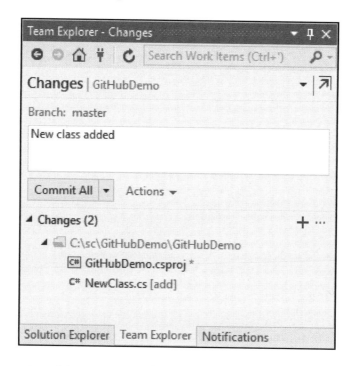

19. One important thing to note is that you have three commit options available to you if you click on the down arrow next to the **Commit All** button. The **Commit All** button will just record the changes you make on your local machine. In other words, the change will not be reflected in the remote repository. The **Commit All and Push** button will record the changes on your local machine and push those changes to your remote GitHub repository. The **Commit All and Sync** button will record the changes on your local machine, then it will pull any changes from the remote repository, and finally it will do the push. You will want to do this if you are working in a team. For this recipe, however, I will just do a **Commit All and Push**, seeing as I am the only developer working on this repo:

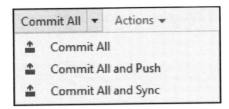

20. When the commit has completed, the **Team Explorer - Synchronization** window will notify you of the successful commit:

21. Heading over to GitHub online, you will see the newly pushed changes reflected in your GitHub repository, along with the commit message:

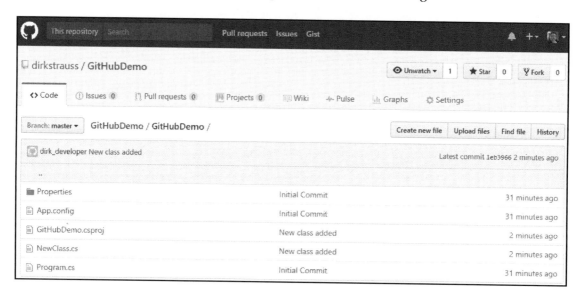

22. GitHub is a fantastic source control solution for any developer. Consider creating an open source project. It is more beneficial than you might imagine.

More and more these days, prospective employers are reviewing developers' GitHub repos when considering applicants for developer positions. Keep that in mind, because a GitHub repo is a resume in itself.

How it works...

The free GitHub account allows you to create public repositories. This means that anyone is able to search for, view, and clone your project from GitHub to their own desktop. This is the central idea behind GitHub. This is obviously a key factor for indie developers and corporates that don't want to spend money. Corporates can afford it more than an indie developer, but I think that some companies prefer to roll their own, rather than use a service provider hosted in the cloud somewhere. This means that they prefer to keep the source control under their control by setting up a source control system on their own corporate servers. Having GitHub as an option for indie developers is an awesome solution. For those that require private repos, the fee isn't a stumbling block either.

Working as a team using GitHub, handling and resolving conflicts in code

GitHub and Team Services really come into their own when working in teams. The effect of collaborative effort is quite powerful. Sometimes though, it can be a bit challenging. Let us have a look at using GitHub to work in a team setup.

Getting ready

We will be using the existing `GitHubDemo` app checked in to GitHub. Let's assume that a new developer (let's call him John) has joined the team. Before you can let him push code to your branch, you need to add him as a collaborator. To do this, log in to GitHub and click on the Settings tab in your `GitHubDemo` repository. Click on **Collaborators** in the menu to the left.

You can then search for collaborators to add by entering their GitHub username, full name, or e-mail address:

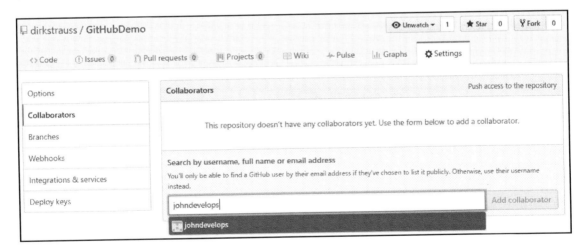

When you are done, click on the **Add collaborator** button to add John as a collaborator to your project:

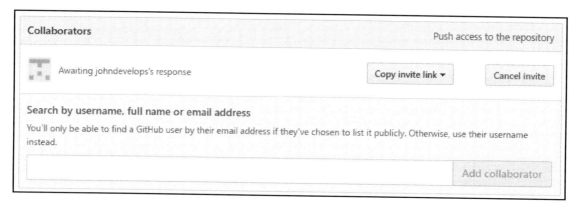

John will receive an e-mail and will first need to respond to your invitation to collaborate.

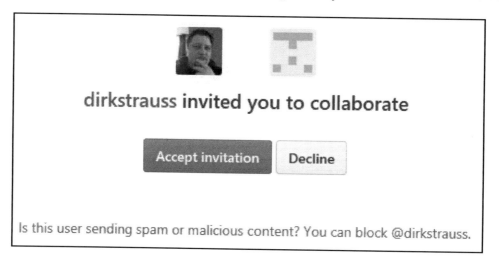

How to do it...

1. John goes about setting up his Visual Studio environment, including getting connected to GitHub, by clicking on **Team** in the menu and clicking on **Manage Connections...**.

2. He logs in to GitHub with his e-mail address and password.

Take note that if you have just signed up to GitHub, you will need to click on the verification e-mail sent to the e-mail address you specified when signing up. Without verifying your e-mail address, you will not be able to log in from Visual Studio.

3. After connecting, John sees his GitHub details loaded:

4. He now wants to work on the GitHubDemo application and finds it on GitHub by searching for it by name:

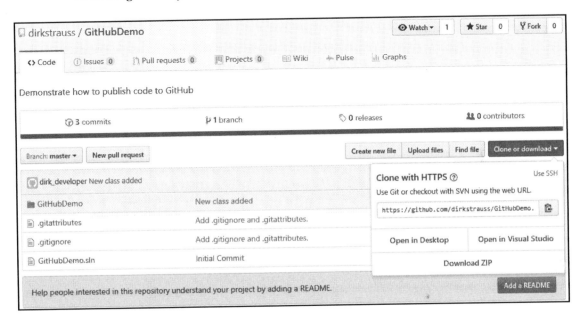

5. He now copies the URL from the **Clone with HTTPS** textbox from the **Clone or download** button:

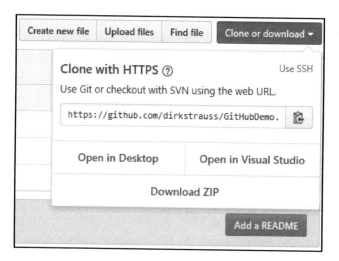

6. Back in Visual Studio, John expands the **Local Git Repositories** and clicks on **Clone**. He pastes the copied URL to the Git Repository path and specifies where the code should be cloned to on his hard drive. He then clicks on **Clone**:

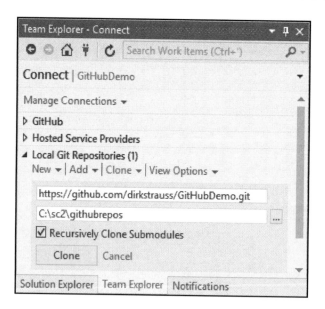

7. When the code is cloned, it will be in the folder path John specified earlier.

8. Time to make some changes to the code. He opens the project in Visual Studio as normal. John decides to work on the `NewClass` class and adds a new function that returns a countdown integer:

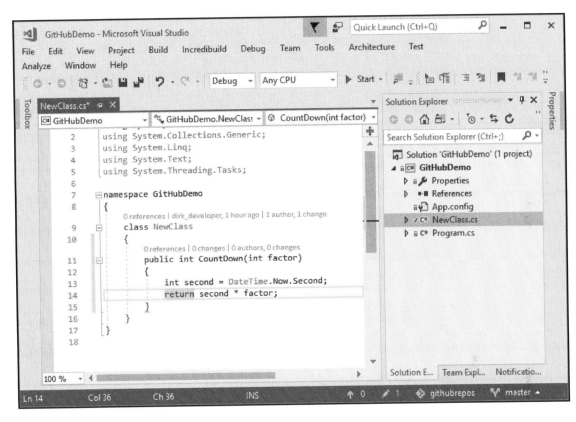

9. After the code change is complete, John prepares to commit the code he just added to the `GitHubDemo` project.

10. After adding a commit message, he then clicks on **Commit All and Sync**.

One important thing to note is that you have three commit options available to you if you click on the down arrow next to the Commit All button. This button will just record the changes you make on your local machine. In other words, the change will not be reflected in the remote repository. The Commit All and Push button will record the changes on your local machine and push those changes to your remote GitHub repository. The Commit All and Sync button will record the changes on your local machine, then it will pull any changes from the remote repository, and finally it will do the push.

11. John's changes are committed to the GitHub repository:

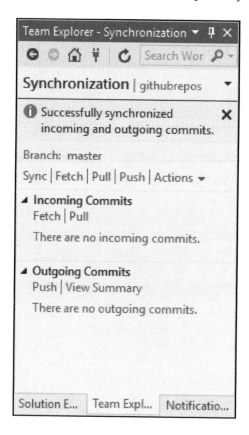

12. On the other side of the office, I am working on the same bit of code. The only problem is that I have added the same method with my own implementation of the `CountDown` logic:

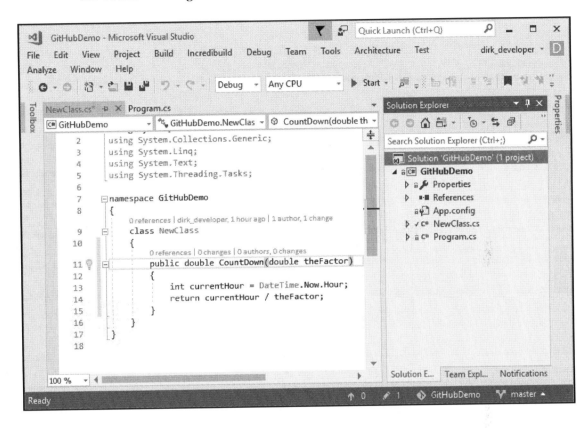

13. I get ready and commit my changes to GitHub:

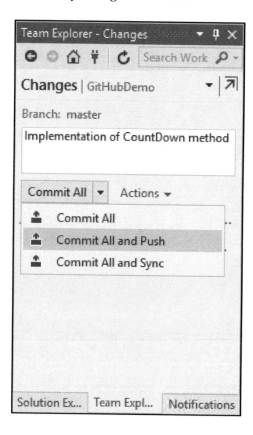

14. GitHub immediately prevents me from doing this. This is because if my code is pushed, the earlier commit by John will be lost. GitHub has a great help file on the subject in GitHub Help at `https://help.github.com/articles/dealing-wi th-non-fast-forward-errors/`.

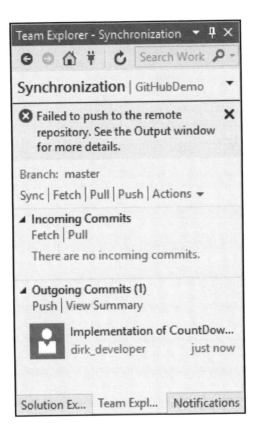

The Output window contains a more descriptive error message:

Error encountered while pushing to the remote repository: rejected Updates were rejected because the remote contains work that you do not have locally. This is usually caused by another repository pushing to the same ref. You may want to first integrate the remote changes before pushing again.

15. To resolve this, click on **Pull** to get the latest commit that John did. Your code will then be in a conflicted state. This sounds bad, but it isn't. It is putting you in control of the decision on which code will be used. You can see that the pull shows that there are conflicted files and also the incoming commit message that John added:

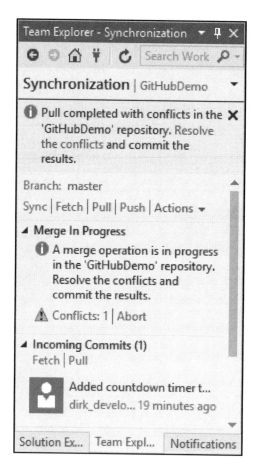

16. To view the conflicts, click on the **Resolve the conflicts** link in the message pop-up:

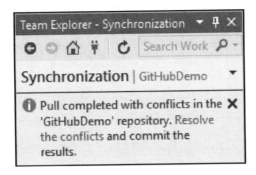

17. You will then see the **Resolve Conflicts** screen listing the conflicted files. Clicking on a file will expand it into a short summary and action options screen. It is always prudent to click on the **Compare Files** link to see the difference between the files in conflict:

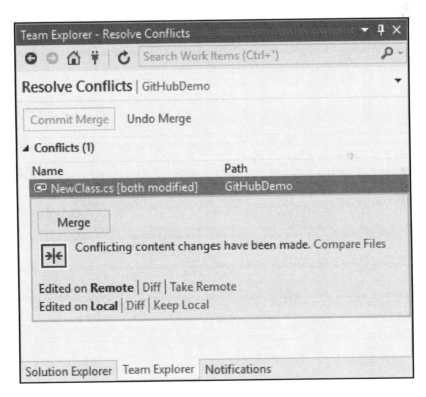

18. The differences in code are immediately evident. The process you follow from here on is subject to how you work together as a team. Usually, the conflict can be quite complex and it is always a good idea to speak to the developer concerned about the way forward:

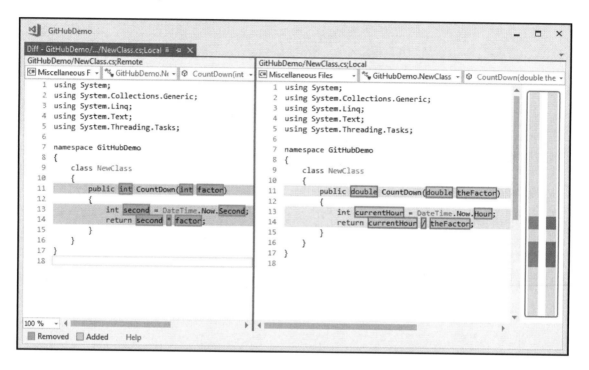

19. In this case, John and I decided that his code was better and more concise. So the decision was made to simply click on **Take Remote** and use John's code. When you have clicked on the link, you need to click on **Commit Merge**:

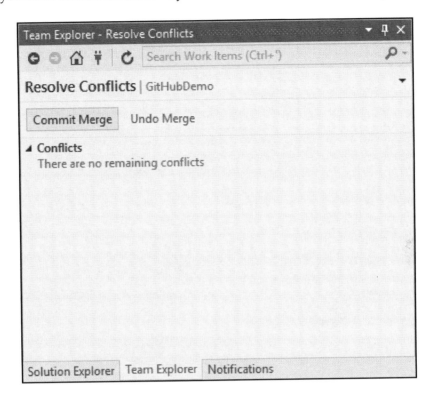

20. After adding a commit message, you can then push your code to the repo. In this case, I simply replaced all my code with John's, but there might be situations when you will be using some of your code and some of another developer's code. GitHub allows us to easily handle these conflicts:

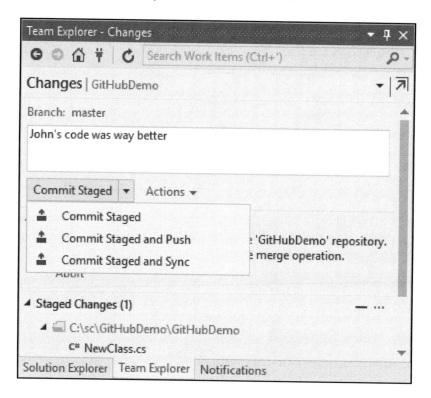

21. After pushing the code to the remote, GitHub notifies you that the code has successfully been synchronized:

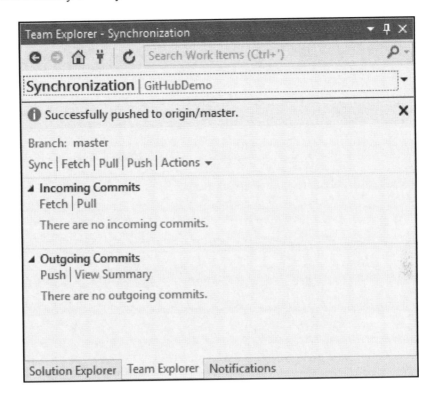

How it works...

GitHub takes the pain out of committing, resolving conflicts, and merging code. It is, without a doubt, an essential tool in any developer's toolkit and essential for development teams. Even if you are not using it professionally, it's a great idea to create a repo for yourself. Start using it to check on the pet projects you work on after hours. Expanding your knowledge beyond what you work with on a day-to-day basis will make you a better developer.

13

Creating a Mobile Application in Visual Studio

Visual Studio is the *tour de force* of **integrated development environments** (**IDEs**). There is no doubt about that. You, as a developer, are able to be as versatile as you like by creating applications for a wide range of platforms. One of these platforms is mobile development. Developers are starting to create mobile applications, but don't want to use a different IDE. With Visual Studio, you don't have to. It will allow you to create Android and (now with **Xamarin**) iOS and Mac applications too.

This chapter will, therefore, take a look at the following concepts:

- Installing Xamarin and other required components on your Windows PC and Mac
- Creating a mobile application using Apache Cordova
- Creating an iOS application using Xamarin.Forms and Visual Studio for Mac

Introduction

If you have not heard about Xamarin, we encourage you to do a Google search for this tool. Traditionally, developers needed to use **Xcode** or **NetBeans** to create iOS and Android applications. The challenge for developers was that it meant learning a new programming language. If you, for example, created an application that you wanted to deploy to iOS, Android, and Windows, you needed to know Objective-C or Swift, Java, and a .NET language.

This also created additional challenges for development, because it meant having to maintain multiple code bases. If a change was to be made in the Windows version of the application, it also had to be made to the iOS and Android code base. Sometimes companies would manage different development teams for each platform. You can imagine the complications involved in managing a change across multiple teams on multiple platforms. This is especially true if you are dealing with a large code base.

Xamarin solves this problem by allowing .NET developers to use standard .NET libraries to create iOS and Android applications using Visual Studio. You, as a .NET developer, can now use the skills you already have to accomplish this. In a nutshell, you would create a shared library for your applications and then have different facades for the different platforms. A second option is to use Xamarin.Forms to create one Visual Studio project and target all three platforms. This makes it very easy to for developers to target multiple platforms.

Installing Xamarin and other required components on your Windows PC and Mac

How does Xamarin work exactly? It does seem like magic, right? I mean, writing C# in Visual Studio and compiling a native iOS, Mac, or Android application on the other side does seem magical. A lot of technology has gone into giving developers the ability to do this. With iOS and Mac applications, the process is somewhat involved. One thing to be aware of if you want to target iOS or Mac is that you will need to use a Mac in order to build your iOS applications. There are services out there that make Macs available for remote testing and compilation (such as MacinCloud, `http://www.macincloud.com/`). These, however, do incur a monthly cost. When Xamarin compiles your C# code, it does so against a special subset of the Mono framework.

 Mono is sponsored by Microsoft and is an open source implementation of the .NET Framework. This is based on the ECMA standards for C# and the **Common Language Runtime**. For more information on the Mono framework, take a look at `http://www.mono-project.com/`.

Looking at iOS specifically, this special subset includes libraries that allow access to iOS platform-specific features. The Xamarin.iOS compiler will take your C# code and compile it into an intermediate language called ECMA CIL. This **common intermediate language (CIL)** is then compiled a second time into native iOS code that an iPhone or iPad can run. You can then also deploy this to a simulator for testing.

Now, you might be wondering why a Mac is needed to compile your application? Why can't it all just happen from within Visual Studio? Well, this is due to a (quite clever) restriction imposed by Apple on the ability of the iOS kernel to generate code at runtime. It simply does not allow that to happen. As you know (this is the extremely simplified explanation), when your C# source code is compiled for testing it is compiled into intermediate language. The **just-in-time (JIT)** compiler then compiles the intermediate language into assembly code that is appropriate for the architecture you are targeting. Because the iOS kernel does not allow this on-demand compilation by a JIT compiler, the code is statically compiled using **ahead-of-time (AOT)** compilation.

To view the limitations of Xamarin.iOS, take a look at the following link: `https://developer.xamarin.com/guides/ios/advanced_topics/limitat ions/`
For a list of available assemblies in Xamarin.iOS, Xamarin.Mac, and Xamarin.Android, take a look at the following support document: `https://developer.xamarin.com/guides/cross-platform/advanced/a vailable-assemblies/`.

The technology behind this is quite impressive. It is no wonder that Microsoft acquired Xamarin and included it as part of Visual Studio. Giving developers this array of choice for cross-platform development is what Microsoft is all about: empowering developers to create world-class applications.

Getting ready

We are going to look at getting Xamarin installed on your Windows PC running Visual Studio 2017 in this recipe. Xamarin can be installed as part of a workload when Visual Studio 2017 is installed. For now, let's assume that Xamarin has not been installed and that you need to do that now, after you have installed Visual Studio. Go to the Visual Studio website at `https://www.visualstudio.com/` and download the installer for the version of Visual Studio you installed.

You can also run the installer from the **New Project** dialog screen in Visual Studio 2017. If you collapse the installed templates, you will see a section that allows you to open the Visual Studio Installer.

You will also need to install Xcode, which is Apple's development environment. This can be downloaded for free from the Mac App Store.

 Note that you will need to have an iTunes login to download Xcode and complete setting up your Mac. Chances are, if you have a Mac, you most definitely will have an iTunes login too.

How to do it...

1. Double-click on the installer you downloaded from the Visual Studio website. You will see that your version of Visual Studio 2017 is displayed and a **Modify** button is visible. Click on the **Modify** button:

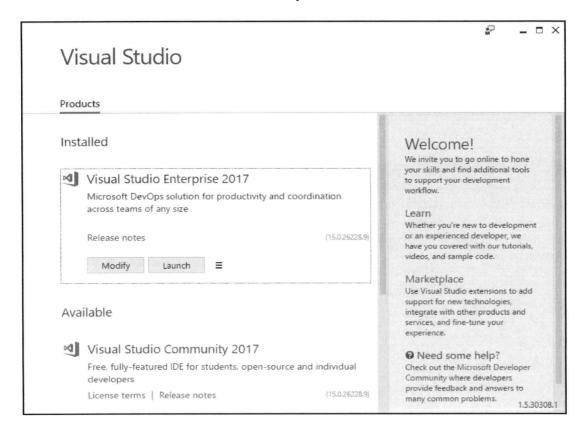

2. This will display the available workloads for you. Under the **Mobile & Gaming** section, ensure that you select **Mobile development with .NET**. Then, click on the **Modify** button in the lower-right corner:

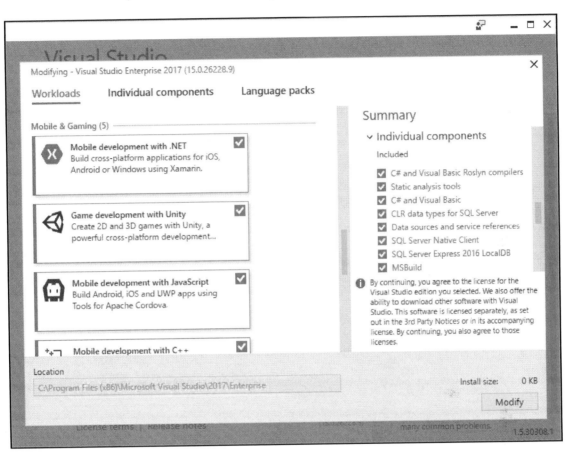

3. There is also a second step we need to take if we want to use Xamarin to target iOS applications. We have to install the required software on a Mac. Head on over to Xamarin's website on your Mac. The URL is `https://www.xamarin.com/`. Click on the **Products** drop-down and select **Xamarin Platform** from the list:

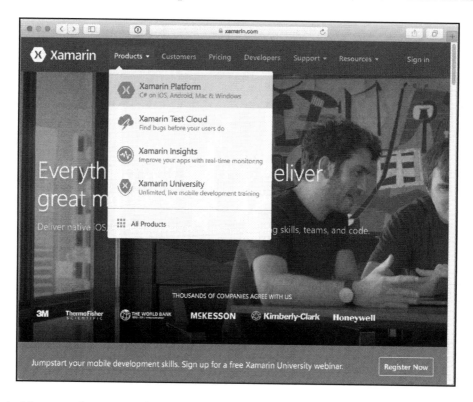

4. You can also access the required page by going to `https://www.xamarin.com/platform`. Clicking on the **Download now for free** button will install something called **Xamarin Studio Community** on your Mac. You need to be aware that when installed on a Mac, Xamarin Studio cannot create Windows apps. It will only allow you to create iOS and Android apps on a Mac. Along with Xamarin Studio, you will also get the Xamarin Mac Agent (previously called the Xamarin build host). This is a required component so that you can link your PC to your Mac in order to build your iOS application. Lastly, the PC and Mac must also be able to connect to each other over a network (more on this later).

5. After downloading the installer on the Mac, the installation is straightforward. You will notice that there are a few options to choose from the installation screen: **Xamarin.Android**, **Xamarin.iOS**, **Xamarin.Mac**, and **Xamarin Workbooks & Inspector**. If you wanted to target Android as a platform, you would install **Xamarin.Android**. To target iOS (iPhone or iPad), you will need to select **Xamarin.iOS**. To create fully native Mac applications, you must select **Xamarin.Mac**. Lastly, **Xamarin Workbooks & Inspector** gives developers an interactive C# console that integrates with app debugging to aid developers when inspecting running apps. For now, we're only interested in **Xamarin.iOS**. Just follow the screen prompts and complete the installation. Depending on your selection, the installer will download the required dependencies and install that on your Mac. Depending on your Internet connection, you might want to go get a cup of coffee:

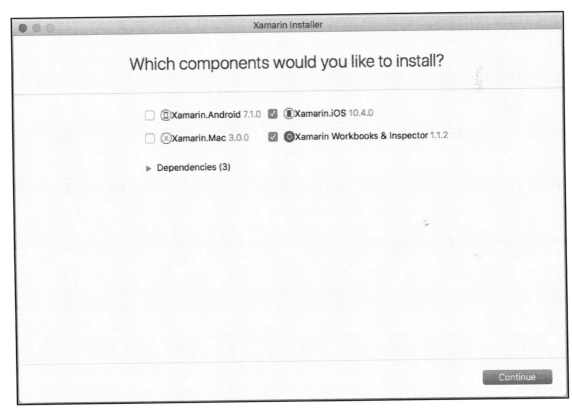

6. Lastly, if you have not installed Xcode from the Mac App Store, you should do so now before continuing:

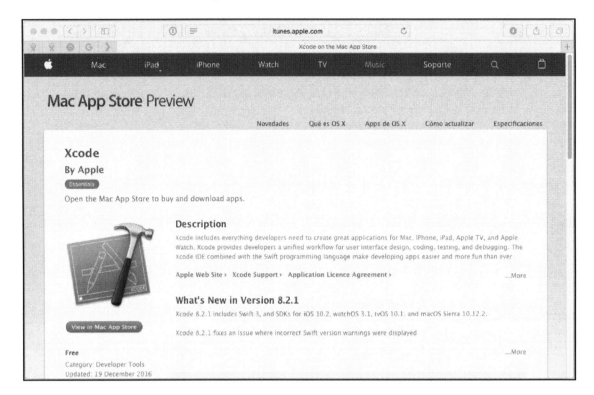

How it works...

The steps we took previously when installing Xamarin will allow us to do target Mac, iOS, and Android (if we selected Xamarin.Android) platforms when developing cross-platform. Previously (before Visual Studio 2015), developers had to learn a new IDE in order to skill themselves up to create applications for other platforms. Personally, I find Xcode (the Apple developer IDE for creating native iOS and Mac applications) a bit of a learning curve. It's not because it is too complicated, but rather because it obviously works differently than what I am used to in Visual Studio. If you are serious about learning another programming language and want to go the Xcode route, take a look at Swift. It is a superb language and one that I found much easier to relate to C# than Objective-C, for example.

If, however, you would rather stick to what you know and are comfortable with, then Xamarin is your best choice for developing cross-platform applications. You also do not have to go out and buy a MacBook to compile your applications on. A Mac mini is more than enough when you want to start developing for iOS and Mac. It is an investment in your development toolset that will stand you in good stead. There are also cloud options (such as MacinCloud) available to you as a developer. With Xamarin, you can stick with C# and develop in an environment that you are familiar with.

There is a third and final option available to developers, and this is one we will be taking a look at in the final recipe of this chapter. The steps in this recipe are for when you need to create applications on your Windows PC and compile them on your Mac or MacinCloud solution.

Creating a mobile application using Apache Cordova

Creating a mobile application using Apache Cordova is not complex at all. If you are familiar with web development, then this will feel quite natural to you. For those of you that have not developed web applications before, this will help you to familiarize yourself with this process. This is because at the very essence of Cordova lies a web application. You reference files such as JS files and CSS files and you work with an `index.html` file that you can debug in a browser.

Cordova applications offer you the flexibility of targeting iOS, Android, or Windows applications. This recipe will illustrate a simple application that displays the current date when the user clicks on a button in the app.

Getting ready

You will need to have installed the **Mobile development with JavaScript** workload as part of the Visual Studio 2017 installation process. For now, let's assume that you did not install it when you installed Visual Studio 2017 and now need to run the installer again.

You can also run the installer from the **New Project** dialog screen in Visual Studio 2017. If you collapse the installed templates, you will see a section that allows you to open the Visual Studio Installer.

Go to the Visual Studio website at `https://www.visualstudio.com/` and download the installer for the version of Visual Studio you have installed. Also take note that you will need to have Google Chrome installed on your machine in order to launch the Cordova application simulator.

How to do it...

1. Double-click on the installer you downloaded from the Visual Studio website. This will launch the installer and list the version of Visual Studio 2017 installed on your machine with a **Modify** button. Click on the **Modify** button:

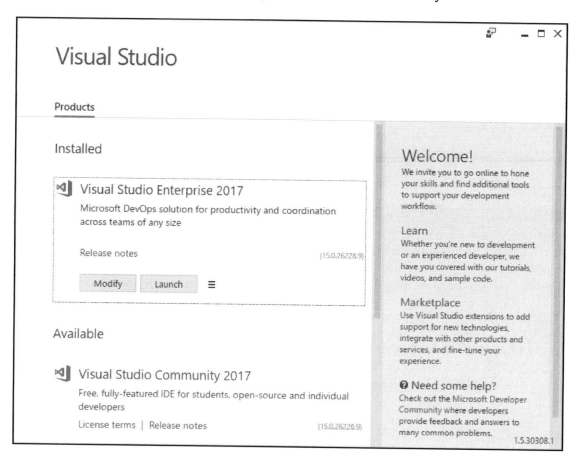

2. From the **Mobile & Gaming** group, select the **Mobile development with JavaScript** workload. Then, click on the **Modify** button. Depending on your specific requirements, additional components might be installed, such as support for the **Android SDK** and the **Google Android Emulator**:

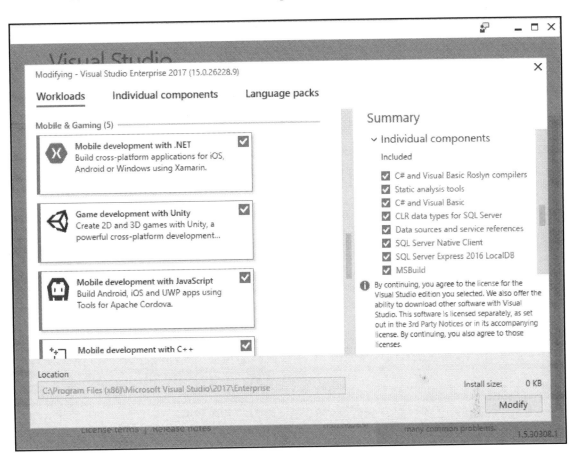

3. Apache Cordova uses web technologies such as HTML, CSS, and JavaScript to build mobile applications that will run on Android, iOS and Windows devices. From Visual Studio, create a new application and select **JavaScript** from the **Other Languages** templates. Then select the **Blank App (Apache Cordova)** template. This is just a blank project that uses **Apache Cordova** to build a mobile app for Android, iOS, and **Universal Windows Platform** (**UWP**). I just called my app **MyCordovaApp**.

4. Once Visual Studio has created your application, you will notice that it has a very specific folder structure:

   - `merges`: Expanding the `merges` folder, you will notice that you have three subfolders called `android`, `ios`, and `windows`. Developers can use these folders to deliver different content based on which mobile platform they are targeting.

   - `www`: This is where most of your development will take place. The `index.html` file will become the main entry point for your Cordova application. When your mobile application is started, Cordova will look for this index file and load that first. You will also notice subfolders under the `www` folder. Think of these as a regular web application folder structure, because that is exactly what they are. The `css` subfolder will contain any style sheets you need to use.
   Any images you need to use in your mobile application will be stored in the `images` subfolder. Lastly, you will add any JavaScript files used by your mobile (web) application in the `scripts` subfolder. If you expand the `scripts` subfolder, you will notice a JavaScript file called `platformOverrides.js`. This is used in conjunction with the `merges` folder to deliver specific JavaScript code based on the mobile platform you are targeting.

   - `res`: The `res` folder will be use to store non-web application resources that might be used by the different native mobile applications. These can be resources such as splash screens, images, icons, signing certificates, and so on:

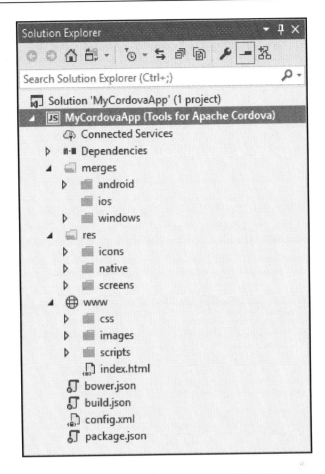

You will also notice several configuration files. These are bower.json, build.json, config.xml, and package.json. While I will not go into each one of these configuration files in detail, I want to briefly mention the config.xml and package.json files. The package.json file is not currently used by Cordova at the time of writing. It is intended to eventually replace the config.xml file. Currently, the config.xml file contains settings specific to your mobile application. Double-click on this file to view the custom editor for the Cordova application. The custom editor avoids the complexities of having to edit the XML file directly by providing a standard Windows form from where you can input the application-specific settings. The settings available to you as a developer are such settings as application name, author name, application description, device orientation, plugin configuration, and so on.

It is imperative that you do not delete the `config.xml` file. Doing so will break your solution and the Cordova SDK will not be able to build and deploy your mobile application without it.

5. At this point, you can select a device from the debug drop-down and run your mobile application. If you had to select **Simulate in Browser - Nexus 7 (Tablet)**, Visual Studio will launch Google Chrome and display the default Cordova application. This is the default for every Cordova application and does not contain any functionality really. It merely lets you know that your Cordova application has started correctly. What is interesting though is that you will see a new tab open up in Visual Studio while your simulator is launched. It is called the **Cordova Plugin Simulation** and defaults to the **Geolocation** plugin. This allows developers to interact with plugins and fire specific events as your application is running in the simulator. Any new plugins added to your Cordova application will expose additional panes in the **Cordova Plugin Simulation**:

6. Next, add the NuGet package **jQuery.mobile** to your solution. NuGet will install **jQuery.1.8.0** and **jquery.mobile.1.4.5** to your solution. At the time this book was written, it was advised that **jQuery.1.8.0** not be upgraded to the latest version due to compatibility reasons:

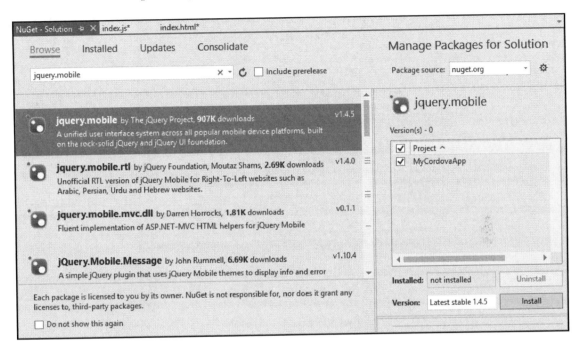

7. In your solution, NuGet will add several JS files to your project's `Scripts` folder. Drag all these JS files to your `www/scripts` folder. Do the same with the project's`Content` folder. Drag all the CSS files and the `images` subfolder to the `www/css` folder:

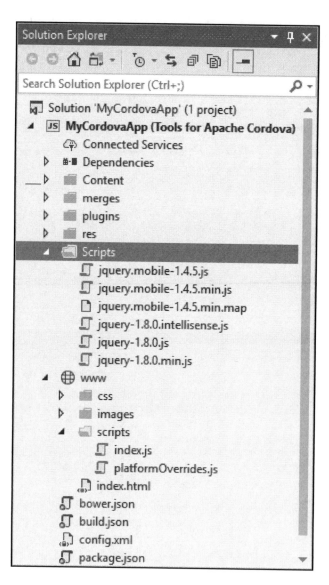

8. Swing back to and open your `index.html` file. You will see a section between the `<body></body>` tags that looks as follows:

```
<div class="app">
  <h1>Apache Cordova</h1>
  <div id="deviceready" class="blink">
    <p class="event listening">Connecting to Device</p>
    <p class="event received">Device is Ready</p>
  </div>
</div>
```

This is the default boilerplate code added by the template and we will not be using it. Replace this with the following code and also add `<script src="scripts/jquery-1.8.0.min.js"></script>` and `<script src="scripts/jquery.mobile-1.4.5.min.js"></script>` to the bottom of the body section where the other script references are.

 Note that your versions of the JS files might differ from the previously referenced versions.

When you are done, your `<body></body>` section should look as follows:

```
<body>
  <div role="main" class="ui-content">
    <form>
      <label id="current-date">The date is:</label>
      <button id="get-date-btn" data-role="button"
        data-icon="search">
        Get Current Date</button>
    </form>
  </div>
  <script src="scripts/jquery-1.8.0.min.js"></script>
  <script src="scripts/jquery.mobile-1.4.5.min.js"></script>
  <script src="cordova.js"></script>
  <script type="text/javascript" src="cordova.js"></script>
  <script type="text/javascript" src=
    "scripts/platformOverrides.js"></script>
  <script type="text/javascript" src="scripts/index.js"></script>
</body>
```

9. Then, between the `<head></head>` tags, add the `<link rel="stylesheet" href="css/jquery.mobile-1.4.5.min.css" />` style reference above the existing `<link rel="stylesheet" type="text/css" href="css/index.css">` reference.

 Note that your versions of the CSS files might differ from the versions referenced earlier.

When you are done, your code should look similar to the following:

```
<head>
  <!--
    Meta references omitted for brevity
  -->
  <link href="css/jquery.mobile-1.4.5.min.css" rel="stylesheet" />
  <link rel="stylesheet" type="text/css" href="css/index.css">
  <title>MyCordovaApp</title>
</head>
```

10. Your application now includes the required jQuery libraries that will make your mobile application mobile and touch optimized. Your mobile application is now also responsive to the device it will be displayed on. We now need to add some basic styling to the application. Open up the `index.css` file referenced in the `<head></head>` section of your `index.html` file. This should be in `www/css/index.css`. Replace the contents with the following code. The `#get-date-btn` is just referencing the button on our form and setting the font size to 22 pixels. The `form` is styled to contain a solid border at the bottom of 1 pixel wide:

```
form {
  border-bottom: 1px solid #ddd;
  padding-bottom: 5px;
}

#get-date-btn {
  font-size: 22px;
}
```

11. We now need to add a click event for when the user taps on the **Get Current Date** button. To do this, open the `index.js` file located at `www/scripts/index.js`. Find the `onDeviceReady()` method and modify the code to look as follows:

```
function onDeviceReady() {
  // Handle the Cordova pause and resume events
  document.addEventListener( 'pause', onPause.bind(
    this ), false );
  document.addEventListener( 'resume', onResume.bind(
    this ), false );

  $('#get-date-btn').click(getCurrentDate);
};
```

12. Think of this code as an event handler for the `get-date-btn` button. It is actually adding a click listener to the button that will call the `getCurrentDate` function whenever the button is tapped by the user. It is probably a good time to mention the `(function () { ... })();` function that contains the `onDeviceReady()` function. This is called an **anonymous self-invoking function**, which is actually just something you can think of as a form load event. You will notice that it adds an event handler for the `onDeviceReady()` method.

13. Lastly, add the `getCurrentDate()` function to the `index.js` file.

For the purposes of this recipe, I'll keep it simple and add the `getCurrentDate()` function to the `index.js` file because the code isn't really that complex. For more complex code, it would be better to create a separate JS file and reference that JS file in your `index.html` page (at the bottom of the `<body></body>` section) along with the other JS file references.

The `getCurrentDate()` function is nothing special. It just gets the date and formats it to a `yyyy/MM/dd` format and displays it in the label on the `index.html` page. Your function should look as follows:

```
function getCurrentDate()
{
  var d = new Date();
  var day = d.getDate();
  var month = d.getMonth();
  var year = d.getFullYear();
  $('#current-date').text("The date is: " + year + "/"
    + month + "/" + day);
}
```

How it works...

You can now start to debug your application. Let's choose a different simulator in Visual Studio. Select **Simulate in Browser - LG G5** and press *F5*:

Chrome will launch and display your Cordova application:

Click on the **Get Current Date** button and the current date will be displayed above the button you just clicked on:

While your simulator is open, open the `index.js` file where you added the `getCurrentDate()` function and place a breakpoint on the line that reads `$('#current-date').text("The date is: " + year + "/" + month + "/" + day);`. Then click on the **Get Current Date** button again:

```
17
18    function getCurrentDate()
19    {
20        var d = new Date();
21        var day = d.getDate();
22        var month = d.getMonth();
23        var year = d.getFullYear();
24        $('#current-date').text("The date is: " + year + "/" + month + "/" + day);
25    }
```

You will notice that your breakpoint is hit and you can now step through your code inspecting variables and debugging your application just like you are used to doing. You can even set conditional breakpoints. This is simply fantastic.

There is so much more to learn surrounding developing applications using Cordova. Web developers will find this process familiar and should easily pick it up. You can now take this application and run it on any platform because it is completely cross-platform. What you can try next is running your Cordova application using one of the Android Emulators available. Play around with this example and add some more functional code. Think of accessing a web service to retrieve values or play around with the styles.

Being able to target different mobile devices from a single solution using Visual Studio allows developers the freedom to experiment and find what solution fits them and their development style the best. Cordova steps up to the plate and offers developers a fantastic solution for those that do not use something such as Xamarin.

Creating an iOS application using Xamarin.Forms and Visual Studio for Mac

Many developers want to try their hand at writing an iOS application. The big drawback has always been learning a new programming language and a new IDE. For some, it is probably not an issue as they want to learn something new. But for many .NET developers, being able to stick to an IDE and programming language they know is immensely empowering. Well, this is exactly what Xamarin.Forms and Visual Studio achieve.

 Please note that I am not including Xamarin.Android here as a consideration. I'm purely focusing on writing native iOS and Mac applications.

Xamarin gives .NET developers the ability to use Visual Studio to write applications that can be run cross-platform easily, without having a separate code base for each. You therefore have a single code base for your application that will run on Windows, iOS/macOS, and Android. If you want to get into developing native iOS/macOS applications, you basically have (to my mind anyway) four viable options. They are as follows:

- Buy yourself a Mac and teach yourself Xcode, Swift, and/or Objective-C.
- Buy yourself a Mac and install Parallels, where you can install Windows, Visual Studio, and other Windows-based software (Mac is not exclusively used for development). You can see a video on the **Developer Community** YouTube channel I created a few years back (`https://www.youtube.com/developercommunity`). In that video, I show you how to install Visual Studio 2013 on a Mac using Parallels.
- Buy yourself a Mac and download **Visual Studio for Mac** (currently still in preview at the time of writing) and install that on your Mac (Mac is exclusively used for developing Android and iOS/macOS applications).
- Buy yourself a Mac and use that to compile iOS/macOS applications developed on your Windows PC running Visual Studio. Do this if you need to create applications that can still target Windows-based platforms in addition to Android and iOS/macOS.

If you are going to be using **Visual Studio for Mac** and Xamarin.Forms, then you will not be able to create Xamarin.Forms projects for Windows and Windows phone because these cannot be build on macOS. Also note that I didn't consider MacinCloud here because somewhere along the development process, I believe that it is really beneficial to own a physical Apple Mac device.

From the points listed earlier, it is clear that you are going to need a Mac. While it is entirely possible to have Visual Studio installed on your Windows PC and connect to the Xamarin Mac agent when the machines are on the same local network, it does become a bit of an inconvenience when you need to try and remotely access the Mac (from your work office, for example). While theoretically this should be possible, you need to do some legwork to make this all work. For one, you will probably need to add some sort of port forwarding on your router to allow remote connections to your Mac. You will also need to assign your Mac a static IP address (or even buy a static IP address for your router) so that if a restart happens due to a power failure when you are working remotely, you will still be able to access your Mac for your Visual Studio builds.

Installing Parallels on your Mac is great, and will really come in handy when you have other Windows-based software that you want to use on your Mac. If you (like me) use your Mac exclusively for development purposes, then Parallels might not be a viable solution. This leaves **Visual Studio for Mac** and is a great option if you only plan to develop iOS/macOS and Android applications.

To download Visual Studio for Mac, head on over to `https://developer.xamarin.com/visual-studio-mac/` and click on the download link. The installation process is somewhat similar to the installation process in the first recipe of this chapter. The difference here is that the actual Visual Studio application will be installed on the Mac and not on a Windows PC on the same network.

Getting ready

After downloading Visual Studio for Mac, start the installation process. This is very similar to the process outlined in the first recipe. It can take a while to complete, so once again, go get yourself a cup of coffee. Creating applications with Visual Studio for Mac is a familiar experience for .NET developers coming from Visual Studio for Windows.

At the heart of Visual Studio for Mac is the Roslyn compiler that is used for refactoring and IntelliSense. The build engine is MSBuild and the debugger engine is the same for Xamarin and .NET Core applications. The software requirements for Xamarin development and Visual Studio for Mac are as follows:

- You will need a Mac running OS X El Capitan (10.11) or macOS Sierra.
- The iOS 10 SDK that ships with Xcode 8 is required. Xcode can be downloaded for free as long as you have a valid iTunes account.
- Visual Studio for Mac requires .NET Core which can be downloaded by following the steps outlined at `https://www.microsoft.com/net/core#macos`. You must complete all the steps listed to ensure that .NET Core is installed correctly. While you are there, make a note to watch a few of Kendra Havens' Channel 9 videos on getting started with .NET Core, at `https://channel9.msdn.com/`. While you are at it, have a look at the other brilliant content on Channel 9.
- If you plan to submit your applications to the Apple App Store, then you will need to purchase a developer license, which is currently priced at $99/year. You can, however, develop your applications without purchasing a developer license.

Note that if you plan to install Visual Studio for Mac alongside Xamarin Studio, then you need to be aware that Visual Studio for Mac requires Mono 4.8. Installing Xamarin Studio will downgrade Mono to an older version. To get around this, you need to opt out of the Mono 4.6 selection during the Xamarin Studio update screen.

With this rather detailed checklist of requirements out of the way, let's get ready to create an iOS application.

How to do it...

1. Launch Visual Studio for Mac and sign in with your Microsoft Account details. You will notice the **Get Started** section that lists a number of useful articles that help developers get up and running with Visual Studio for Mac:

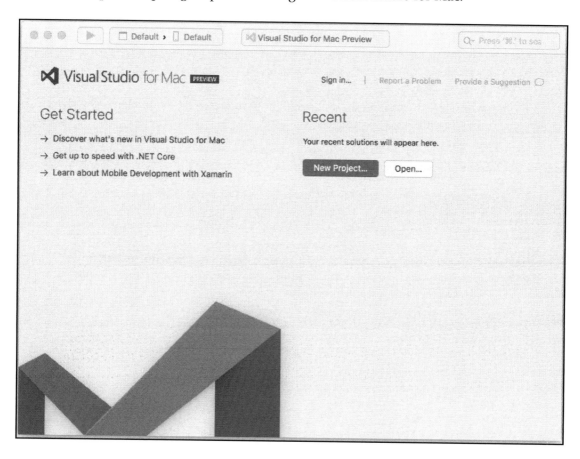

2. Next, click on **New Project...** and select the **Forms App** project from the **Xamarin.Forms** group in the **Multiplatform App** templates. Then, click on **Next**:

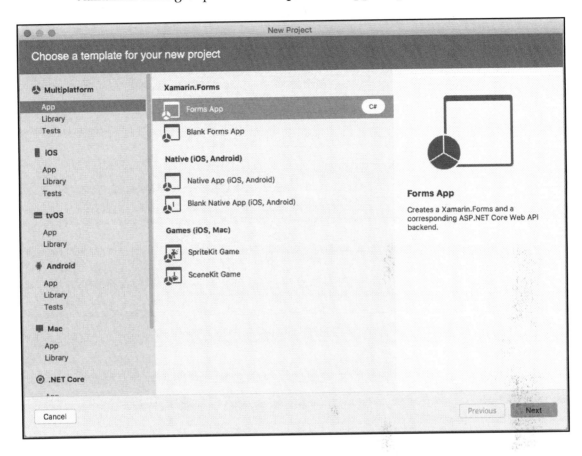

3. We then need to give our application a name and an **Organization Identifier**. I simply called my app `HelloWorld` and then selected only **iOS** under **Target Platforms**. Click on **Next** to continue:

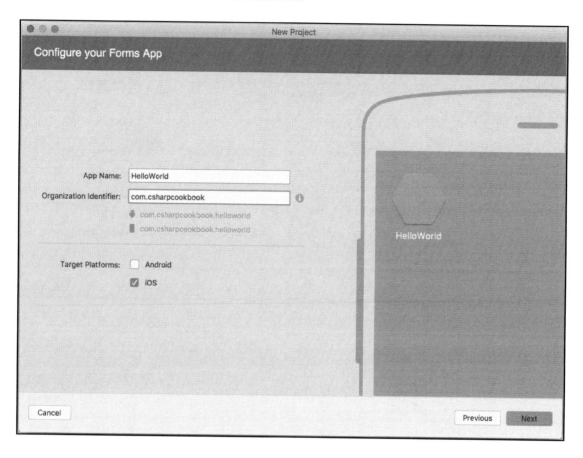

4. Lastly, decide whether you want to configure your project to use Git for version control and **Xamarin Test Cloud**. When you have configured what you need to, click on **Create**:

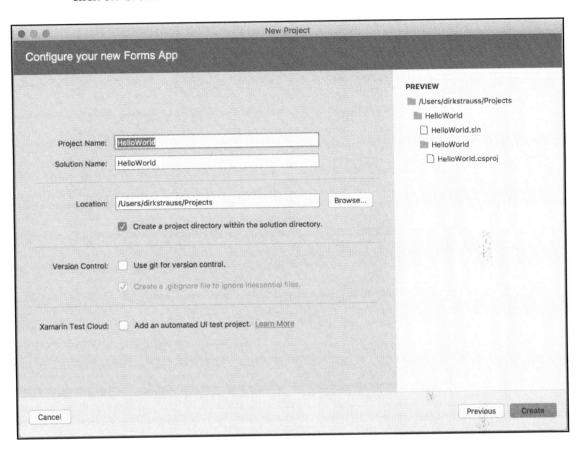

5. When your project is created, you will notice that you can select the device you want to simulate by clicking on the down arrow next to the Debug button:

6. This will list the different simulators available to you, as well as any devices tethered to your Mac (in this case, my iPhone):

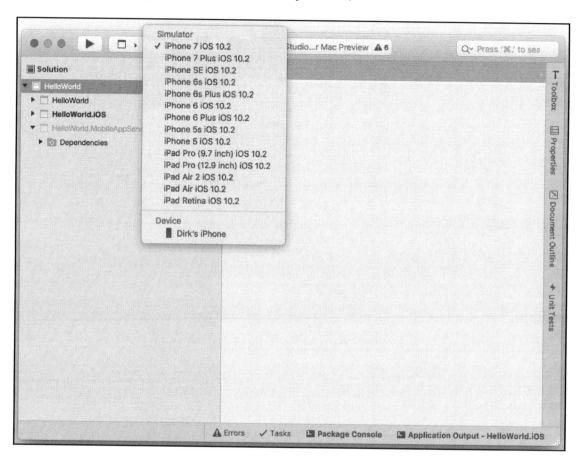

7. Clicking on the Run button will launch the simulator for the selected device and display the default application created for you when you created the **Xamarin.Forms** iOS application:

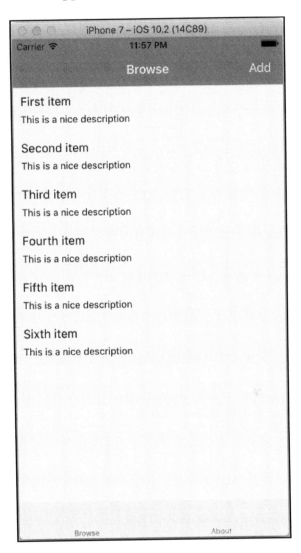

8. The application in the simulator is fully functional and you can interact with it to get a feel for how the simulator works. As mentioned earlier, if you have an iOS device tethered to your Mac, you can even launch the application on your device to test it. Clicking on the **About** tab, for example, will display the **About** page:

9. Click on the Stop button in Visual Studio for Mac and go back to your solution. Expand the `ViewModels` and `Views` folders. You will see a very familiar structure:

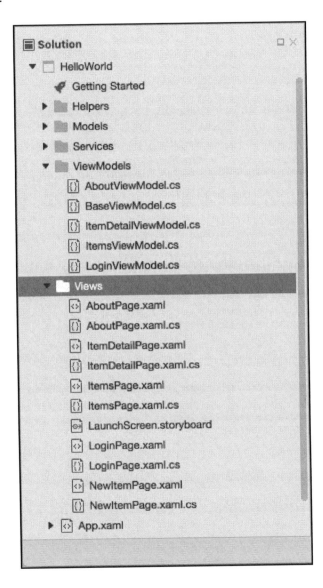

10. In the `ViewModels` folder, open the `AboutViewModel.cs` file. In the constructor `AboutViewModel()`, you will see the following code:

```
public AboutViewModel()
{
  Title = "About";
  OpenWebCommand = new Command(() => Device.OpenUri(new
    Uri("https://xamarin.com/platform")));
}
```

11. For now, just to illustrate the use of C#, change the code here to look like the following code listing. Do you notice the first line of code? The section after `var titleText =` is an interpolated string `$"Hello World – The date is {DateTime.Now.ToString("MMMM dd yyyy")}";`. Interpolated strings were introduced in C# 6.0. Click on the Play button to launch the application in the simulator:

```
public AboutViewModel()
{
  var titleText = $"Hello World – The date is {
    DateTime.Now.ToString("MMMM dd yyyy")}";
  Title = titleText;
  OpenWebCommand = new Command(() => Device.OpenUri(new
    Uri("https://xamarin.com/platform")));
}
```

12. Now, click on the **About** tab again and look at the title. The title has changed to display **Hello World** and the current date:

How it works...

Well, I will be the first to admit that the code we wrote was not earth-shattering at all. In fact, we basically piggybacked on an existing application and just modified a little bit of code to display Hello World and the current date. One thing that you need to remember here though is that we have written C# code and compiled that to a native iOS application.

There is still much to learn. We have not even scratched the surface with what is available now with Visual Studio for Mac, Xamarin.Forms and cross-platform C# applications. Xamarin has really good documentation that will assist you as you navigate the new causeways of developing applications using Xamarin. A nice case study to read through is the Tasky case study, which can be found at `https://developer.xamarin.com/guides/cross-platform/application_fundamentals/building_cross_platform_applications/case_study-tasky/`. This will give you a good idea about what is involved with developing a cross-platform application using Xamarin.

Why don't you try to play around a bit more with the application we just created? See what is possible and what differences there are in approaching database logic and reading user input, for example. Visual Studio for Mac has opened a new world for developers, making it easier than ever to get started developing native iOS applications.

14

Writing Secure Code and Debugging in Visual Studio

In this chapter, we will take a look at some examples of being more efficient as a developer when it comes to debugging your code. We will also be looking at how to write secure code. Writing secure code can be a challenge, but consider the following: if part of your code security involves making sure that passwords are securely stored, why write that code over and over between projects? Write the code once and implement it in every new project you create. The concepts we will be looking at are as follows:

- Encrypting and storing passwords correctly
- Using SecureString in code
- Securing sensitive parts of the App.config/web.config
- Preventing SQL injection attacks
- Using IntelliTrace, diagnostic tools, and historical debugging
- Setting conditional breakpoints
- Using PerfTips to identify bottlenecks in code

Introduction

Something that many developers tend to miss is the need to write secure code. Development deadlines and other project-related pressures cause developers to put delivering code above doing it the right way. Many of you might not agree with me, but believe me when I say that I have heard the excuse of, "We do not have the budget for this," one too many times. This is usually when the development budget has been determined by other stakeholders and the developer not consulted.

Consider a situation where a consultant tells the developer that they have sold a system to a customer. That system now needs to be developed. Furthermore, the developer is told that they have *x* amount of hours to complete the development. A document outlining the requirements is given to the developer and the developer is given the go-ahead to begin, and to complete development in the required time.

This scenario is the reality many developers face. You might think that this scenario can't possibly exist, or perhaps you are reading this and relate to the scenario as being how the process currently works in your company. Whatever the case may be, this is something that happens today in software development.

So, how do developers combat project suicide (I call these projects this because projects approached like this rarely succeed)? Start by creating reusable code. Think of processes you repeat often enough to warrant writing a reusable DLL for. Did you know that you can create Visual Studio templates? If you have a standard project structure you use, create a template from it and reuse it for each new project, thereby speeding up delivery and cutting down on bugs.

A few considerations for project templates are database layers, security layers, common validation code (does this data table contain any data?), common extension methods, and so on.

Encrypting and storing passwords correctly

One thing I have often seen is badly stored passwords. Just because the password is stored in a database on your server, does not make it secure. So, what do badly stored passwords look like?

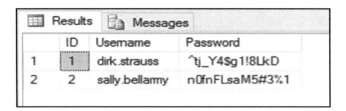

Secure passwords stored badly are no longer secure. The passwords in the previous screenshot are the actual user passwords. Entering the first password, ^tj_Y4$g1!8LkD at the login screen will give the user access to the system. Passwords should be stored securely in the database. In fact, you need to employ salted password hashing. You should be able to encrypt the user's password, but never decrypt it.

So, how do you decrypt the password to match it to the password the user enters on the login screen? Well, you don't. You always hash the password the user enters at the login screen. If it matches the hash of their real password stored in the database, you give them access to the system.

Getting ready

The SQL tables in this recipe are for illustration only and are not writtento by the code in the recipe. The database can be found in the _database scripts folder that accompanies the source code for this book.

How to do it...

1. The easiest way is to create a console application and then add a new class library by right-clicking on your solution, and selecting **Add** and then **New Project** from the context menu.

2. From the **Add New Project** dialog screen, select **Class Library** from the installed templates and call your class Chapter15.

3. Your new class library will be added to your solution with a default name of Class1.cs, which we renamed Recipes.cs in order to distinguish the code properly. You can, however, rename your class whatever you like if that makes more sense to you.

4. To rename your class, simply click on the class name in the **Solution Explorer** and select **Rename** from the context menu.

5. Visual Studio will ask you to confirm a rename of all references to the code element **Class1** in the project. Just click on **Yes**.

6. The following class is added to your `Chapter15` library project:

```
namespace Chapter15
{
  public static class Recipes
  {

  }
}
```

7. Add the following `using` statement to your class:

```
using System.Security.Cryptography;
```

8. Next, you need to add two properties to the class. These properties will store the salt and the hash. Usually you will write these values to the database along with the username, but, for the purposes of this recipe, we will simply add them to the static properties. Also add two methods to the class called `RegisterUser()` and `ValidateLogin()`. Both methods take as parameters the `username` and `password` variables:

```
public static class Recipes
{
  public static string saltValue { get; set; }
  public static string hashValue { get; set; }

  public static void RegisterUser(string password, string
    username)
  {

  }

  public static void ValidateLogin(string password,
    string username)
  {

  }
}
```

9. Starting with the `RegisterUser()` method, here we do a number of things. To list the steps in the method:

    1. We generate a truly random, cryptographically strong salt value using `RNGCryptoServiceProvider`.

2. Add the salt to the password and hash the salted password using SHA256.

It doesn't matter if you add the salt before or after the password. Just remember to be consistent each time you do it.

3. Store the salt value and the hash value along with the username in the database.

In order to cut down on code, I have not actually added code to write the hash and salt values to the database. I simply added them to the properties created earlier. In a real-world situation, you would always write these to the database.

This is a very secure way to handle user passwords in your application:

```
public static void RegisterUser(string password, string  username)
{
    // Create a truly random salt using RNGCryptoServiceProvider.
    RNGCryptoServiceProvider csprng = new RNGCryptoServiceProvider();
    byte[] salt = new byte[32];
    csprng.GetBytes(salt);

    // Get the salt value
    saltValue = Convert.ToBase64String(salt);
    // Salt the password
    byte[] saltedPassword = Encoding.UTF8.GetBytes(
        saltValue + password);

    // Hash the salted password using SHA256
    SHA256Managed hashstring = new SHA256Managed();
    byte[] hash = hashstring.ComputeHash(saltedPassword);

    // Save both the salt and the hash in the user's database record.
    saltValue = Convert.ToBase64String(salt);
    hashValue = Convert.ToBase64String(hash);
}
```

10. The next method we need to create is the `ValidateLogin()` method. Here, we take the username and validate that first. If the user entered the username incorrectly, do not tell them so. This would alert someone trying to compromise the system that they have the wrong username and that as soon as they get a wrong password notification, they know that the username is correct. The steps in this method are as follows:

    1. Get the salt and hash values for the entered username from the database.
    2. Salt the password the user entered at the login screen with the salt read from the database.
    3. Hash the salted password using the same hashing algorithm when the user registered.
    4. Compare the hash value read from the database to the hash value generated in the method. If the two hashes match, then the password is correctly entered and the user validated.

Note that we never decrypt the password from the database. If you have code decrypting user passwords and matching the password entered, you need to reconsider and rewrite your password logic. A system should never be able to decrypt user passwords.

```
public static void ValidateLogin(string password, string username)
{
  // Read the user's salt value from the database
  string saltValueFromDB = saltValue;

  // Read the user's hash value from the database
  string hashValueFromDB = hashValue;

  byte[] saltedPassword = Encoding.UTF8.GetBytes(
    saltValueFromDB + password);

  // Hash the salted password using SHA256
  SHA256Managed hashstring = new SHA256Managed();
  byte[] hash = hashstring.ComputeHash(saltedPassword);

  string hashToCompare = Convert.ToBase64String(hash);

  if (hashValueFromDB.Equals(hashToCompare))
    Console.WriteLine("User Validated.");
  else
    Console.WriteLine("Login credentials incorrect. User not
      validated.");
}
```

11. To test the code, add a reference to the `Chapter15` class in your `CodeSamples` project.

12. Because we created a static class, you can add the new `using static` to your `Program.cs` file:

    ```
    using static Chapter15.Recipes;
    ```

13. Test the code by calling the `RegisterUser()` method and pass it the `username` and `password` variable. After that, call the `ValidateLogin()` method and see whether the password matches the hash. This would obviously not happen at the same time in a real production system:

    ```
    string username = "dirk.strauss";
    string password = "^tj_Y4$g1!8LkD";
    RegisterUser(password, username);

    ValidateLogin(password, username);
    Console.ReadLine();
    ```

14. When you debug the code, you will see the user has been validated:

15. Lastly, modify the code slightly and set the `password` variable to something else. This will mimic a user entering an incorrect password:

```
string username = "dirk.strauss";
string password = "^tj_Y4$g1!8LkD";
RegisterUser(password, username);

password = "WrongPassword";
ValidateLogin(password, username);
Console.ReadLine();
```

16. When you debug the application, you will see that the user is not validated:

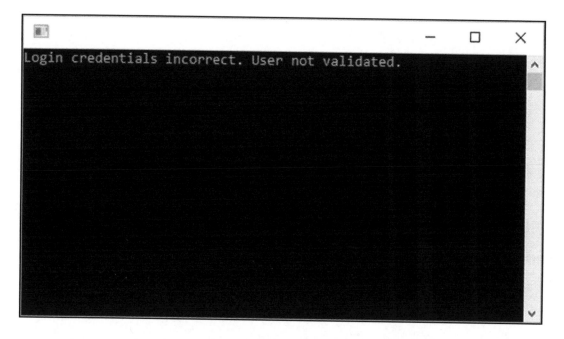

How it works...

Nowhere in the code did we decrypt the password. In fact, the password is never stored anywhere. We always worked with the hash of the password. Here are the important points to take away from this recipe:

- Never use the `Random` class in C# to generate your salt. Always use the `RNGCryptoServiceProvider` class.

- Never reuse the same salt in your code. So don't create a constant with your salt and use it to salt all the passwords in your system.
- Never tell the user that the password is incorrect if the password didn't match. Also, never tell the user that they entered an incorrect username. This prevents someone trying to compromise the system after discovering that they got one of the two login credentials correct. Rather, if either the username or password has been entered incorrectly, notify the user that their login credentials are incorrect. This could mean that either the username or password (or both) has been entered incorrectly.
- You can't get the passwords from the hash or salt stored in the database. Therefore, if the database was compromised, the password data stored within it would not be at risk. The encryption of the user's password is a one-way operation, meaning that it can never be decrypted. Also important to note is that, even if the source code was compromised and stolen by someone with malicious intent, you would not be able to use the code to decipher the encrypted data in the database.
- Combine the previous methods with a strong password policy (because even in 2016, there are still users that think using `13tm31n` for a password is good enough), and you have a very good password encryption routine.

When we look at the user access table, the correct way to store user credentials would look something like this:

	ID	Username	Salt	Hash
1	1	dirk.strauss	KxZH/jO8OFbNBvAiUJDnTHwGGMJ384+Tlq1JbKnKYY=	Togax/WIna6Y8wblyiSvX7GRQBf4MQ+foBfobSILzo=
2	2	sally.bellamy	9qSLUCH+VLQYa5DIlwiclpQoadyiVKIlxqqsuabN3k0=	vOBzPiM2Z+qxed7n8gVlKGfnm3o6lvqXIRkrWR2hM9k=

The salt and hash are stored alongside the username, and are secure because they can't be decrypted to expose the actual password.

> If you sign up for a service on the Internet and they send you a confirmation either via e-mail or text message and display your password in this message in plain text, then you should seriously consider closing your account. If a system can read your password and send it to you in plain text, so can anybody else. Never use the same password for all your logins.

Using SecureString in code

Securing your application against malicious attacks is not an easy task. It is the constant struggle between writing secure code while minimizing bugs (which hackers usually exploit) and black hats writing more and more sophisticated methods to compromise systems and networks. I personally believe that higher learning institutions need to teach IT students two things:

- How to use and integrate with a popular ERP system
- Proper software security principles

In fact, I believe that secure programming 101 must not simply be a module or topic in a given IT course, but a whole course on its own. It needs to be handled with the seriousness and respect it deserves and needs to preferably be taught by someone who can actually hack a system or network.

White hats teaching students how to compromise systems, exploit vulnerable code, and infiltrate networks will make a big difference in changing the way future software developers approach programming. It comes down to developers knowing what not to do when programming defensively. It is quite possible that some of those students might go on to become black hats themselves, but they would have done that irrespective of whether they took a class on hacking secure programming or not.

Getting ready

The code might look a little funny in some places. This is because SecureString is using unmanaged memory to store the sensitive information. Rest assured that SecureString is well supported and used within the .NET Framework, as can be seen from the instantiation of the SqlCredential object used in creating connections to a database:

```
SqlCredential cred = new SqlCredential()
            SqlCredential(string userId, SecureString password)
            Creates an object of type SqlCredential.
            userId: The user id.
```

How to do it...

1. Start by adding a new Windows forms project to your solution.
2. Call the project `winformSecure` and click on the **OK** button.
3. In the **Toolbox**, search for the **TextBox** control and add it to your form.
4. Lastly, add a button control to your form. You can resize this form, however you like to look more like a login form:

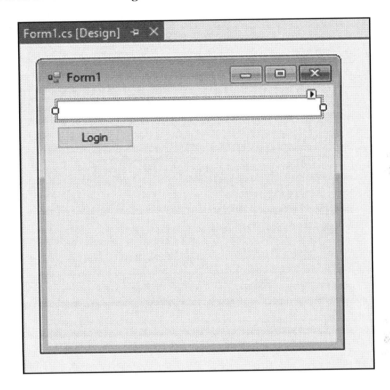

5. With the textbox control selected on the Windows forms, open up the **Properties** panel and click on the **Events** button (it looks like a lightning bolt). In the **Key** group, double-click on the **KeyPress** event to create the handler in the code behind:

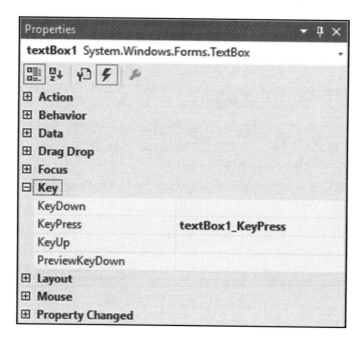

The code that is created for you is the **KeyPress** event handler for the textbox control. This will fire whenever a user presses a key on the keyboard:

```
private void textBox1_KeyPress(object sender,  KeyPressEventArgs e)
{

}
```

6. Back in the **Properties** panel, expand the **Behavior** group and change the value of **UseSystemPasswordChar** to True:

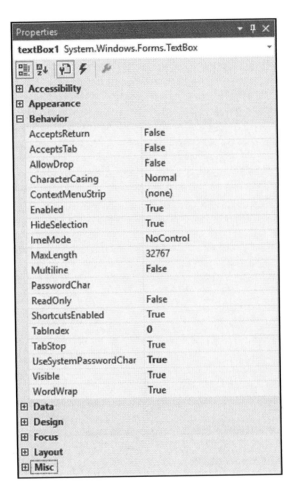

7. In the code behind, add the following using statement:

```
using System.Runtime.InteropServices;
```

8. Add the SecureString variable as a global variable to your Windows forms:

```
SecureString secure = new SecureString();
```

9. Then, in the `KeyPress` event, append the `KeyChar` value to the `SecureString` variable every time the user presses a key. You might want to add code to ignore certain key presses, but this is beyond the scope of this recipe:

```
private void textBox1_KeyPress(object sender,  KeyPressEventArgs e)
{
   secure.AppendChar(e.KeyChar);
}
```

10. Then, in the **Login** button's event handler, add the following code to read the value from the `SecureString` object. Here, we are working with unmanaged memory and unmanaged code:

```
private void btnLogin_Click(object sender, EventArgs e)
{
   IntPtr unmanagedPtr = IntPtr.Zero;

   try
   {
     if (secure == null)
     throw new ArgumentNullException("Password not defined");
     unmanagedPtr = Marshal.SecureStringToGlobalAllocUnicode(
        secure);
     MessageBox.Show($"SecureString password to validate is
                  {Marshal.PtrToStringUni(unmanagedPtr)}");
   }
   catch(Exception ex)
   {
     MessageBox.Show(ex.Message);
   }
   finally
   {
     Marshal.ZeroFreeGlobalAllocUnicode(unmanagedPtr);
     secure.Dispose();
   }
}
```

11. Run your Windows forms application and type in a password:

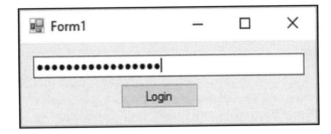

12. Then click on the **Login** button. You will then see the password you typed in displayed in the message box:

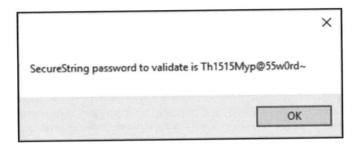

How it works...

It has become almost a habit for many developers to use System.String to store sensitive information such as passwords. The problem with this approach is that System.String is immutable. This means that the object created in memory by System.String can't be changed. If you modify the variable, a new object is created in memory. You also cannot determine when the object created by System.String will be removed from memory during garbage collection. Conversely, using the SecureString object, you will encrypt sensitive information and, when that object is no longer needed, it is deleted from memory. SecureString encrypts and decrypts your sensitive data in unmanaged memory.

Now, I need to be clear regarding one thing here. `SecureString` is by no means foolproof. If your system contains a virus with the sole purpose of compromising the `SecureString` operations, using it doesn't help much (be sure to use proper anti-virus software anyway). At some point during the code execution, the string representation of your password (or sensitive information) is visible. Secondly, if a hacker somehow found a way to inspect your heap or log your key strokes, the password might be visible. The use of `SecureString`, however, makes this window of opportunity for a hacker much smaller. The window of opportunity reduces because there are less attack vectors (points of entry for a hacker) thereby reducing your attack surface (sum of all points of attack by a hacker).

The bottom line is this: `SecureString` is there for a reason. As a software developer concerned about security, you should be using `SecureString`.

Securing sensitive parts of the App.config/web.config

As a developer, you will undoubtedly work with sensitive information such as passwords. How you handle this information during development is very important. In the past, I have received copies of a client's live database to use for testing. This does pose a very real security risk for your client.

Often, we keep settings in a `web.config` file (when working with web applications). For this example, though, I will be demonstrating a console application that uses an `App.config` file. The same logic can be applied to a `web.config` file too.

Getting ready

Creating a console application is the quickest way to demonstrate this recipe. If, however, you want to follow along using a web application (and securing a `web.config` file), you can do so.

How to do it...

1. In the console application, locate the `App.config` file. This is the file that contains the sensitive data.

2. If you open the `App.config` file, you will see that, within the `appSettings` tag, there is a key added called `Secret`. This information should probably not be in the `App.config` to start off with. The problem here is that it might be checked into your source control. Imagine that on GitHub?

```xml
<?xml version="1.0" encoding="utf-8"?>
<configuration>
  <startup>
    <supportedRuntime version="v4.0" sku=".NETFramework,
    Version=v4.6.1"/>
  </startup>
  <appSettings>
    <add key="name" value="Dirk"/>
    <add key="lastname" value="Strauss"/>
    <add key="Secret" value="letMeIn"/>
  </appSettings>
</configuration>
```

3. To overcome this vulnerability, we need to move the sensitive data out of the `App.config` file into another file. To do this, we specify a path to a file that will contain the sensitive data we want to remove from the `App.config` file.

```
<appSettings file="C:\temp\secret\secret.config">:
```

 You might be wondering why not simply just encrypt the information. Well, that is a given really. The reason this value is in plain text is just to demonstrate a concept here. You would probably encrypt this value anyway in a real-world situation. You would not, however, want this sensitive information sitting on a server in a code repository somewhere, even if it is encrypted. Be safe, move it out of your solution.

4. When you have added the path to the secure file, remove the key containing the sensitive information:

```
 1    <?xml version="1.0" encoding="utf-8"?>
 2    <configuration>
 3        <startup>
 4            <supportedRuntime version="v4.0" sku=".NETFramework,Version=v4.6.1"/>
 5        </startup>
 6        <appSettings file="C:\temp\secret\secret.config">
 7            <add key="name" value="Dirk"/>
 8            <add key="lastname" value="Strauss"/>
 9        </appSettings>
10    </configuration>
```

5. Navigate to the path you specified in the App.config file property. Create your secret.config file and open it up for editing:

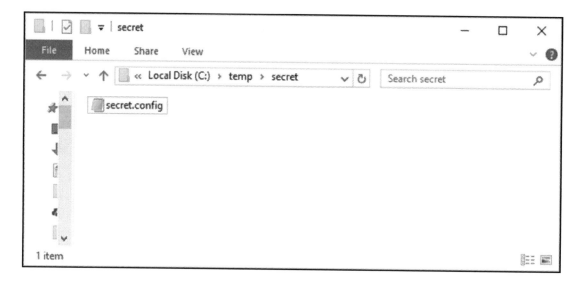

6. Inside this file, repeat the `appSettings` section and add the `Secret` key to it. What happens now is that, when your console application runs, it reads the `appSettings` section in your solution and finds the reference to the secret file. It then looks for the secret file and merges it with the `App.config` in your solution:

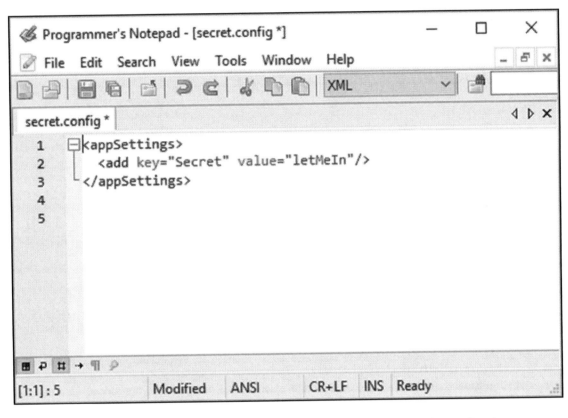

7. To see that this merge works, add a reference to your console application.

8. Search for and add `System.Configuration` to your references:

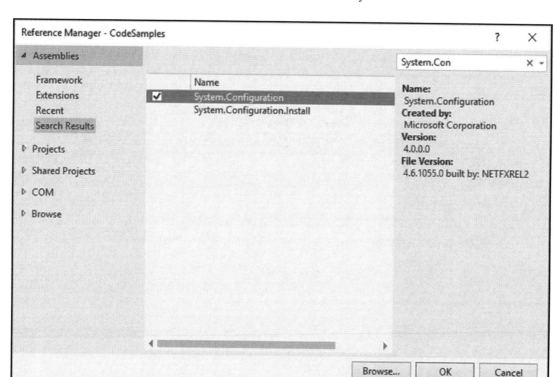

9. When you have added the reference, your solution references will list **System.Configuration**.

10. To the top of your `Program.cs` file, add the following `using` statement:

```
using System.Configuration;
```

11. Add the following code to read the `Secret` key setting from your `App.config` file. Only this time, it will read the merged file, which is made up of your `App.config` and your `secret.config` file:

```
string sSecret = ConfigurationManager.AppSettings["Secret"];
Console.WriteLine(sSecret);
Console.ReadLine();
```

12. Run your console application, and you will see that the sensitive data has been read from the `secret.config` file, which was merged with the `App.config` file at runtime:

How it works...

Something I need to point out here is that this technique will also work for `web.config` files. If you need to remove sensitive information from your configuration file, move it to another file so that it doesn't get included in your source control check-in or deployment.

Preventing SQL injection attacks

SQL injection attacks are a very real problem. There are too many applications that still make themselves vulnerable to this kind of attack. If you develop a web application or website, you should be vigilant about bad database operations. Vulnerable in-line SQL exposes the database to a SQL injection attack. A SQL injection attack is where an attacker modifies SQL statements via a web form input box to produce a different result than originally intended. This is usually attempted on a form where the web application is supposed to access the database to authenticate the user login. By not sanitizing the user input, you are exposing your data to exploits such as this.

The accepted solution to mitigate SQL injection attacks is to create a parameterized stored procedure, and call that from your code.

Getting ready

You need to create the CookbookDB database in your SQL Server before continuing this recipe. You will find the script in the _database scripts folder in the accompanying source code.

How to do it...

1. For this recipe, I am using SQL Server 2012. The concept is the same if you are using an older version of SQL Server. After you have created the CookbookDB database, you will see that there is a table called UserDisplayData under the Tables folder:

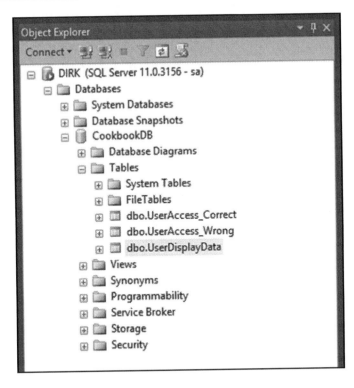

2. The `UserDisplayData` table is simply used to illustrate the concept of querying using a parameterized stored procedure. It would not have any real benefit in a production database, because it only returns a screen name:

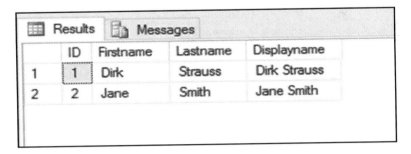

3. We need to create a stored procedure to select data from this table for a specific ID (user ID). Click on the `Programmability` node to expand it:

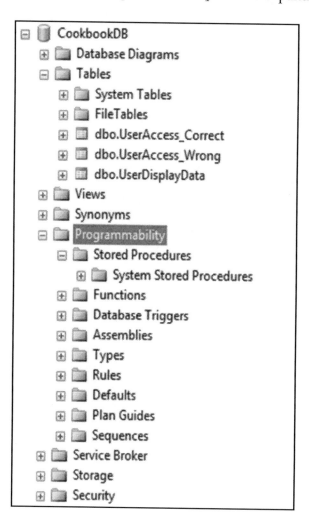

4. Next, right-click on the `Stored Procedures` node and select **New Stored Procedure...** from the context menu:

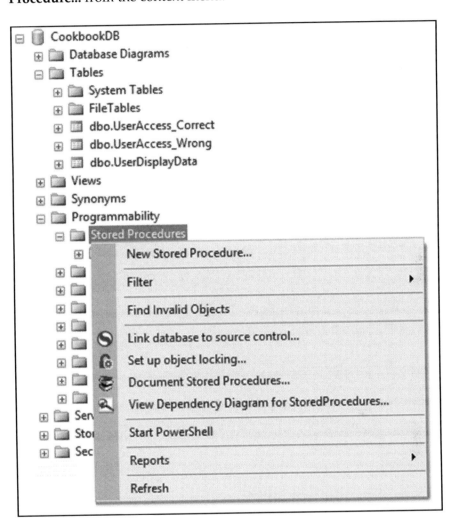

5. SQL Server will create the following stored procedure template for you. This template consists of a section where you can comment on the particular stored procedure, as well as a section to add parameters you might need, and obviously a section that you need to add the actual SQL statement to:

```
SET ANSI_NULLS ON
GO
SET QUOTED_IDENTIFIER ON
GO
-- =============================================
-- Author:          <Author,,Name>
-- Create date:     <Create Date,,>
-- Description:     <Description,,>
-- =============================================
CREATE PROCEDURE <Procedure_Name, sysname, ProcedureName>
    -- Add the parameters for the stored procedure here
    <@Param1, sysname, @p1> <Datatype_For_Param1, , int> =
    <Default_Value_For_Param1, , 0>,
    <@Param2, sysname, @p2> <Datatype_For_Param2, , int> =
<Default_Value_For_Param2, , 0>
AS
BEGIN
-- SET NOCOUNT ON added to prevent extra result sets       from
-- interfering with SELECT statements.
SET NOCOUNT ON;

-- Insert statements for procedure here
SELECT <@Param1, sysname, @p1>, <@Param2, sysname, @p2>
END
GO
```

6. Give the stored procedure a suitable name that will describe the action or intent of the stored procedure:

```
CREATE PROCEDURE cb_ReadCurrentUserDisplayData
```

There are many people that do prefix their stored procedures, and I'm one of those. I like to keep my stored procedures grouped. I, therefore, name my stored procedures in the format *[prefix]_[tablename_or_module]_[stored_procedure_action]*. Having said that, I generally avoid using `sp_` as a prefix to my stored procedures. There are a lot of opinions on the Internet as to why this is a bad idea. It is generally believed that using `sp_` as a stored procedure prefix impacts on performance because it is used as the stored procedure prefix in the master database. For the purposes of this recipe, I have just kept to a simple name for the stored procedure.

7. Define a parameter for this stored procedure. By doing this, you are telling the database that when this stored procedure is called, it will pass through a value of type integer that is stored in a parameter caller `@userID`:

   ```
   @userID INT
   ```

8. You now define the SQL statement to be used by this stored procedure. We are just going to do a straightforward `SELECT` statement:

   ```
   SELECT
       Firstname, Lastname, Displayname
   FROM
       dbo.UserDisplayData
   WHERE
       ID = @userID
   ```

   You will notice that my `SELECT` statement contains the specific column names instead of a `SELECT * FROM`. Doing a `SELECT *` is considered bad practice. You would usually not want to return all the column values from a table. If you want all the column values, then it is better to explicitly list the columns by name instead of just getting all. Using `SELECT *` returns unnecessary columns and increases the overhead on the server. This does make a difference in the bigger scheme of things, especially when the database starts getting a lot of traffic. The thought of having to type out the column names for a large table is definitely not something I would look forward to. You can, however, use the following tricks to make it easy for you to add the column names to your SQL `SELECT` statement. You can right-click on the database table and select **Script Table As** to create one of several SQL statements. Secondly, you can expand the `Table` node and expand the table you wish to write the statement for. You will then see a node called `Columns`. Drag the `Columns` node onto the query editor. That will insert all the column names into the query editor for you.

9. When you have completed adding the code to your stored procedure, it will look like this:

```
SET ANSI_NULLS ON
GO
SET QUOTED_IDENTIFIER ON
GO
-- =============================================
-- Author:        <Dirk Strauss>
-- Create date:   <2 April 2016>
-- Description:   <Read the user data for the specific user ID supplied as parameter>
-- =============================================
CREATE PROCEDURE cb_ReadCurrentUserDisplayData
        @userID INT
AS
BEGIN
        -- SET NOCOUNT ON added to prevent extra result sets from
        -- interfering with SELECT statements.
        SET NOCOUNT ON;

        SELECT
            Firstname, Lastname, Displayname
        FROM
            dbo.UserDisplayData
        WHERE
            ID = @userID
END
GO
```

10. To create the stored procedure, you need to click on the **Execute** button. Be certain that you have the correct database selected when clicking on the **Execute** button:

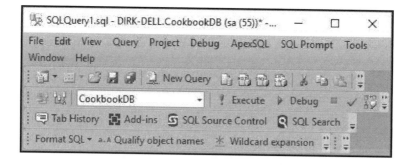

11. The stored procedure will then be created under the `Stored Procedures` node in SQL Server:

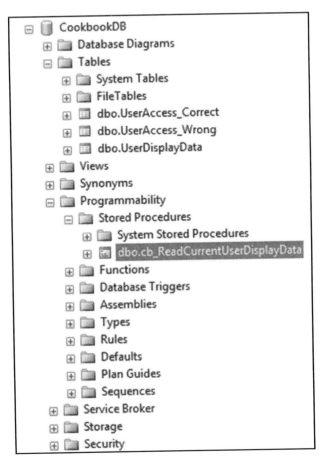

12. We have now come halfway through this task. It is time to construct the code that we will use in our application to query the database. We will be adding this code directly to the `Program.cs` file of your console application. While this code isn't considered best practice (hardcoding the server credentials), it serves merely to illustrate the concept of calling a parameterized stored procedure from C#.

13. To start, add the following `using` statement to the top of your console application:

```
using System.Data.SqlClient;
```

14. We then add the variables to contain the credentials we need to log on to the server:

```
int intUserID = 1;
int cmdTimeout = 15;
string server = "DIRK";
string db = "CookbookDB";
string uid = "dirk";
string password = "uR^GP2ABG19@!R";
```

15. We now use `SecureString` to store the password and add it to a `SqlCredential` object:

```
SecureString secpw = new SecureString();
if (password.Length > 0)
{
   foreach (var c in password.ToCharArray()) secpw.AppendChar(c);
}
secpw.MakeReadOnly();

string dbConn = $"Data Source={server};Initial Catalog={db};";
SqlCredential cred = new SqlCredential(uid, secpw);
```

 For more on `SecureString`, see the *Using SecureString in code* recipe of this chapter.

16. We now create a `SqlConnection` object inside a `using` statement. This ensures that the SQL connection is closed when the `using` statement moves out of scope:

```
using (SqlConnection conn = new SqlConnection(dbConn,  cred))
{
   try
   {

   }
   catch (Exception ex)
   {
      Console.WriteLine(ex.Message);
   }
}
Console.ReadLine();
```

17. Inside the `try`, add the following code to open the connection string and create a `SqlCommand` object that takes the open connection and name of the stored procedure as parameters. You can use the shortcut method of creating the actual SQL parameter to pass to the stored procedure:

```
cmd.Parameters.Add("userID", SqlDbType.Int).Value = intUserID;
```

Because I'm just passing a parameter of type integer to the stored procedure, I'm not defining a length for this parameter:

```
cmd.Parameters.Add("userID", SqlDbType.Int).Value = intUserID;
```

▲ 3 of 4 ▼ SqlParameter SqlParameterCollection.Add(string parameterName, SqlDbType **sqlDbType**, int size)
Adds a SqlParameter to the SqlParameterCollection, given the specified parameter name, SqlDbType and size.
sqlDbType: *The SqlDbType of the SqlParameter to add to the collection.*

If, however, you ever need to define a parameter of type `VarChar(MAX)`, you would need to define the size of the parameter type by adding –1. Let's say, for example, you need to store a student's essay in the database; the code would then look as follows for the `VarChar(MAX)`:

```
cmd.Parameters.Add("essay", SqlDbType.VarChar, -1).Value =
    essayValue;
```

18. After we have added our parameter with its value to the `SqlCommand` object, we specify a timeout value, execute the `SqlDataReader`, and load it into a `DataTable`. The value is then output to the console application:

```
conn.Open();
SqlCommand cmd = new SqlCommand("cb_ReadCurrentUserDisplayData",
    conn);
cmd.CommandType = CommandType.StoredProcedure;
cmd.Parameters.Add("userID", SqlDbType.Int).Value = intUserID;
cmd.CommandTimeout = cmdTimeout;
var returnData = cmd.ExecuteReader();
var dtData = new DataTable();
dtData.Load(returnData);

if (dtData.Rows.Count != 0)
    Console.WriteLine(dtData.Rows[0]["Displayname"]);
```

19. After you have added all the code to your console application, the correct completed code will look as follows:

```
int intUserID = 1;
int cmdTimeout = 15;
string server = "DIRK";
string db = "CookbookDB";
string uid = "dirk";
string password = "uR^GP2ABG19@!R";
SecureString secpw = new SecureString();
if (password.Length > 0)
{
    foreach (var c in password.ToCharArray())
        secpw.AppendChar(c);
}
secpw.MakeReadOnly();

string dbConn = $"Data Source={server};Initial Catalog={db};";

SqlCredential cred = new SqlCredential(uid, secpw);
using (SqlConnection conn = new SqlConnection(dbConn, cred))
{
    try
    {
        conn.Open();
        SqlCommand cmd = new SqlCommand(
            "cb_ReadCurrentUserDisplayData", conn);
        cmd.CommandType = CommandType.StoredProcedure;
        cmd.Parameters.Add("userID", SqlDbType.Int).Value = intUserID;
        cmd.CommandTimeout = cmdTimeout;
        var returnData = cmd.ExecuteReader();
        var dtData = new DataTable();
        dtData.Load(returnData);
        if (dtData.Rows.Count != 0)
            Console.WriteLine(dtData.Rows[0]["Displayname"]);
    }
    catch (Exception ex)
    {
        Console.WriteLine(ex.Message);
    }
}
Console.ReadLine();
```

20. Run your console application and you will see the display name output to the screen:

How it works...

By creating a parameterized SQL query, the compiler correctly substitutes the arguments before running the SQL statement against the database. It will prevent malicious data changing your SQL statement in order to exact a malicious result. This is because the SqlCommand object does not directly insert the parameter values into the statement.

To sum it all up, using parameterized stored procedures means no more Little Bobby Tables.

Using IntelliTrace, diagnostic tools, and historical debugging

The trusty old bug has been the bane of software developers and engineers for more than 140 years. Yes, you read that right. It was in fact Thomas Edison that coined the term "bug" in the late 1870s. It appeared in many of his notebook entries where he describes for example that the incandescent lightbulb still had many "bugs left".

His efforts to debug his inventions are quite legendary. Consider the true grit and determination it took for a man already in his mid-sixties to work 112-hour working weeks. He and his seven-person team (it is a common misconception that there were only six because the seventh member didn't appear in the group photograph) became known as the insomnia squad during a 5-week stint that resulted in very little sleep.

These days, thanks to the advances of technology, software developers have a vast array of debugging tools (inside and outside of Visual Studio) at their disposal. So does debugging really matter? Of course it does. It is part of what we as software developers do. If we don't debug, well, here are some examples:

- In 2004, the **Electronic Data Systems (EDS)** child support system in the UK overpaid almost 2 million people, while underpaying almost a million, and resulted in billions of dollars in uncollected child support payments. The incompatibility between EDS and another system it relied on resulted in taxpayers losing money and negatively affecting the lives of so many single parents.
- The initial release of Apple Maps in 2012. Enough said. While bemusing for many, I still find myself using Google Maps for turn-by-turn directions when in an unfamiliar city or area.
- The Therac-25 radiation therapy machine used electrons to target tumors in patients. Unfortunately, a race condition in the software caused the machine to deliver lethal overdoses of radiation in several patients.

Examples of software bugs affecting the lives of millions of people can be found all over the Internet. We're not simply talking about the run-of-the-mill bugs either. Sometimes, we're faced with seemingly insurmountable issues. It is the comfort of knowing how to use some of the tools available that makes the difference between a stable application and one that is totally unusable.

Getting ready

Note that IntelliTrace is only available in the Enterprise edition of Visual Studio. See the `htt ps://www.visualstudio.com/vs/compare/` link for comparisons between the versions of Visual Studio. IntelliTrace is not a new feature in Visual Studio. It has evolved over time (since Visual Studio 2010) into what we have available today.

How to do it...

1. To start off, go to **Tools**, **Options**.
2. Expand the **IntelliTrace** node and click on **General**. Ensure that **Enable IntelliTrace** is checked. Also, make sure that the **IntelliTrace events and call information** option is selected. Click on **OK**:

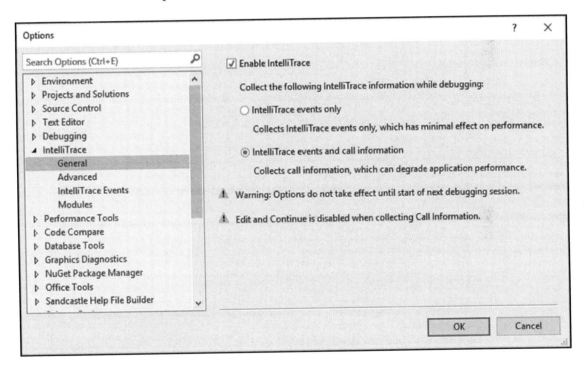

3. In the `Recipes.cs` file, you might need to add the following `using` statements:

```
using System.Diagnostics;
using System.Reflection;
using System.IO;
```

4. Add a method called `ErrorInception()` to the `Recipes` class. Also, add the code to read the base path and assume that there is a folder called `log`. Do not create this folder on your hard drive. We want an exception to be thrown. Lastly, add another method called `LogException()` that does nothing:

```
public static void ErrorInception()
{
    string basepath = Path.GetDirectoryName(
        Assembly.GetEntryAssembly().Location);
    var full = Path.Combine(basepath, "log");
}

private static void LogException(string message)
{

}
```

5. Add the following code to your `ErrorInception()` method after the full path has been determined. Here, we are trying to open the log file. This is where the exception will occur:

```
try
{
    for (int i = 0; i <= 3; i++)
    {
        // do work
        File.Open($"{full}log.txt", FileMode.Append);
    }
}
catch (Exception ex)
{
    StackTrace st = new StackTrace();
    StackFrame sf = st.GetFrame(0);
    MethodBase currentMethodName = sf.GetMethod();
    ex.Data.Add("Date", DateTime.Now);
    LogException(ex.Message);
}
```

6. When you have added all your code, your code should look like this:

```
public static void ErrorInception()
{
  string basepath = Path.GetDirectoryName(
    Assembly.GetEntryAssembly().Location);
  var full = Path.Combine(basepath, "log");

  try
  {
    for (int i = 0; i <= 3; i++)
    {
      // do work
      File.Open($"{full}log.txt", FileMode.Append);
    }
  }
  catch (Exception ex)
  {
    StackTrace st = new StackTrace();
    StackFrame sf = st.GetFrame(0);
    MethodBase currentMethodName = sf.GetMethod();
    ex.Data.Add("Date", DateTime.Now);
    LogException(ex.Message);
  }
}

private static void LogException(string message)
{

}
```

7. In the `Program.cs` file, call the `ErrorInception()` method. Right after that, do a `Console.ReadLine()` so that our console application will pause there. Do not add any breakpoints anywhere to your code:

```
ErrorInception();
Console.ReadLine();
```

8. Start debugging your application. The exception is thrown and the application continues running, a condition often experienced with much more complex applications. At this point, you would expect a log file to be appended with the fictitious data of the app, but nothing happened. It is, at this point, that you stop your application and start adding breakpoints all over your code in a hit and miss-type exercise. I say hit and miss because you probably won't know exactly where the error is. This is especially true if your code file contains a few thousand lines of code. Well now with IntelliTrace and historical debugging, you just need to click on the **Break All** button:

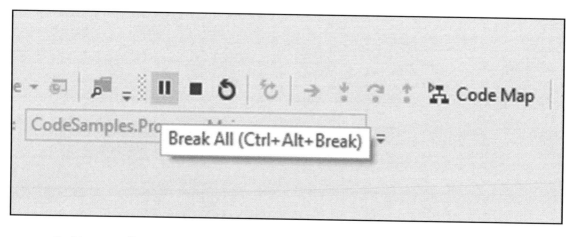

9. Your application is now essentially paused. If you don't see the **Diagnostic Tools** window, hold down *Ctrl + Alt + F2*.

10. Visual Studio now displays the **Diagnostic Tools** window. Immediately, you can see that there is a problem indicated by the red diamond icon on the **Events** section. In the **Events** tab at the bottom, you can click on the exception:

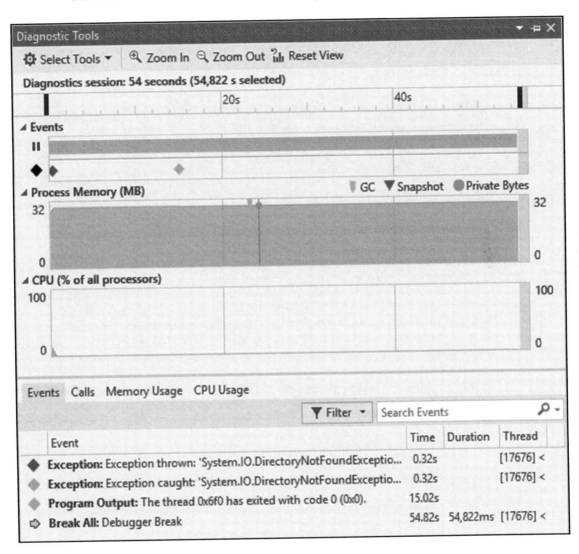

11. Doing this expands the exception details where you can see that the log file was not found. Visual Studio, however, goes one step further with historical debugging:

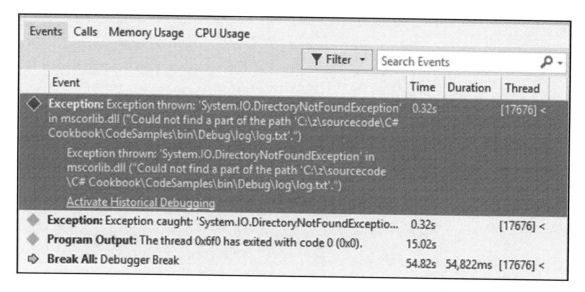

12. You will see a link at the bottom of the exception details that says **Activate Historical Debugging**. Click on this link. This allows you to see the actual line of code that caused this exception in the code editor. It also allows you to view the history of the applications state in the **Locals** window, call stack, and other windows. You can now see the specific line of code that caused the exception in your code editor. In the **Locals** window, you can also see what the path was that the application used to look for the log file. This kind of debugging experience is immensely powerful and allows developers to go straight to the source of the error. This leads to increased productivity and better code:

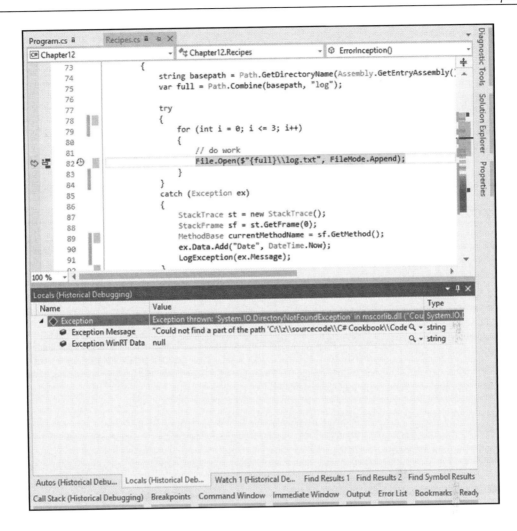

How it works...

So what is the takeaway here? If you only remember one thing, remember this. Once the users of your system lose faith in the abilities and potential of that system due to bugs, that confidence is almost impossible to regain. Even if you resurrect your system from the ashes, after it was laid low by bugs and other issues, to produce a flawless product, your users will not be easily swayed. This is because in their mind, the system is buggy.

I once had to take over a system partially developed by a senior developer who was leaving the company. She had an excellent specification and a well presented prototype shown to the customer. The only problem was that she left the company shortly after the system's phase one was implemented. When the bugs came popping up, the client naturally asked for her assistance.

Telling the client that the developer (who had been solely responsible for building a relationship with the client) had left the company did not bode well to instill a sense of confidence. Having a single developer involved was the first mistake of this particular project anyway.

Secondly, phase two was about to be developed by yours truly, who was also the only developer assigned to this client. This had to be done while building on top of the buggy phase one. So, I was fixing bugs while developing new features for the system. Luckily this time round, I had a fantastic project manager called Rory Shelton as my wingman. Together, we were dumped in the deep end and Rory did a fantastic job managing the client's expectations while being totally transparent with the client regarding the challenges we were facing.

The users were unfortunately already disillusioned with the provided system and didn't trust the software. This trust was never fully regained. If we had IntelliTrace and historical debugging back in 2007, I definitely would have been able to track down the issues in a code base that was unfamiliar to me.

Always debug your software. When you find no more bugs, debug it again. Then give the system to my mom (love you mom). You, as the developer of that system, know which buttons to click on and what data to enter, and in which order things need to happen. My mom doesn't and I can assure you that a user unfamiliar with a system can break it quicker than you can brew a fresh cup of coffee.

Visual Studio provides developers with a very powerful and feature rich set of debugging tools. Use them.

Setting conditional breakpoints

Conditional breakpoints are another hidden gem when it comes to debugging. This allows you to specify one or several conditions. When one of these conditions is met, the code will stop at the breakpoint. Using conditional breakpoints is really easy.

Getting ready

There is nothing you specifically need to prepare to use this recipe.

How to do it...

1. Add the following code to your `Program.cs` file. We are simply creating a list of integers and looping through that list:

```
List<int> myList = new List<int>() { 1, 4, 6, 9, 11 };
foreach(int num in myList)
{
    Console.WriteLine(num);
}
Console.ReadLine();
```

2. Next, place a breakpoint on the `Console.WriteLine(num)` line of code inside the loop:

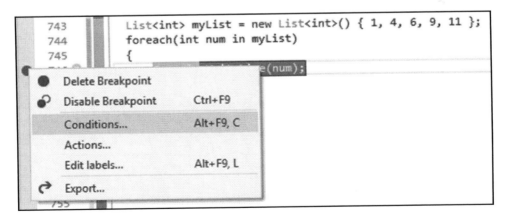

3. Right-click on the breakpoint and select **Conditions...** from the context menu:

4. You will now see that Visual Studio opens a **Breakpoint Settings** window. Here we specify that the breakpoint needs to be hit only when the value of num is 9. You can add several conditions and specify different conditions. The condition logic is really flexible:

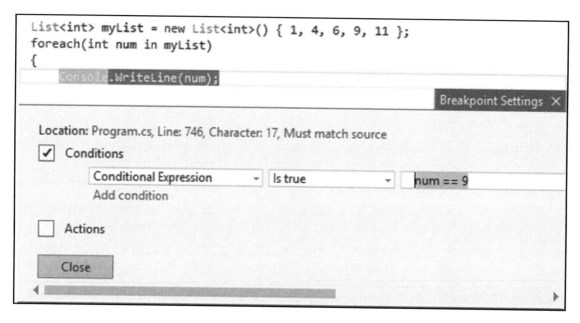

5. Debug your console application. You will see that when the breakpoint is hit, the value of num is 9:

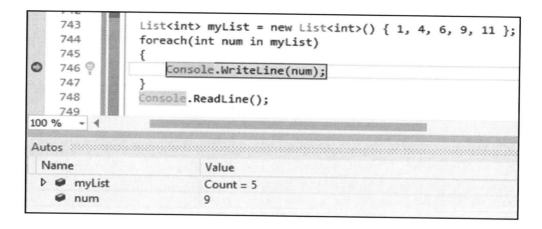

How it works...

The condition is evaluated on every loop. When the condition is true, the breakpoint will be hit. In the example illustrated in this recipe, the true benefit of a conditional breakpoint is somewhat lost because it is a very small list. Consider this though. You are binding a data grid. Items on the grid are given specific icons based on the status of the item. Your grid contains hundreds of items, because this is a hierarchical grid. You identify the primary ID of the item which is bound to the grid. This primary ID is then passed to other code logic to determine the status, which determines the icon displayed.

To debug and pressing *F10* through hundreds of loops is not productive in any event. With conditional breakpoints, you can specify a value for the primary ID, and only break when the loop hits that value. You can then go straight to the item that is being displayed incorrectly.

Using PerfTips to identify bottlenecks in code

PerfTips are definitely one of my favorite features of Visual Studio. Explaining what they do doesn't do them justice. You have to see them in action.

Getting ready

Do not confuse PerfTips with CodeLens. It is a separate option from CodeLens in Visual Studio.

How to do it...

1. PerfTips are enabled by default. But just in case you are not seeing any PerfTips, go to **Tools | Options**, and expand the **Debugging** node. Under **General**, to the bottom of the settings page, you will see an option called **Show elapsed time PerfTip while debugging**. Ensure that this option is checked:

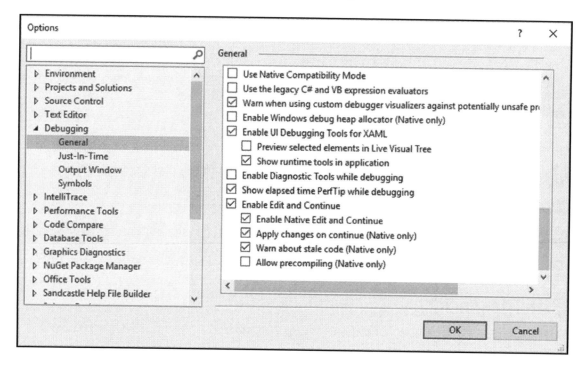

2. We will create a few simple methods that mimic long-running tasks. To do this, we will just sleep the thread for a couple of seconds. In the `Recipes.cs` file, add the following code:

```
public static void RunFastTask()
{
    RunLongerTask();
}

private static void RunLongerTask()
{
    Thread.Sleep(3000);
    BottleNeck();
}
```

```
private static void BottleNeck()
{
    Thread.Sleep(8000);
}
```

3. In your console application, call the static method `RunFastTask()` and place a breakpoint on this line of code:

```
RunFastTask();
Thread.Sleep(1000);
```

4. Start debugging your console application. Your breakpoint will stop on the `RunFastTask()` method. Hit *F10* to step over this method:

```
RunFastTask();

Thread.Sleep(1000);
}
```

5. You will notice that 11 seconds later, the next line will be highlighted and the PerfTip will be displayed. The PerfTip displays the time it took for the previous line of code to execute. So, the debugger that now sits on the `Thread.Sleep`, shows that the `RunFastTask()` method took 11 seconds to complete. The task is clearly not very fast:

```
RunFastTask();

Thread.Sleep(1000);  ≤11 022ms elapsed
}
```

6. Stepping into the `RunFastTask()` method, you can place further breakpoints and step over them one by one to find the method that is causing the longest delay. As you can see, PerfTips allow developers to quickly and easily identify bottlenecks in code:

```csharp
1 reference
public static void RunFastTask()
{
    RunLongerTask();
}

1 reference
private static void RunLongerTask()
{
    Thread.Sleep(3000);
    BottleNeck();
}

1 reference
private static void BottleNeck()
{
    Thread.Sleep(8000);
}  ≤8 001ms elapsed
```

How it works...

There are many tools on the market that do this and much more, allowing developers to view all sorts of code metrics. PerfTips, however, allow you to see issues on the fly while you are stepping through your code as per your normal debugging tasks. It is, in my opinion, an indispensable debugging tool.

15

Creating Microservices on Azure Service Fabric

This chapter deals with the exciting world of microservices and **Azure Service Fabric**. In this chapter, we will cover the following recipes:

- Downloading and installing Service Fabric
- Creating a Service Fabric application with a stateless actor service
- Using Service Fabric Explorer

Introduction

Traditionally, developers wrote applications in a monolithic manner. This means one single executable that is broken up into components via classes and so on. Monolithic applications require a great deal of testing, and deployment is tedious due to the bulkiness of the monolithic application. Even though you might have multiple developer teams, they all need to have a solid understanding of the application as a whole.

Microservices is a technology that aims to address the issues surrounding monolithic applications and the traditional way of developing applications. With microservices, you can break the application into smaller bits (services) that can function on their own without being dependent on any of the other services. These smaller services can be stateless or stateful and are also smaller in scale of functionality, making them easier to develop, test, and deploy. You can also version each microservice independently from the others. If one microservice is receiving more load than the others, you can scale only that service up to meet the demands placed on it. With monolithic applications, you would have to try and scale the whole application up in order to meet the demands for a single component within the application.

Take, for example, the workings of a popular online web store. It could consist of a shopping cart, shopper profile, order management, backend login, inventory management, billing, returns, and much more. Traditionally, a single web application is created to provide all these services. With microservices, you can isolate each service as a standalone, self-contained bit of functionality and code base. You can also dedicate a team of developers to work on a single portion of the web store. If this team is responsible for the inventory-management microservice, they would handle every aspect of it. This, for example, means everything from writing code and enhancing functionality to testing and deployment.

Another excellent side effect of microservices is that it allows you to easily isolate any faults you might come across. Finally, you can also create microservices in any technology you want (C#, Java, and VB.NET), as they are language-independent.

Azure Service Fabric allows you to scale your microservices easily and increases application availability because it implements failover. When microservices are used with the Service Fabric, microservices become a very powerful technology. Think of Azure Service Fabric as a **Platform as a Service** (**PaaS**) solution on top of which your microservices sit. We call the collection that the microservices live on a Service Fabric cluster. Each microservice lives on a virtual machine, which is referred to as a node in the Service Fabric cluster. This Service Fabric cluster can live in the cloud or on a local machine. If a node becomes unavailable due to any reason, the Service Fabric cluster will automatically redistribute the microservices to the other nodes so that the application remains available.

Finally, here is a word on the differences between stateful and stateless microservices. You are able to create a microservice as stateless or stateful. When a microservice relies on an external data store to persist data, it is stateless in nature. This simply means that the microservice does not maintain its state internally. A stateful microservice, on the other hand, maintains its own state by storing it locally on the server it resides on. As you can imagine, stateful microservices are nicely suited for financial transactions. If a node had to go down for whatever reason, the state of that transaction will be persisted when the failover happens and continue where it left off on the new node.

Downloading and installing Service Fabric

You will have to install and set up a local Service Fabric cluster on your PC before you can create and test Service Fabric applications. The local Service Fabric cluster is a fully functional cluster, as it would be in a live environment.

Getting ready

We will download and install the **Microsoft Azure Service Fabric SDK** from the Azure site. This will allow you to create a local Service Fabric cluster on your local development machine. For more information, have a look at `https://docs.microsoft.com/en-us/azur` `e/service-fabric/service-fabric-get-started`.

The Service Fabric tools are now part of the **Azure development and management** workload in Visual Studio 2017. Enable this workload when you install Visual Studio 2017. You will also need to enable the **ASP.NET and web development** workload:

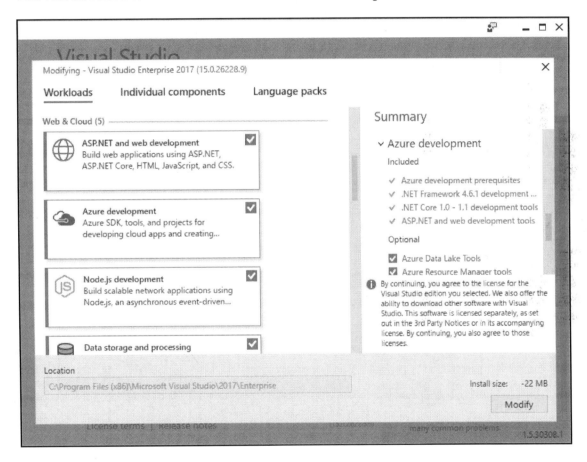

Note that if you do not have the original installer for Visual Studio anymore, and didn't enable the **Azure Development and Management** workload during installation, you can still enable this. Download the web platform installer for the version of Visual Studio 2017 you have and click on it. This will launch the installer, but will allow you to modify your existing Visual Studio 2017 installation. You can also run the installer from the **New Project** dialog screen in Visual Studio 2017. If you collapse the installed templates, you will see a section that allows you to open the Visual Studio Installer.

In addition to that, you can install the **Microsoft Azure Service Fabric SDK** using the Web Platform Installer from the preceding link. It will read **Install the Microsoft Azure Service Fabric SDK**. For the best installation experience, it is advisable to launch the Web Platform Installer using Internet Explorer or Edge browsers.

How to do it...

1. From the Microsoft Azure site, download the **Microsoft Azure Service Fabric SDK** and access other resources, such as documentation via the Service Fabric learning path, from `https://azure.microsoft.com/en-us/documentation/lea rning-paths/service-fabric/`. When you click on the WPI launcher, you should see the following screen:

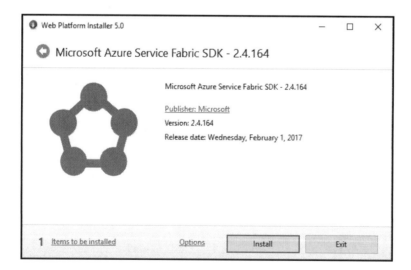

2. You will need to accept the license terms before the installation begins.

3. The web platform installer then starts downloading **Microsoft Azure Service Fabric Runtime**. Allow this process to complete.

4. After the download has completed, the installation process will begin:

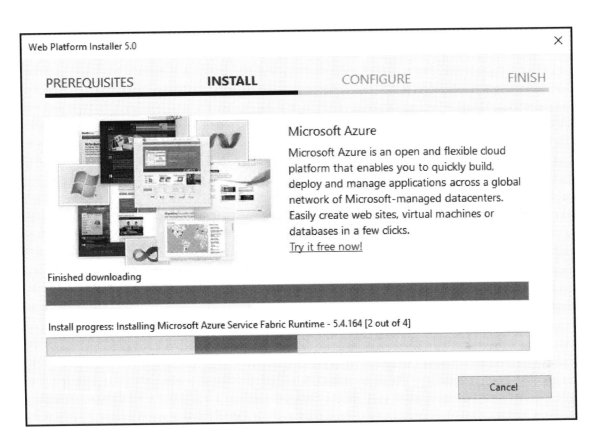

5. When the installation has completed, the following products will have been installed, which is also evident in the following screenshot:

- **Microsoft Visual C++ 2012 SP1 Redistributable Package**
- **Microsoft Azure Service Fabric Runtime**
- **Microsoft Azure Service Fabric SDK**

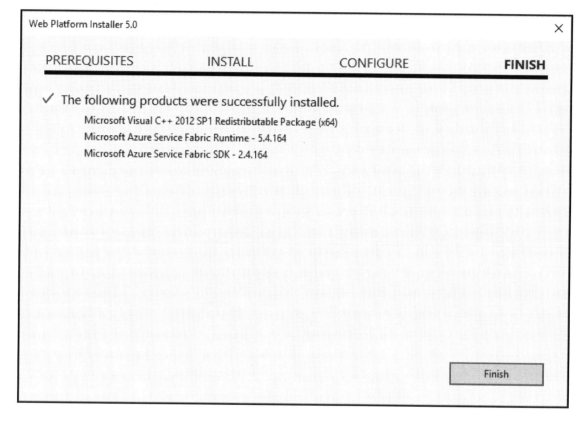

 Your installation might differ from the screenshot, depending on your specific pre-installed components.

6. The next task is to open PowerShell as the administrator. In the Windows 10 Start menu, type the word `PowerShell`, and the search will immediately return the desktop application as a result. Right-click on the desktop application and select **Run as administrator** from the context menu:

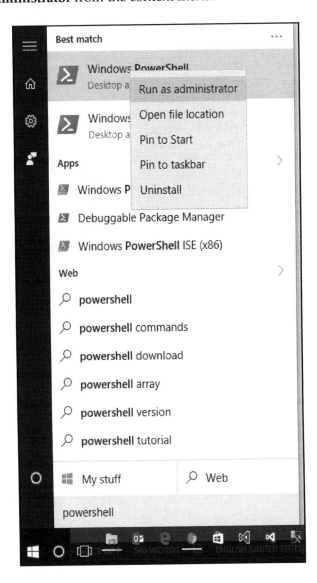

7. Once Windows PowerShell has opened up, run the `Set-ExecutionPolicy -ExecutionPolicy Unrestricted -Force -Scope CurrentUser` command. The reason for this is that Service Fabric uses PowerShell scripts for the creation of the local development cluster. It is also used for the deployment of Visual Studio developed apps. Running this command prevents Windows from blocking those scripts:

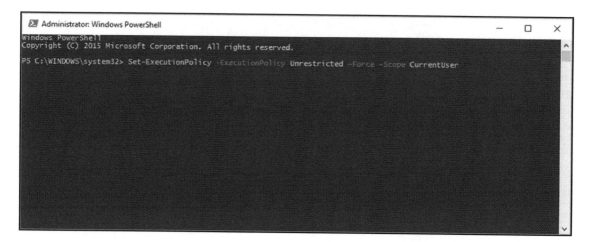

8. Next, create the local Service Fabric cluster. Enter the `& "$ENV:ProgramFiles\Microsoft SDKs\Service Fabric\ClusterSetup\DevClusterSetup.ps1"` command.

This will create the local cluster needed to host Service Fabric applications:

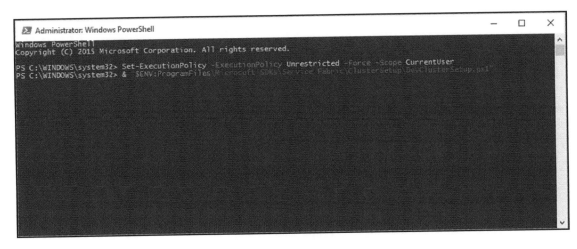

B06434_17_07

9. After the cluster is created, PowerShell will start the service:

10. The process might take several minutes. Be sure to let it complete:

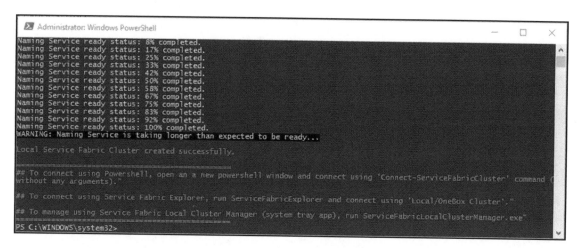

11. Once the naming service is ready, you can close PowerShell:

12. To view the created cluster, you can navigate to
    `http://localhost:19080/Explorer` on your local machine.

This will give you a snapshot of the cluster's health and state. It will also show any applications running in the cluster:

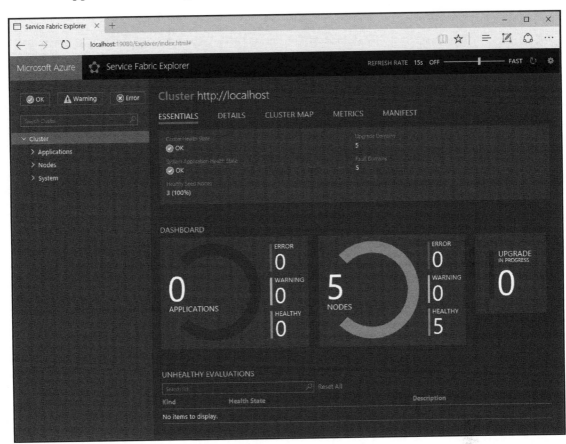

How it works...

As you can see, the Service Fabric cluster is essential for creating and running applications created in Visual Studio. This will allow us to test applications directly on your local machine before publishing them to the cloud. As mentioned earlier, this isn't a watered-down version of the Service Fabric cluster. It is exactly the same version that would be installed on any one of the machines that you would install your Service Fabric applications on.

Creating a Service Fabric application with a stateless actor service

As part of the introduction to this chapter, we looked at the difference between stateful and stateless microservices. The Service Fabric application templates available are then further divided into **Reliable Services** (stateful/stateless) and **Reliable Actors**. When to use which one is something that will depend on the specific business requirement of your application.

To put it simply though, if you wanted to create a service that should be exposed to many users of your application at any one time, a Reliable Service would probably be a good fit. Think of a service exposing the latest exchange rates that can be consumed by many users or applications at once.

Again, looking back to the introduction of this chapter, we used the example of an online web store with a shopping cart. A Reliable Actor could be a good fit for every customer buying items, so you could have a shopping cart actor. The Reliable Actor as part of the Service Fabric framework is based on the Virtual Actor pattern. Have a look at the article on the Virtual Actor pattern at http://research.microsoft.com/en-us/projects/orleans/.

To show you how easy it is to create a microservice using a stateless actor service as an example, we will use Visual Studio to publish a service to the Service Fabric cluster and call that service from a console (client) application.

Getting ready

To complete this recipe, you must ensure that you have installed your local Service Fabric cluster on your local machine. You also need to ensure that the **Azure Development and Management** workload in Visual Studio 2017 has been installed. Enable this workload when you install Visual Studio 2017. If you did not install the workload as part of Visual Studio 2017, you can do so by clicking on the Web Platform Installer for Visual Studio 2017 and maintaining the installation.

How to do it...

1. In Visual Studio, create a new project by going to **File** | **New** | **Project**.

2. From the **Visual C#** node, expand the nodes until you see the **Cloud** node. When you click on it, you will see that Visual Studio now lists a new **Service Fabric Application** template. Select the **Service Fabric Application** template, call it sfApp, and click on **OK**:

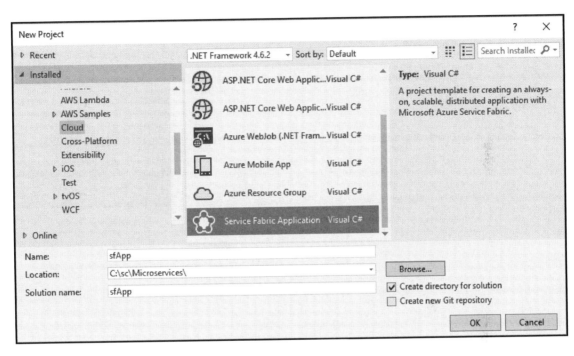

3. Next, select **Actor Service** from the **Service Templates** window that pops up. We just called ours `UtilitiesActor`:

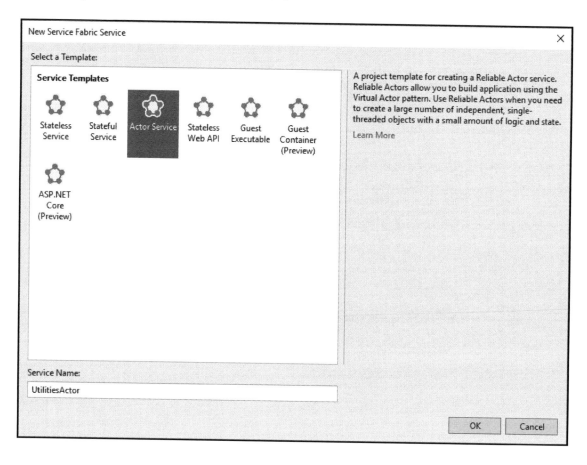

4. Once your solution is created, you will notice that it consists of three projects:

- sfApp
- UtilitiesActor
- UtilitiesActor.Interfaces

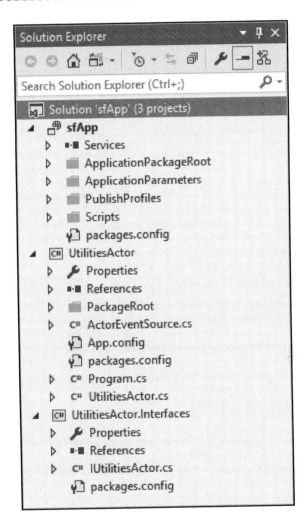

5. We will start off by modifying the `IUtilitiesActor` interface in the `UtilitiesActor.Interfaces` project. This interface will simply require that `UtilitiesActor` implements a method called `ValidateEmailAsync` that takes an e-mail address as a parameter and returns a Boolean value indicating whether it is a valid e-mail address or not:

```
namespace UtilitiesActor.Interfaces
{
  public interface IUtilitiesActor : IActor
  {
    Task<bool> ValidateEmailAsync(string emailToValidate);
  }
}
```

6. Next, open up your `UtilitiesActor` project and view the class `UtilitiesActor.cs`. Look for the internal class definition `internal class UtilitiesActor : Actor, IUtilitiesActor` around line 22. The `IUtilitiesActor` interface name will be underlined with a red squiggly line because it does not implement the interface member `ValidateEmailAsync()`.

7. Using *Ctrl + .* (period), implement the interface. Remove all the other unnecessary default code (if any).

8. The implemented interface code inserted for you should look like the following. At the moment, it only contains `NotImplementedException`. It is here that we will implement the code to validate the e-mail address:

```
namespace UtilitiesActor
{
  internal class UtilitiesActor : StatelessActor, IUtilitiesActor
  {
    public UtilitiesActor(ActorService actorService,
      ActorId actorId) : base(actorService, actorId)
    {
    }
    public async Task<bool> ValidateEmailAsync(string
      emailToValidate)
    {
      throw new NotImplementedException();
    }
  }
}
```

9. We will use a regular expression to validate the e-mail address passed to this method via the parameter. Regular expressions are very powerful. I have, however, in all my years of programming, never written my own expression. These are readily available on the Internet, and you can create a utilities class (or extension methods class) for your own projects to reuse. You can make use of regular expressions and other code that are often used.

Finally, you will notice the `ActorEventSource` code. This is simply just to create **Event Tracing for Windows (ETW)** events that will help you see what is happening in your application from the diagnostic events window in Visual Studio. To open the diagnostic events window, go to **View**, **Other Windows** and click on **Diagnostic Events**:

```
public async Task<bool> ValidateEmailAsync(string emailToValidate)
{
    ActorEventSource.Current.ActorMessage(this, "Email Validation");
    return await Task.FromResult(Regex.IsMatch(emailToValidate,
    @"A(?:[a-z0-9!#$%&'*+/=?^_&grave;{|}~-]+(?:.[
    a-z0-9!#$%&'*+/=?^_&grave;{|}~-]+)  *@(?:[a-z0-9](?:[a-z0-9-]
    *[a-z0-9])?.)+[a-z0-9](?:[a-z0-9-]*[a-z0-9])?)
    Z", RegexOptions.IgnoreCase));
}
```

10. Be sure to add a reference to the `System.Text.RegularExpressions` namespace. Without it, you will not be able to use the regular expressions. If you add the regular expression in your code without adding the reference, Visual Studio will display a red squiggly line under the `Regex` method.

11. Using *Ctrl* + . (period), add the `using` statement to your project. This will bring the regular expression namespace into scope.

12. Now that we have created the interface and also added the implementation of that interface, it is time to add a client application that we will use for testing. Right-click on your solution and add a new project.

13. The easiest way is to add a simple console application. Call your client application sfApp.Client and click on the **OK** button.

14. After you have added your console application to your solution, your solution should look like this:

15. You will now need to add references to your client application. Right-click the References node in your sfApp.Client project and select **Add Reference** from the context menu.

16. Start off by adding a reference to the UtilitiesActor.Interfaces project.

17. You will also need to add references to several Service Fabric **dynamic link libraries (DLLs)**. When you created your Service Fabric application, it should have added a folder called `packages` to your project folder structure. Browse to this folder and add your Service Fabric DLLs from there. After you have added the required DLLs, your project should look like this:

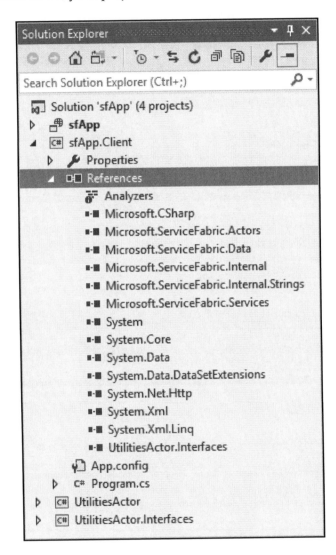

18. In the `Program.cs` file of your console application, you need to add the following code to the `Main` method:

```
namespace sfApp.Client
{
  class Program
  {
    static void Main(string[] args)
    {
      var actProxy = ActorProxy.Create<IUtilitiesActor>
        (ActorId.CreateRandom(), "fabric:/sfApp");
      WriteLine("Utilities Actor {0} - Valid Email?:{1}",
      actProxy.GetActorId(), actProxy.ValidateEmailAsync(
      "validemail@gmail.com").Result);
      WriteLine("Utilities Actor {0} - Valid Email?:{1}",
      actProxy.GetActorId(), actProxy.ValidateEmailAsync(
      "invalid@email@gmail.com").Result);
      ReadLine();
    }
  }
}
```

Be sure to add the following `using` statements to your console application:

```
using Microsoft.ServiceFabric.Actors;
using Microsoft.ServiceFabric.Actors.Client;
using UtilitiesActor.Interfaces;
using static System.Console;
```

All we are doing is creating a proxy for our actor and writing the output of the e-mail validation to the console window. Your client application is now ready.

How it works...

Before we can run the client application, however, we need to publish our service first. In **Solution Explorer**, right-click on the sfApp service and click on **Publish...** from the context menu:

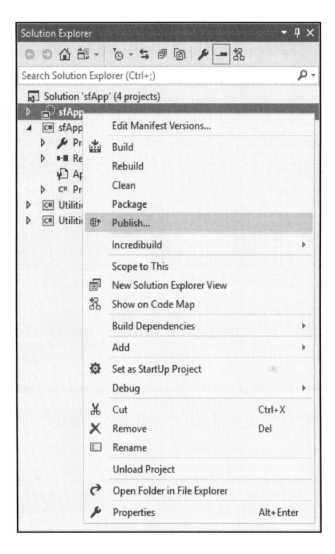

The **Publish Service Fabric Application** window will now be displayed. Click on the **Select...** button next to the **Connection Endpoint** textbox. Select **Local Cluster** as your **Connection Endpoint** and click on **OK.** Change **Target profile** and **Application Parameters File** to `Local.1Node.xml`. When you are done, click on the **Publish** button:

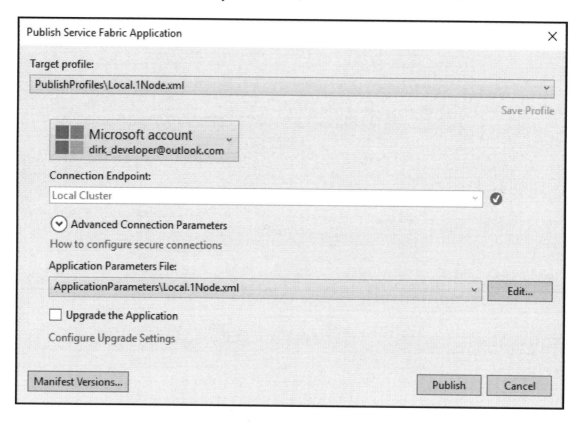

If you navigate to `http://localhost:19080/Explorer`, you will notice that the service you created has been published to your local Service Fabric cluster:

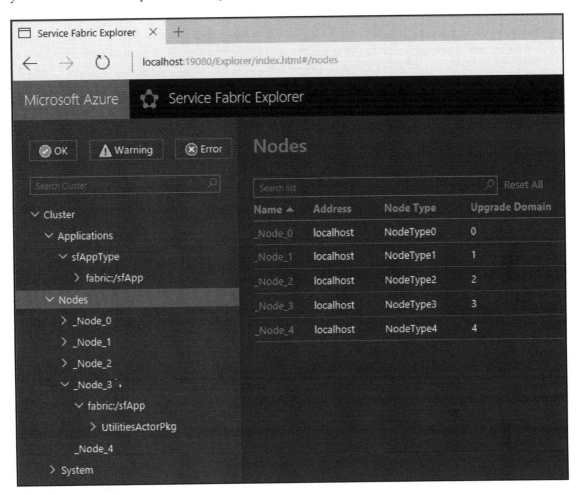

You are now ready to run your client application. Right-click on the `sfApp.Client` project and select **Debug** and **Start new instance** from the context menu. The console application calls the `validate` method to check the e-mail addresses and displays the results to the console window. The results are as expected:

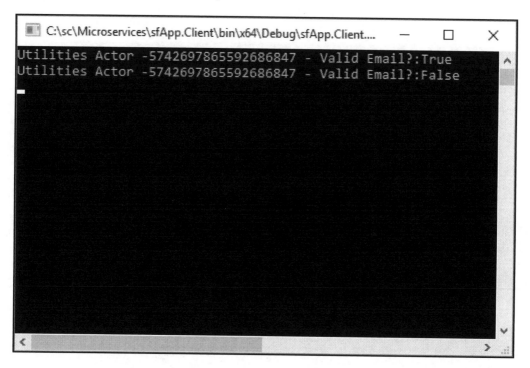

If you receive a `System.BadImageFormatException` when trying to run your console application, check to see what platform your console application is targeting. You might have compiled your console application as **Any CPU** while the other projects in your solution target **x64**. Modify this from the Configuration Manager and make the console application also target **x64**.

We can, however, be more specific when creating the actor ID. In the previous code listing, we used the `CreateRandom()` method to generate an `ActorId`. We can now give it a specific name. Modify your proxy code and create a new `ActorId` instance and give it any string value. In the following code listing, I just called mine `Utilities`:

```
var actProxy = ActorProxy.Create<IUtilitiesActor>(new ActorId("Utilities"),
"fabric:/sfApp");
```

The `ActorId` method can take a parameter of type `Guid`, `long`, or `string`.

When you debug your client application again, you will notice that `Utilities Actor` now has a logical name (the same name you passed as string value when creating a new `ActorId` instance):

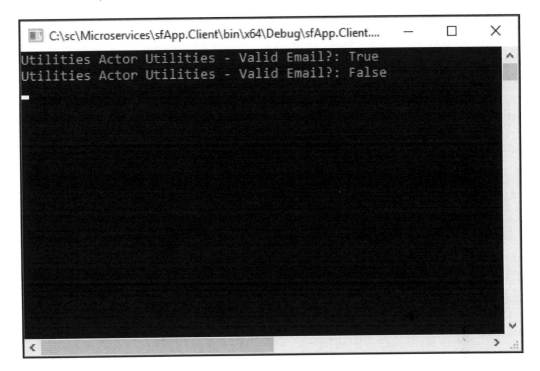

Creating your Service Fabric application and publishing it locally is a perfect solution for testing your application before publishing it to the cloud. Creating small, independent microservices allows developers many benefits related to testing, debugging, and deploying efficient and robust code that your applications can leverage to ensure maximum availability.

Using Service Fabric Explorer

There is another tool that you can use to visualize the Service Fabric cluster. It is a standalone tool that you can find by navigating to the local installation path at `%Program Files%\Microsoft SDKs\Service Fabric\Tools\ServiceFabricExplorer` and clicking on `ServiceFabricExplorer.exe`. When you run the application, it will automatically connect to your local Service Fabric cluster. It can display rich information regarding the applications on the cluster, the cluster nodes, heath status of the applications and nodes, and any load on the applications in the cluster.

Getting ready

You must have already completed the installation of Service Fabric on your local machine for Service Fabric Explorer to work. If you have not done so yet, follow the *Downloading and installing Service Fabric* recipe in this chapter.

How to do it...

1. When you start Service Fabric Explorer, the following window will appear:

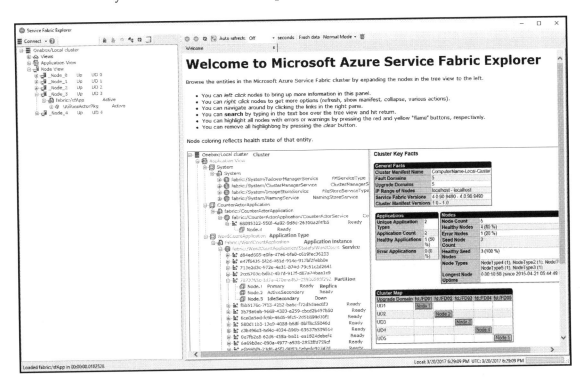

2. Note that the tree view to the left displays **Application View** and **Node View**:

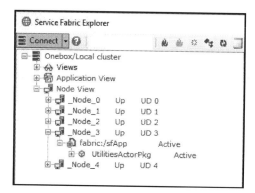

3. The pane on the right-hand side will display information regarding the local cluster. This makes it easy for you to see the overall health of the local Service Cluster:

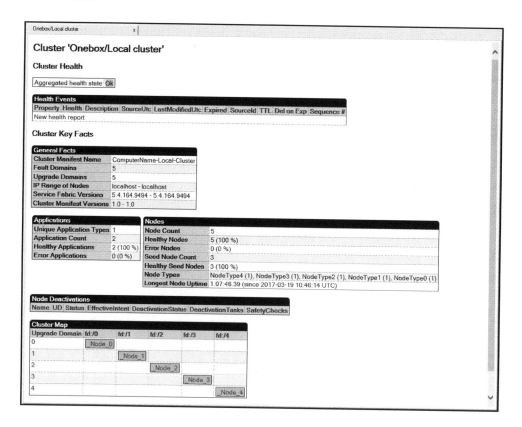

4. When you expand **Application View**, you will notice that our `sfApp` service has been published. Expanding it even further, you will see that the `sfApp` service has been published on **Node_3**. Expand **Node View** and **Node_3** to see the service active on that node:

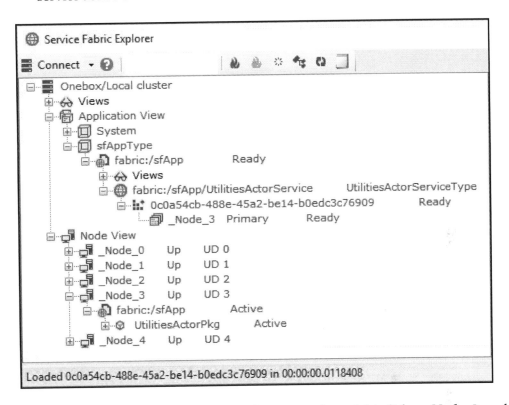

5. To illustrate the scalability of microservices, right-click on **Node_3**, and from the context menu select **Activate / Deactivate** and **Deactivate (remove data)** on the node. Then, click on the Refresh button at the top of the window to refresh the nodes and applications.

6. If you now go ahead and expand **Application View** and look at the service again, you will notice that the Service Fabric cluster noticed that **Node_3** was disabled. It then automatically pushed the service onto a new, healthy node (in this case, **Node_2**):

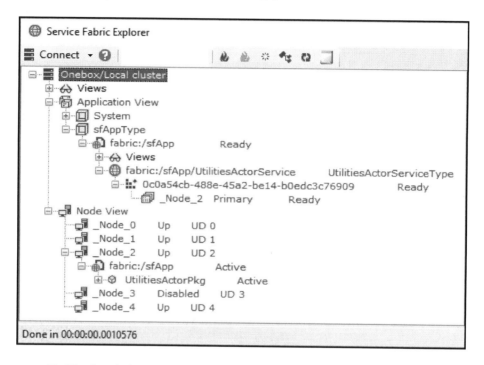

7. The local cluster nodes view in the right panel of Service Fabric Explorer also reports that **Node_3** is disabled. Click on **Node View** to see this:

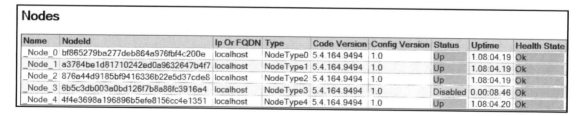

Name	NodeId	Ip Or FQDN	Type	Code Version	Config Version	Status	Uptime	Health State
_Node_0	bf865279ba277deb864a976fbf4c200e	localhost	NodeType0	5.4.164.9494	1.0	Up	1.08:04.19	Ok
_Node_1	a3784be1d81710242ed0a9632647b4f7	localhost	NodeType1	5.4.164.9494	1.0	Up	1.08:04.19	Ok
_Node_2	876a44d9185bf9416336b22e5d37cde8	localhost	NodeType2	5.4.164.9494	1.0	Up	1.08:04.19	Ok
_Node_3	6b5c3db003a0bd126f7b8a86fc3916a4	localhost	NodeType3	5.4.164.9494	1.0	Disabled	0.00:08.46	Ok
_Node_4	4f4e3698a196896b5efe8156cc4e1351	localhost	NodeType4	5.4.164.9494	1.0	Up	1.08:04.20	Ok

Nodes

How it works...

Service Fabric Explorer will allow you to see information on the selected node, and you will be able to drill down and see a rich amount of information regarding the Service Fabric cluster applications. It just another utility for administrators to use apart from the Service Fabric Explorer available in the browser.

There is some heated debate as to the manner in which developers should approach the microservices architecture. There are some that believe that when your goal as a developer is a microservices architecture for your application, you need to approach it from a monolith-first perspective. That is to say, write the big monolithic application first because that process is a familiar approach to development. After you have done that, plan and carve up the monolithic application into smaller microservices. The argument here is that the time to market is much quicker when creating a monolithic application. A quicker time to market means a quicker return on your investment.

Then the other side of the argument is that starting with a monolith is exactly the wrong approach to follow. The correct time to start thinking about how to carve up your application into pieces is at the design phase. The concession is made, however, that the development team will probably need to understand the system they are required to build. Another concession is made in the fact that it would probably be better to start off with a microservices approach when creating a second version of the existing monolith. A monolithic application by definition has all the parts tightly coupled to each other. How much time would it take to break these into smaller microservices?

Whichever approach you decide to take, it is one that must be decided on after careful consideration of all the facts involving all the stakeholders. Unfortunately, there is no formula or hard and fast rule to aid you in your decision. The decision regarding architecture of an application (monolithic versus microservices) will vary from project to project.

16

Azure and Serverless Computing

Right about now, I bet that there are some of you coming to this chapter asking, "What does serverless computing even mean?" The name is confusing, I agree. It makes no sense (to me anyway), but when you understand the concept it kind of makes sense. In this chapter, we will have a look at what the term Serverless Computing means. We will also take a look at:

- Creating an Azure Function
- Providing print functionality with DocRaptor
- Using AWS and S3
- Creating C# lambda functions with AWS

Introduction

Serverless does not mean the lack of a server, but rather you (or the application) does not know which server is used to provide some functionality to an application. Serverless, therefore, describes an application that depends on some 3rd party app or service that lives in the cloud to provide some logic or functionality to the application.

Let us use the example of a student research portal. Students research a certain topic and create documents in the portal related to what they need to research. They can then load print credits against their profile and print the saved documents they need. After a page is printed, the print credit is deducted from their profile.

While this is a very simple example, I am using it to illustrate the concept of serverless computing. We can split the application up into various components. These are as follows:

1. Login authentication
2. Purchasing print credits
3. Updating remaining print credits
4. Printing documents

 There could be several other components required not mentioned here, but this is not the real world. We are just creating this hypothetical application to illustrate the concept of serverless computing.

Why write the code to provide login authentication in your application when there are already third-party services out there that do just that? Similarly, why write code to print documents when there are services that provide quite rich functionality you can just consume in your application? Anything specific such as the purchasing and loading of student print credits, can be created using an Azure Function. The topic of serverless computing is broad and still in its infancy. There is much to learn and experience. Let's take the first steps and explore what benefits this can have for developers.

Creating an Azure function

Why Azure Functions? Imagine that you have an application that needs to provide some specific functionality, but that still scales up when the call rate to your function increases. This is where Azure Functions provide a benefit. With Azure Functions, you only pay for the compute that your function needs at a specific instance in time, and it is immediately available.

To get started, head on over to `https://azure.microsoft.com/en-us/services/function` `s` and create a free account.

 Because you only pay for the actual computing time you use when running Azure Functions, it is imperative that your code is as optimized as possible. If you refactor the Azure Function code and gain a 40% code execution improvement, you are directly saving 40% in your monthly expense. The more you refactor and improve your code, the more money you will save.

Getting ready

You need to have an Azure account set up. If you don't have one, you can set one up for free. From the Azure portal, on the left-side menu, click on **New** to get started:

In the search box, type in `Function App` and hit the *Enter* button. The first result should be **Function App**. Select that.

When you select the **Function App**, you will see this screen pop out to the right. The description perfectly describes what Azure Functions do. Click the **Create** button at the bottom of this form.

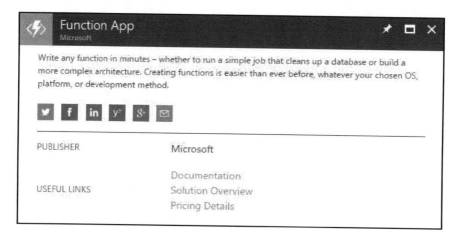

You now see a form that allows you to give your function a name and select the **Resource Group** and other settings. Click on the **Create** button when you are done.

How to do it...

1. After Azure has created the new **Function App,** you will then be able to create an Azure Function. All that we are going to do is to create an Azure Function that will be triggered whenever something happens on a GitHub repository. Click on the **Create your own custom function** link.

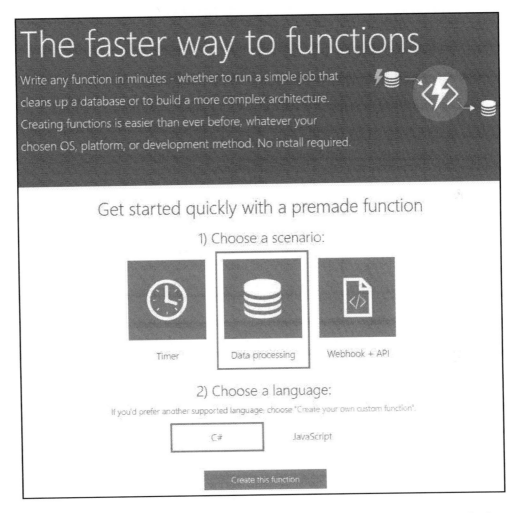

 According to the Microsoft Azure site, the following are supported when writing Azure Functions: JavaScript, C#, F#, and scripting options such as Python, PHP, Bash, Batch, and PowerShell.

2. You will now see that you are given a choice between several templates. Choose **C#** from the **Language** selection and **API & Webhooks** from the **Scenario** selection and then select the **GitHubWebHook-CSharp** template. Azure will now ask you to give your function a name. I called mine `GithubAzureFunctionWebHook`. Click on the **Create** button to create the function.

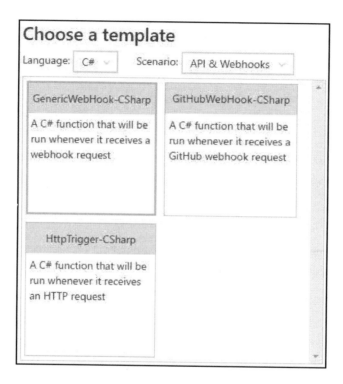

3. When your function is created, you will see that it has added some default code for you in the online code editor.

```
using System.Net;

public static async Task<HttpResponseMessage> Run
                    (HttpRequestMessage req, TraceWriter log)
{
    log.Info("C# HTTP trigger function processed a request.");

    // Get request body
    dynamic data = await req.Content.ReadAsAsync<object>();

    // Extract github comment from request body
```

```
string gitHubComment = data?.comment?.body;

return req.CreateResponse(HttpStatusCode.OK, "From Github:" +
                          gitHubComment);
}
```

4. Preceding the `return` statement, add the following line of code: `log.Info($"Message from GitHub: {gitHubComment}");`. This is so that we will see what was sent from GitHub.

5. Your code should now look as follows. Note that there are two links that allow you to get the function URL and the GitHub secret. Click on those links and copy the values of each to Notepad. Click on the **Save and run** button.

 Your Azure Function URL should be something like: `https://funccredits.azurewebsites.net/api/GithubAzureFunctionWebHook`

---

run.csx   Save   ▶ Save and run   </> Get function URL   </> Get GitHub secret

```
 1  using System.Net;
 2
 3  public static async Task<HttpResponseMessage> Run(HttpRequestMessage req, Trace
 4  {
 5      log.Info("C# HTTP trigger function processed a request.");
 6
 7      // Get request body
 8      dynamic data = await req.Content.ReadAsAsync<object>();
 9
10      // Extract github comment from request body
11      string gitHubComment = data?.comment?.body;
12      log.Info($"Message from GitHub: {gitHubComment}");
13
14      return req.CreateResponse(HttpStatusCode.OK, "From Github:" + gitHubComment
15  }
```

---

6. Head on over to GitHub at `https://github.com/`. If you don't have an account, create one and create a repository (GitHub is free for open source projects). Go to the repository you created, and click on the **Settings** tab. To the left, you will see a link called **Webhooks**. Click on that link.

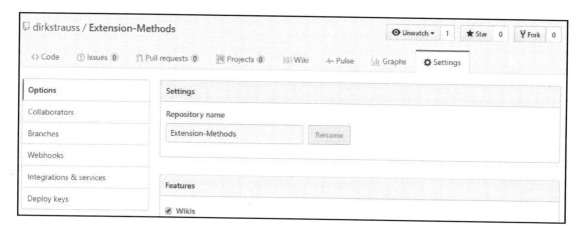

7. You will now see a button to the right called **Add webhook**. Click on that button.

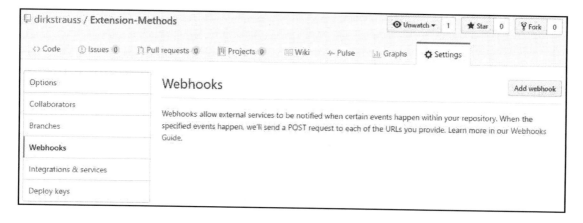

8. Add the Azure Function URL you copied earlier to the **Payload URL** field. Change the **Content type** to **application/json** and add the GitHub secret you copied earlier to the **Secret** field. Select **Send me everything** and click on the **Add webhook** button.

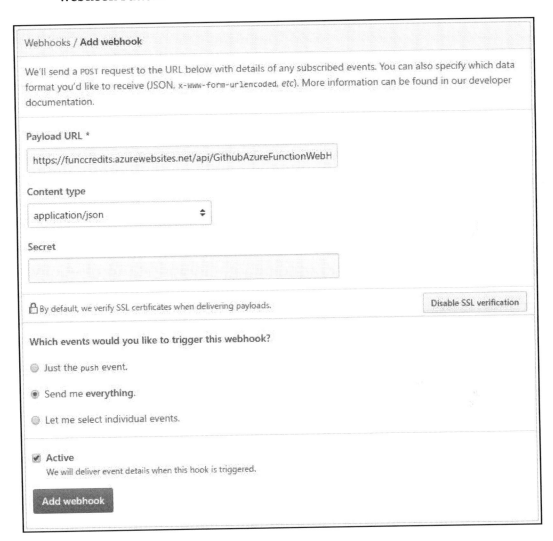

How it works...

Still in your GitHub repository, open a file and add a comment to it. Click on the **Comment on this commit** button.

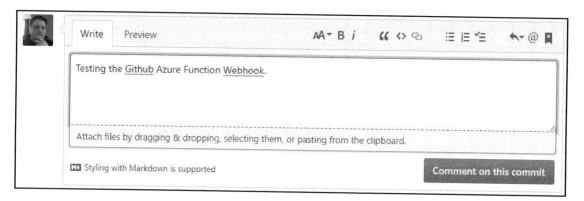

Swing back to your Azure Function and take a look at the **Logs** window. This window is directly below the code window. You will see that the comment we posted in GitHub pops up in the log output of the Azure Function.

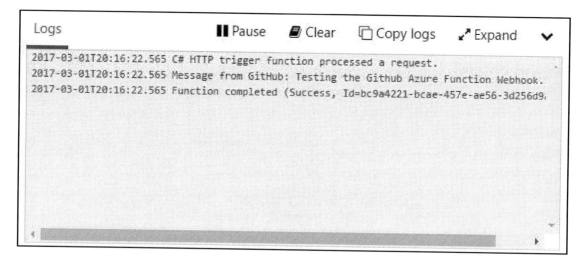

 If nothing appears in the log window, ensure that you have clicked on the **Run** button of the Azure Function. If all else fails, click on the **Run** button at the bottom of the **Test** window.

While this is a very simple example, the usefulness of Azure Functions should become evident to you. You will also notice that the function has a `.csx` extension. What is important to note is that Azure Functions share a few core concepts and components irrespective of which programming language you choose to code it in. At the end of the day, a function is the primary concept here. You also have a `function.json` file that contains JSON configuration data. You can see this and other files by clicking on the **View files** link to the right.

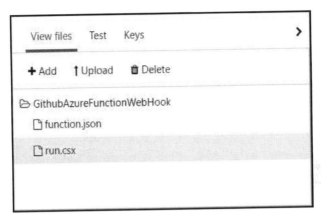

Clicking on the `function.json` file, you will see the contents of the JSON file. Changing the `disabled` property to `true` will effectively stop the function from executing if called. You will also notice the `bindings` property. Here, you configure your web hook. All these settings can be set from within the **Integrate** and other sections of the Azure Function.

```json
{
    "bindings": [
        {
            "type": "httpTrigger",
            "direction": "in",
            "webHookType": "github",
            "name": "req"
        },
        {
            "type": "http",
            "direction": "out",
            "name": "res"
        }
    ],
    "disabled": false
}
```

Azure Functions and the benefits exposed to developers is an exciting concept. This is one area of your programming repertoire that will surely keep you busy for many hours as you explore more intricate and complex tasks.

Providing print functionality with DocRaptor

Printing from a web application has always been tricky. This is much easier these days with the availability of numerous third-party controls that provide print functionality to your application. The reality, however, is that I have come across many projects where, when they were developed, used a third-party control to provide print functionality. At the time it was developed, the third-party control was good and did exactly what they needed.

Having this functionality available to the application means that the companies that purchase the licenses for these third-party controls, rarely continue renewing their licenses. Within a few years, however, this results in a web application that contains old and dated print technology. While there is nothing wrong with this, it does have some drawbacks.

The developers are usually stuck with maintaining an aging code base, which is locked into this third-party control. Any change in requirements, and you'll find that developers are faced with making code work within the limitations of the third-party controls. Alternatively, they need to approach the powers that be and suggest that the third-party controls be updated to the latest version. This means that the small change needed in the print module, turns out to be more costly than anyone had budgeted.

Real world: I used to work for a company that would have consultants quote customers on what a change to some application functionality would cost. After the quote was given and accepted, it was handed to development to make it work within the allotted time frame and budget. This resulted in developers having to hack code to make it work and meet budget and deadlines because of a lack of proper project management skills. Replacing third-party controls would be virtually impossible because the budget was already set without input from development.

I agree that there are some developers that do a very good job of providing and maintaining functionality in an aging code base. I also really love third-party controls and the functionality they provide. There are a select few big players that a developer can choose from. But here is the catch: why purchase a suite of third-party controls, when all you need is the ability to print an invoice for example? Using this logic, serverless make much more sense in many cases (this one included).

Getting ready

This example will take a look at a service called DocRaptor. The service isn't free, but consider the cost of writing and maintaining code to provide print functionality in your web application. Consider the cost of buying third-party controls to provide the same functionality. It all comes down to what makes the most sense for you as a developer.

Create a basic web application and go to **Tools**, **NuGet Package Manager**, **Package Manager Console**. Type the following command in the console to install the DocRaptor NuGet package.

```
Install-Package DocRaptor
```

Once DocRaptor is installed, you can head on over to their web page (http://docraptor.com/) to read through some of the API documentation or you can also swing by the GitHub page (https://github.com/DocRaptor/docraptor-csharp) for additional information.

It will be better to have a look at the source code accompanying this book in order to copy the code for this recipe.

How to do it...

1. Add an aspx web page that contains invoice details. I have simply taken from the example on DocRaptor's site and modified it slightly. Call this page `InvoicePrint.aspx`.

I have included the CSS in a style sheet called `invoice.css`. Be sure to get this from the source code accompanying this book.

There are a few ways you could approach this code. This is not necessarily the only way to create the web pages. If you are using .NET Core MVC, your approach would probably be different. However if you do this, remember that this code is just to illustrate the concept here.

```
<%@ Page Language="C#" AutoEventWireup="true"
CodeBehind="InvoicePrint.aspx.cs" Inherits="Serverless.InvoicePrint" %>

<!DOCTYPE html>

<html xmlns="http://www.w3.org/1999/xhtml">
  <head runat="server">
    <title>Invoice</title>
    <meta http-equiv="content-type" content="text/html;
     charset=utf-8"/>
    <link href="css/invoice.css" rel="stylesheet" />
    <script type="text/javascript">
     function ToggleErrorDisplay()
     {
       if ($("#errorDetails").is(":visible")) {
         $("#errorDetails").hide();
       } else {
         $("#errorDetails").show();
       }
     }

     function TogglePrintResult() {
       if ($("#printDetails").is(":visible")) {
         $("#printDetails").hide();
       } else {
         $("#printDetails").show();
       }
     }
    </script>
  </head>
  <body>
    <form runat="server">
      <div id="container">
        <div id="main">
          <div id="header">
            <div id="header_info black">The Software Company
              <span class="black">|</span> (072)-412-5920
              <span class="black">|</span> software.com</div>
          </div>
          <h1 class="black" id="quote_name">Invoice INV00015</h1>
          <div id="client" style="float: right">
            <div id="client_header">client:</div>
            <p class="address black">
```

```
          Mr. Wyle E. Coyote
     </p>
</div>
<table id="phase_details">
  <thead>
    <tr>
      <th class="title">Stock Code</th>
      <th class="description">Item Description</th>
      <th class="price">price</th>
    </tr>
  </thead>
  <tr class="first black">
    <td>BCR902I45</td>
    <td>Acme Company Roadrunner Catch'em Kit</td>
    <td class="price">
      <div class="price_container">$300</div>
    </td>
  </tr>
  <tr>
    <td></td>
    <td>Booster Skates</td>
    <td class="price">
      <div class="price_container">$200</div>
    </td>
  </tr>
  <tr>
    <td></td>
    <td>Emergency Parachute</td>
    <td class="price">
        <div class="price_container">$100</div>
    </td>
  </tr>
  <tr class="last">
    <td></td>
    <td></td>
    <td></td>
  </tr>
  <tr class="first black">
    <td>BFT547J78</td>
    <td>Very Sneaky Trick Seed Kit</td>
    <td class="price">
      <div class="price_container">$800</div>
    </td>
  </tr>
  <tr>
    <td></td>
    <td>Giant Magnet and Lead Roadrunner Seeds</td>
    <td class="price">
```

```
              <div class="price_container">$500</div>
            </td>
          </tr>
          <tr>
            <td></td>
            <td>Rollerblades</td>
            <td class="price">
              <div class="price_container">$300</div>
            </td>
          </tr>
          <tr class="last">
            <td></td>
            <td></td>
            <td></td>
          </tr>
        </table>
      </div>
      <div id="total_price">
        <h2>TOTAL: <span class="price black">$1100</span></h2>
      </div>
      <div id="print_link">
        <asp:LinkButton ID="lnkPrintInvoice" runat="server"
          Text="Print this invoice" OnClick="lnkPrintInvoice_Click">
        </asp:LinkButton>
      </div>
      <div id="errorDetails">
        <asp:Label ID="lblErrorDetails" runat="server">
        </asp:Label>
      </div>
      <div id="printDetails">
        <asp:Label ID="lblPrintDetails" runat="server">
        </asp:Label>
      </div>
    </div>
  </form>

</body>
</html>
```

2. I also created a print friendly version of the invoice page called `invoice.html`.

3. The next step is to create a click event for the link button. Add the following code to the click event. You will notice that I have just hard coded the path to generate the PDF document to as: `C:\temp\invoiceDownloads`. You need to make sure that you change this path if you want to output to a different path (or get a path relative to the server you're on).

```
Configuration.Default.Username = "YOUR_API_KEY_HERE";
```

```
DocApi docraptor = new DocApi();

 Doc doc = new Doc(
    Test: true,
    Name: "docraptor-csharp.pdf",
    DocumentType: Doc.DocumentTypeEnum.Pdf,
    DocumentContent: GetInvoiceContent()
);

byte[] create_response = docraptor.CreateDoc(doc);
File.WriteAllBytes(@"C:\temp\invoiceDownloads\invoice.pdf",
                   create_response);
```

4. Make sure that you include the following namespaces in your web page:

```
using System;
using System.Web.UI;
using DocRaptor.Client;
using DocRaptor.Model;
using DocRaptor.Api;
using System.IO;
using System.Net;
using System.Text;
```

5. Lastly, get the HTML content of the print friendly page called invoice.html. The URL in the code below will differ on your machine because your port number will probably be different.

```
private string GetInvoiceContent()
{
   WebRequest req = WebRequest.Create
                        ("http://localhost:37464/invoice.html");
   WebResponse resp = req.GetResponse();
   Stream st = resp.GetResponseStream();
   StreamReader sr = new StreamReader(st, Encoding.ASCII);
   return sr.ReadToEnd();
}
```

How it works...

Run your web application and see the basic invoice displayed on the web page. Make sure that you have set your `InvoicePrint.aspx` page as the start page for your web application. Click on the **Print this invoice** link.

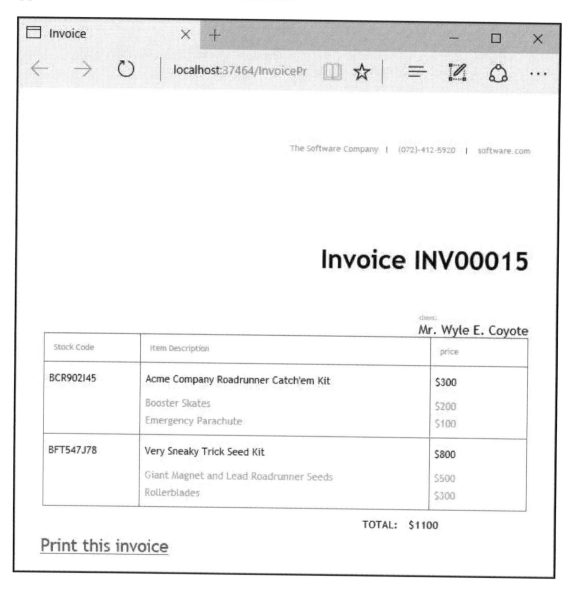

You will see that the invoice is created in the output path you specified.

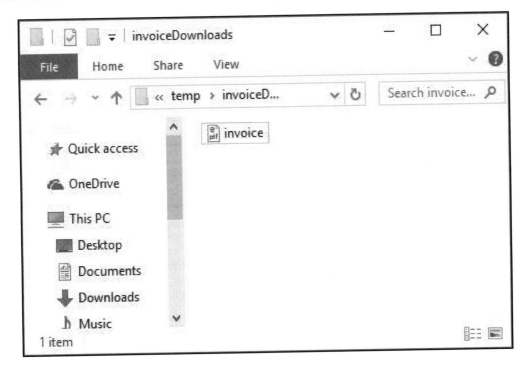

Click on the PDF document to open the invoice.

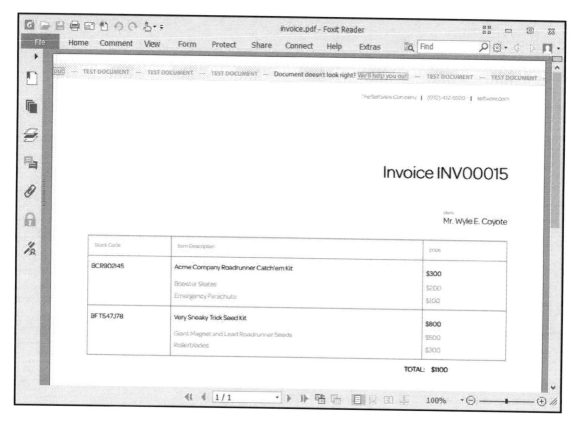

DocRaptor provides a service that is really useful to developers creating web solutions. If you need to create PDF or Excel documents from your application, DocRaptor can benefit your team. The test document used in this example is free to use without it being deducted from your monthly quota (if you are on a paid plan).

In the true serverless sense of the word, DocRaptor provides functionality to you without you having to write a lot of extra code. It is super easy to implement and super easy to maintain. The preceding example is really basic, but you can pass DocRaptor a URL instead of the `DocumentContent` to print the page you want. From the developer's perspective, they don't care how DocRaptor does what they do. It just works. And this is the idea behind serverless computing.

Developers can implement solutions in their applications easily, effortlessly, and in record time, using minimal code while adding a lot of value to the application they're developing. The functionality being implemented can also easily scale as demand increases. There are, however, overage charges on the professional plan. Lastly, creating a few PDF documents will probably not make much of a difference in server computing power. Consider then that DocRaptor is used by some large companies that probably generate thousands of documents each month. All those document generation requests do not get processed by the customer using DocRaptor, but by the DocRaptor servers themselves.

You are then left with being able to develop a lightweight, streamlined web application that will not place huge demand on your server as volumes increase.

Using AWS and S3

This chapter can't be considered complete without looking at Amazon Web Services (AWS). The topic of AWS is really vast. There is a lot of functionality provided by the platform. Developers can harness this in their applications and provide rich functionality with minimal code on their part. AWS also has really good documentation that developers can review to get up to speed quickly. S3 is Amazon's Simple Storage Service and allows you to store and retrieve data in the cloud.

I enjoy playing Minecraft with my kids. Some of the things they create are mind boggling, especially since my daughter (who plays as CupcakeSparkle) is 7 years old and my son (who plays as Cheetah) is only 4 years old. My daughter has been playing Minecraft since she was 5 and as you can imagine, she has created quite a few incredible structures. Joseph Garrett is by far my kids' favorite YouTuber who plays as Stampy Cat. They watch his Let's Play videos religiously (including Building Time with Squid Nugget). We often have Building Time competitions of our own and Stampy Cat and his lovely world serve as an inspiration for my kids in everything they do in Minecraft.

Here is the picture of Stampy Cat that my daughter built.

Here is the picture of Squid Nugget that my son built.

So, I want to create a place to upload some of their Minecraft pictures, screenshots, and other documents related to our Minecraft adventures. For this, we will use S3.

Getting ready

This chapter assumes that you have signed up for an AWS account using the free tier. For more details regarding the free tier, navigate to `https://aws.amazon.com/free/`. One section I want to highlight though is the following:

The Amazon Web Services (AWS) Free Tier is designed to enable you to get hands-on experience with AWS Cloud Services. The AWS Free Tier includes services with a free tier available for 12 months following your AWS sign-up date, as well as additional service offers that do not automatically expire at the end of your 12 month AWS Free Tier term.

In order to sign up, you need to provide your credit card information. When the free tier period expires (or if your application exceeds the usage limitations), you will be charged the pay-as-you-go service rates. Regarding S3 specifically, the free tier allows 5GB of storage, 20,000 get requests and 2,000 put requests. First you will need to create an S3 bucket. From the **Services** selection, locate the **Storage** group and click on **S3**.

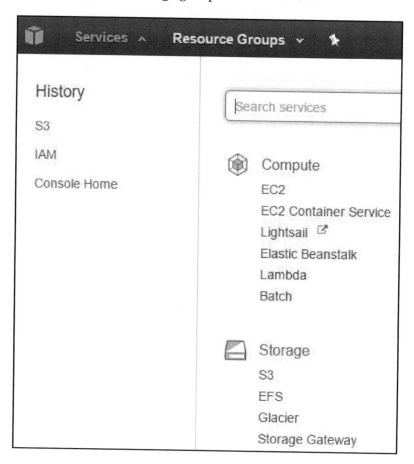

Create your first bucket. I named mine `familyvaultdocs` and selected the **EU (Frankfurt)** region. Click on **Next** until you have completed the creation of the bucket.

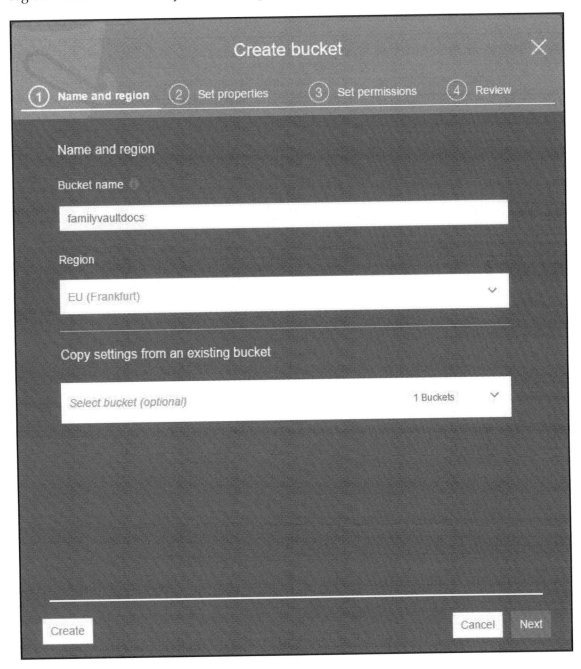

After the bucket is created, you can review the permissions for the bucket. For simplicity's sake I have selected that **Everyone** has **Read** and **Write** permissions for **Object access** and **Permissions access**.

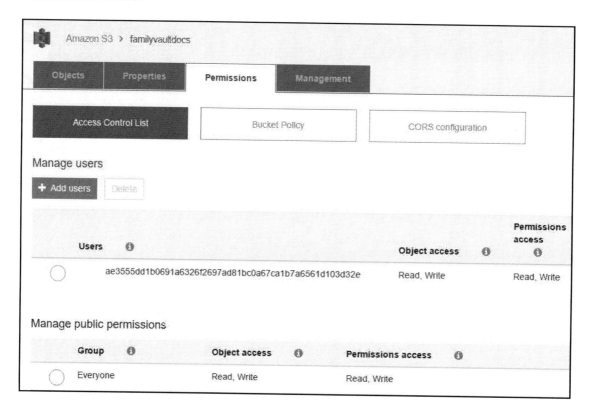

Lastly, you will also need to create an access key and secret key for your application. From the **Services**, look for the **Security, Identity & Compliance** group and click on **IAM (Identity and Access Management)**. Add a user with the **Access type** of **Programmatic access**. This will provide you with the **access key ID** and **secret access key** you need.

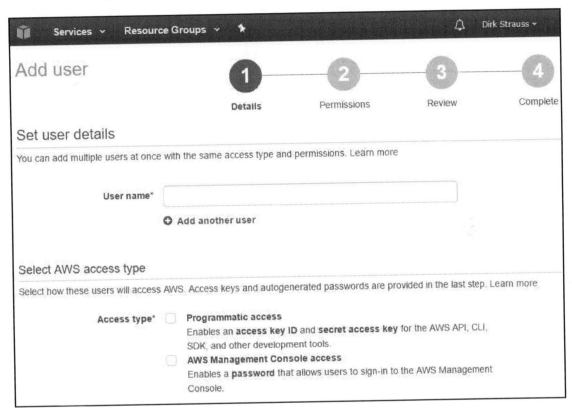

With your bucket created, user permissions set to **Everyone** and access keys created, let's write some code.

How to do it...

1. We will just create a console application that will upload the picture to the S3 bucket we created earlier. Start off by opening the NuGet Package Manager and adding the **AWSSDK** NuGet package to your Console Application.

It might be worth your while to have a look at the AWS SDK for .NET at the following link `https://aws.amazon.com/sdk-for-net/`. This helps developers get up to speed quickly with the SDK.

2. Next, create a class called `StampysLovelyWorld` and a method called `SaveStampy()`. There is really nothing complicated about the code. Create a client object that specifies the region of your bucket, create the `TransferUtilityUploadRequest` object that specifies the file to upload, the bucket name and directory and, lastly, upload the file to the bucket via a `TransferUtility`.

 The AWS `RegionEndpoint` enumeration for **EU (Frankfurt)** is `EUCentral1`. Refer to the following link on the AWS Regions and Endpoints `https://docs.aws.amazon.com/general/latest/gr/rande.html`.

In reality, we would probably enumerate the contents of a folder or even allow the user to select several files. This class is only to illustrate the concept of uploading a file to our bucket. As you will see, this code is really uncomplicated.

```
internal static class StampysLovelyWorld
{
  public static void SaveStampy(string fileToSave,
                                string bucket,
                                string bucketDirectory,
                                string bucketFilename)
  {
    IAmazonS3 client = AWSClientFactory.CreateAmazonS3Client
                            (RegionEndpoint.EUCentral1);

    TransferUtility utility = new TransferUtility(client);
    TransferUtilityUploadRequest request = new
                        TransferUtilityUploadRequest();

    request.BucketName = bucket + "/" + bucketDirectory;
    request.Key = bucketFilename;
    request.FilePath = fileToSave;
    utility.Upload(request);
  }
}
```

3. In the `static void Main` method of the console application, specify the bucket name you created earlier, a folder to create in the bucket and the filename you want in the S3 folder. Pass these along with the path to your file, to the `SaveStampy()` method in the `StampysLovelyWorld` class.

```
static void Main(string[] args)
{
    string uploadFile = "C:\Users\dirk\Pictures\Saved
                         Pictures\StampyCat.png";
    string S3Bucket = "familyvaultdocs";
    string S3Folder = "MinecraftPictures";
    string uploadedFilename = $"{DateTime.Now.ToString("yyyymmdd")}
                             - StampyCat.png";
    StampysLovelyWorld.SaveStampy(uploadFile, S3Bucket, S3Folder,
                                  uploadedFilename);

    WriteLine("uploaded");
    ReadLine();
}
```

4. The last thing we need to do is add the access key and secret key to the **App.config** file of our console application. Just add an `<appSettings>` section and add the keys listed here. You will obviously use the access key and secret key you generated in the **IAM** earlier.

```
<?xml version="1.0" encoding="utf-8" ?>
<configuration>
  <appSettings>
    <add key="AWSProfileName" value="profile1"/>
    <add key="AWSAccessKey" value="AKIAJ6Q2Q77IHJX7STWA"/>
    <add key="AWSSecretKey" value="uFBN6xtuWCSf9zR9WzQKrh1vk
                                   zU2PEuosTTy5qhc"/>
  </appSettings>
  <startup>
    <supportedRuntime version="v4.0" sku=".NETFramework,
        Version=v4.6.2" />
  </startup>
</configuration>
```

5. Run your console application. After the file is uploaded, your console application will just display the text **uploaded** in the output.

How it works...

Swing back to your `familyvaultdocs` bucket in AWS and click on the refresh icon next to the **EU (Frankfurt)** region. You will see the folder `MinecraftPictures` you specified in code.

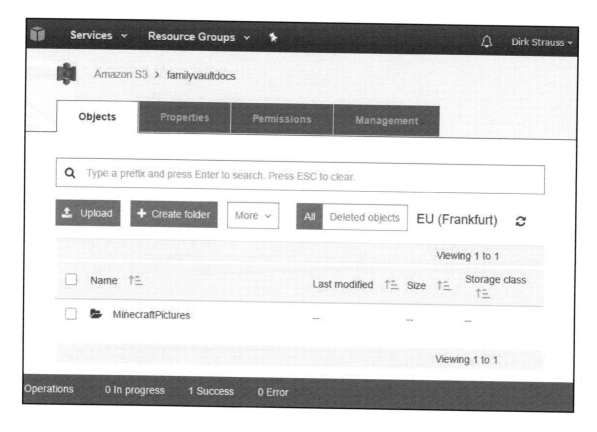

Clicking on the folder, you will see the contents listed. I previously uploaded the
`SquidNugget.png` image, but the `StampyCat.png` image we uploaded in our code sample
has been prefixed with the date as specified in code.

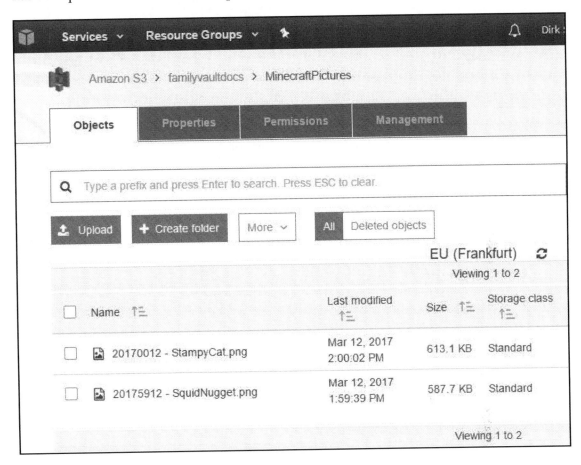

The code is run and the files are added almost immediately. Admittedly they aren't very big files, but this goes to show how easy it is to add a simple storage service to AWS and integrate that with a .NET application.

Creating C# Lambda functions with AWS

On the 1st of December 2016, Amazon announced that C# was now a supported language for AWS Lambda. This is therefore really fresh off the press, so to speak, and developers can experiment with using AWS Lambda in their .NET applications. AWS Lambda allows you to deploy your code to AWS and not have to worry about the machines the code runs on or even worry about the scaling of those machines when demand increases. Your code will just work. This is really great for mobile developers. Up until December, AWS Lambda only supported Node.js, Pythos, and Java. Let's take a look at how to create a Lambda function in Visual Studio 2017 using C#.

Getting ready

You need to ensure that you have downloaded and installed the preview of the AWS Toolkit for Visual Studio 2017. At the time of this writing, the toolkit could be found at this link: `https://aws.amazon.com/blogs/developer/preview-of-the-aws-toolkit-for-visual-studio-2017/`.

If you are using an earlier version of Visual Studio, download the AWS Toolkit from this link: `https://aws.amazon.com/visualstudio/`. This version of the toolkit supports Visual Studio 2015 and also allows you to download legacy versions for Visual Studio 2010-2012 and Visual Studio 2008. After you have downloaded and installed the toolkit, you are ready to create your first AWS Lambda function.

How to do it...

1. Launch Visual Studio and create a new project. Under the **Visual C#** templates, you will see a new type called **AWS Lambda**. Click on the **AWS Lambda Project (.NET Core)** template. That's right, these are .NET Core apps.

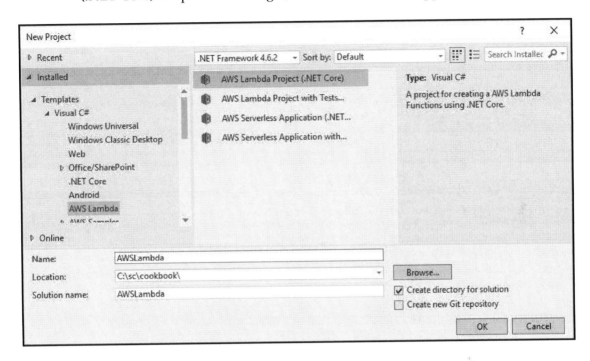

2. The next screen will allow us to select a blueprint. For our purposes, we will just select a **Simple S3 Function** blueprint that responds to S3 event notifications.

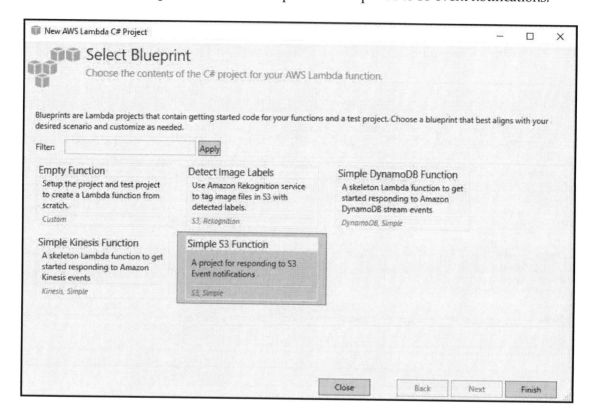

3. The function is created and your **Solution Explorer** in Visual Studio will look as follows.

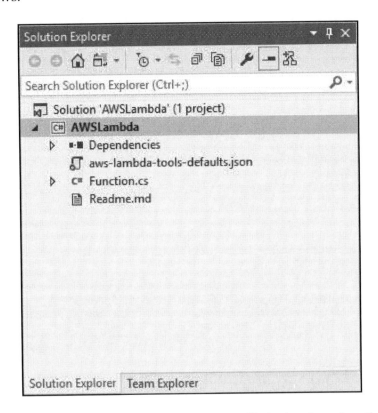

4. The code that is added to the `Function.cs` file is simply a class that has at its heart a method called `FunctionHandler()`. You will also notice an assembly attribute at the top of the class as follows: `[assembly: LambdaSerializerAttribute(typeof(Amazon.Lambda.Serialization.Json.JsonSerializer))]`. This is required and registers the Lambda JSON serializer that is using `Newtonsoft.Json` to create our typed class. Since this code just works, I will not spend much time on explaining it.

```
public async Task<string> FunctionHandler(S3Event evnt,
                                          ILambdaContext context)
{
  var s3Event = evnt.Records?[0].S3;
  if(s3Event == null)
  {
    return null;
  }
```

```
try
{
  var response = await this.S3Client.GetObjectMetadataAsync
                  (s3Event.Bucket.Name, s3Event.Object.Key);
  return response.Headers.ContentType;
}
catch(Exception e)
{
  context.Logger.LogLine($"Error getting object
    {s3Event.Object.Key} from bucket {s3Event.Bucket.Name}.
    Make sure they exist and your bucket is in the same
    region as this function.");
  context.Logger.LogLine(e.Message);
  context.Logger.LogLine(e.StackTrace);
  throw;
}
}
```

5. You can now publish the function to AWS directly from within Visual Studio. Right-click on the project that you created and from the context menu, select **Publish to AWS Lambda....**

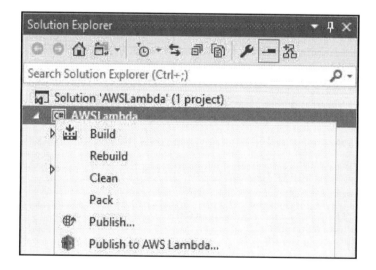

6. You now need to complete the deployment wizard. Give your function a name, and if you do not have an account profile selected, add one.

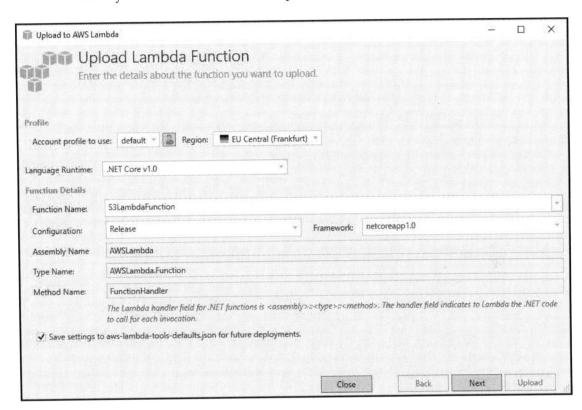

 For your AWS Lambda function, be sure to select the same region as that of your S3 bucket created in the previous recipe.

7. Adding an account profile is really easy. This is the account you configured in IAM.

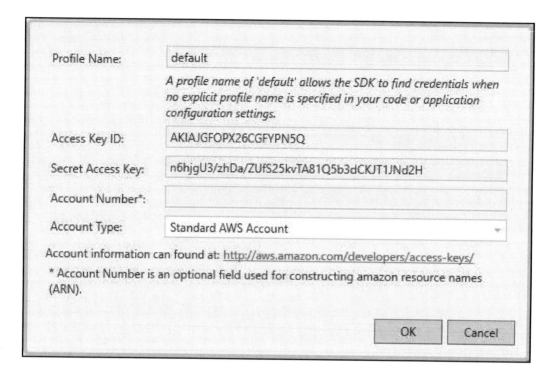

Profile Name: **default**

A profile name of 'default' allows the SDK to find credentials when no explicit profile name is specified in your code or application configuration settings.

Access Key ID: AKIAJGFOPX26CGFYPN5Q

Secret Access Key: n6hjgU3/zhDa/ZUfS25kvTA81Q5b3dCKJT1JNd2H

Account Number*:

Account Type: Standard AWS Account

Account information can found at: http://aws.amazon.com/developers/access-keys/

* Account Number is an optional field used for constructing amazon resource names (ARN).

OK   Cancel

8. Clicking next will allow you to select the IAM Role Name that provides access permissions to S3 and our function. This is configured in the **IAM (Identity and Access Management)**.

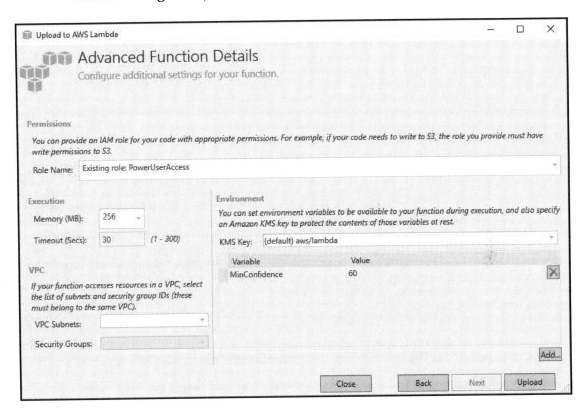

9. Click on **Upload** to upload the function to AWS.

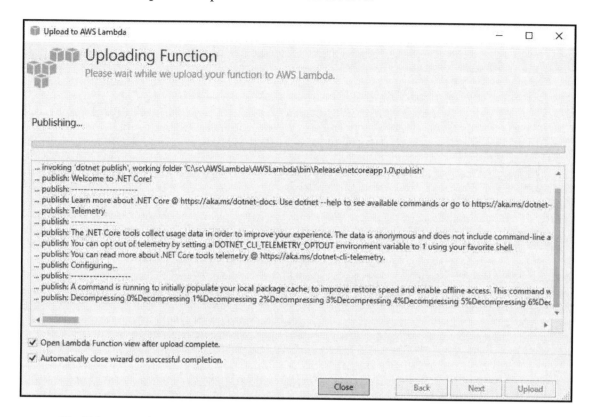

10. Take note, however, that there might be several permission issues encountered at this step. You might encounter something like the following:

```
Error creating Lambda function: User:
arn:aws:iam::932141661806:user/S3Lambda is not authorized to perform:
lambda:CreateFunction on resource: arn:aws:lambda:eu-
central-1:932141661806:function:S3LambdaFunction
```

You can in fact receive several such errors when trying to upload your function to AWS. The Identity and Access Management area in AWS is your friend here. You should have a look at the user you are using (in this case the user is **S3Lambda**) and review the permissions attributed to the user. Here, the error is informing us that the user **S3Lambda** does not have permission to create the function on AWS for the **S3LambdaFunction** resource. Modify your permissions and try uploading again.

How it works...

After you have uploaded your function to AWS, click on the **View** menu in Visual Studio and select the **AWS Explorer**. Expanding the AWS Lambda node will show us the function we previously uploaded. If you see an error when expanding the node, you might need to give your user the **ListFunctions** permission. Expanding the AWS Identity and Access Management node will also show you the users, groups and roles you have configured. You can easily test your AWS Lambda function from within Visual Studio here by selecting one of the **Example Requests** and clicking on the **Invoke** button.

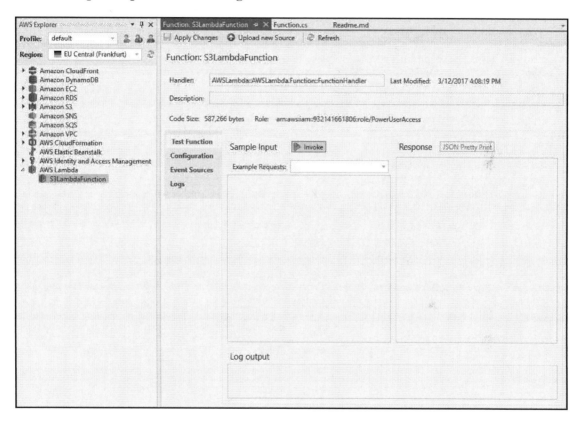

What we want to do, however, is hook up our S3 that stores files to send events to our function. Click on the **Event Sources** tab and click the **Add** button. Select **Amazon S3** as the **Source Type** and select the `familyvaultdocs` bucket we created in the previous recipe. When you are done, click on the **OK** button.

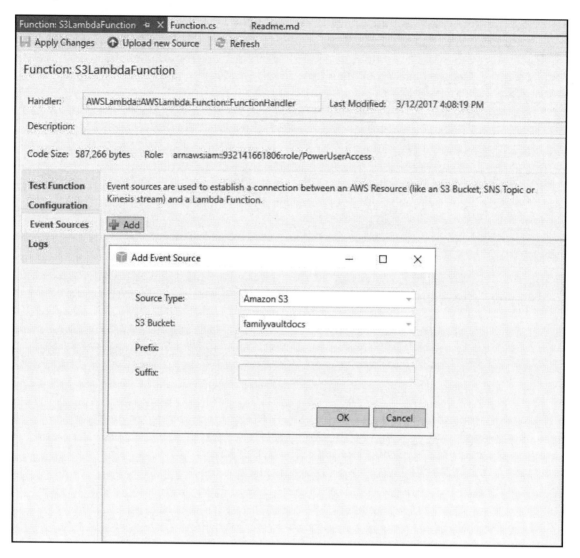

Running the console application in the previous recipe to upload a new file to our S3 bucket will trigger our Lambda function. We can confirm this by looking at the **Logs** section in our function view.

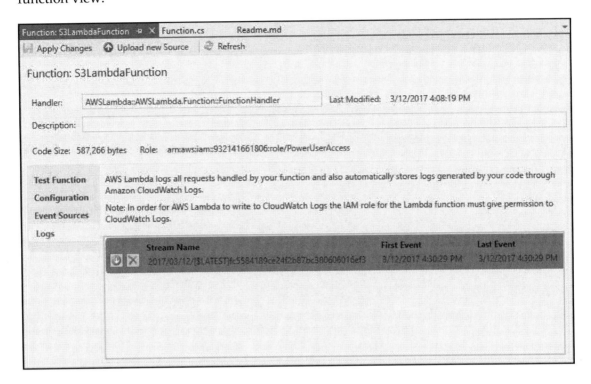

You can also upload files from the **AWS Explorer**. Expand the **Amazon S3** node and click on the **Upload File** button to the bucket.

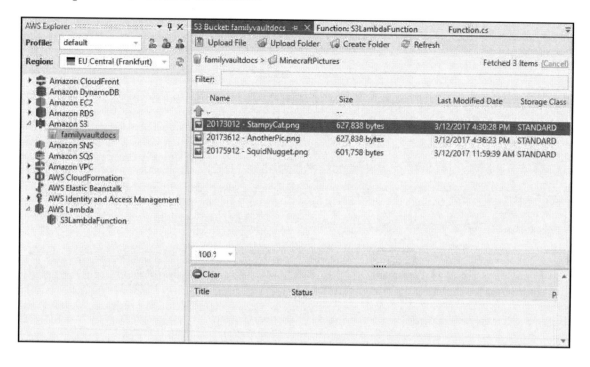

Your file is uploaded and the progress is shown in the status window at the bottom.

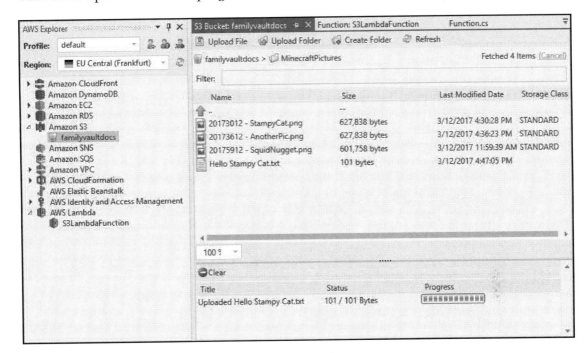

While this example is not too complicated (with the exception of the permission settings perhaps), it does illustrate the concept of AWS Lambda functions. We can use the function to do a host of actions when triggered from something as simple as an event in an S3 bucket. Start to combine functionality and you can create a very powerful, serverless module to support and enhance your applications.

It does not matter if you are using AWS, Azure or something such as DocRaptor (or any of the other 3rd party services available). Serverless computing is here to stay and C# Lambda functions will change the face of development in a big way.

Index

Made in the USA
Middletown, DE
11 April 2019